Princess Resurrection

2

Yasunori Mitsunaga

Translated by
Satsuki Yamashita

Adapted by
Joshua Hale Fialkov

Lettered by
North Market Street Graphics

Ballantine Books · New York

Princess Resurrection volume 2 is a work of fiction. Names, characters, places, and incidents are the products of the author's imagination or are used fictitiously. Any resemblance to actual events, locales, or persons, living or dead, is entirely coincidental.

A Del Rey Trade Paperback Original

Published in the United States by Del Rey Books, an imprint of The Random House Publishing Group, a division of Random House, Inc., New York.

Publication rights arranged through Kodansha Ltd.

First published in Japan in 2006 by Kodansha Ltd., Tokyo.

ISBN 978-0-345-49682-9

Printed in the United States of America

www.delreymanga.com

9 8 7 6 5 4 3 2 1

Translator: Satsuki Yamashita
Adapter: Joshua Hale Fialkov
Lettering: North Market Street Graphics

Contents

That is not dead
which can eternal lie,
and with strange eons
even death may die.

Honorifics Explained

Throughout the Del Rey Manga books, you will find Japanese honorifics left intact in the translations. For those not familiar with how the Japanese use honorifics and, more important, how they differ from American honorifics, we present this brief overview.

Politeness has always been a critical facet of Japanese culture. Ever since the feudal era, when Japan was a highly stratified society, use of honorifics—which can be defined as polite speech that indicates relationship or status—has played an essential role in the Japanese language. When addressing someone in Japanese, an honorific usually takes the form of a suffix attached to one's name (example: "Asuna-san"), is used as a title at the end of one's name, or appears in place of the name itself (example: "Negi-sensei," or simply "Sensei!").

Honorifics can be expressions of respect or endearment. In the context of manga and anime, honorifics give insight into the nature of the relationship between characters. Many English translations leave out these important honorifics and therefore distort the feel of the original Japanese. Because Japanese honorifics contain nuances that English honorifics lack, it is our policy at Del Rey not to translate them. Here, instead, is a guide to some of the honorifics you may encounter in Del Rey Manga.

-san: This is the most common honorific and is equivalent to Mr., Miss, Ms., or Mrs. It is the all-purpose honorific and can be used in any situation where politeness is required.

-sama: This is one level higher than "-san" and is used to confer great respect.

-dono: This comes from the word "tono," which means "lord." It is an even higher level than "-sama" and confers utmost respect.

-kun: This suffix is used at the end of boys' names to express familiarity or endearment. It is also sometimes used by men among friends, or when addressing someone younger or of a lower station.

-chan: This is used to express endearment, mostly toward girls. It is also used for little boys, pets, and even among lovers. It gives a sense of childish cuteness.

Bozu: This is an informal way to refer to a boy, similar to the English terms "kid" and "squirt."

Sempai/
Senpai: This title suggests that the addressee is one's senior in a group or organization. It is most often used in a school setting, where underclassmen refer to their upperclassmen as "sempai." It can also be used in the workplace, such as when a newer employee addresses an employee who has seniority in the company.

Kohai: This is the opposite of "sempai" and is used toward underclassmen in school or newcomers in the workplace. It connotes that the addressee is of a lower station.

Sensei: Literally meaning "one who has come before," this title is used for teachers, doctors, or masters of any profession or art.

[blank]: This is usually forgotten in these lists, but it is perhaps the most significant difference between Japanese and English. The lack of honorific means that the speaker has permission to address the person in a very intimate way. Usually, only family, spouses, or very close friends have this kind of permission. Known as *yobisute,* it can be gratifying when someone who has earned the intimacy starts to call one by one's name without an honorific. But when that intimacy hasn't been earned, it can be very insulting.

Princess Resurrection

2

Yasunori Mitsunaga

Contents

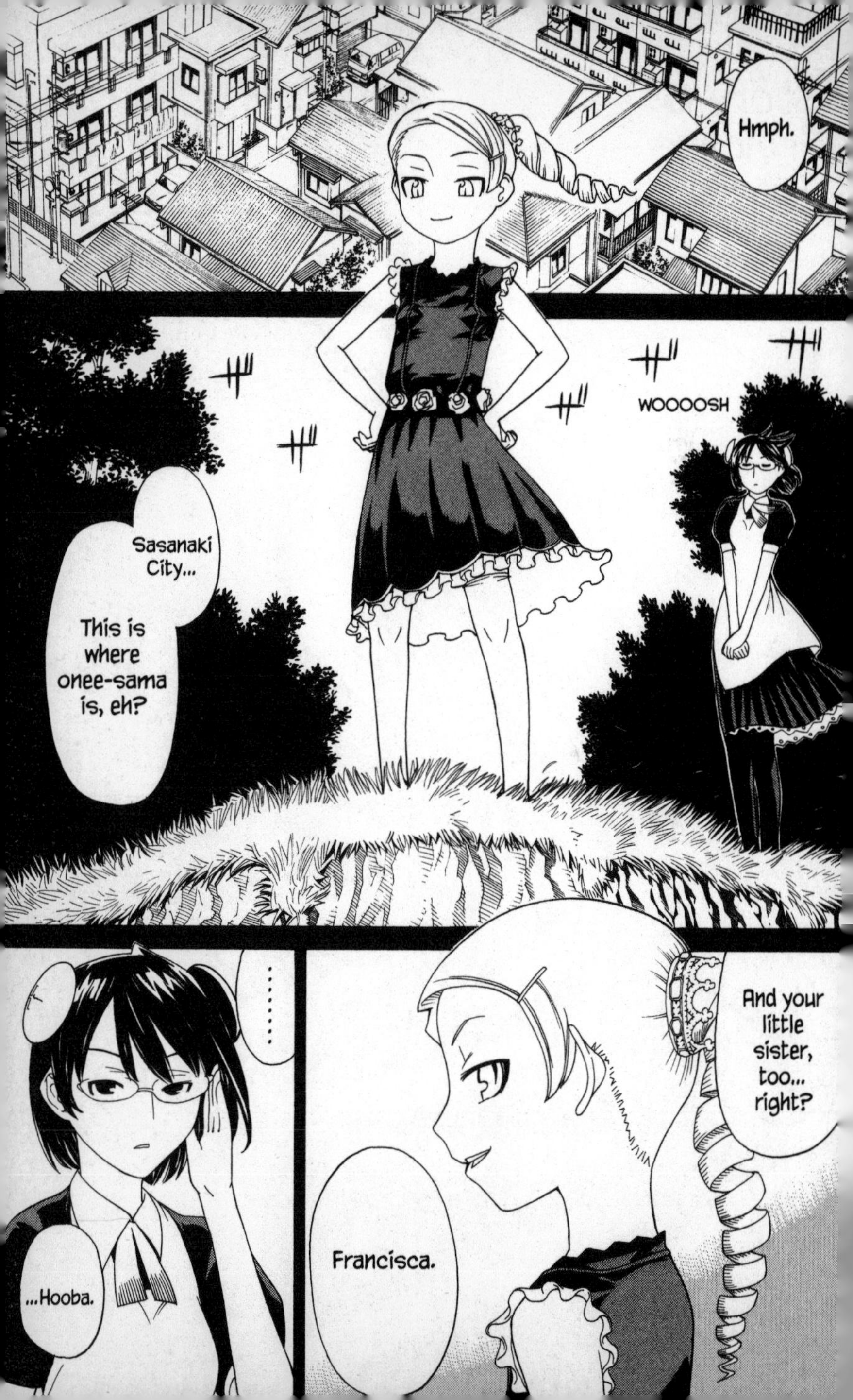
Hmph.
WOOOOSH
Sasanaki City...
This is where onee-sama is, eh?
And your little sister, too... right?
Francisca.
......
...Hooba.

Story 6: Princess Alliance

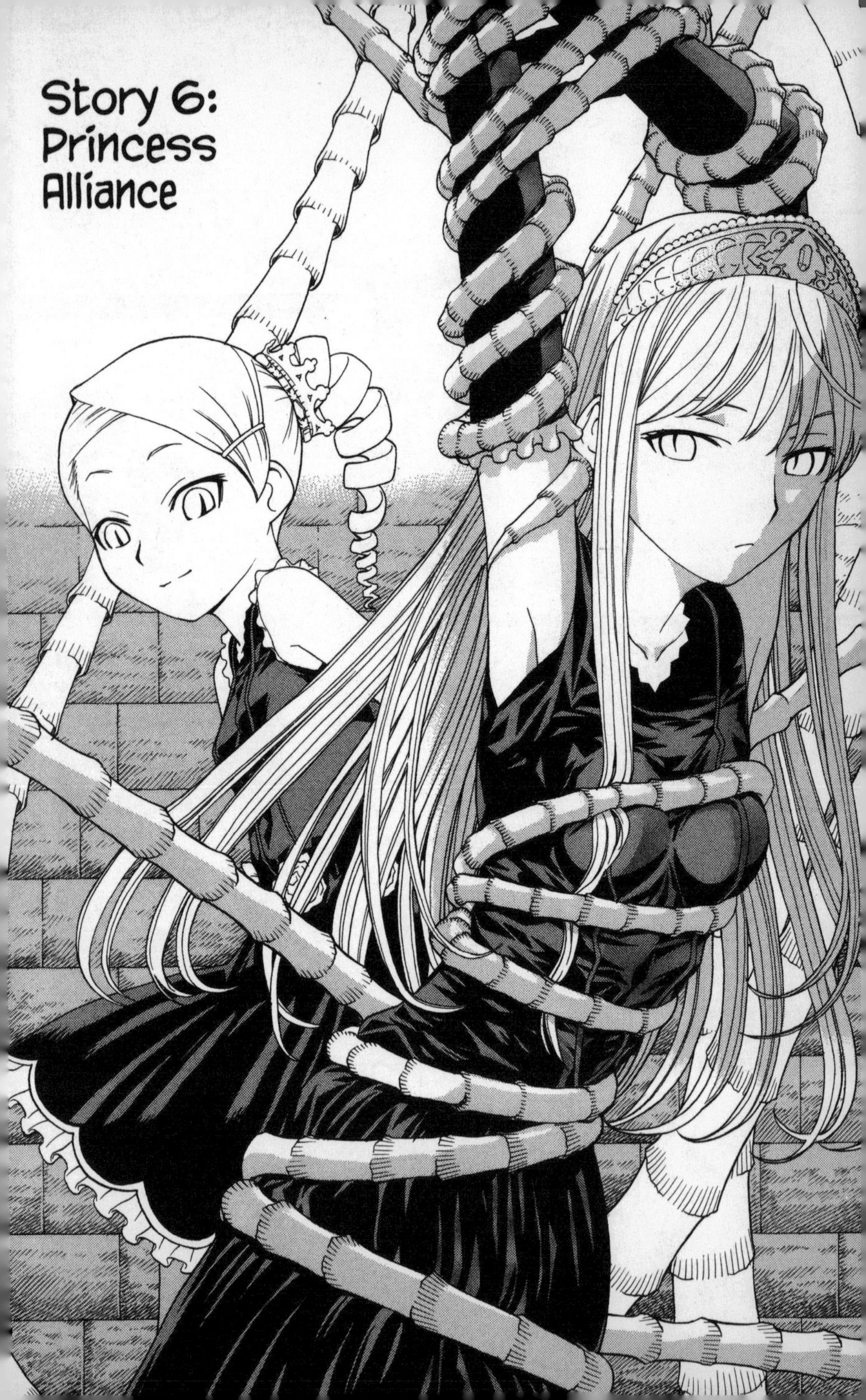

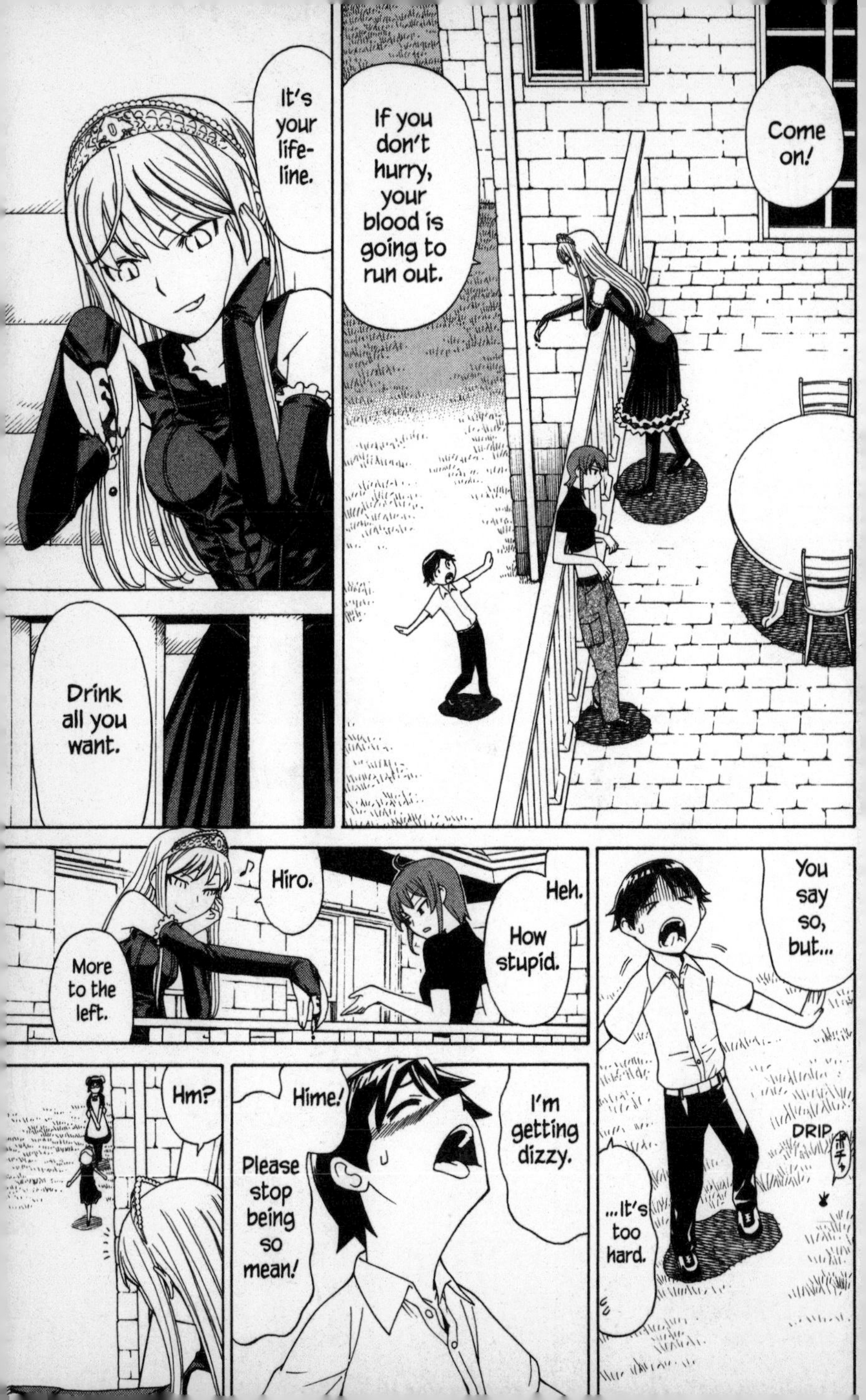
Come on!
If you don't hurry, your blood is going to run out.
It's your lifeline.
Drink all you want.
You say so, but...
DRIP
...It's too hard.
Heh.
How stupid.
Hiro.
More to the left.
I'm getting dizzy.
Hime!
Please stop being so mean!
Hm?

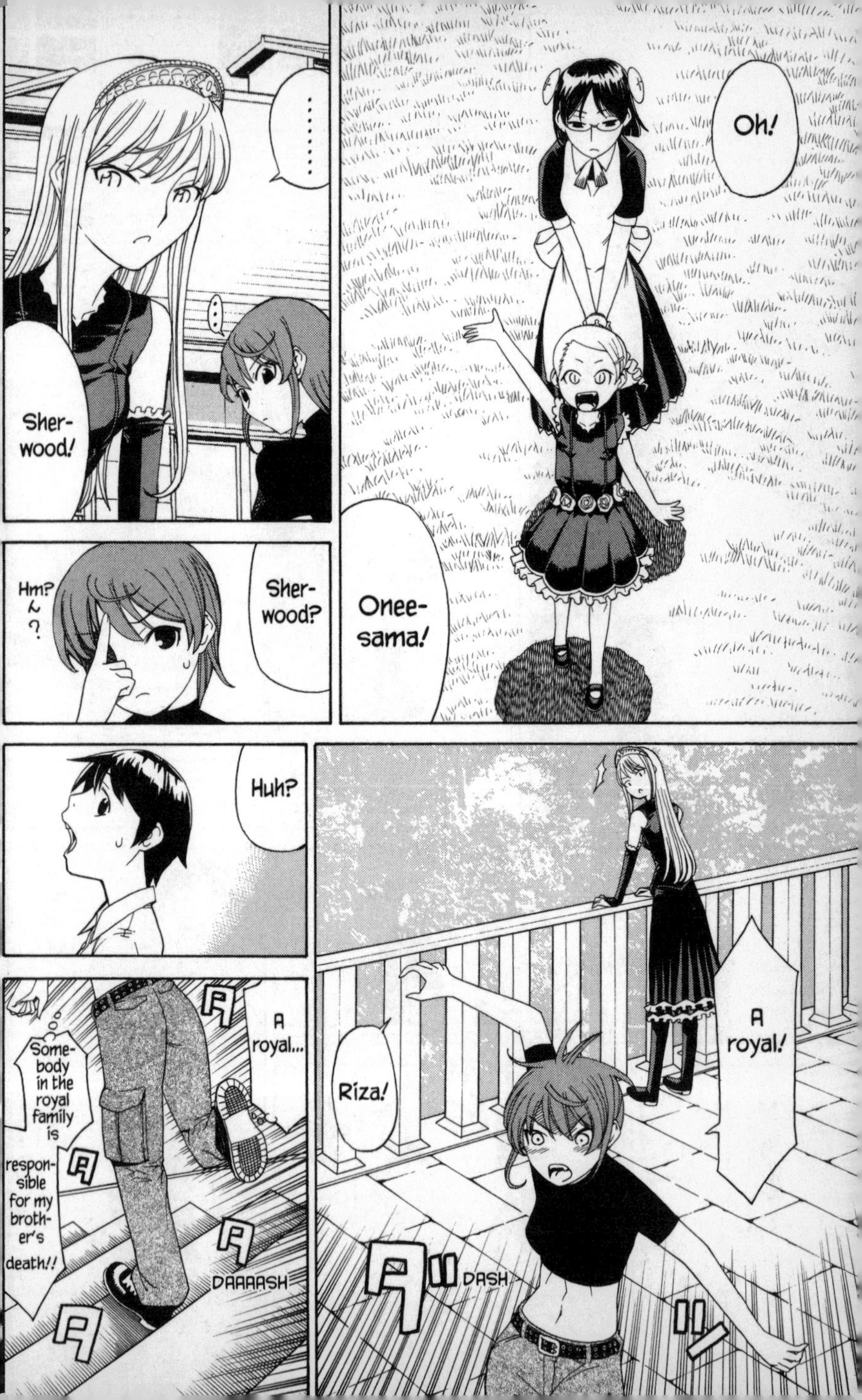
Oh!
Onee-sama!
......
...
Sher-wood!
Sher-wood?
Hm? ん？
A royal!
Riza!
DASH
Huh?
A royal...
Somebody in the royal family is responsible for my brother's death!!
DAAAASH

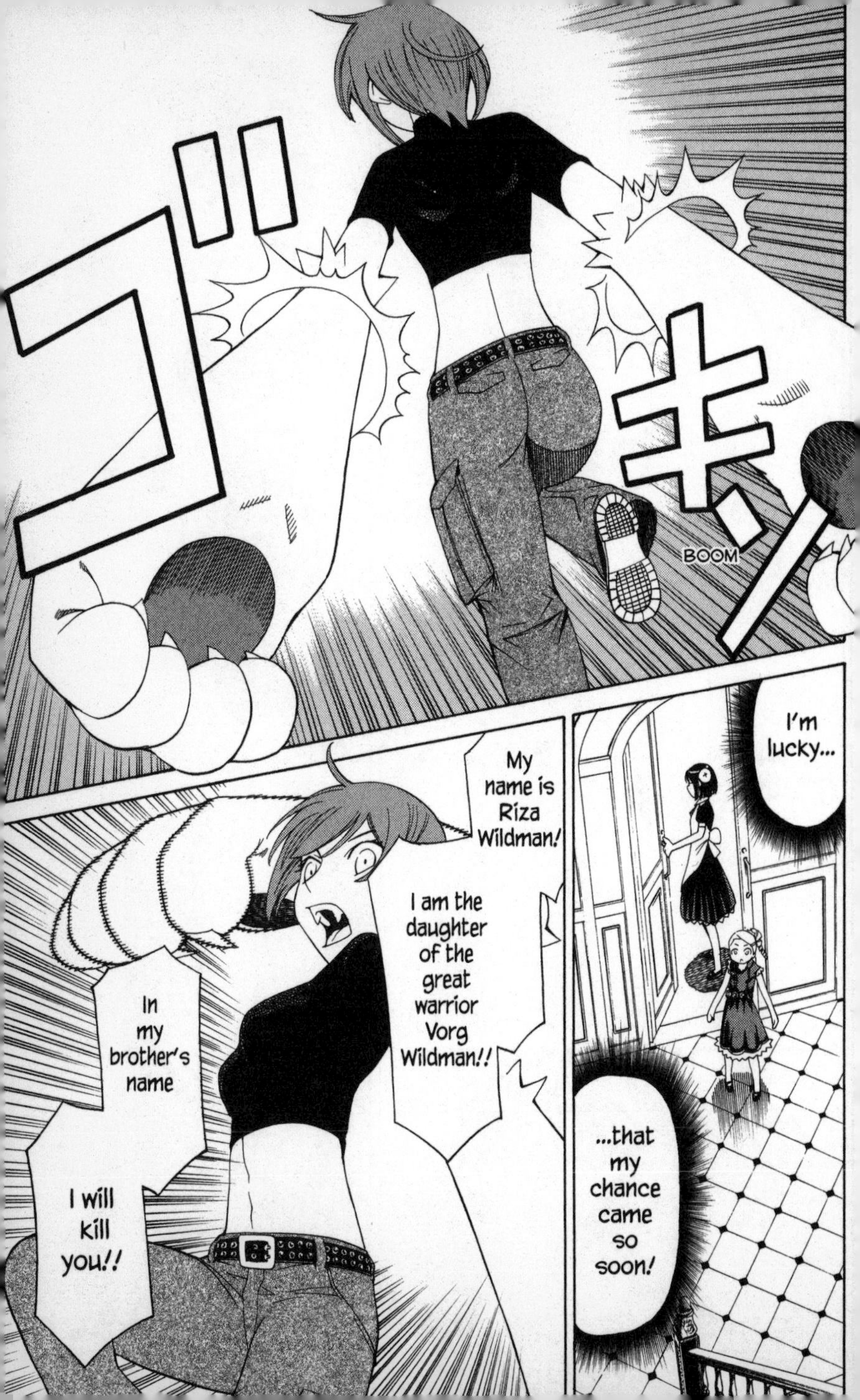
ゴキッ
BOOM
I'm lucky...
...that my chance came so soon!
My name is Riza Wildman!
I am the daughter of the great warrior Vorg Wildman!!
In my brother's name
I will kill you!!

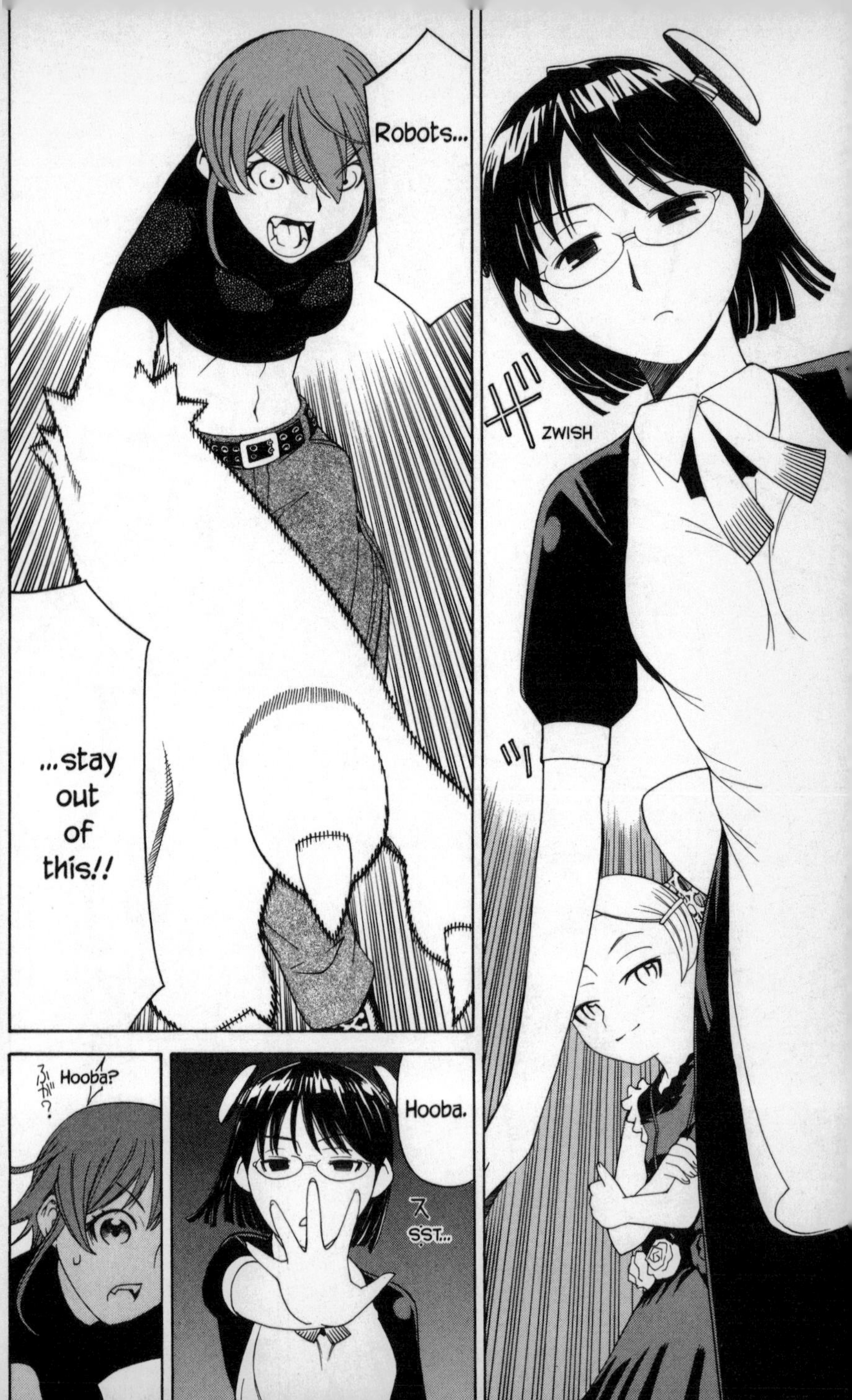

ザ
ZWISH
ッ
Robots...
...stay out of this!!
Hooba.
ス
SST...
ふが?
Hooba?

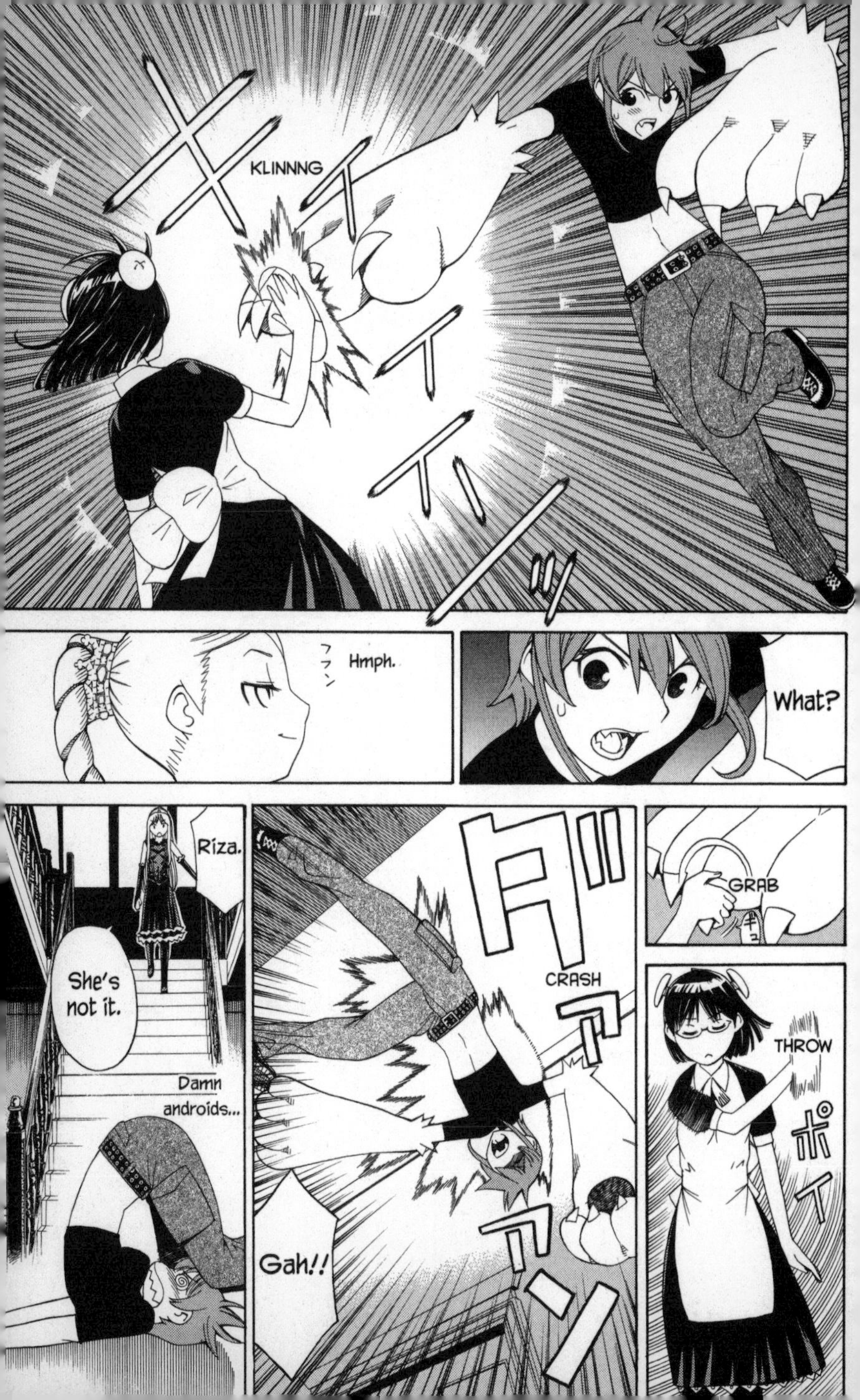
KLINNNG
What?
Hmph.
GRAB
THROW
CRASH
Gah!!
Riza.
She's not it.
Damn androids...

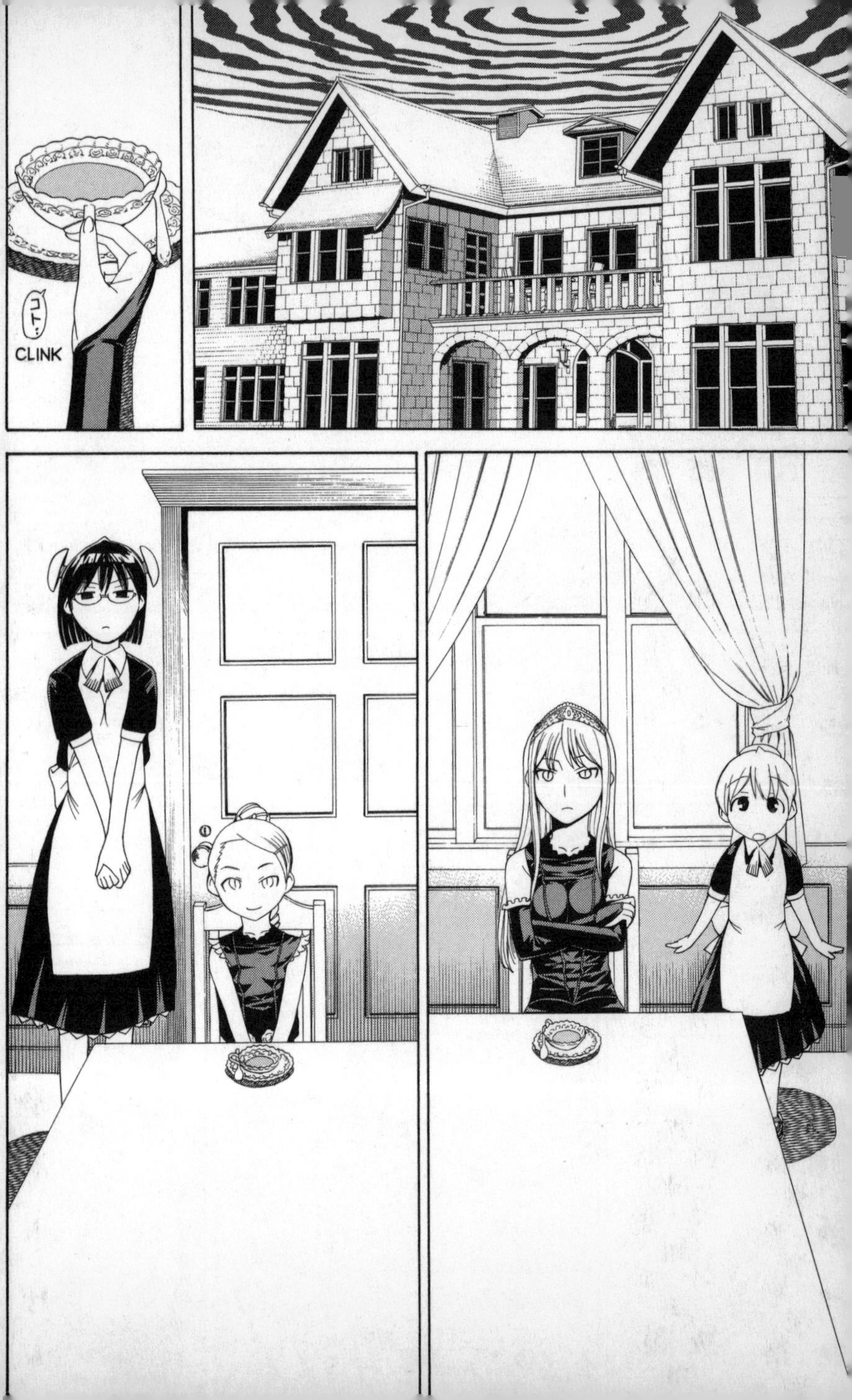
コト
CLINK

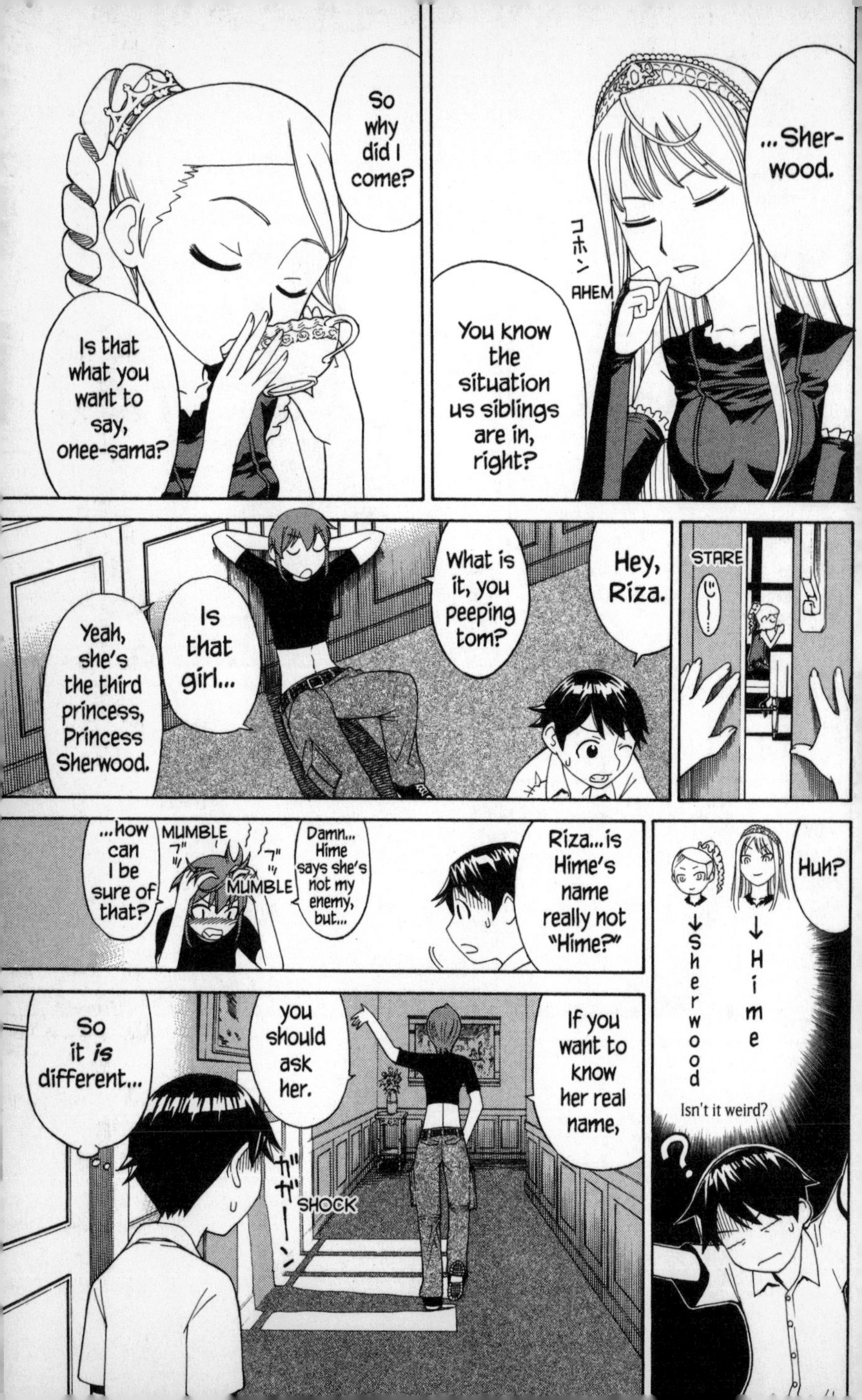

...Sher-wood.
コホン
AHEM
You know the situation us siblings are in, right?
So why did I come?
Is that what you want to say, onee-sama?
STARE
じー…
Hey, Riza.
What is it, you peeping tom?
Is that girl...
Yeah, she's the third princess, Princess Sherwood.
Huh?
↓Hime
↓Sherwood
Isn't it weird?
Riza...is Hime's name really not "Hime?"
Damn... Hime says she's not my enemy, but...
MUMBLE
MUMBLE
...how can I be sure of that?
If you want to know her real name,
you should ask her.
SHOCK
So it *is* different...

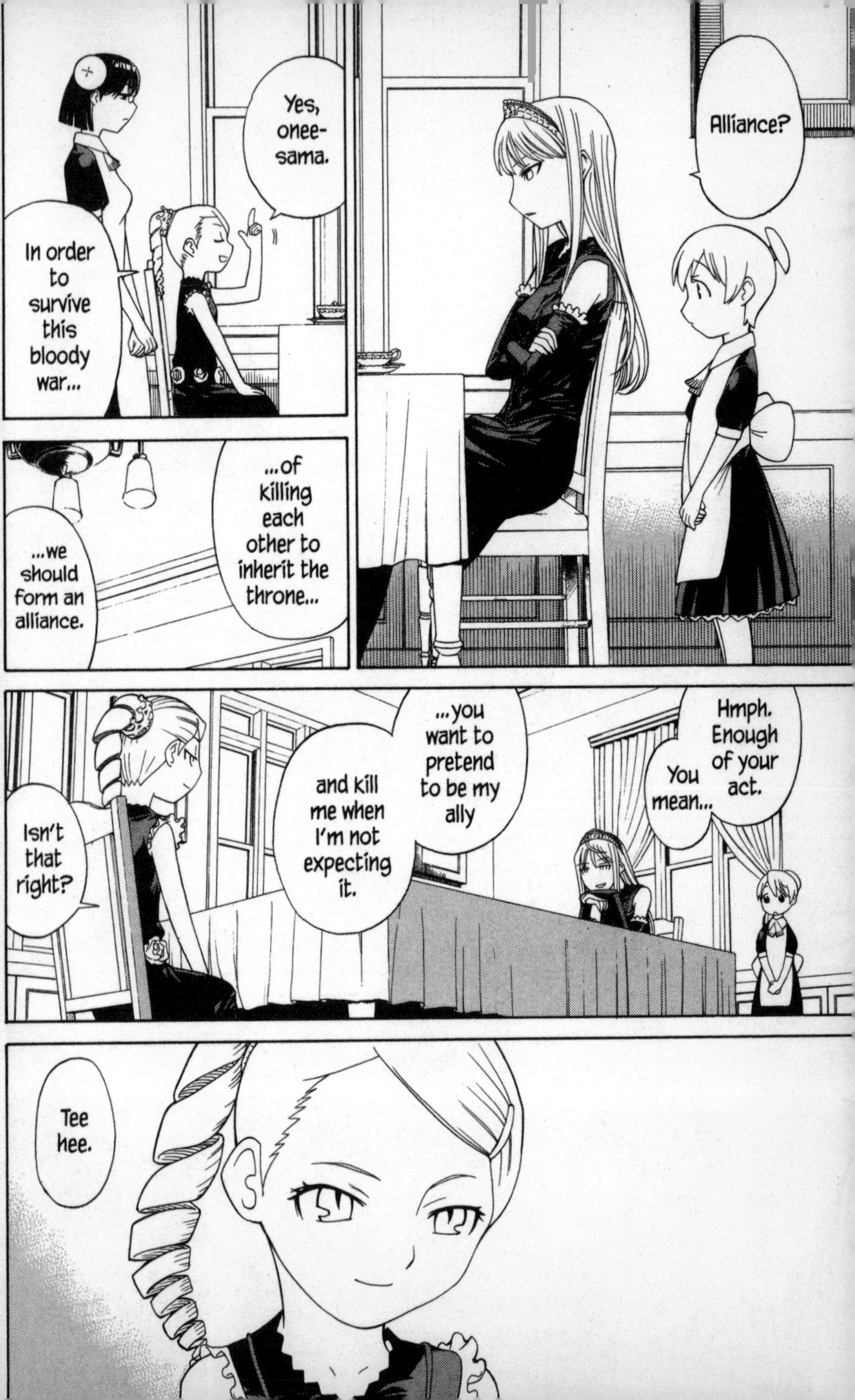
Alliance?
Yes, onee-sama.
In order to survive this bloody war...
...of killing each other to inherit the throne...
...we should form an alliance.
Hmph. Enough of your act.
You mean...
...you want to pretend to be my ally
and kill me when I'm not expecting it.
Isn't that right?
Tee hee.

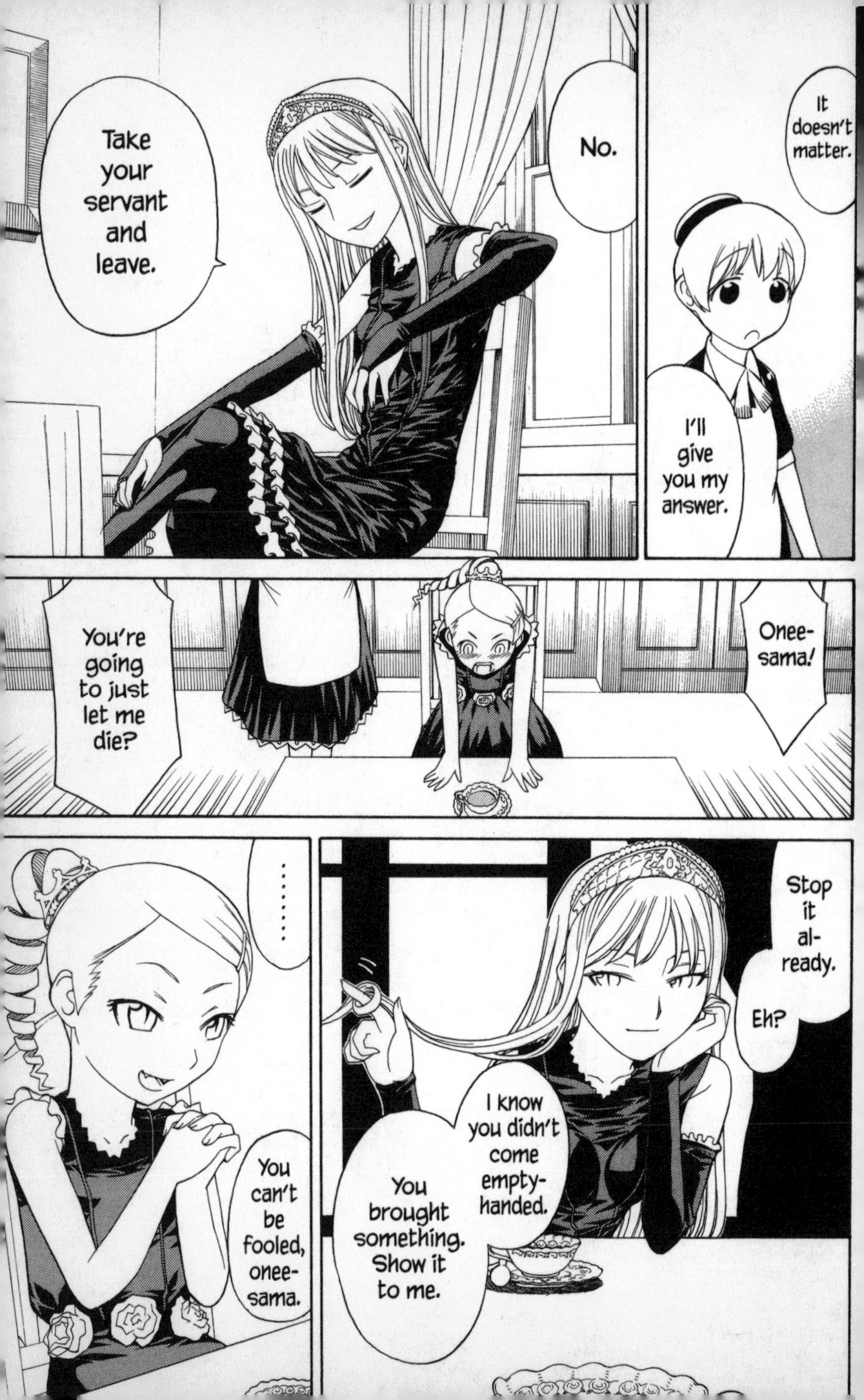

It doesn't matter.
I'll give you my answer.
No.
Take your servant and leave.
Onee-sama!
You're going to just let me die?
Stop it al-ready.
Eh?
I know you didn't come empty-handed.
You brought something. Show it to me.
......
You can't be fooled, onee-sama.

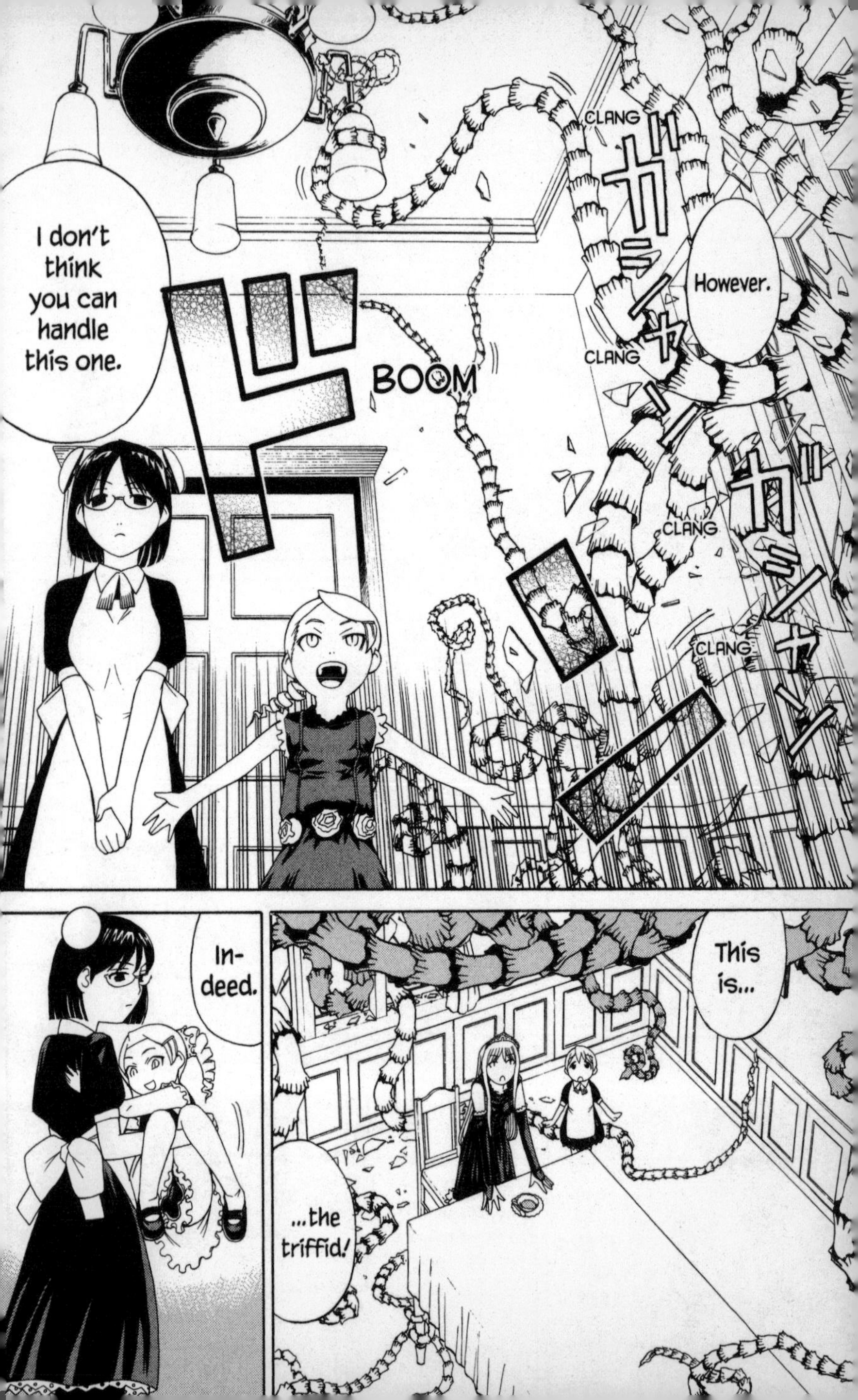
CLANG
However.
CLANG
CLANG
CLANG
BOOM
I don't think you can handle this one.
This is...
...the triffid!
In-deed.

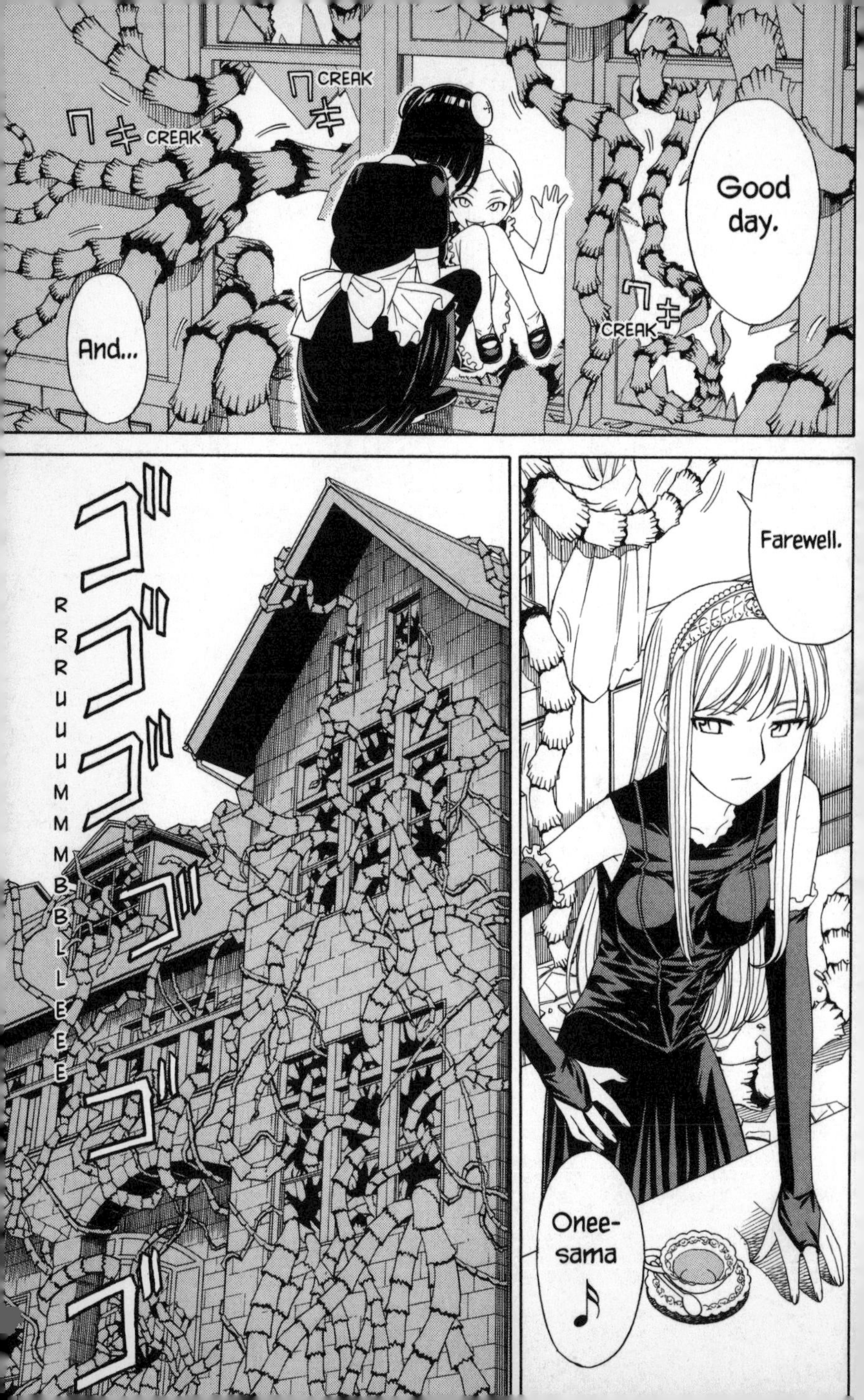

CREAK
CREAK
Good day.
CREAK
And...
Farewell.
Onee-sama ♪
RRRUUUMMMBBLLEEE

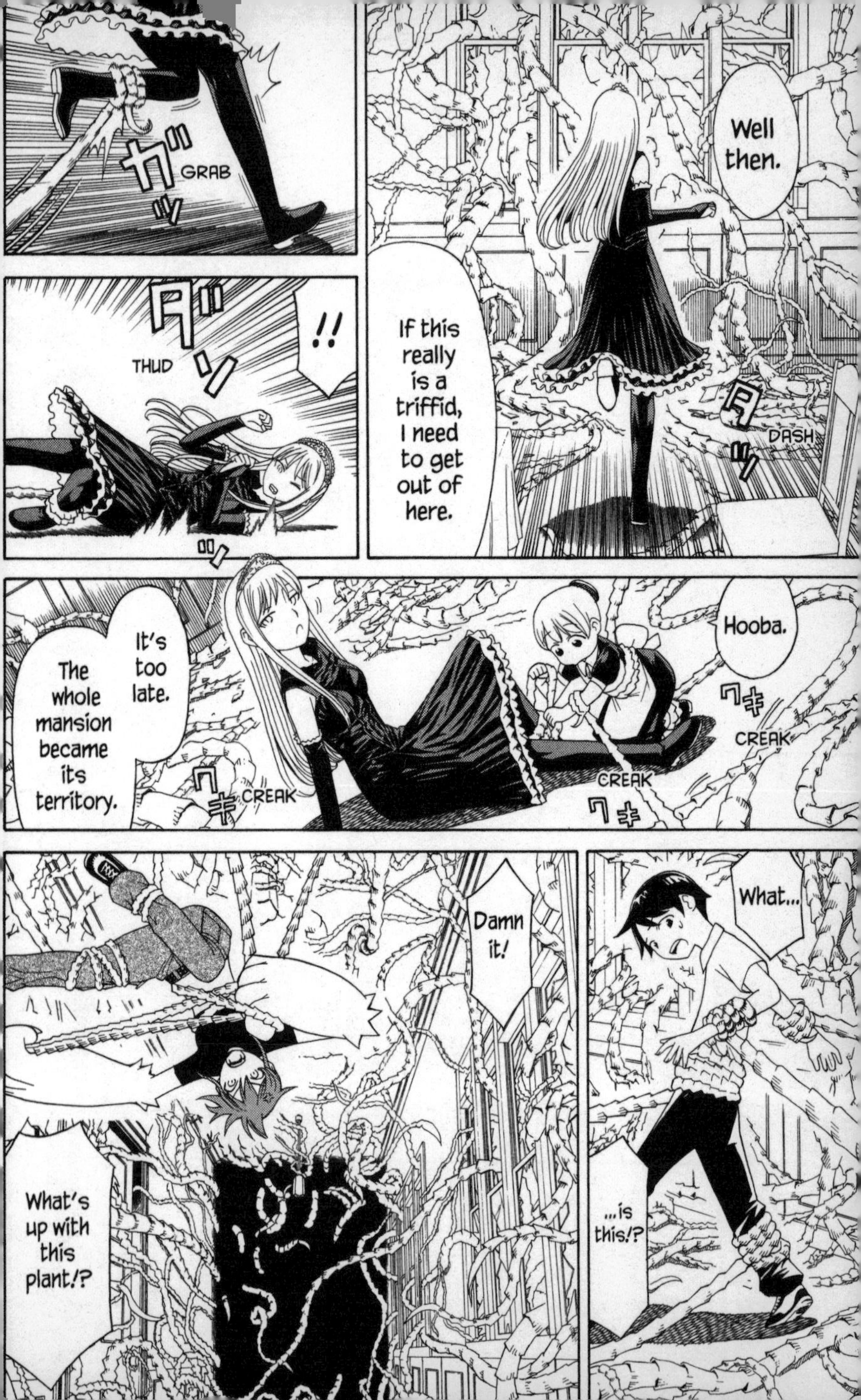
Well then.
If this really is a triffid, I need to get out of here.
DASH
GRAB
!!
THUD
Hooba.
CREAK
CREAK
It's too late.
The whole mansion became its territory.
CREAK
What...
...is this!?
Damn it!
What's up with this plant!?

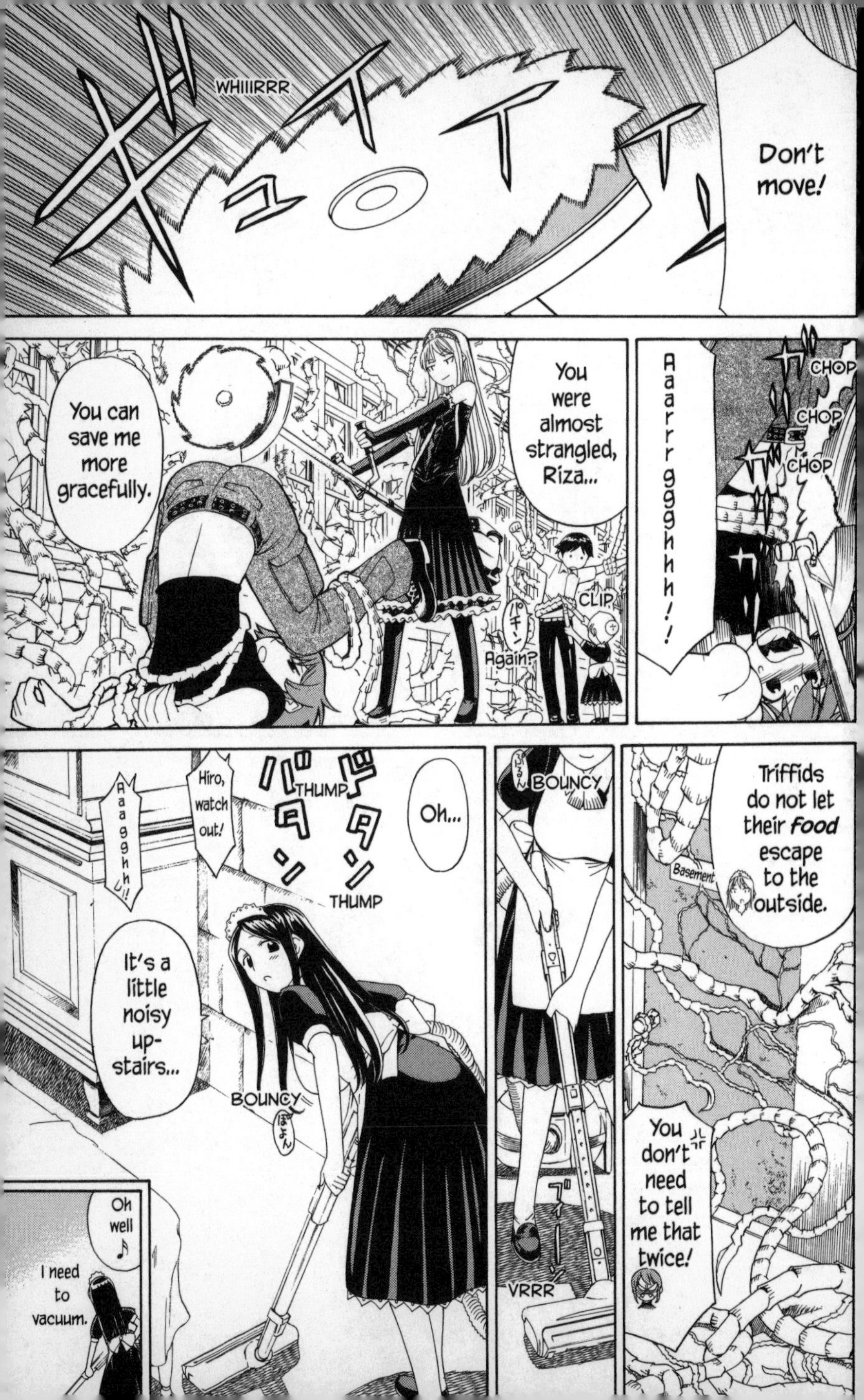
Don't move!
WHIIIRRR
Aaarrrggghhh!!
CHOP
CHOP
CHOP
You were almost strangled, Riza...
CLIP
Again?
You can save me more gracefully.
Triffids do not let their *food* escape to the outside.
Basement
You don't need to tell me that twice!
BOUNCY
VRRR
Oh...
THUMP
THUMP
Hiro, watch out!
Aaagghh!!
It's a little noisy upstairs...
BOUNCY
Oh well ♪
I need to vacuum.

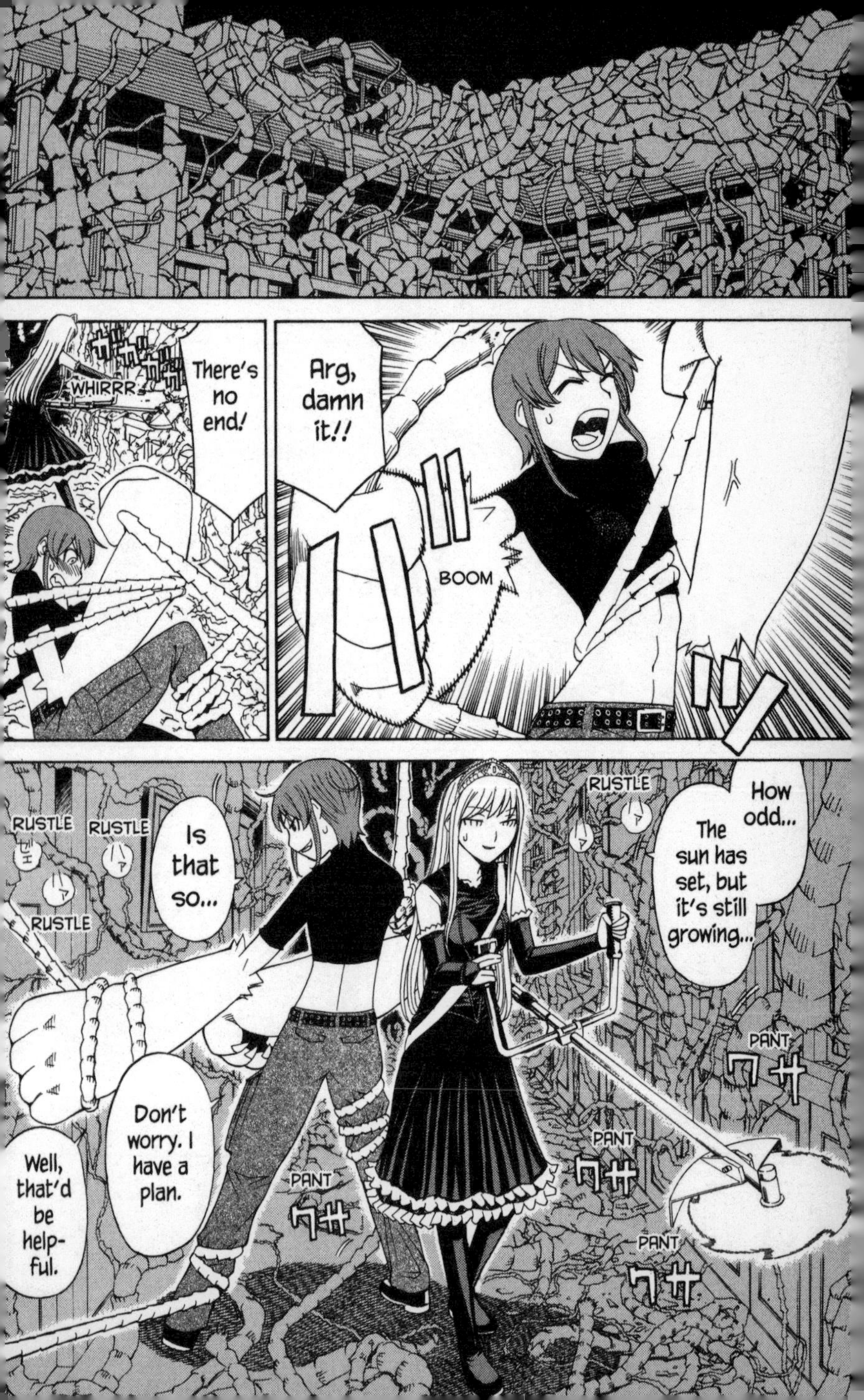
Arg, damn it!!
BOOM
There's no end!
WHIRRR
RUSTLE
How odd... The sun has set, but it's still growing...
Is that so...
RUSTLE
RUSTLE
RUSTLE
PANT
PANT
PANT
PANT
Don't worry. I have a plan.
Well, that'd be helpful.

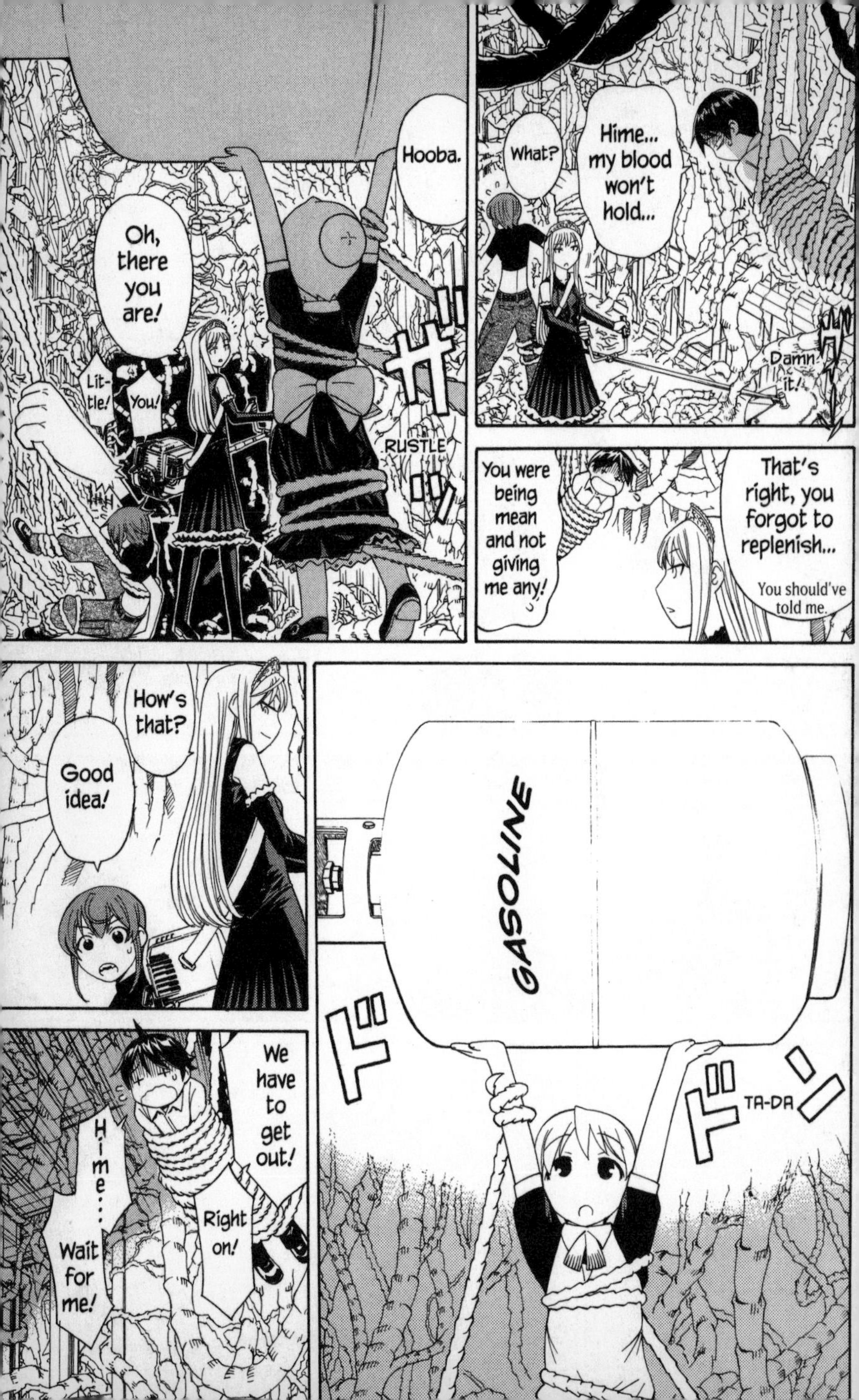
Hime... my blood won't hold...
What?
Damn it!
That's right, you forgot to replenish...
You should've told me.
You were being mean and not giving me any!
Hooba.
Oh, there you are!
You!
Lit-tle!
RUSTLE
GASOLINE
TA-DA
How's that?
Good idea!
We have to get out!
Right on!
Hime... Wait for me!

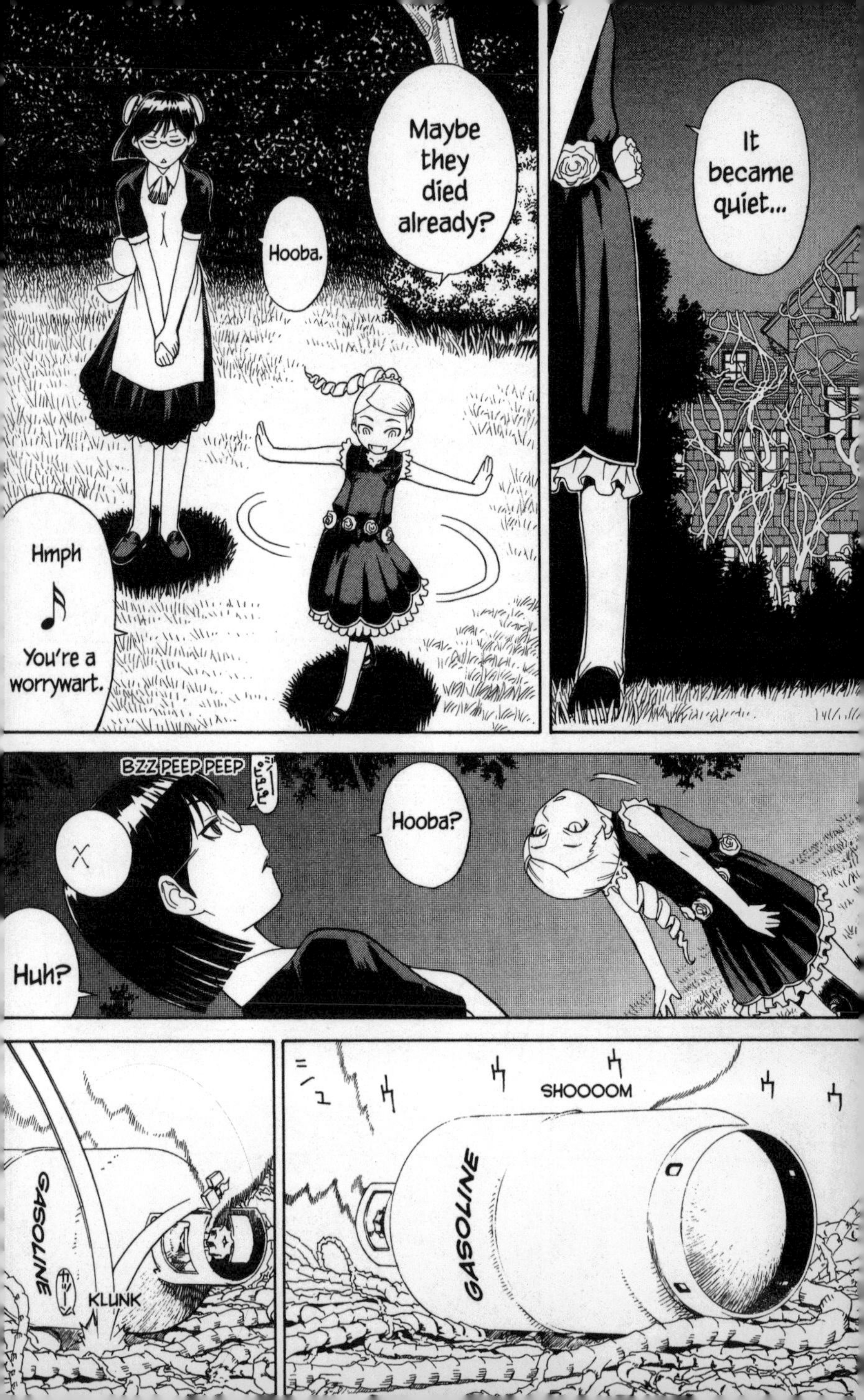
It became quiet...
Maybe they died already?
Hooba.
Hmph ♪ You're a worrywart.
BZZ PEEP PEEP
Hooba?
Huh?
SHOOOOM
GASOLINE
GASOLINE
KLUNK

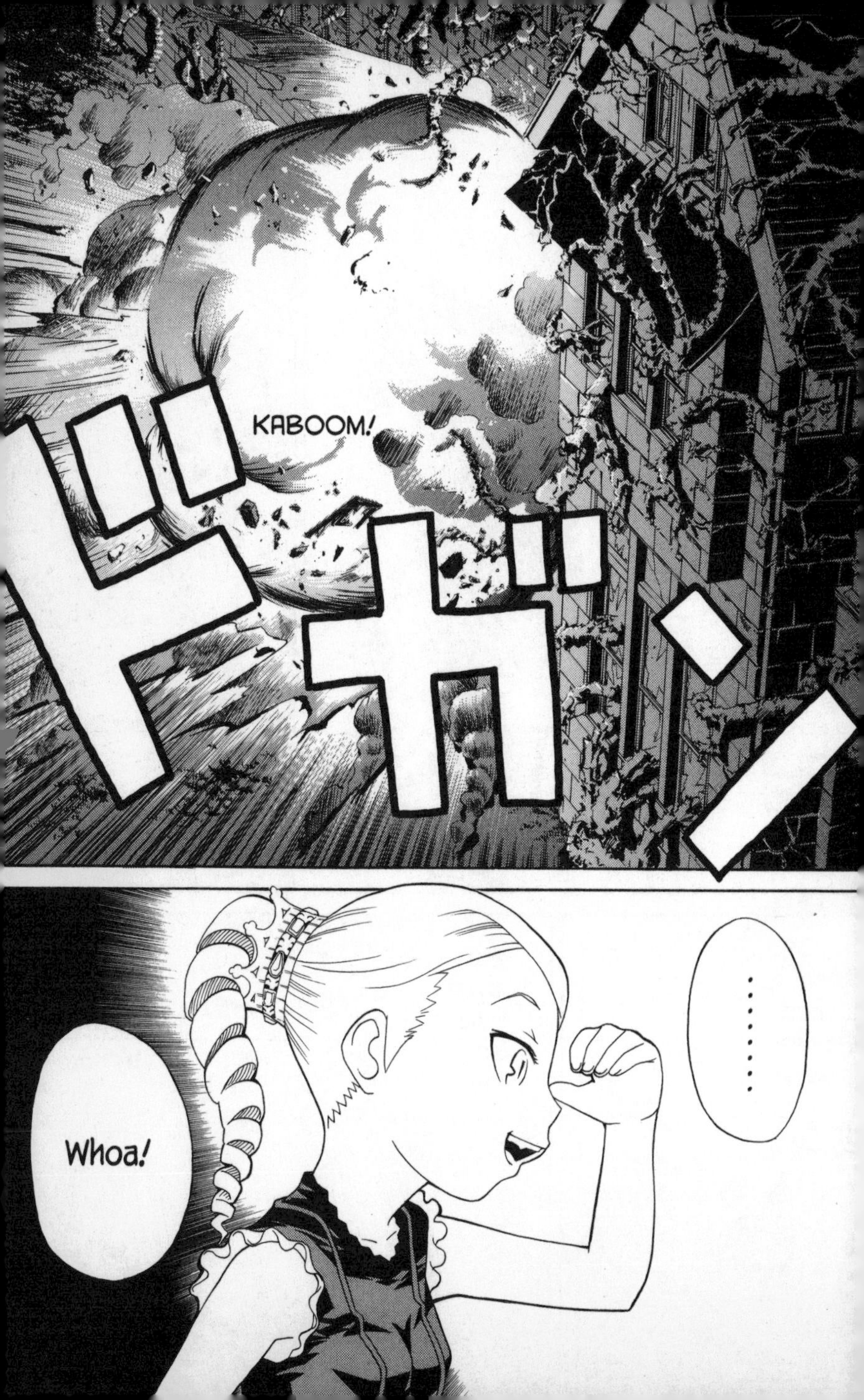
ドガン
KABOOM!
....
Whoa!

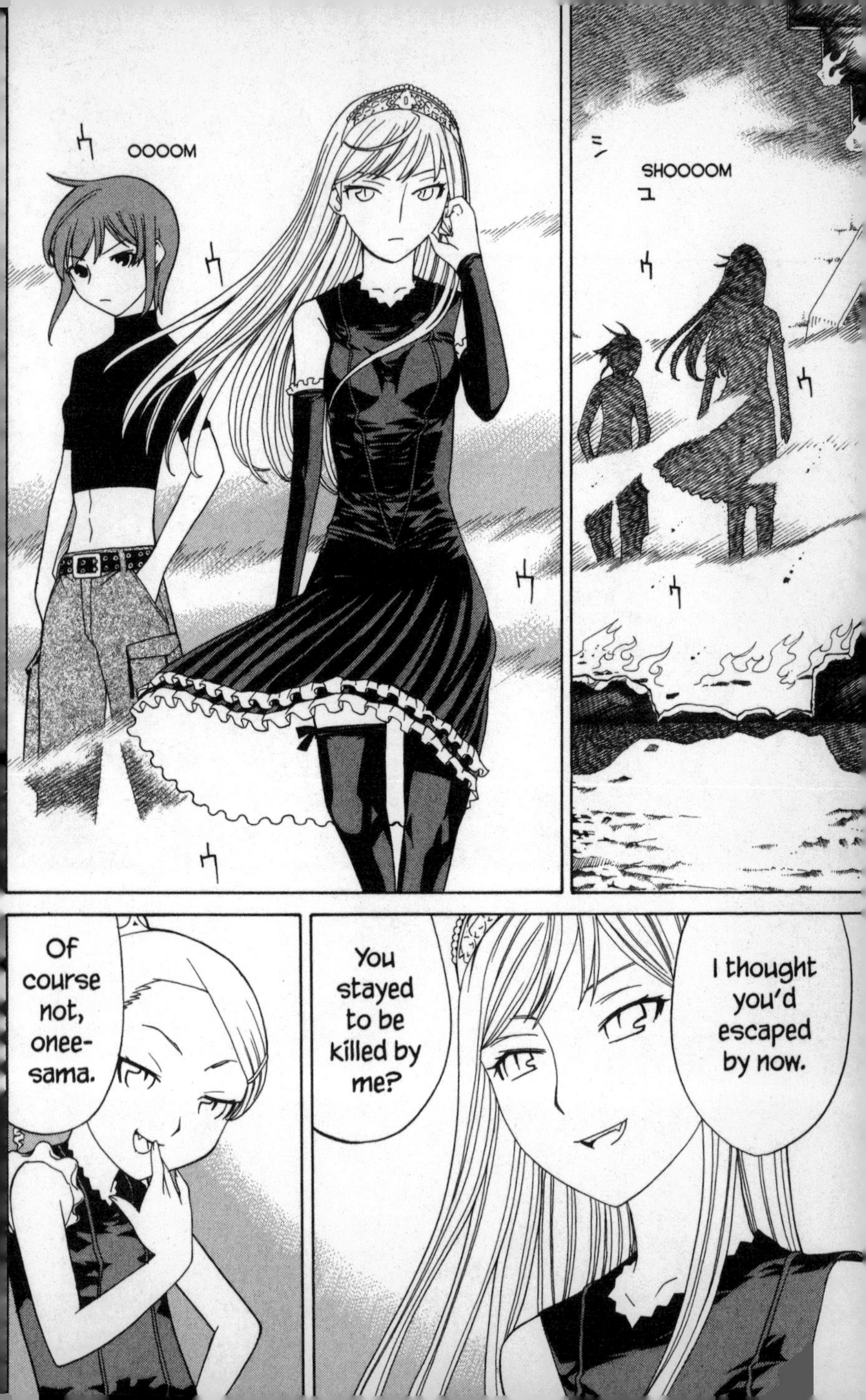
SHOOOOM
OOOOM
I thought you'd escaped by now.
You stayed to be killed by me?
Of course not, onee-sama.

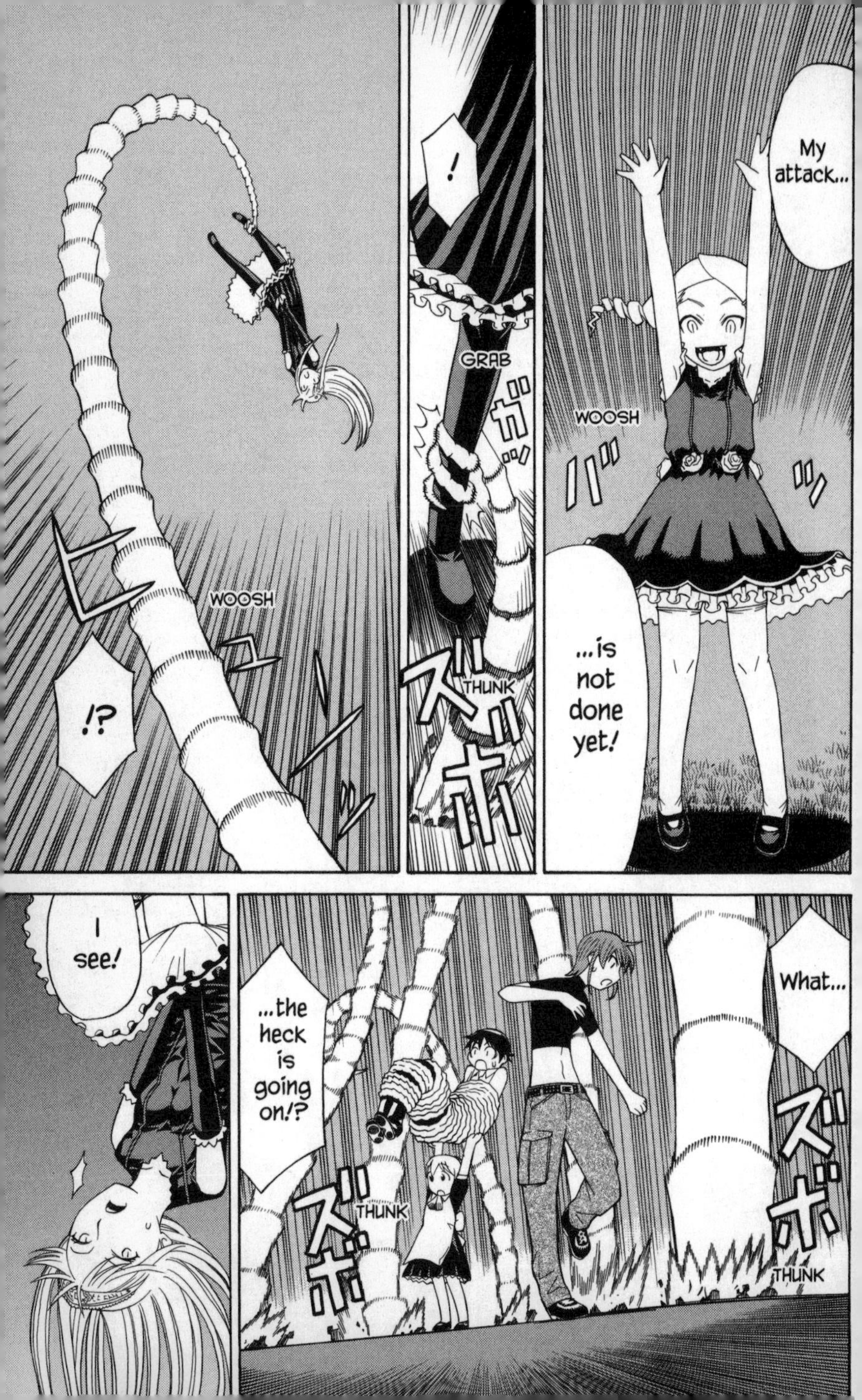
My attack...
...is not done yet!
WOOSH
バッ
!
GRAB
ガッ
THUNK
ズボ
WOOSH
ヒュンッ
!?
What...
...the heck is going on!?
THUNK
ズボ
THUNK
ズボ
I see!

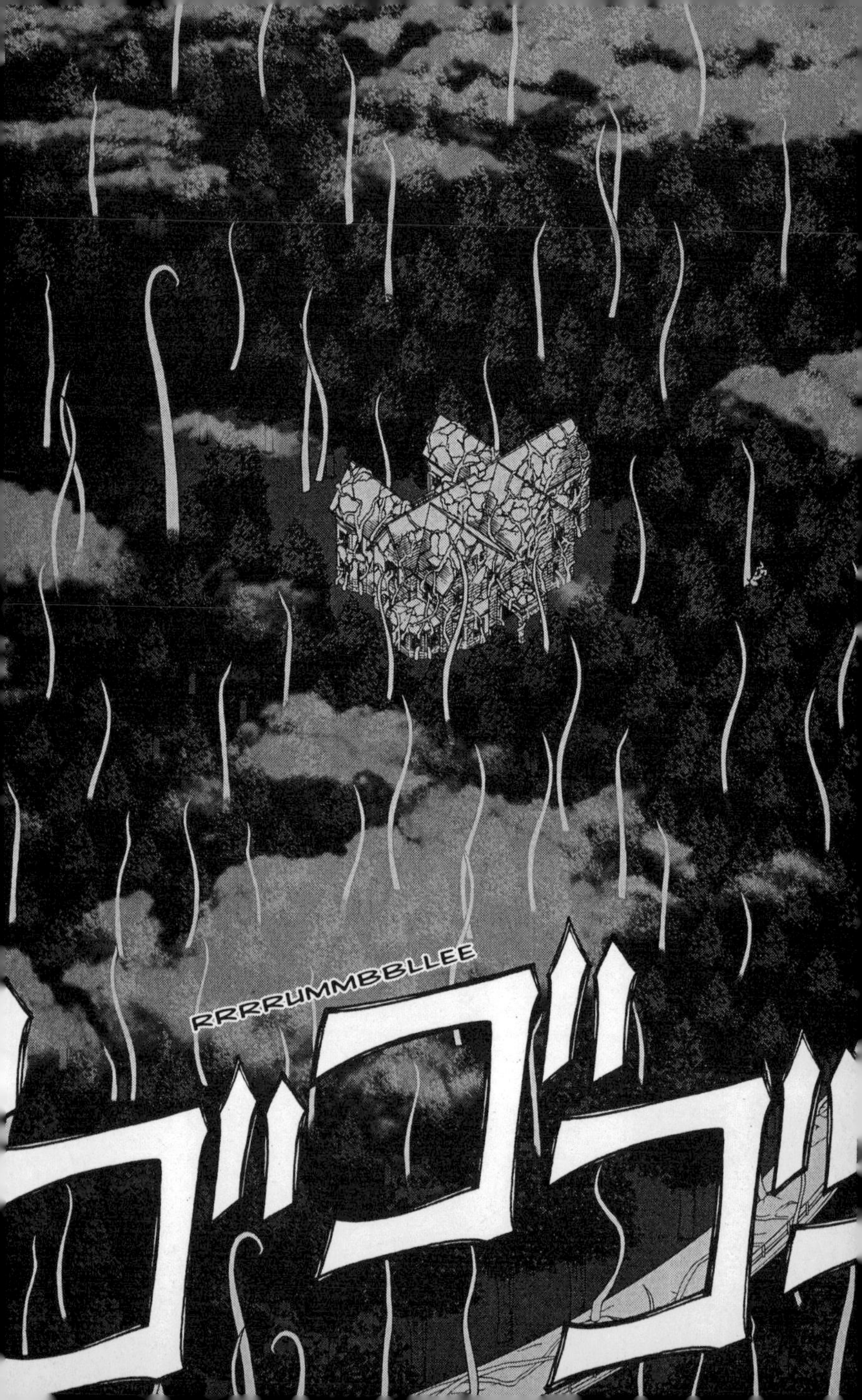
RRRRUMMBBLLEE

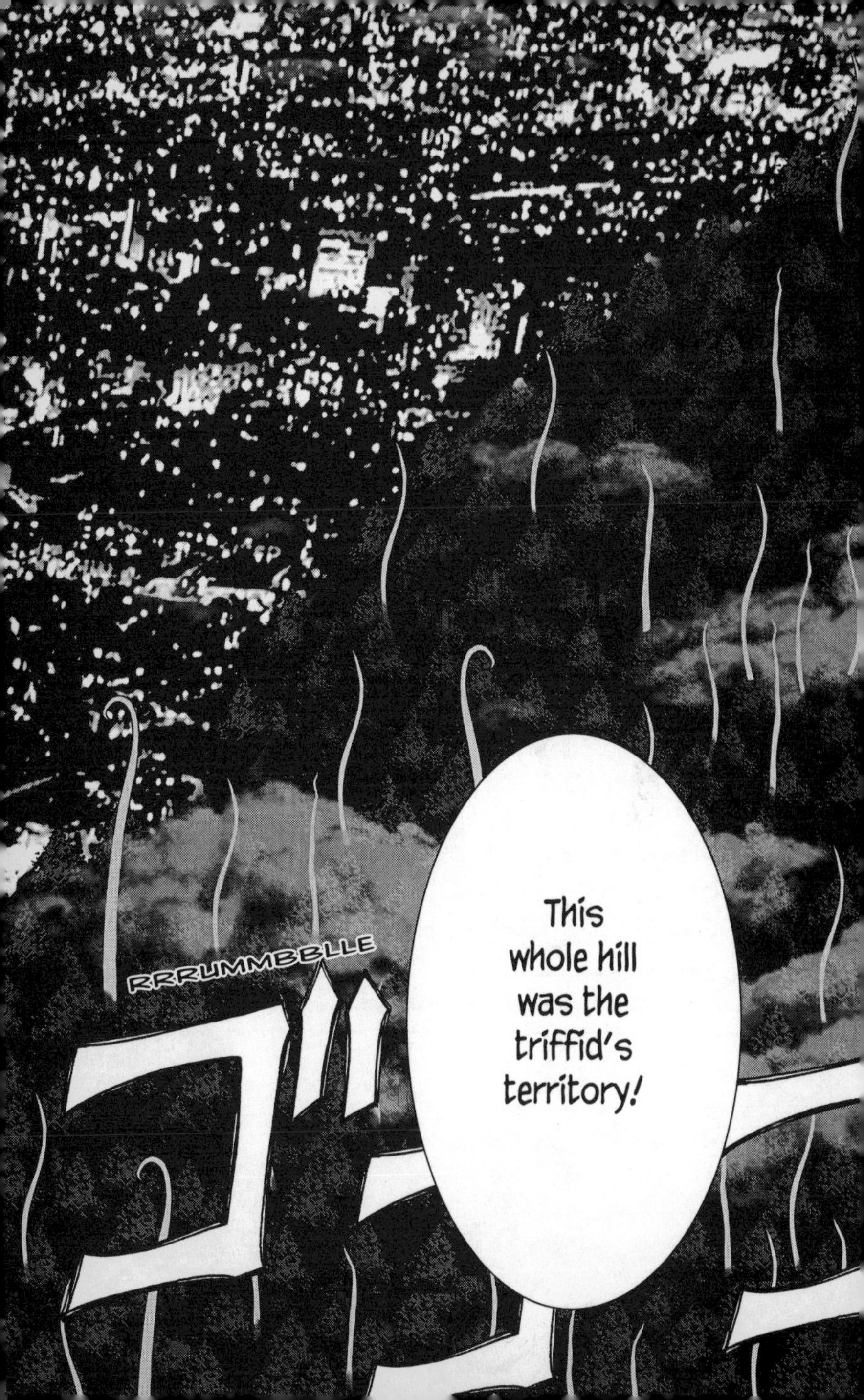
This whole hill was the triffid's territory!
RRRUMMBBLLE

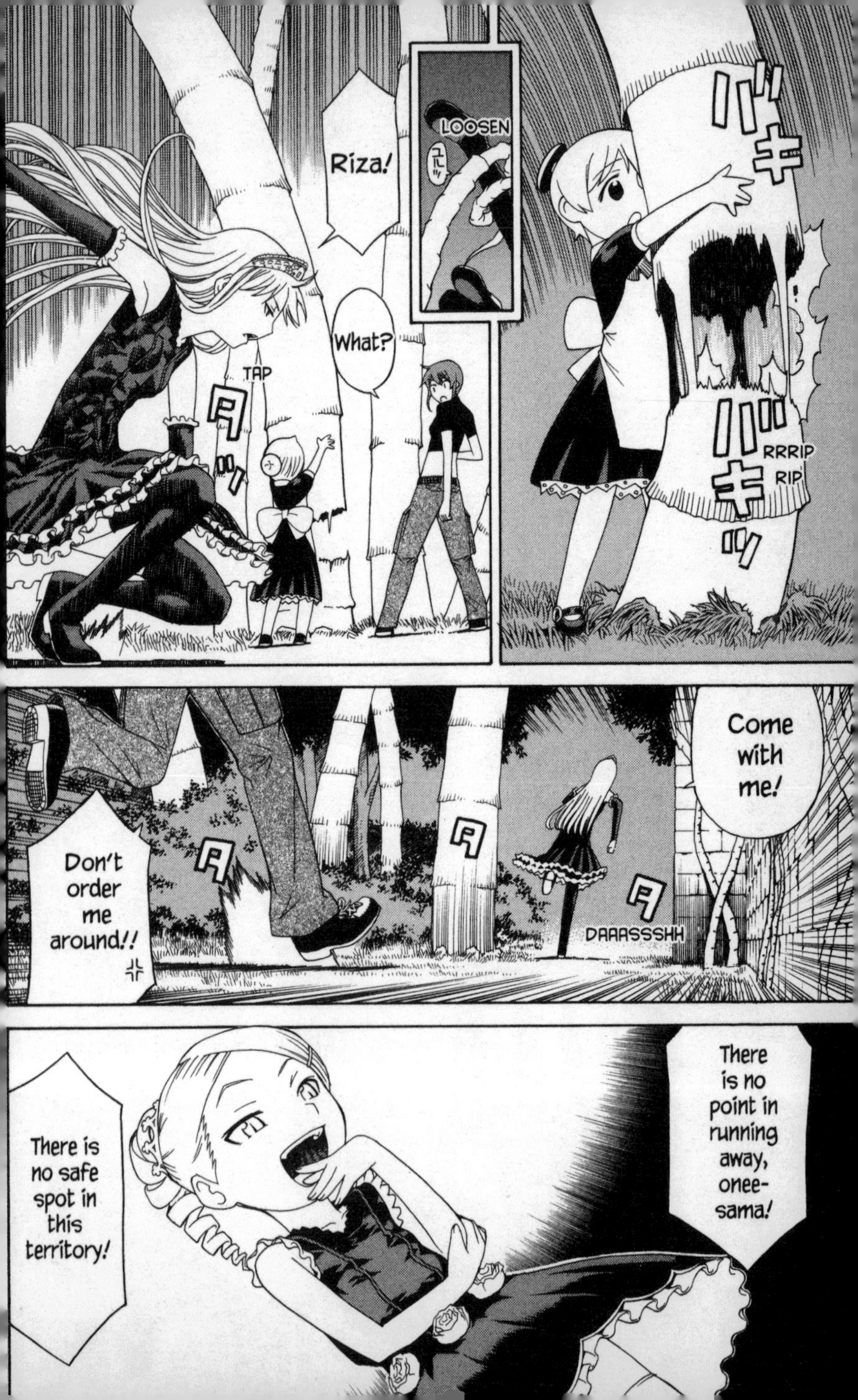
RRRIP
RIP
LOOSEN
Riza!
What?
TAP
Come with me!
DAAASSSHH
Don't order me around!!
There is no point in running away, onee-sama!
There is no safe spot in this territory!

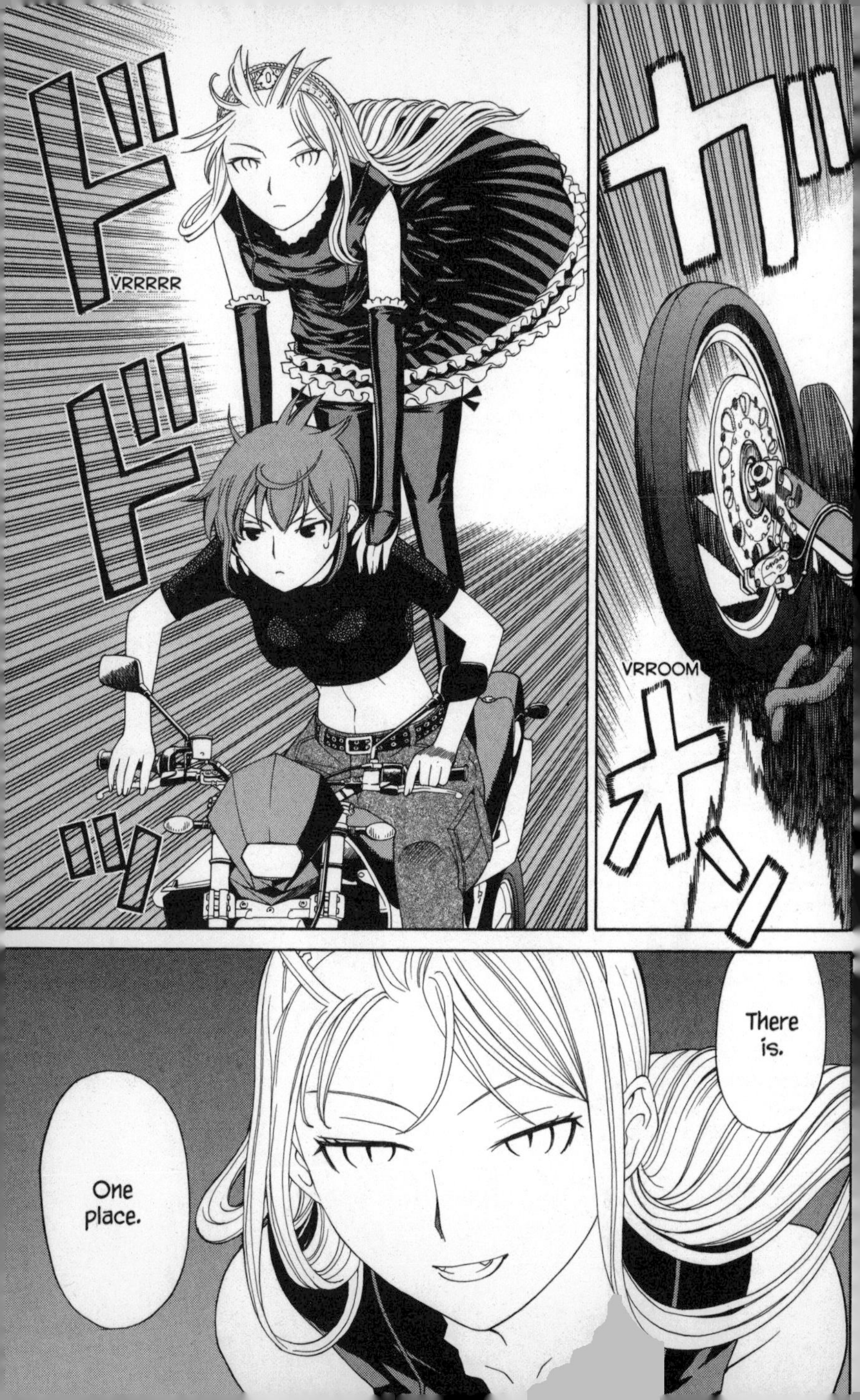

VRROOM
VRRRRR
There is.
One place.

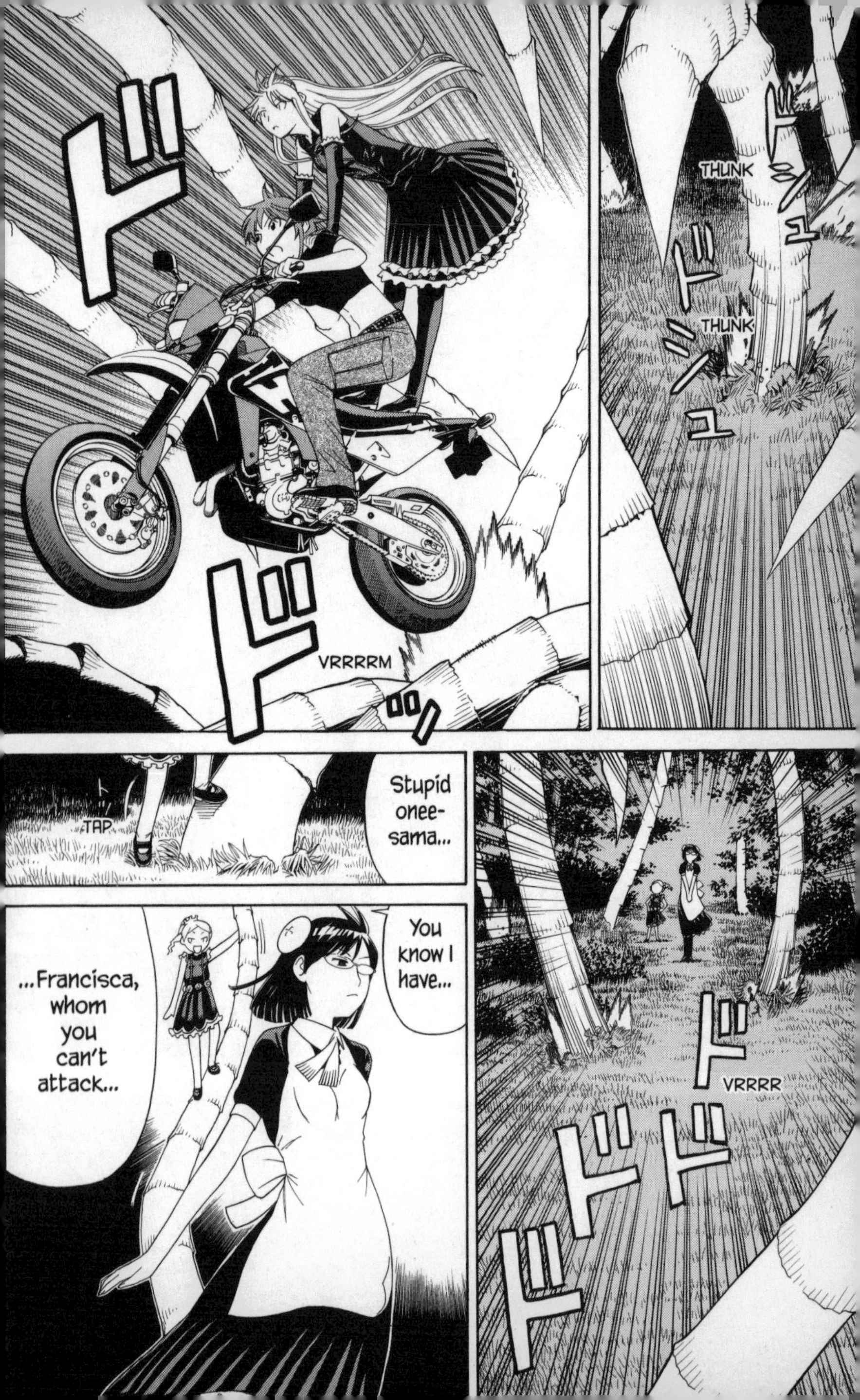
THUNK
THUNK
VRRRRM
VRRRR
TAP
Stupid onee-sama...
You know I have...
...Francisca, whom you can't attack...

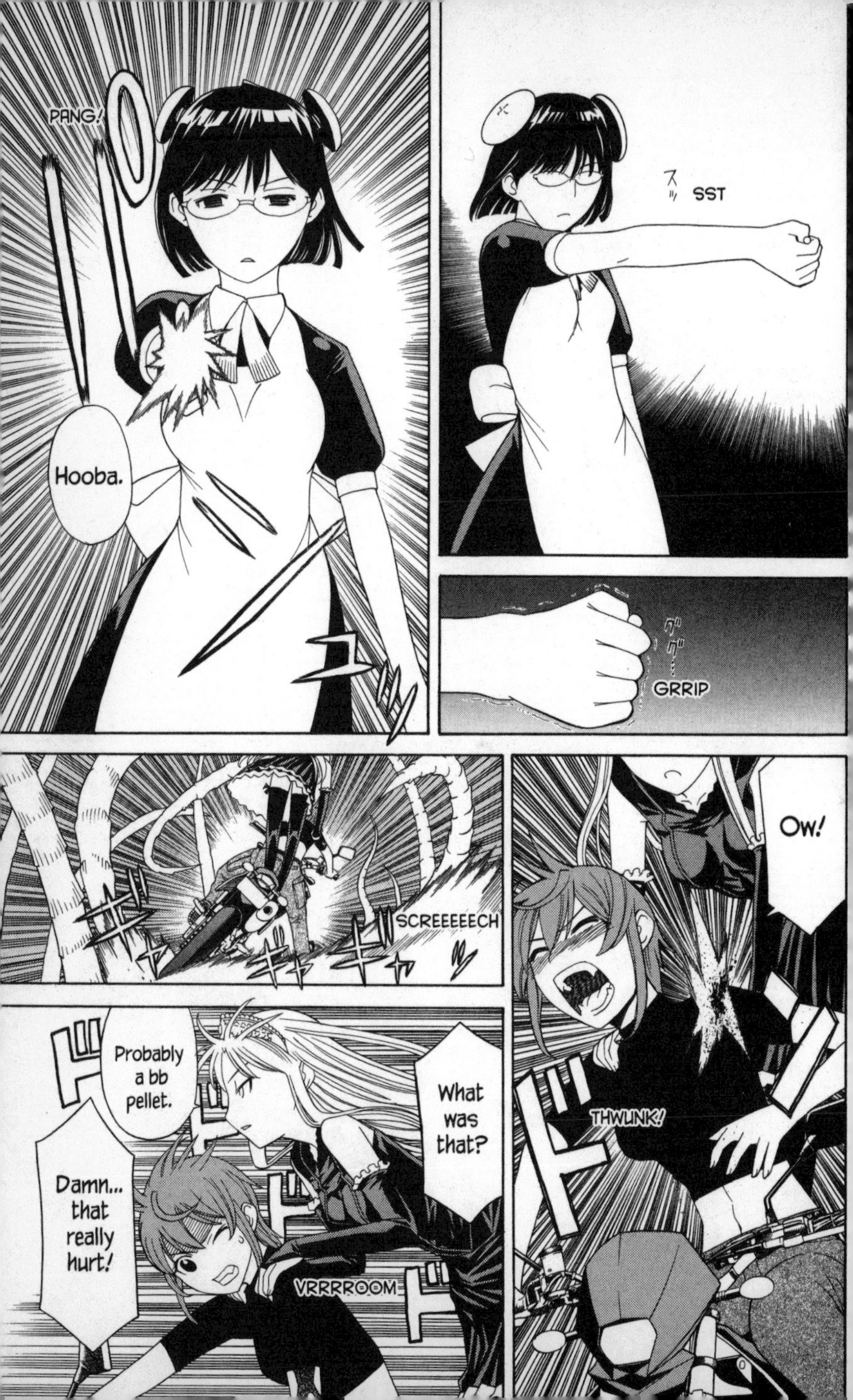
スッ
SST
GRRIP
PANG!
Hooba.
Ow!
THWUNK!
SCREEEEECH
What was that?
Probably a bb pellet.
Damn... that really hurt!
VRRRROOM

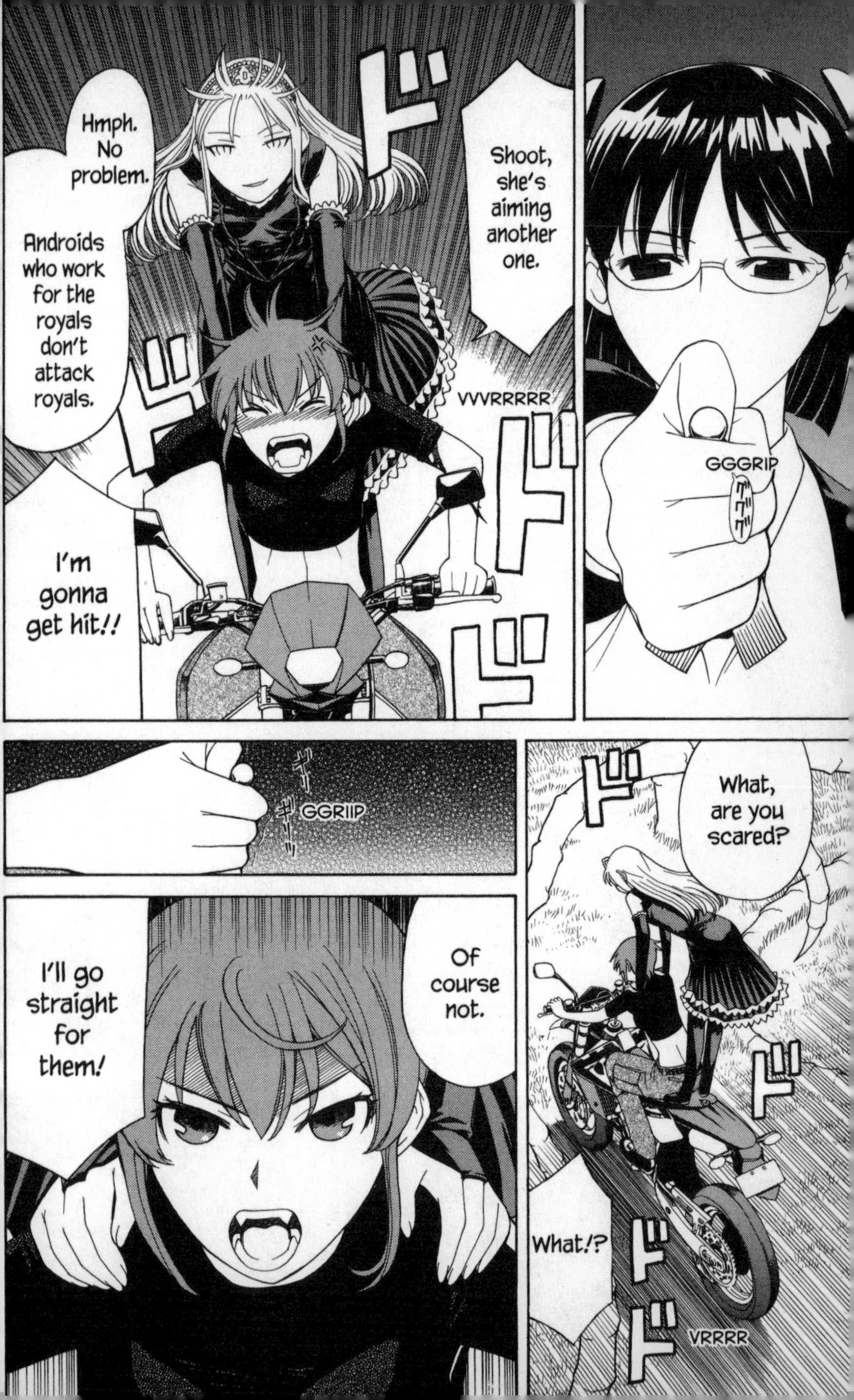
GGGRIP
Shoot, she's aiming another one.
Hmph. No problem.
Androids who work for the royals don't attack royals.
VVVRRRR
I'm gonna get hit!!
What, are you scared?
What!?
VRRRR
GGRIIP
Of course not.
I'll go straight for them!

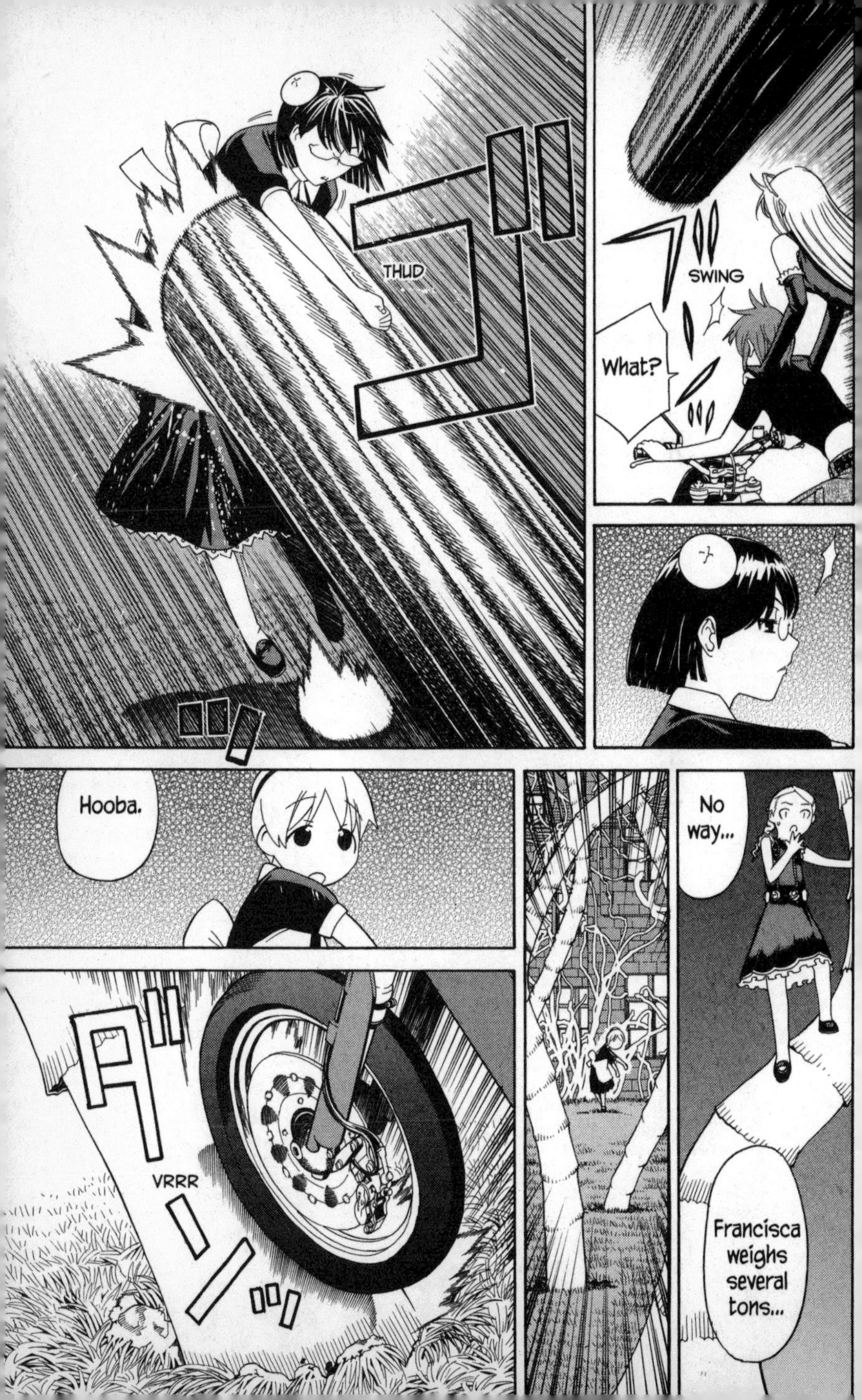
SWING
What?
THUD
No way...
Francisca weighs several tons...
Hooba.
VRRR

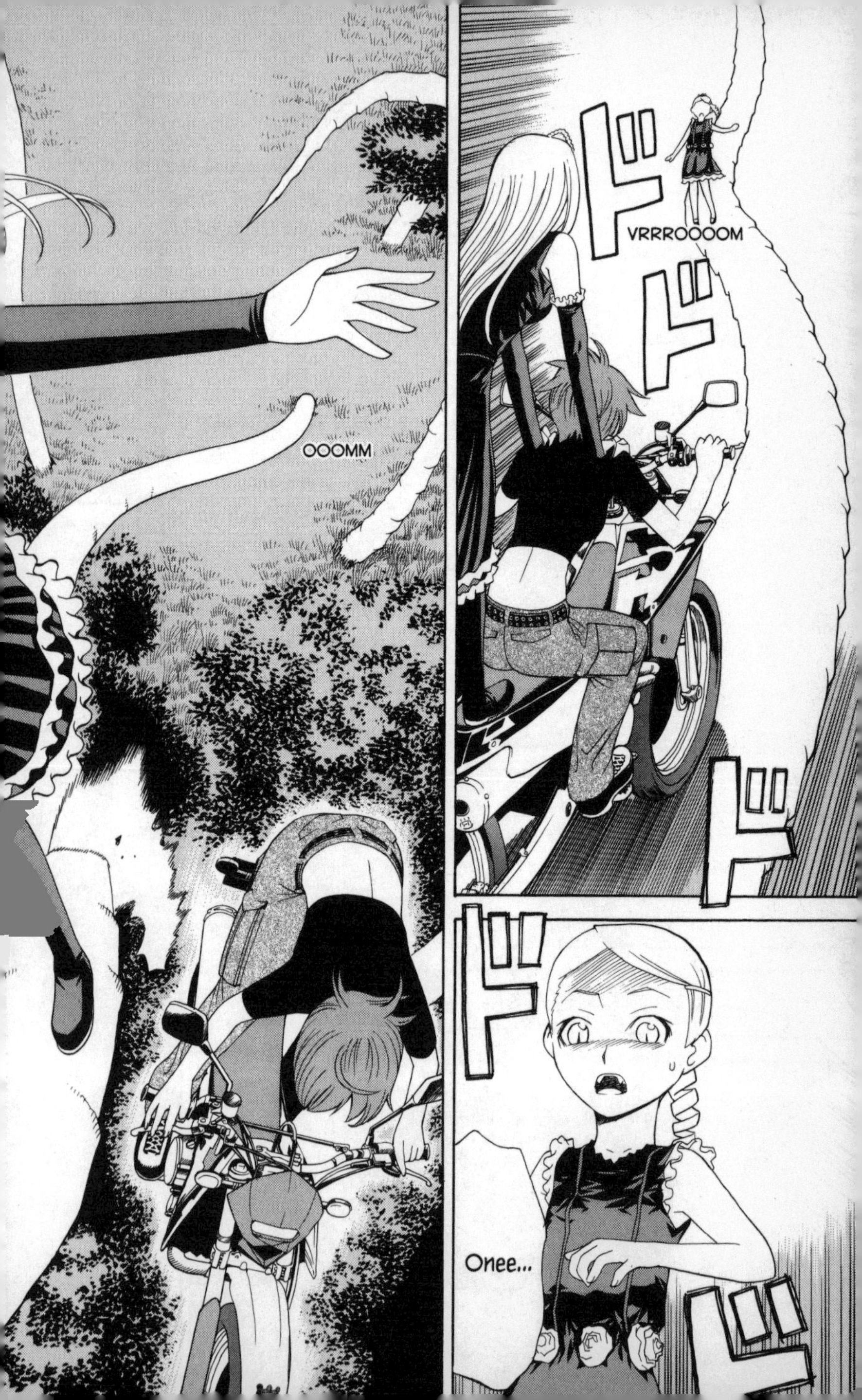
ド
VRRROOOOM
ド
ド
ド
Onee...
ド
OOOMM

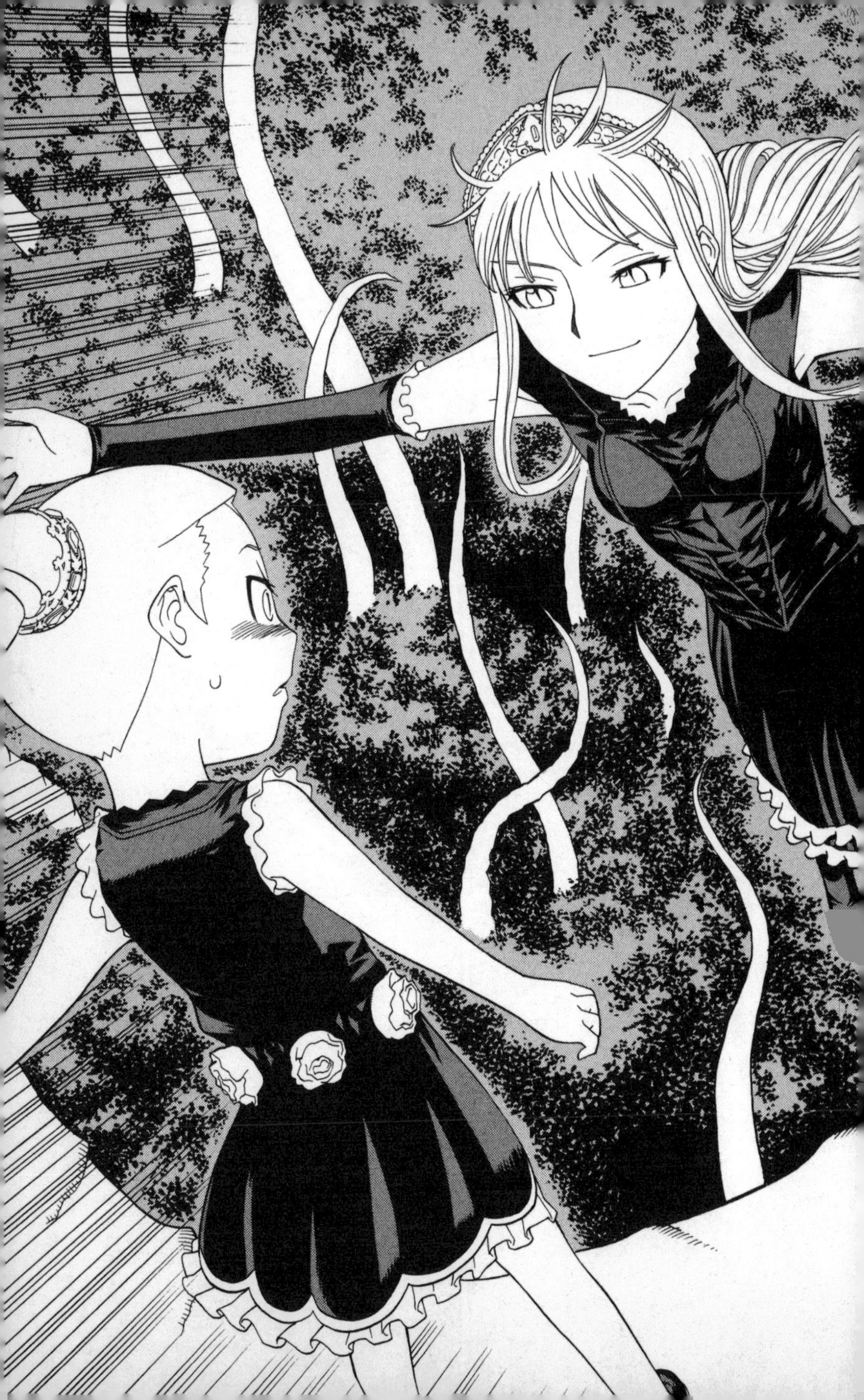

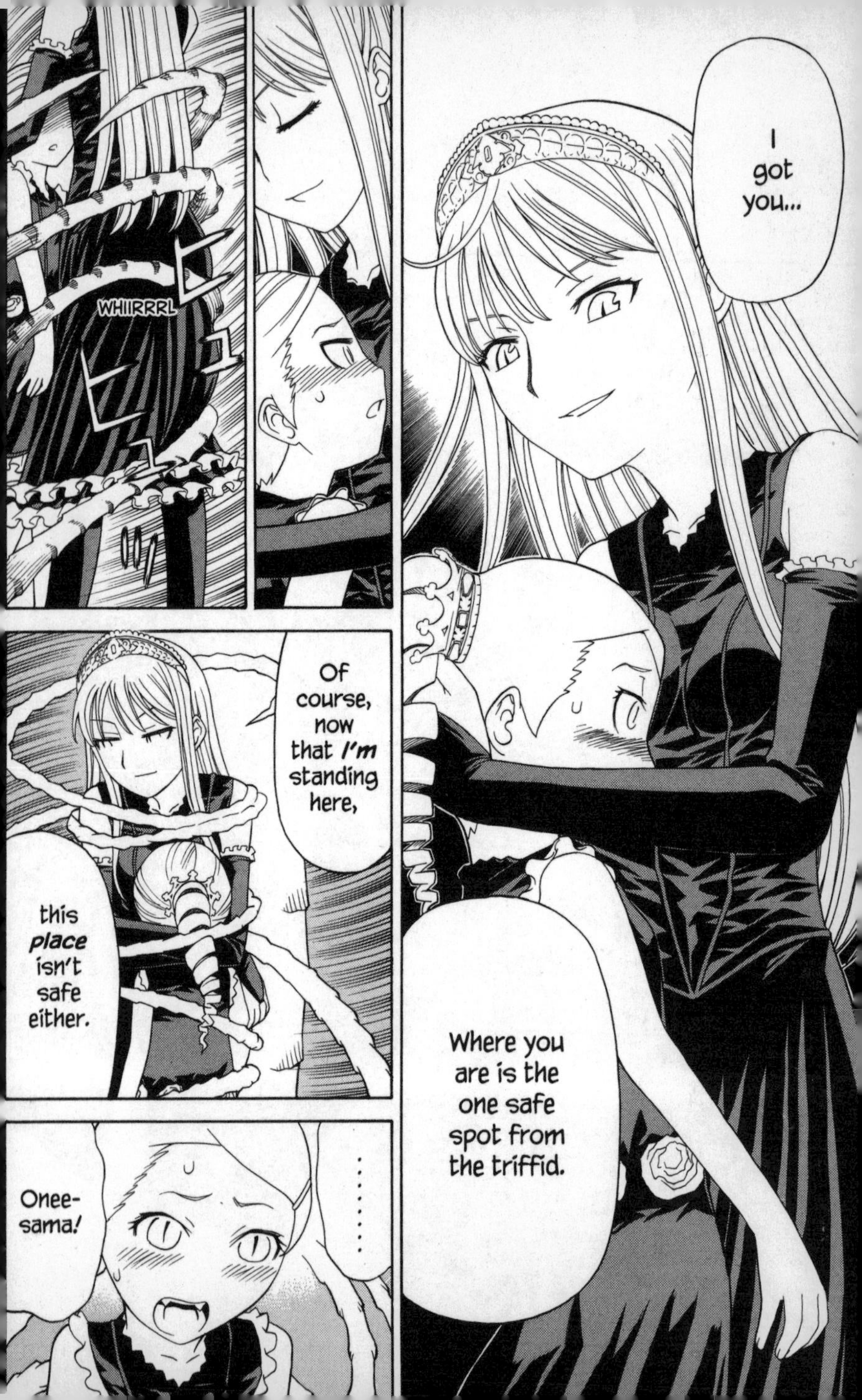
I got you...
Where you are is the one safe spot from the triffid.
WHIIRRRL
Of course, now that *I'm* standing here,
this *place* isn't safe either.
......
Onee-sama!

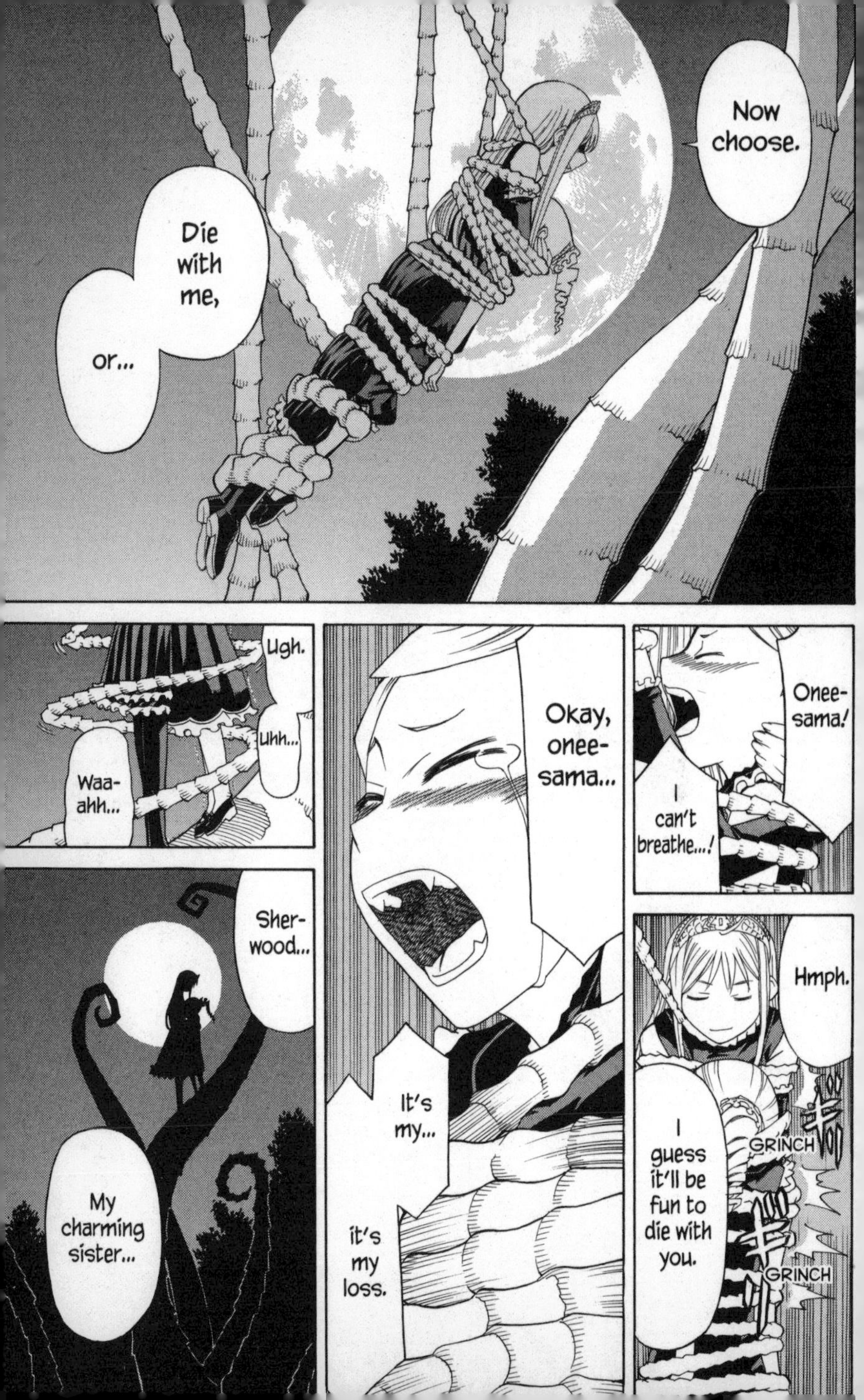

Now choose.
Die with me,
or...
Onee-sama!
I can't breathe...!
Hmph.
I guess it'll be fun to die with you.
GRINCH
GRINCH
Okay, onee-sama...
It's my...
it's my loss.
Ugh.
uhh...
Waa-ahh...
Sher-wood...
My charming sister...

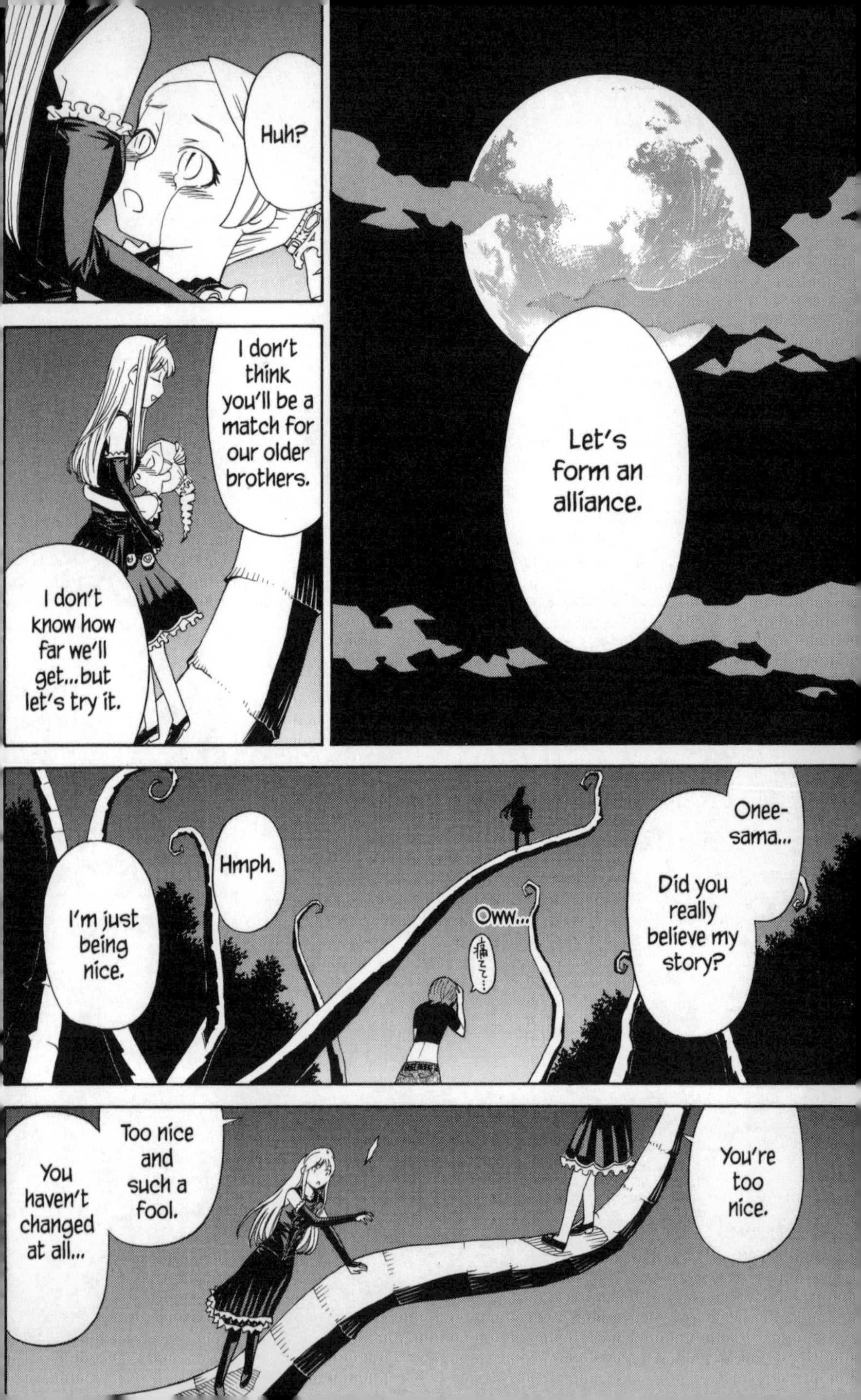
Let's form an alliance.
Huh?
I don't think you'll be a match for our older brothers.
I don't know how far we'll get...but let's try it.
Onee-sama...
Did you really believe my story?
Oww...
痛てて…
Hmph.
I'm just being nice.
You're too nice.
Too nice and such a fool.
You haven't changed at all...

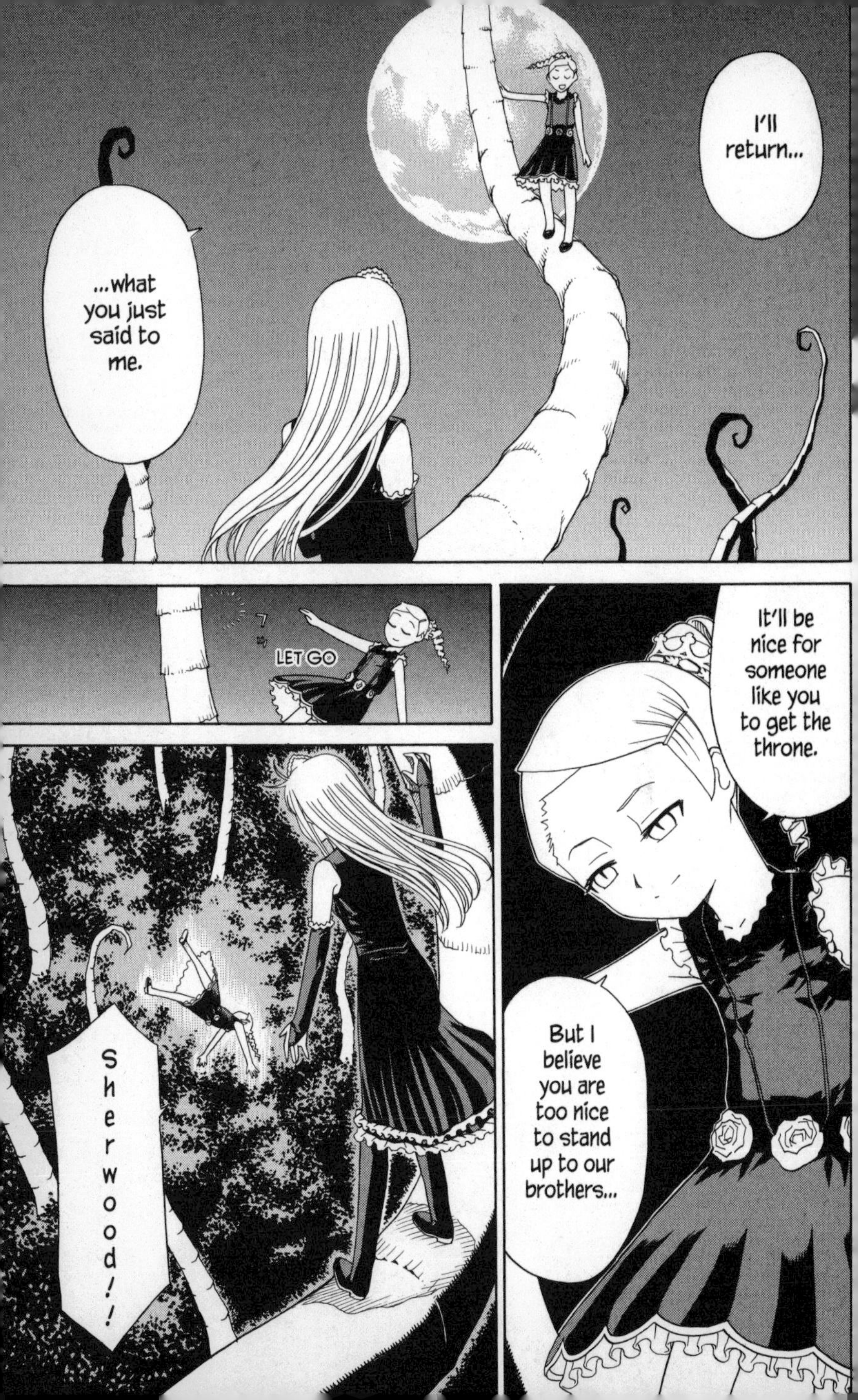
I'll return...
...what you just said to me.
It'll be nice for someone like you to get the throne.
But I believe you are too nice to stand up to our brothers...
LET GO
Sherwood!!

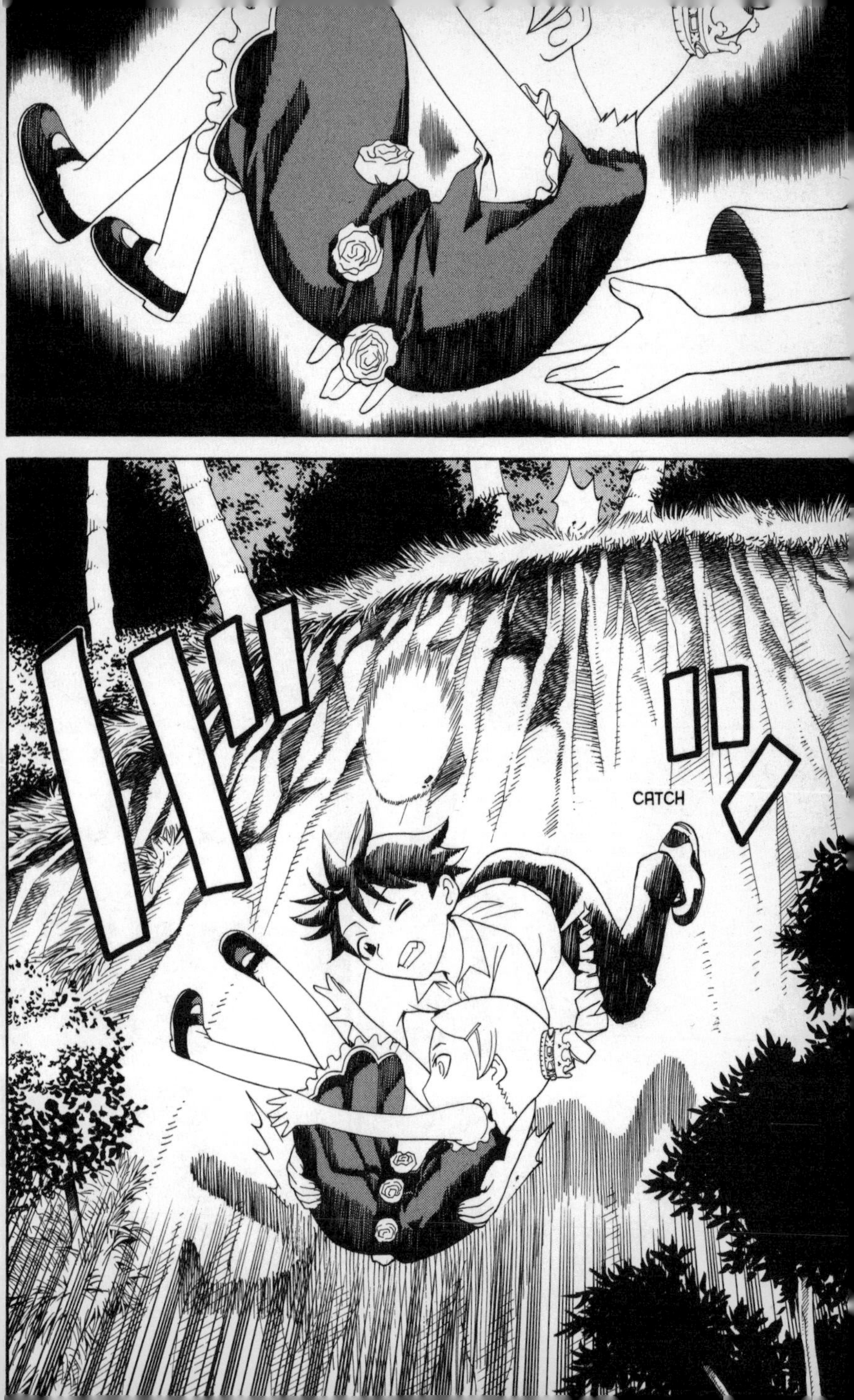
CATCH

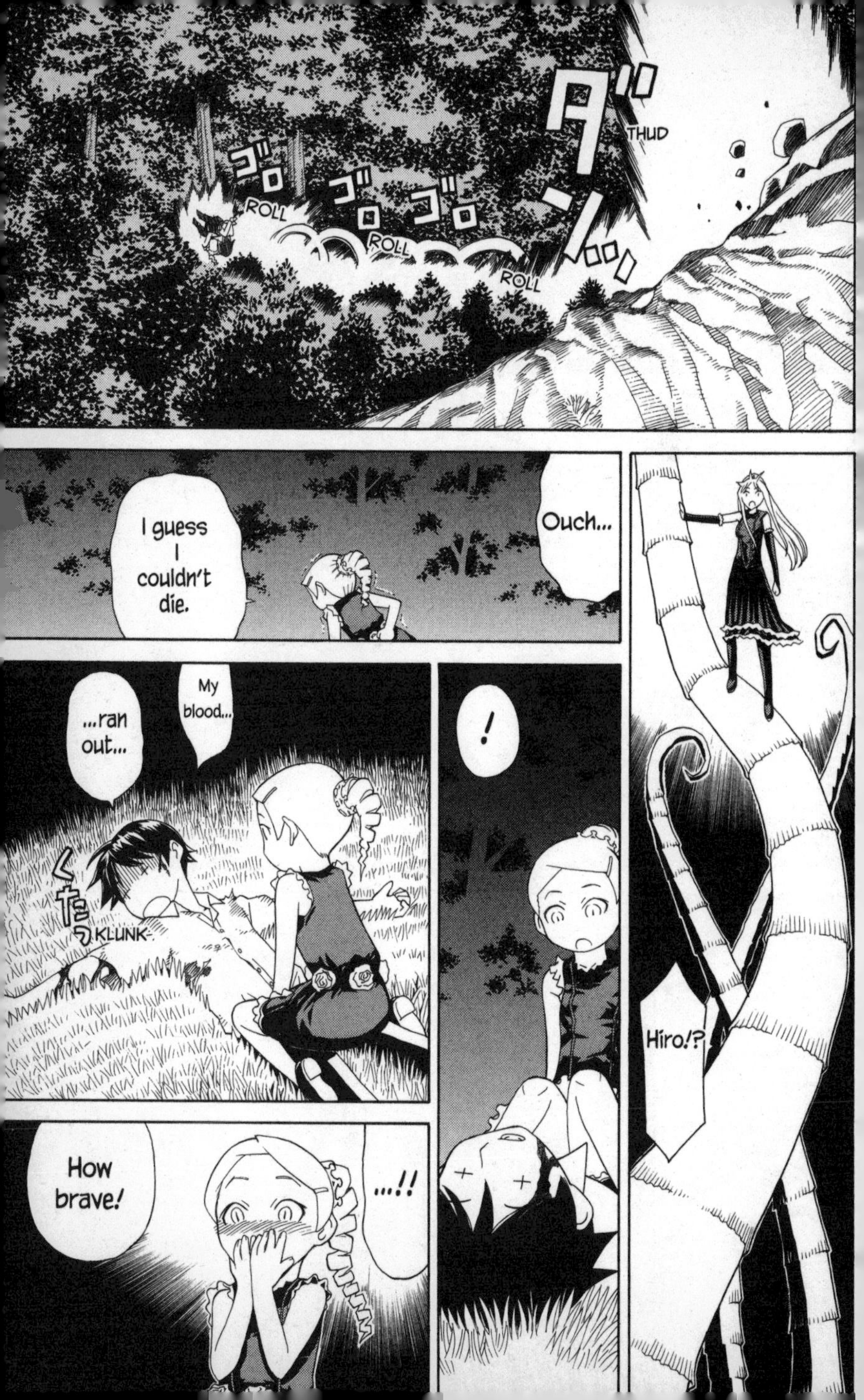

ダン THUD
ゴロ ROLL
ゴロ ROLL
ゴロ ROLL
Hiro!?
Ouch...
I guess I couldn't die.
!
My blood...
...ran out...
くたっ KLUNK
...!!
How brave!

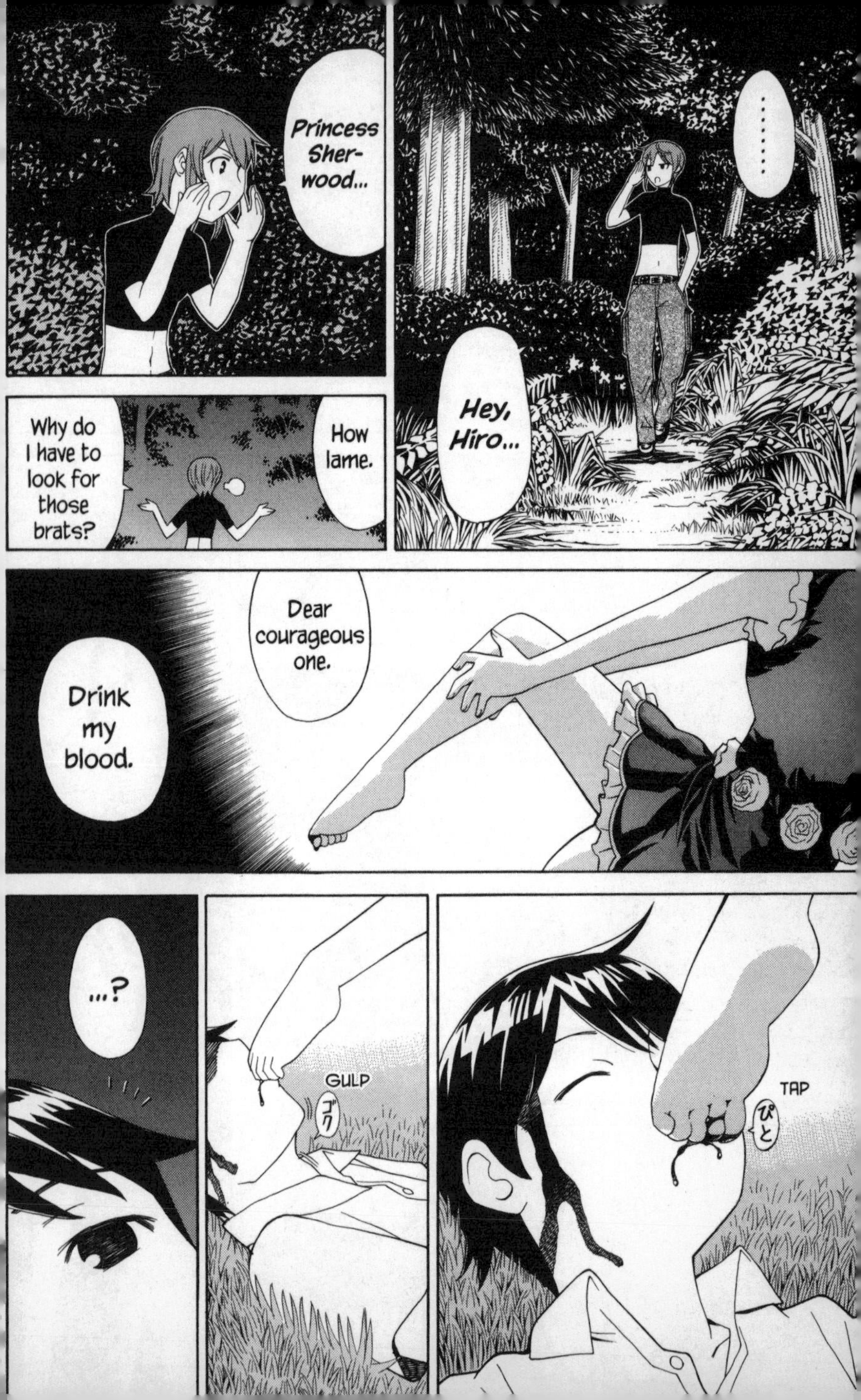
......
Hey, Hiro...
Princess Sherwood...
How lame.
Why do I have to look for those brats?
Dear courageous one.
Drink my blood.
TAP
ぴと
GULP
ゴク
...?

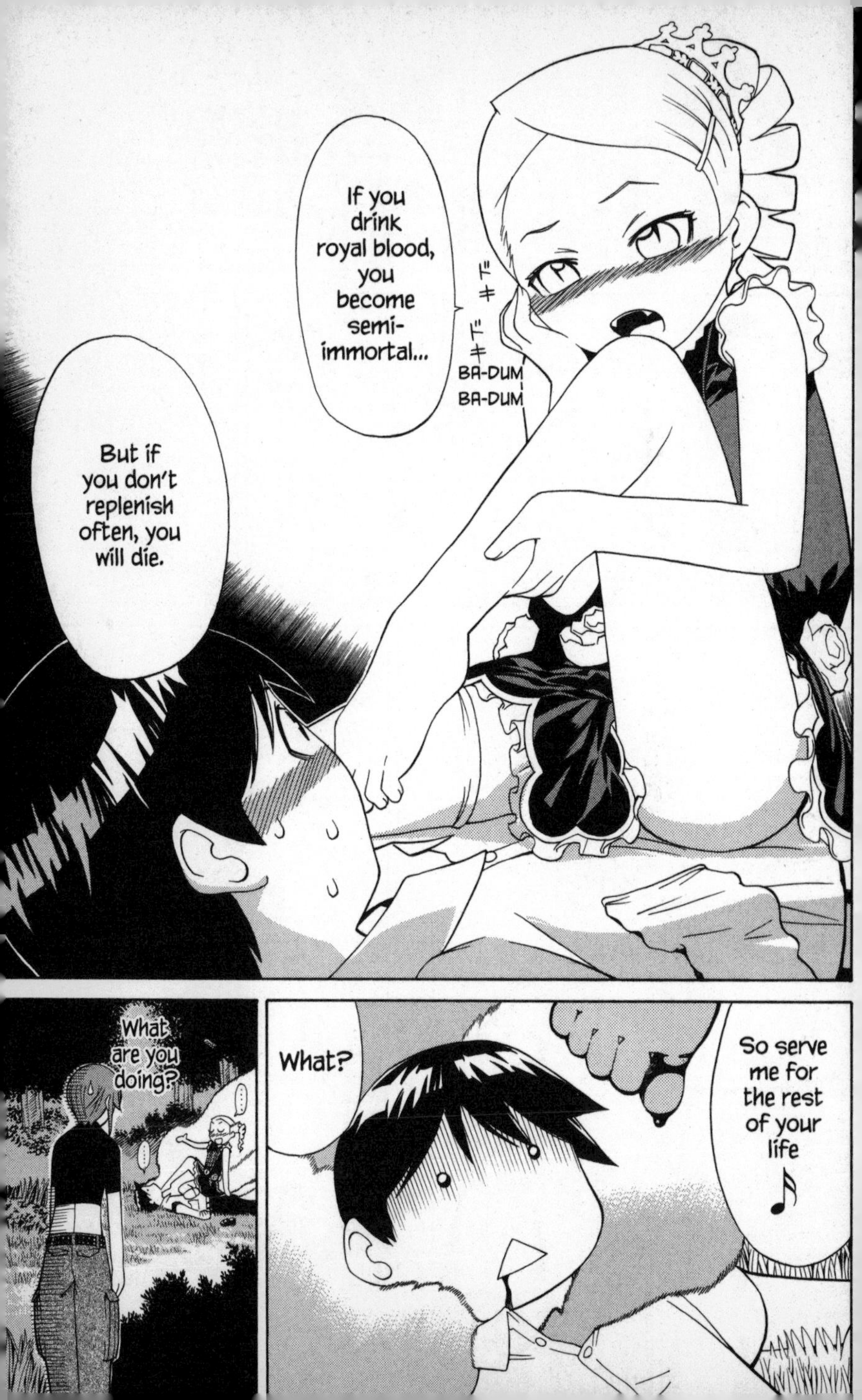
If you drink royal blood, you become semi-immortal...
ドキドキ
BA-DUM BA-DUM
But if you don't replenish often, you will die.
So serve me for the rest of your life ♪
What?
What are you doing?
...
...

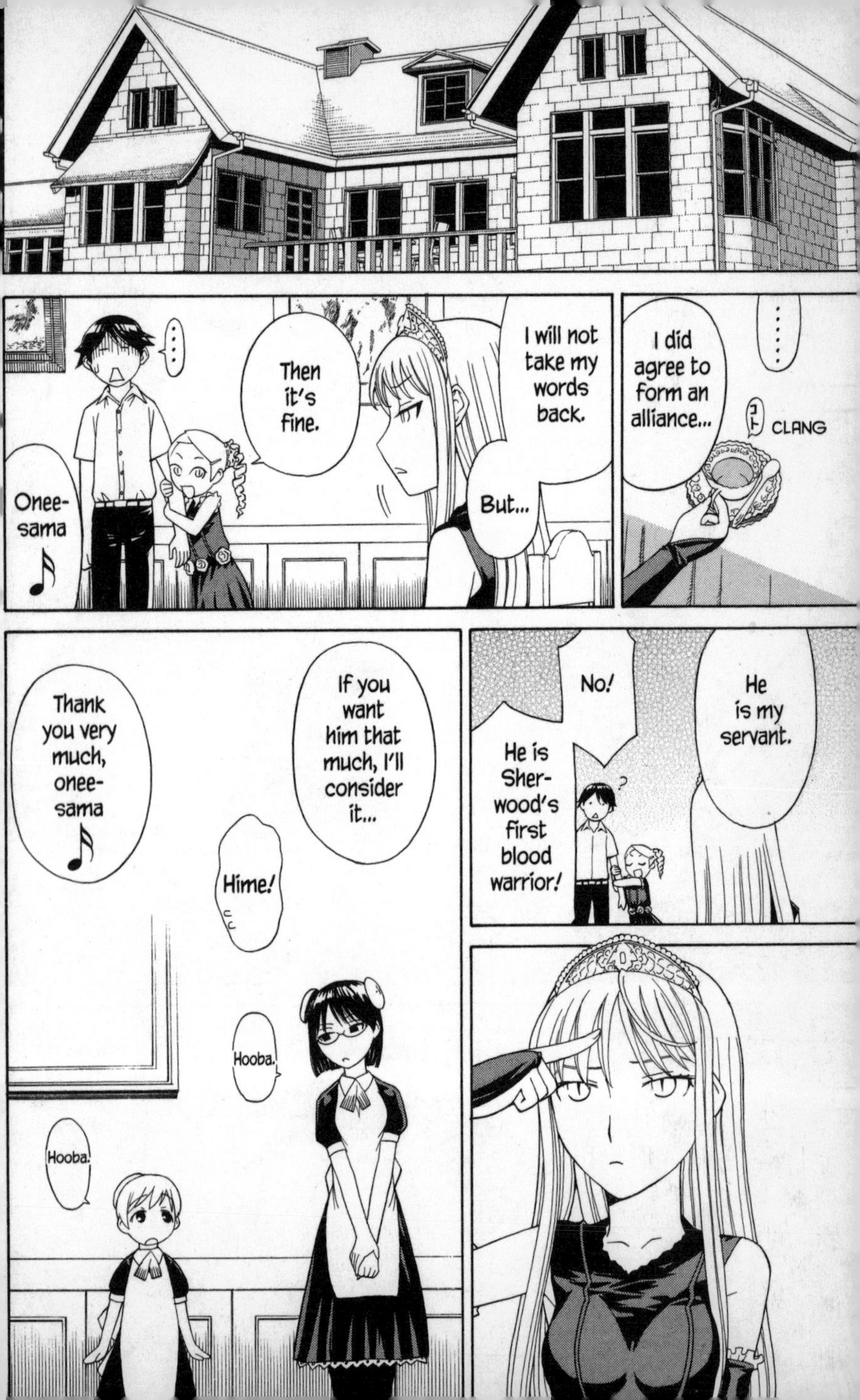
......
I did agree to form an alliance...
CLANG
I will not take my words back.
But...
Then it's fine.
....
Onee-sama ♪
He is my servant.
No!
He is Sherwood's first blood warrior!
If you want him that much, I'll consider it...
Thank you very much, onee-sama ♪
Hime!
Hooba.
Hooba.

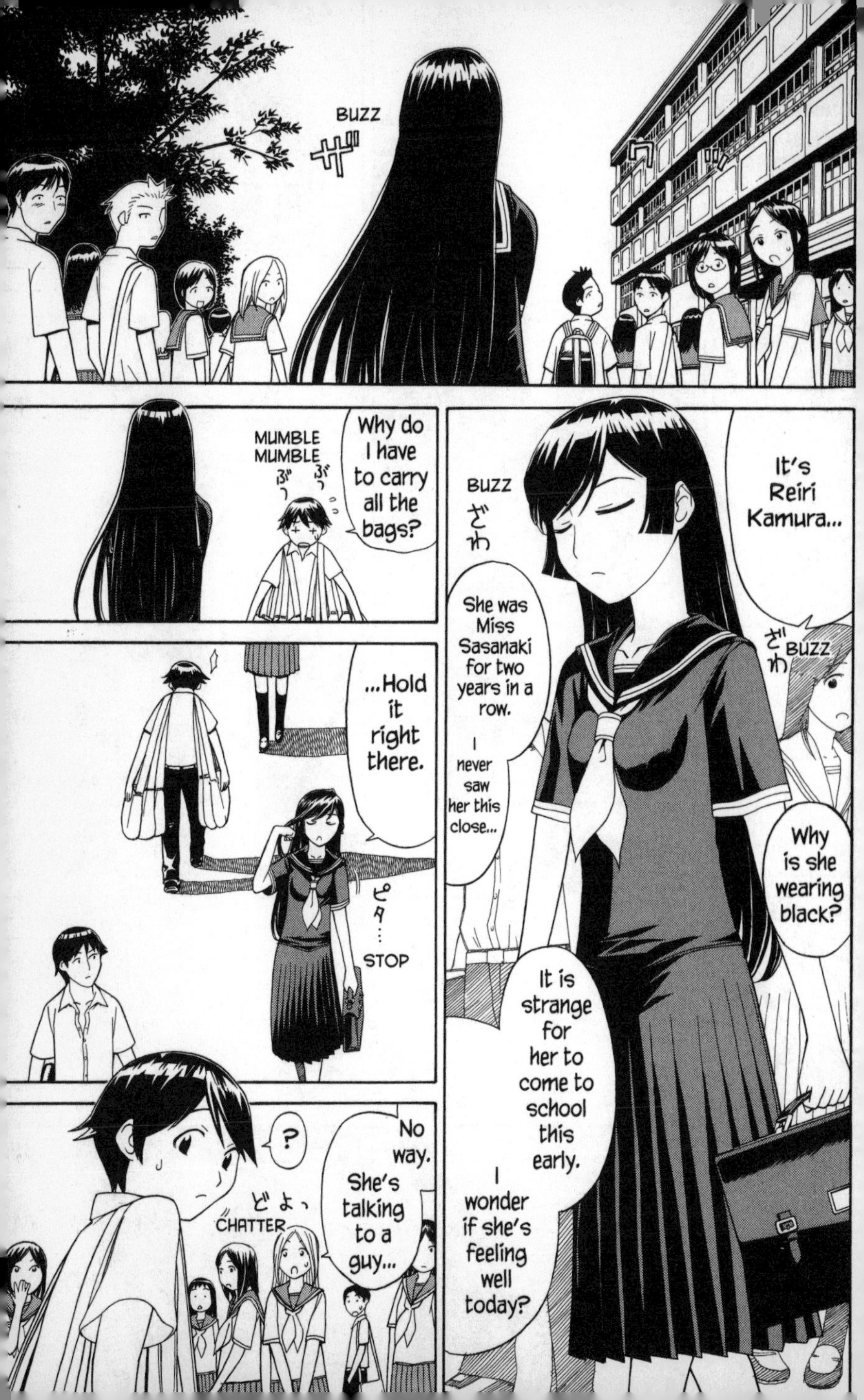

BUZZ
ザ
It's Reiri Kamura...
ざわ BUZZ
BUZZ ざわ
She was Miss Sasanaki for two years in a row.
I never saw her this close...
Why is she wearing black?
It is strange for her to come to school this early.
I wonder if she's feeling well today?
Why do I have to carry all the bags?
MUMBLE MUMBLE
ぶつ ぶつ
...Hold it right there.
ピタ...
STOP
No way. She's talking to a guy...
?
どよっ
CHATTER

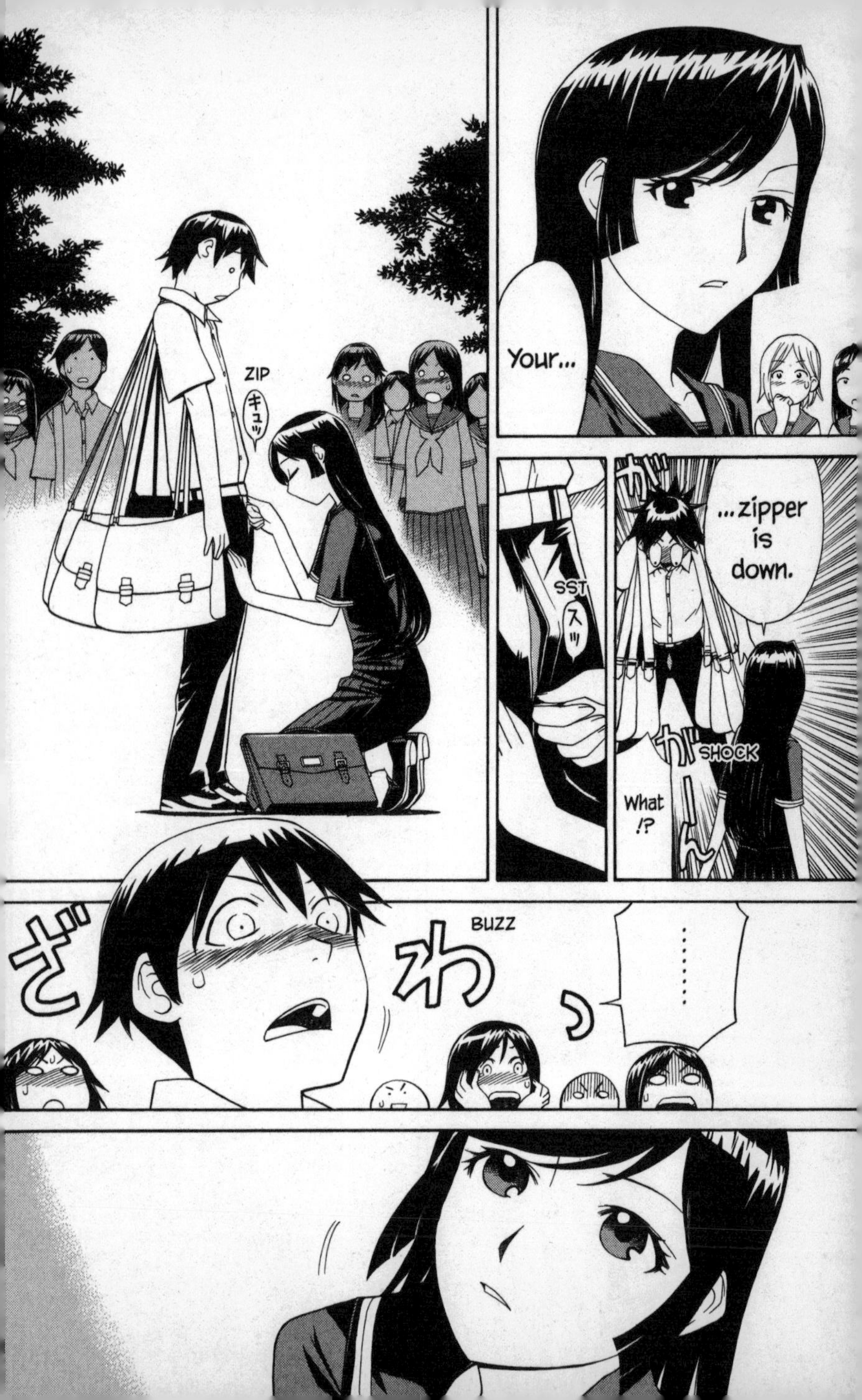
Your...
...zipper is down.
がーん
SHOCK
What !?
SST
スッ
ZIP
キュッ
ざわっ
BUZZ
......

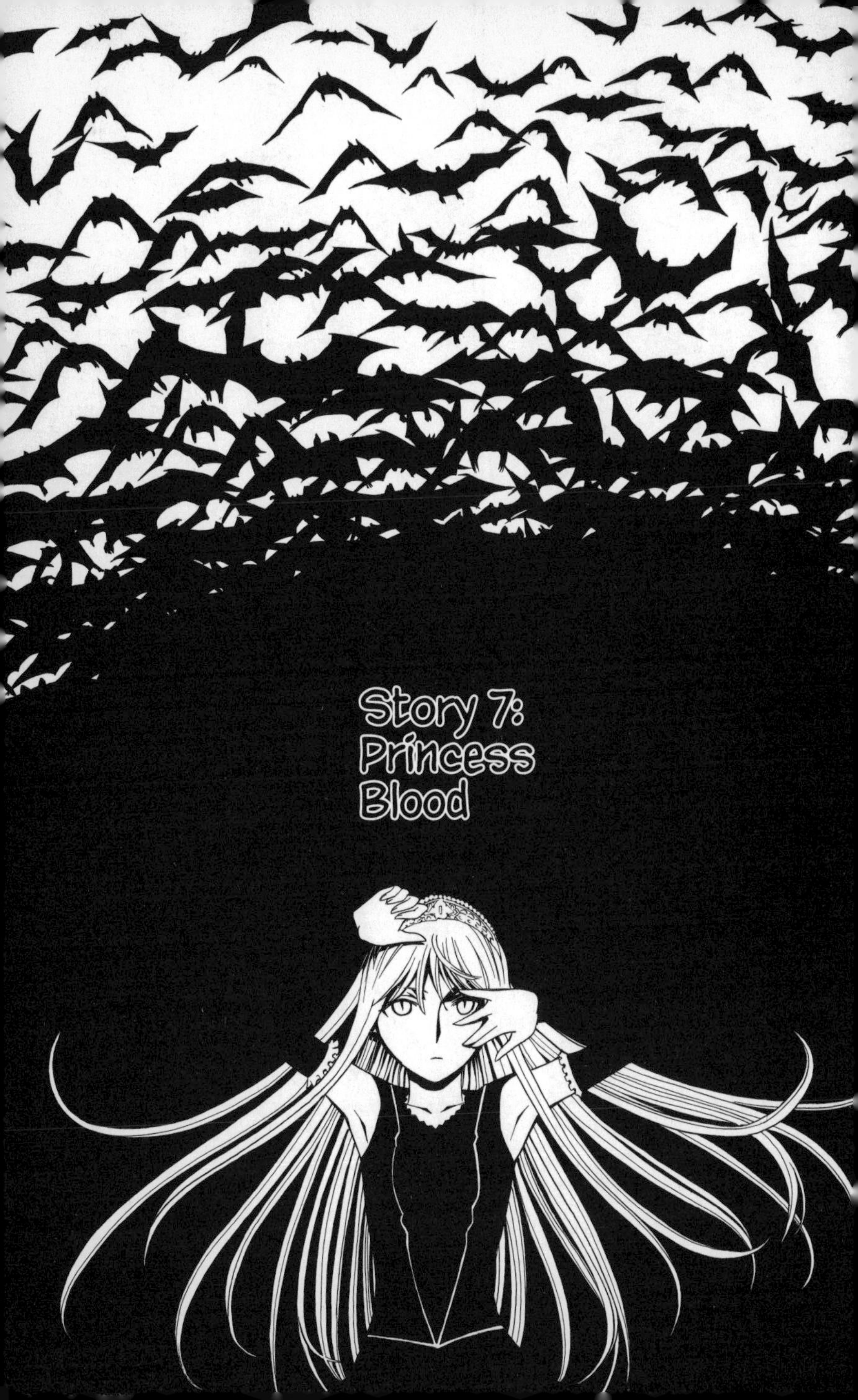
Story 7:
Princess
Blood

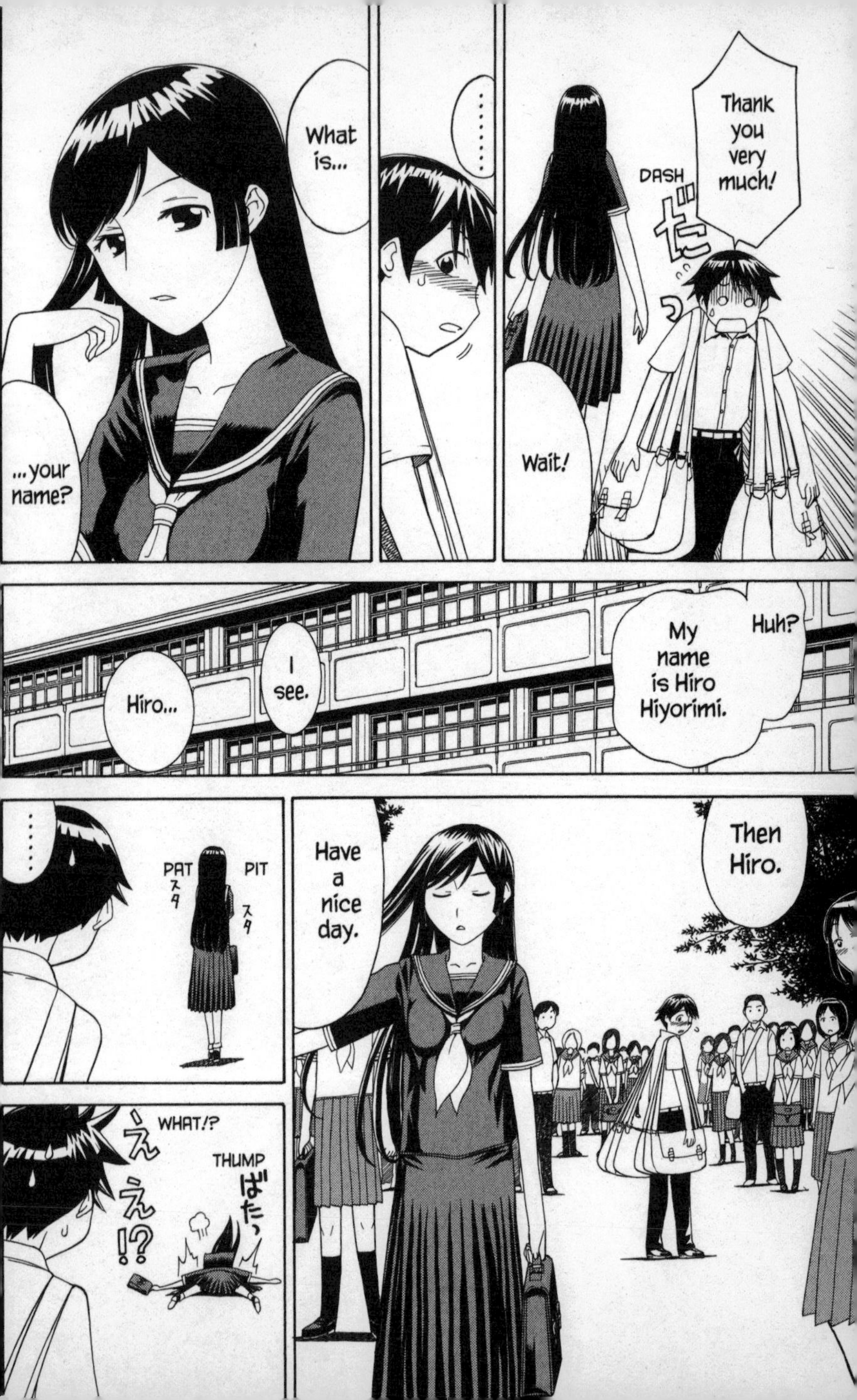
Thank you very much!
DASH
だっ
Wait!
......
What is...
...your name?
Huh?
My name is Hiro Hiyorimi.
I see.
Hiro...
Then Hiro.
Have a nice day.
......
PIT
スタ
PAT
スタ
WHAT!?
ええ!?
THUMP
ばたっ

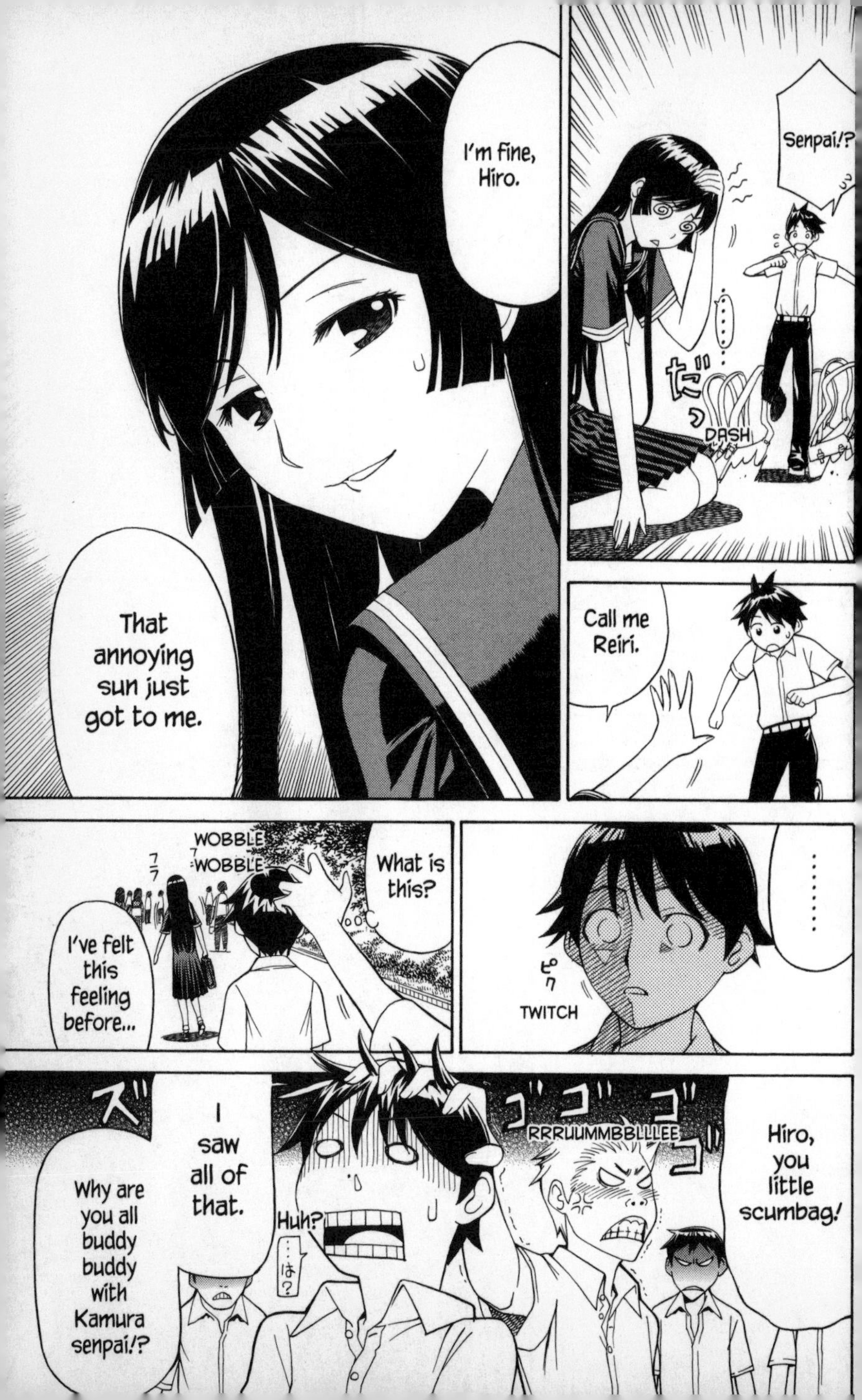
Senpai!?
......
だっ
DASH
Call me Reiri.
I'm fine, Hiro.
That annoying sun just got to me.
....
ピク
TWITCH
What is this?
WOBBLE WOBBLE
I've felt this feeling before...
Hiro, you little scumbag!
RRRUUMMBBLLLEE
I saw all of that.
Huh?
...は?
Why are you all buddy buddy with Kamura senpai!?

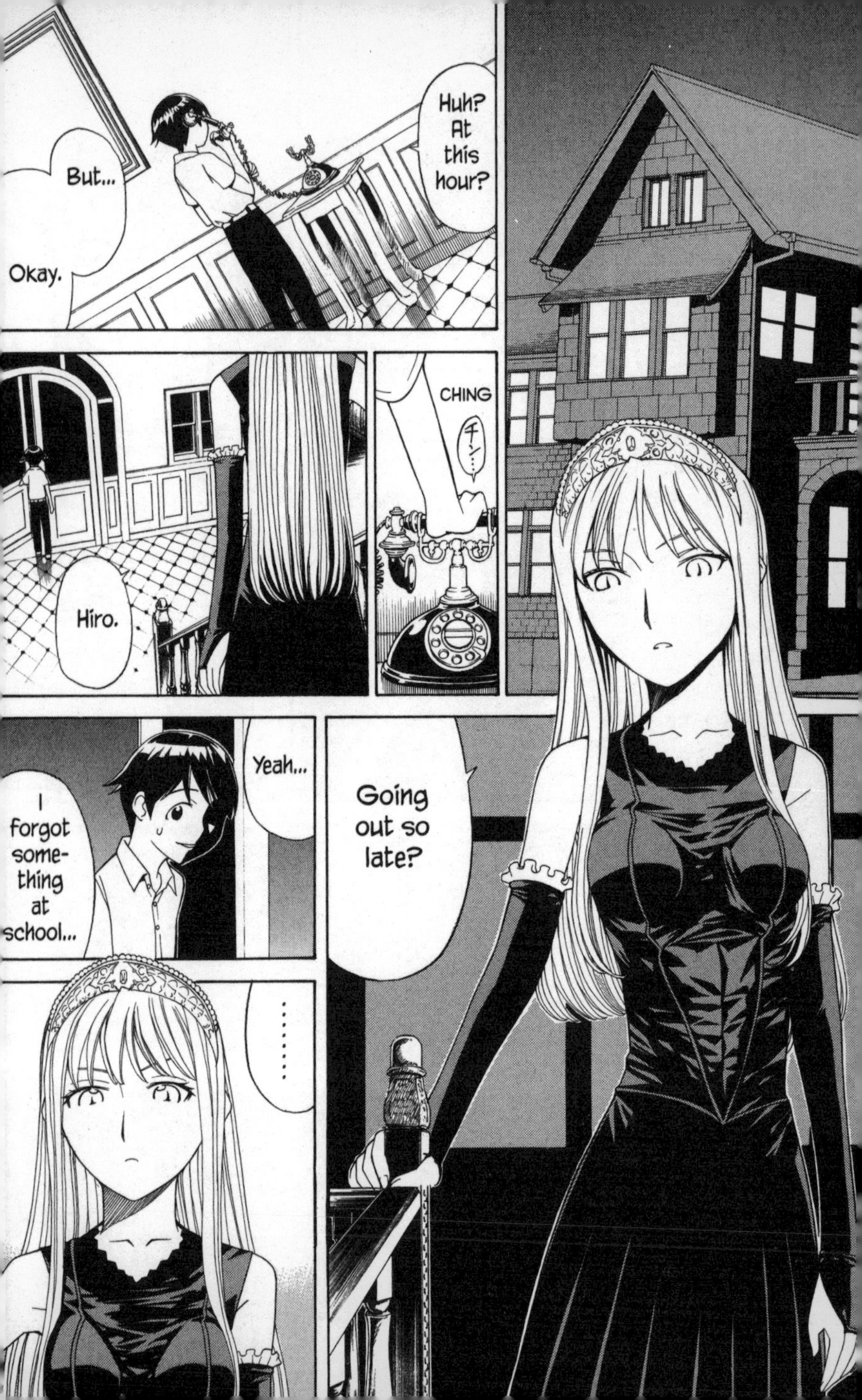
Huh? At this hour?
But...
Okay.
CHING
チン…
Hiro.
Going out so late?
Yeah...
I forgot some-thing at school...
......

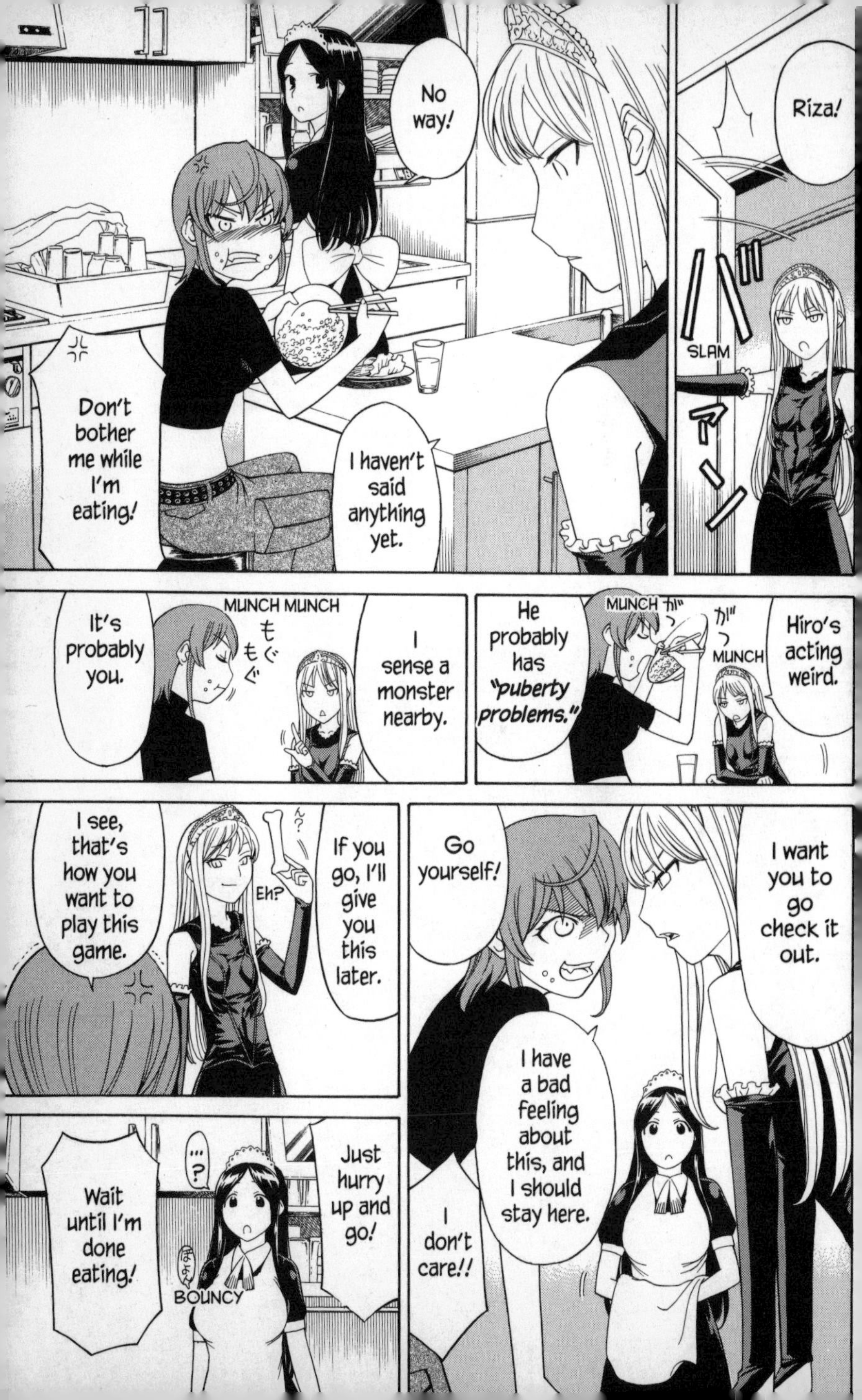
Riza!
SLAM
バアン
No way!
I haven't said anything yet.
Don't bother me while I'm eating!
Hiro's acting weird.
MUNCH がつ
MUNCH がつ
He probably has *"puberty problems."*
I sense a monster nearby.
MUNCH MUNCH もぐもぐ
It's probably you.
I want you to go check it out.
Go yourself!
I have a bad feeling about this, and I should stay here.
I don't care!!
ん?
If you go, I'll give you this later.
Eh?
I see, that's how you want to play this game.
Just hurry up and go!
...?
Wait until I'm done eating!
BOUNCY

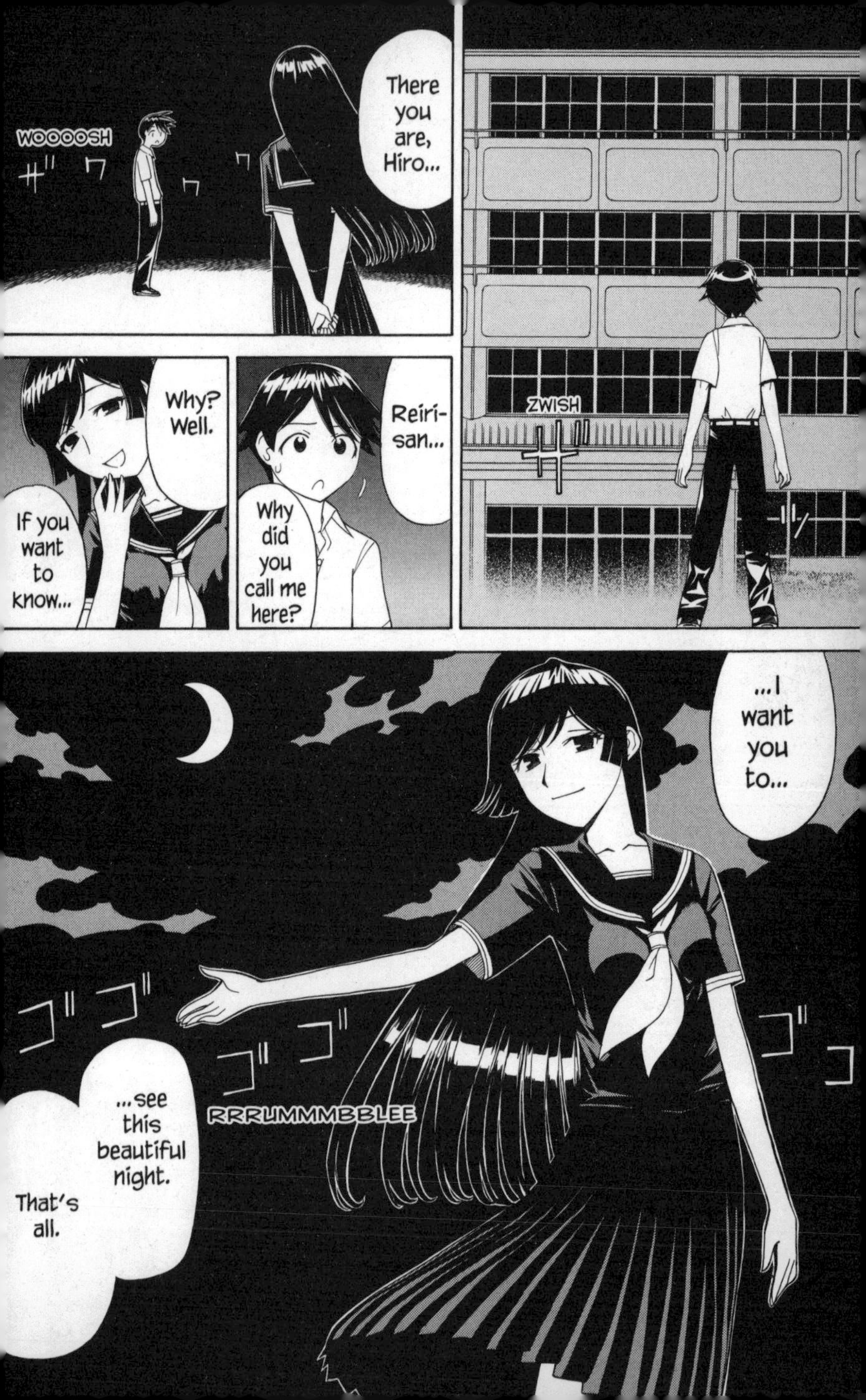
ZWISH
There you are, Hiro...
WOOOOSH
Reiri-san...
Why did you call me here?
Why? Well.
If you want to know...
...I want you to...
...see this beautiful night.
RRRUMMMBBLEE
That's all.

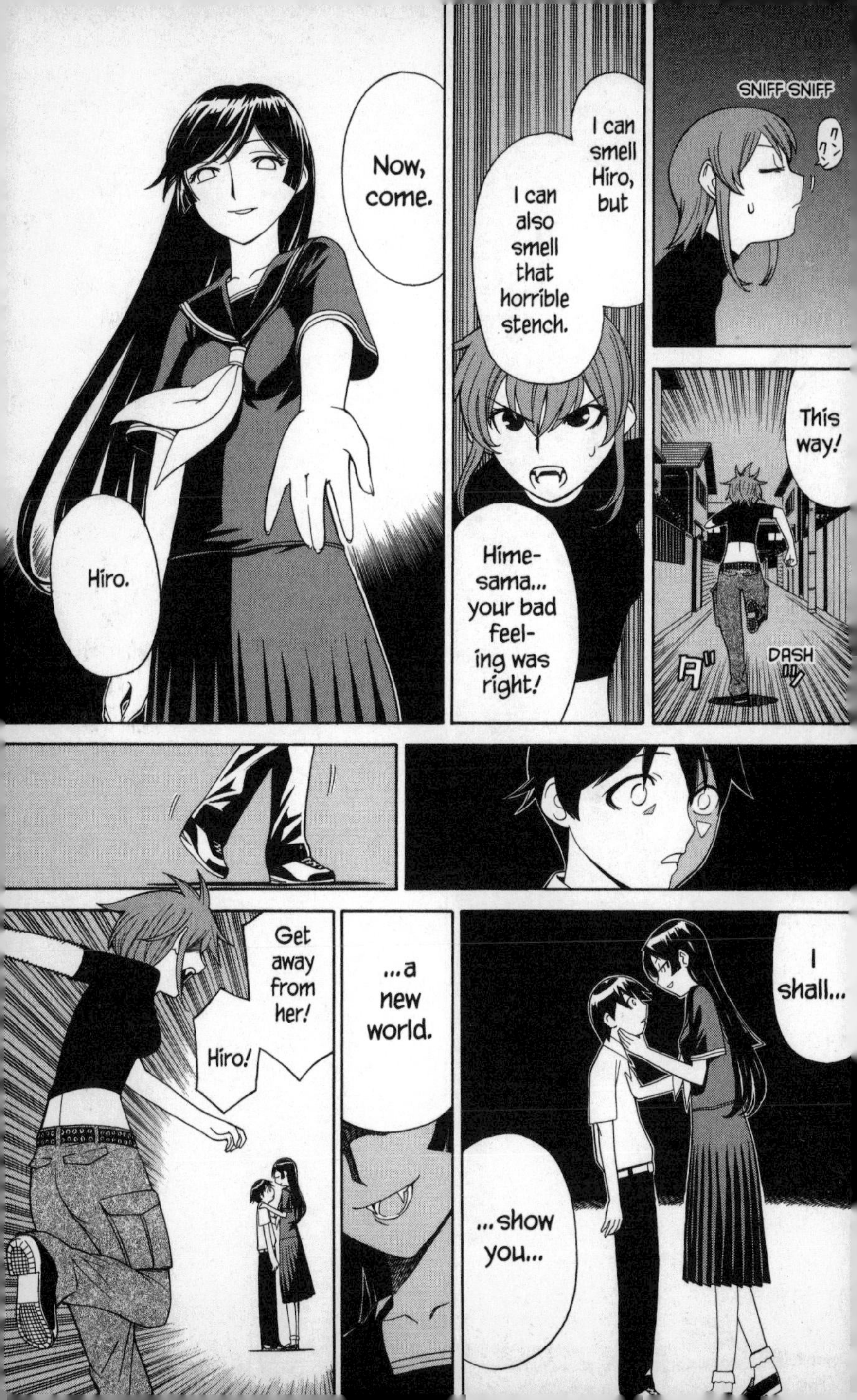

SNIFF SNIFF
This way!
DASH
I can smell Hiro, but
I can also smell that horrible stench.
Hime-sama... your bad feeling was right!
Now, come.
Hiro.
I shall...
...show you...
...a new world.
Get away from her!
Hiro!

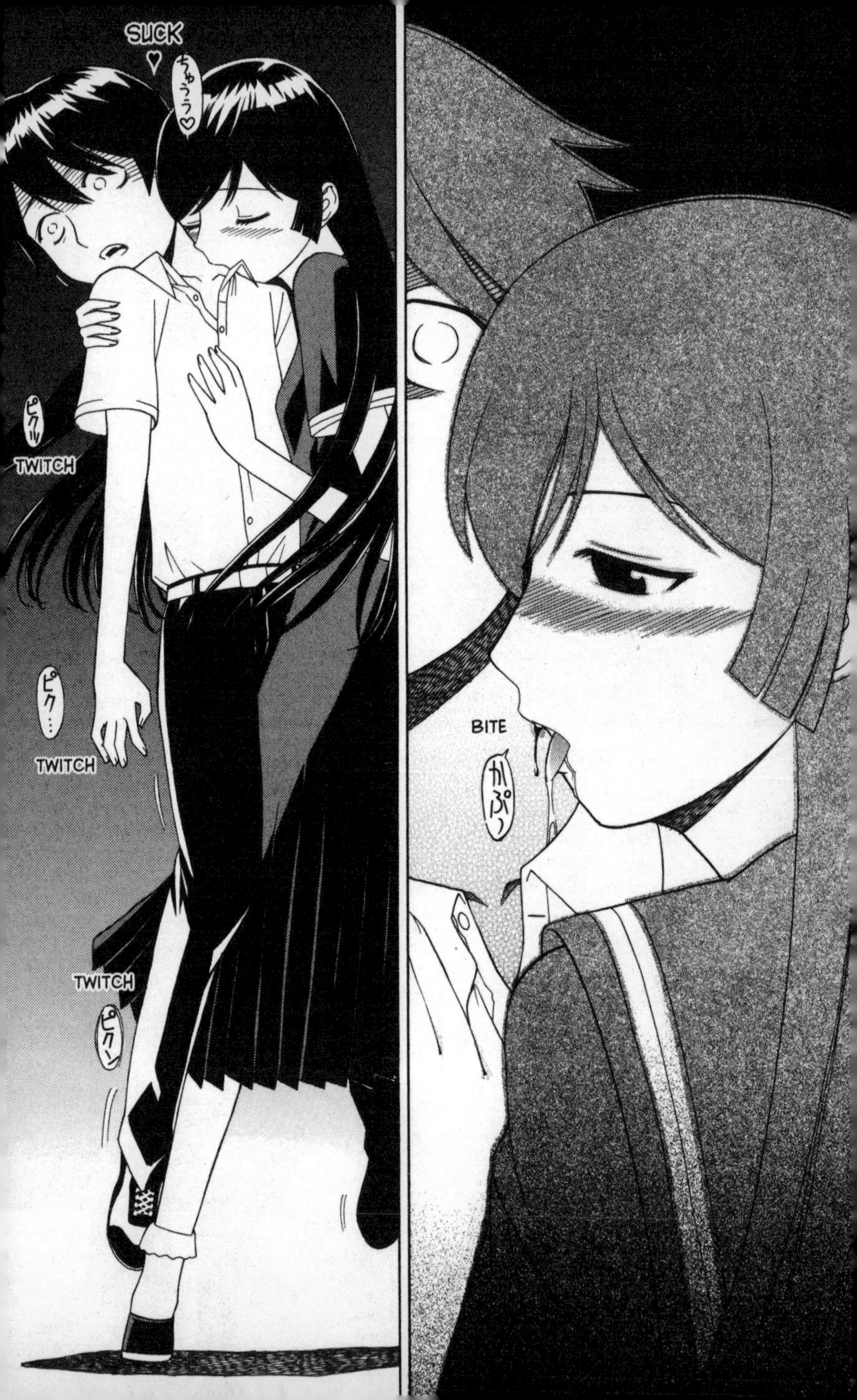
BITE
かぷっ
SUCK ♥
ちゅうう♡
ピクッ
TWITCH
ピク…
TWITCH
TWITCH
ピクン

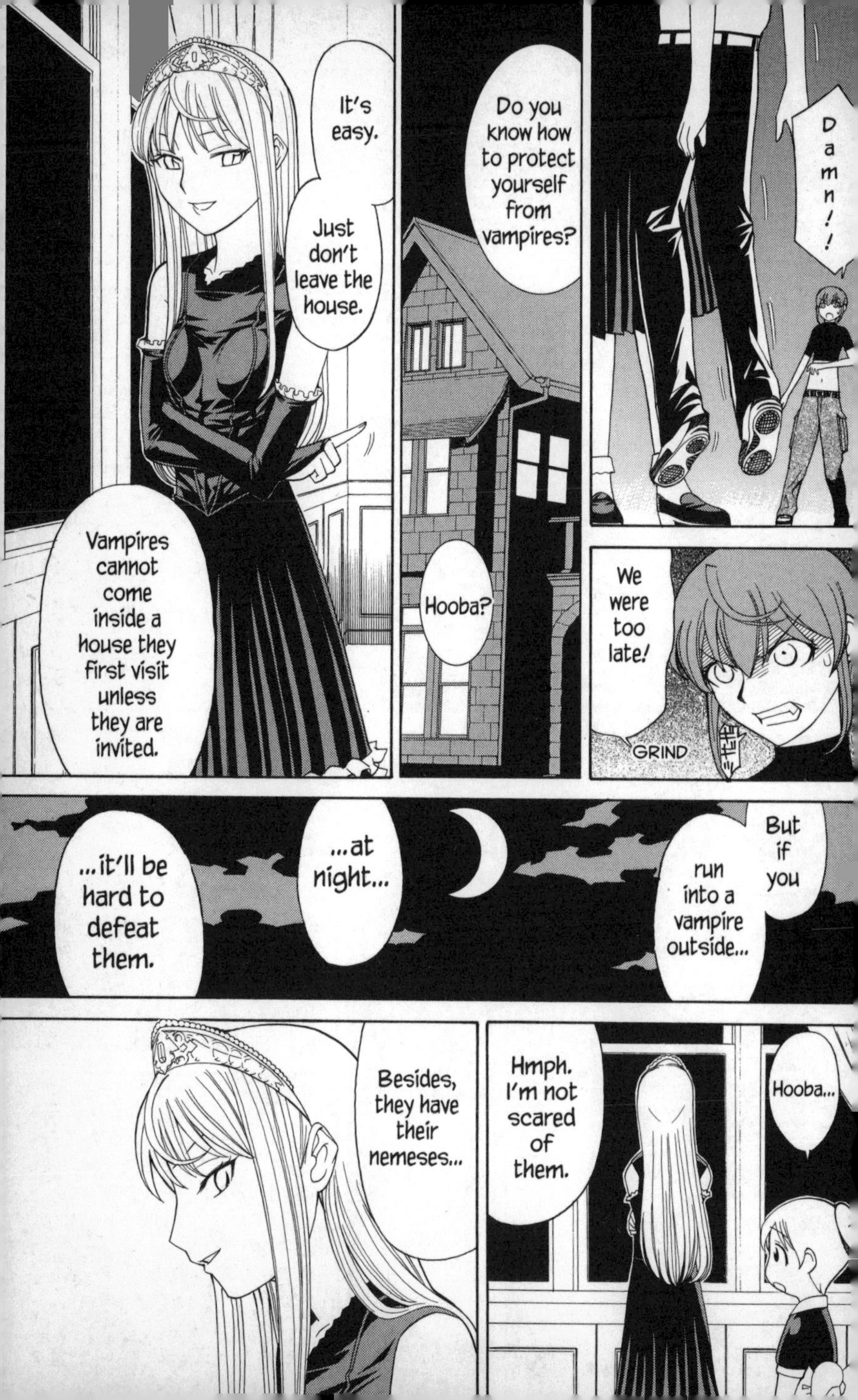
Damn!!
We were too late!
GRIND
Do you know how to protect yourself from vampires?
Hooba?
It's easy.
Just don't leave the house.
Vampires cannot come inside a house they first visit unless they are invited.
But if you run into a vampire outside...
...at night...
...it'll be hard to defeat them.
Hooba...
Hmph. I'm not scared of them.
Besides, they have their nemeses...

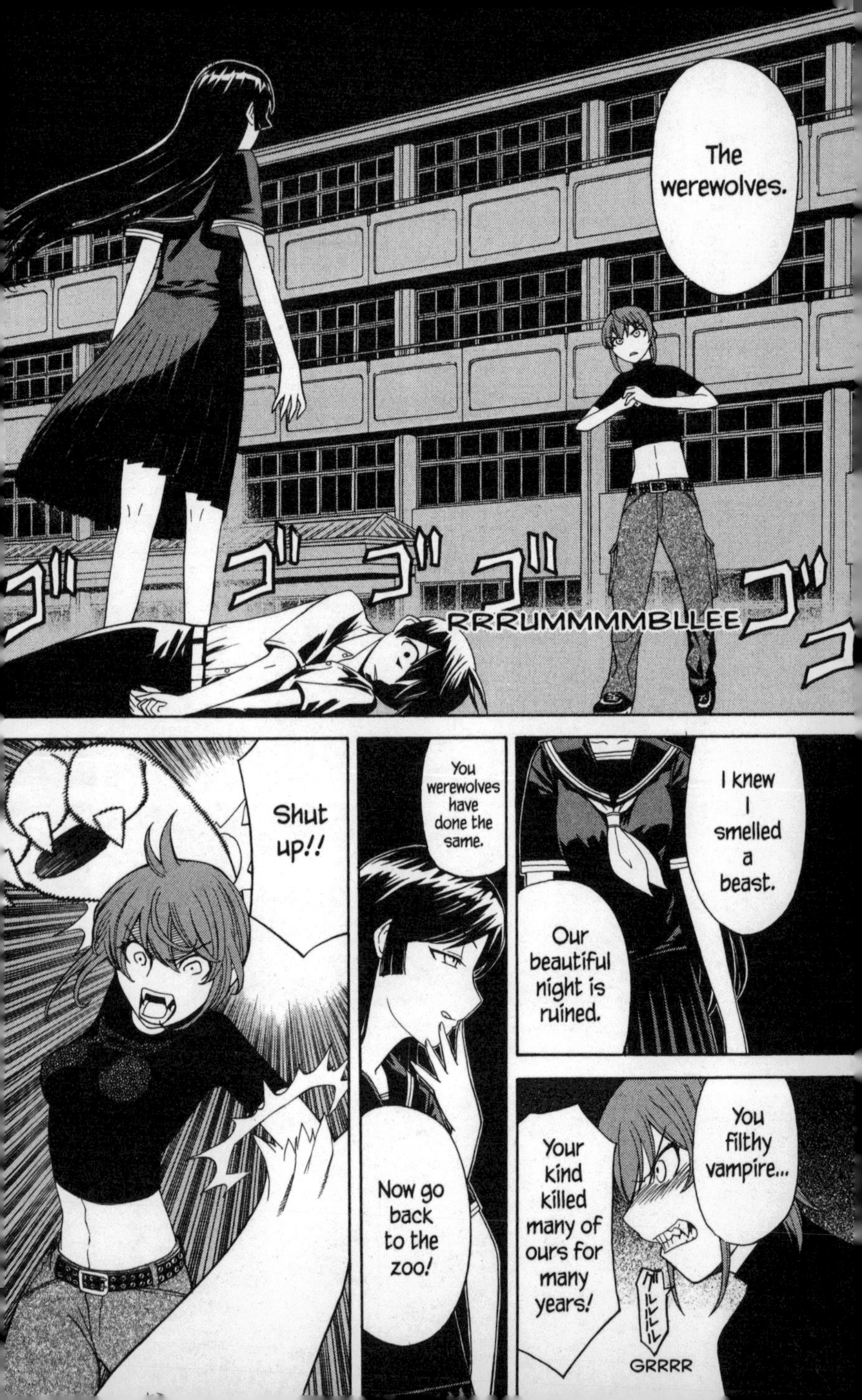
The werewolves.
RRRUMMMMMBLLEE
I knew I smelled a beast.
Our beautiful night is ruined.
You filthy vampire...
Your kind killed many of ours for many years!
GRRRR
You werewolves have done the same.
Now go back to the zoo!
Shut up!!

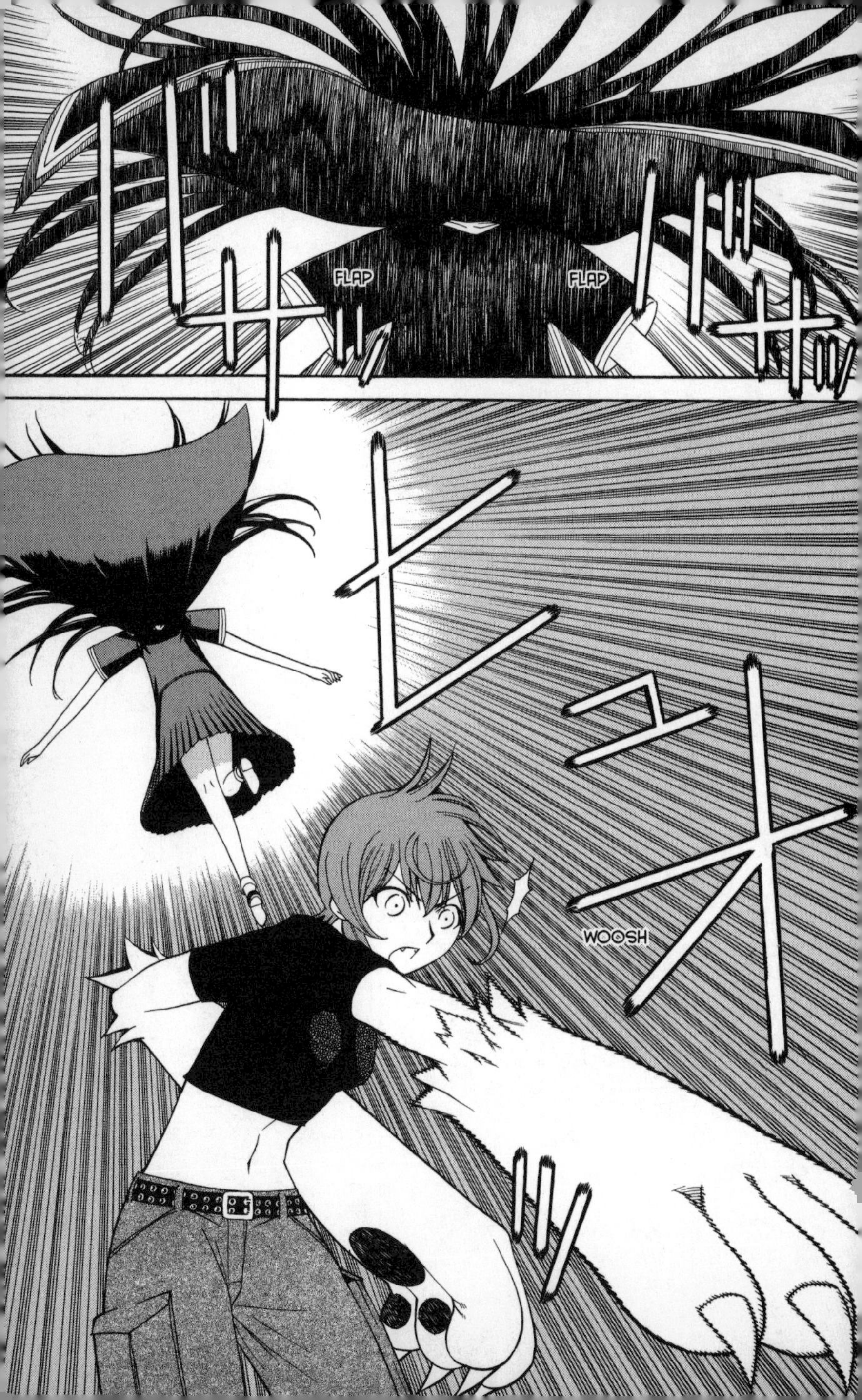
FLAP
FLAP
WOOSH

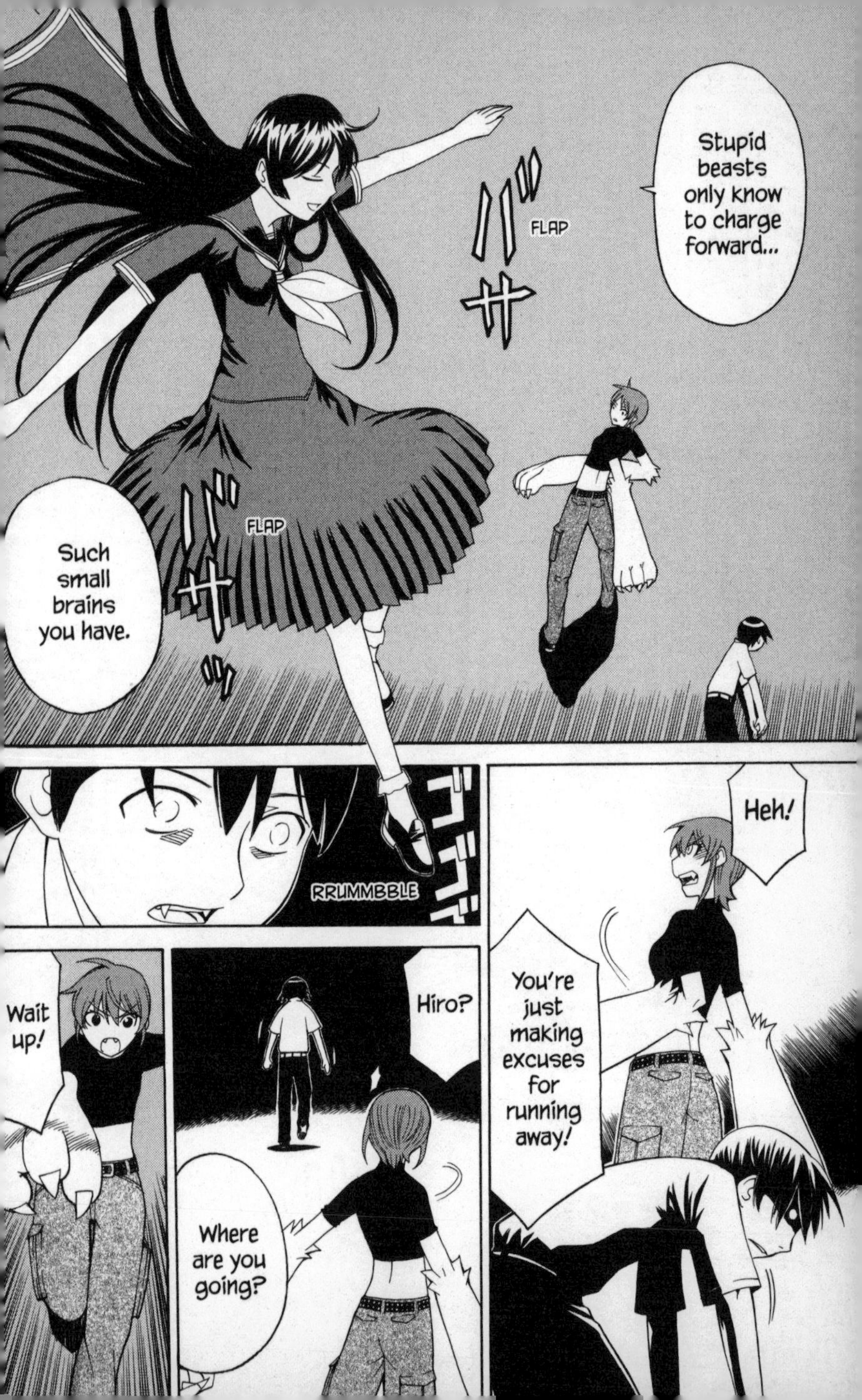
Stupid beasts only know to charge forward...
FLAP
FLAP
Such small brains you have.
Heh!
You're just making excuses for running away!
RRUMMBBLE
Hiro?
Where are you going?
Wait up!

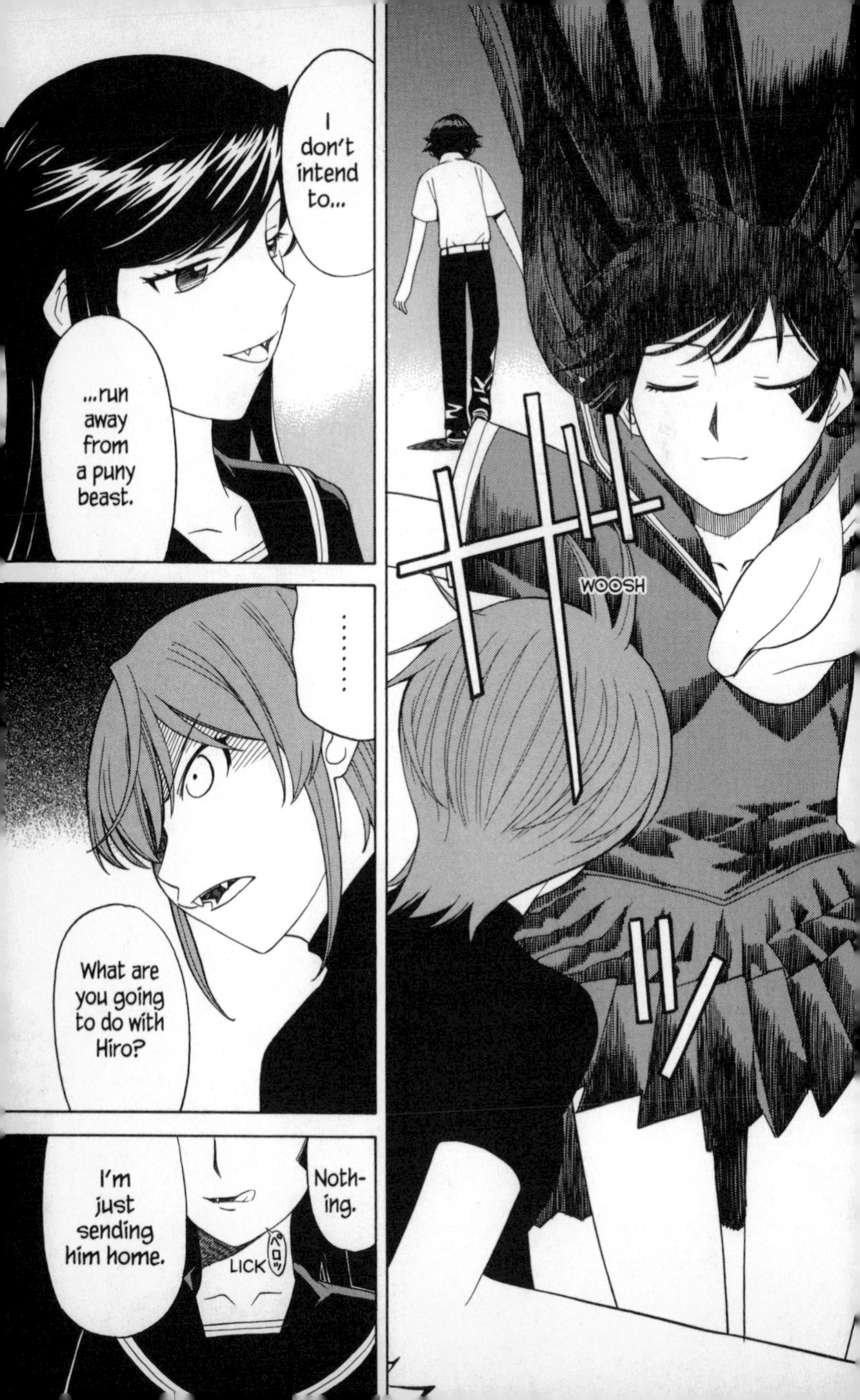
WOOSH
I don't intend to...
...run away from a puny beast.
......
What are you going to do with Hiro?
Noth-ing.
I'm just sending him home.
LICK

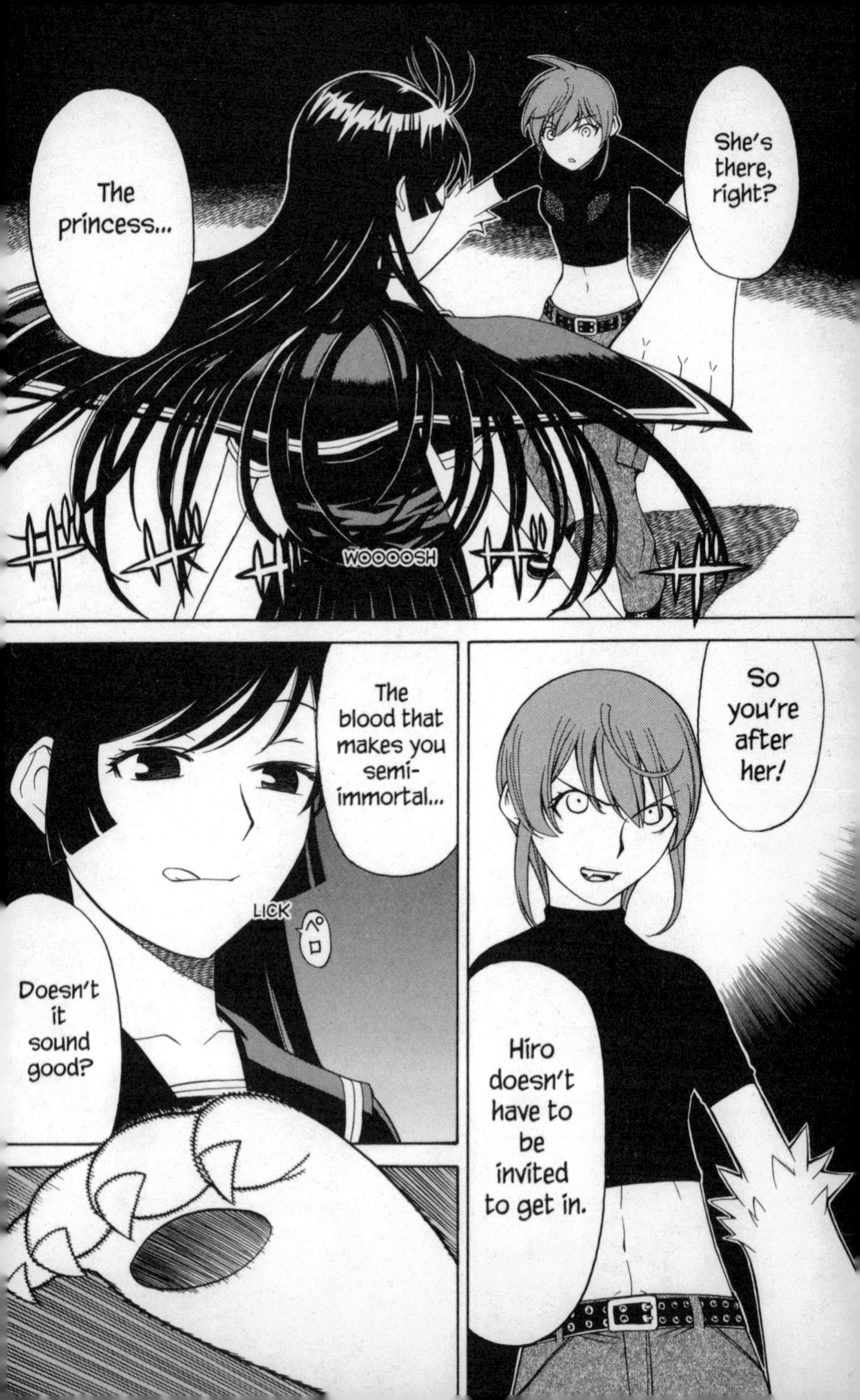
She's there, right?
The princess...
WOOOOSH
So you're after her!
Hiro doesn't have to be invited to get in.
The blood that makes you semi-immortal...
LICK
ペロ
Doesn't it sound good?

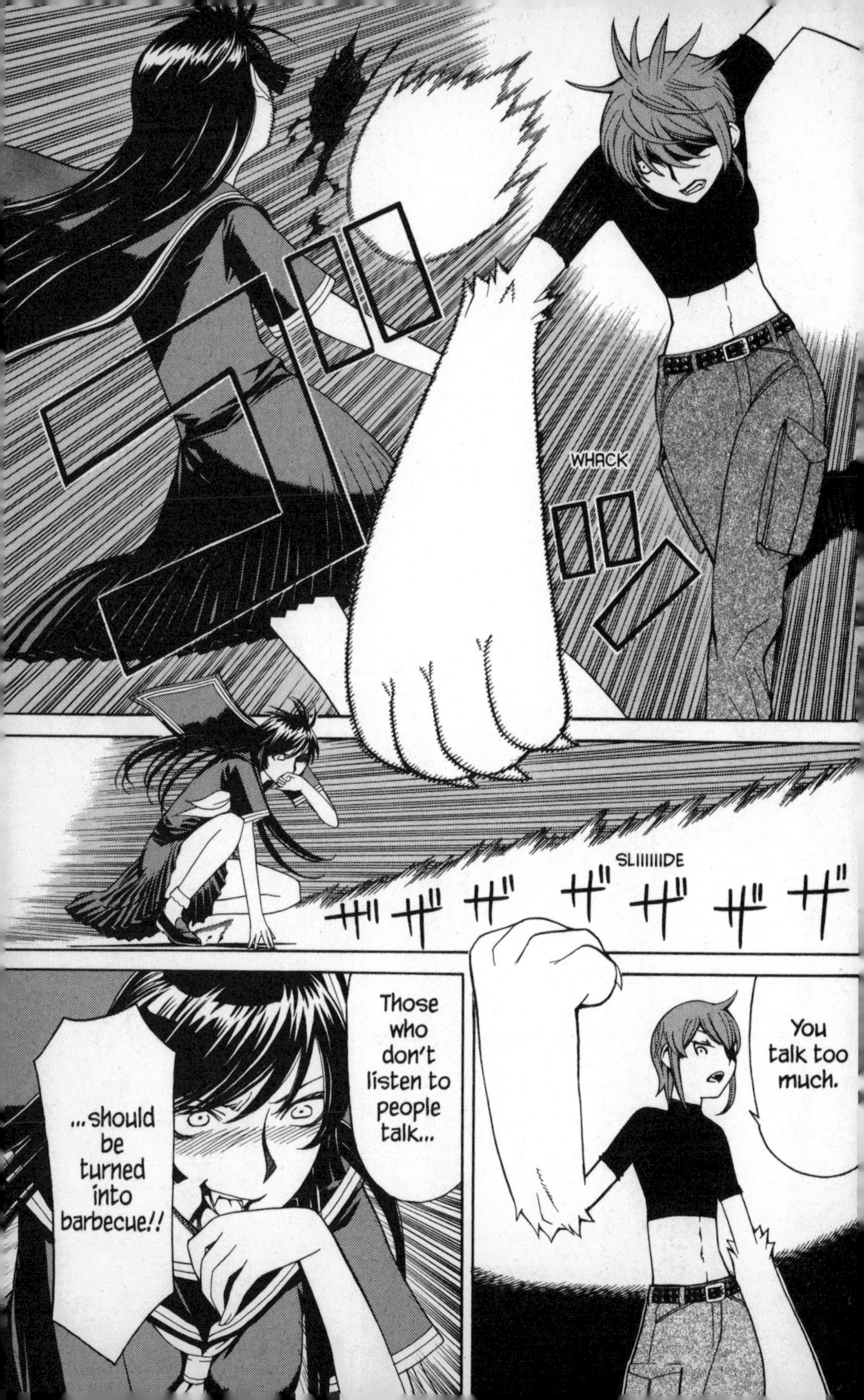
WHACK
SLIIIIIIDE
ザザザザザザザ
You talk too much.
Those who don't listen to people talk...
...should be turned into barbecue!!

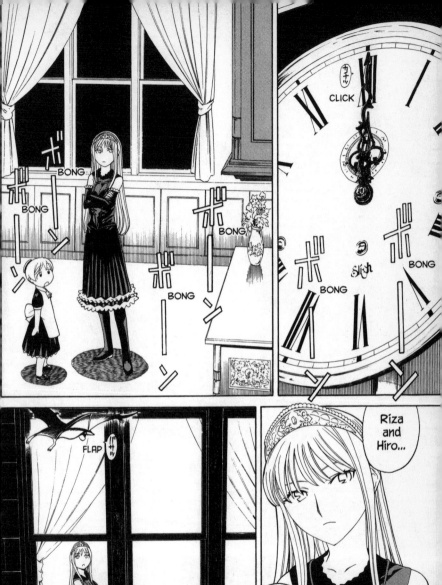

CLICK

BONG
BONG
BONG
BONG
BONG
BONG
Slish

FLAP

Riza and Hiro...

...are not coming home.

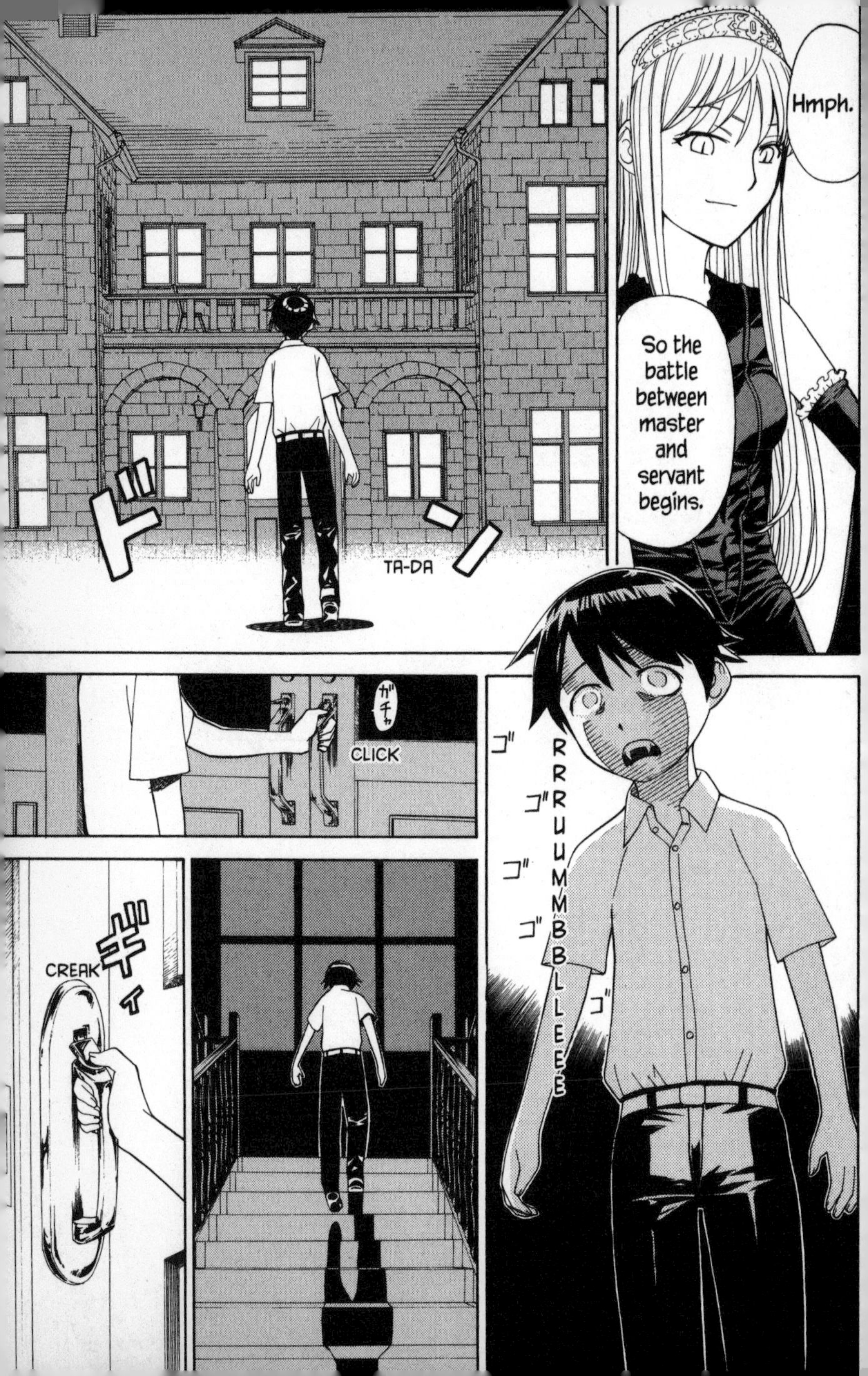
Hmph.
So the battle between master and servant begins.
ドーン
TA-DA
ゴ゛
ゴ゛
ゴ゛
ゴ゛
ゴ゛
RRRUUMMBBLLEEE
ガチャ
CLICK
ギィ
CREAK

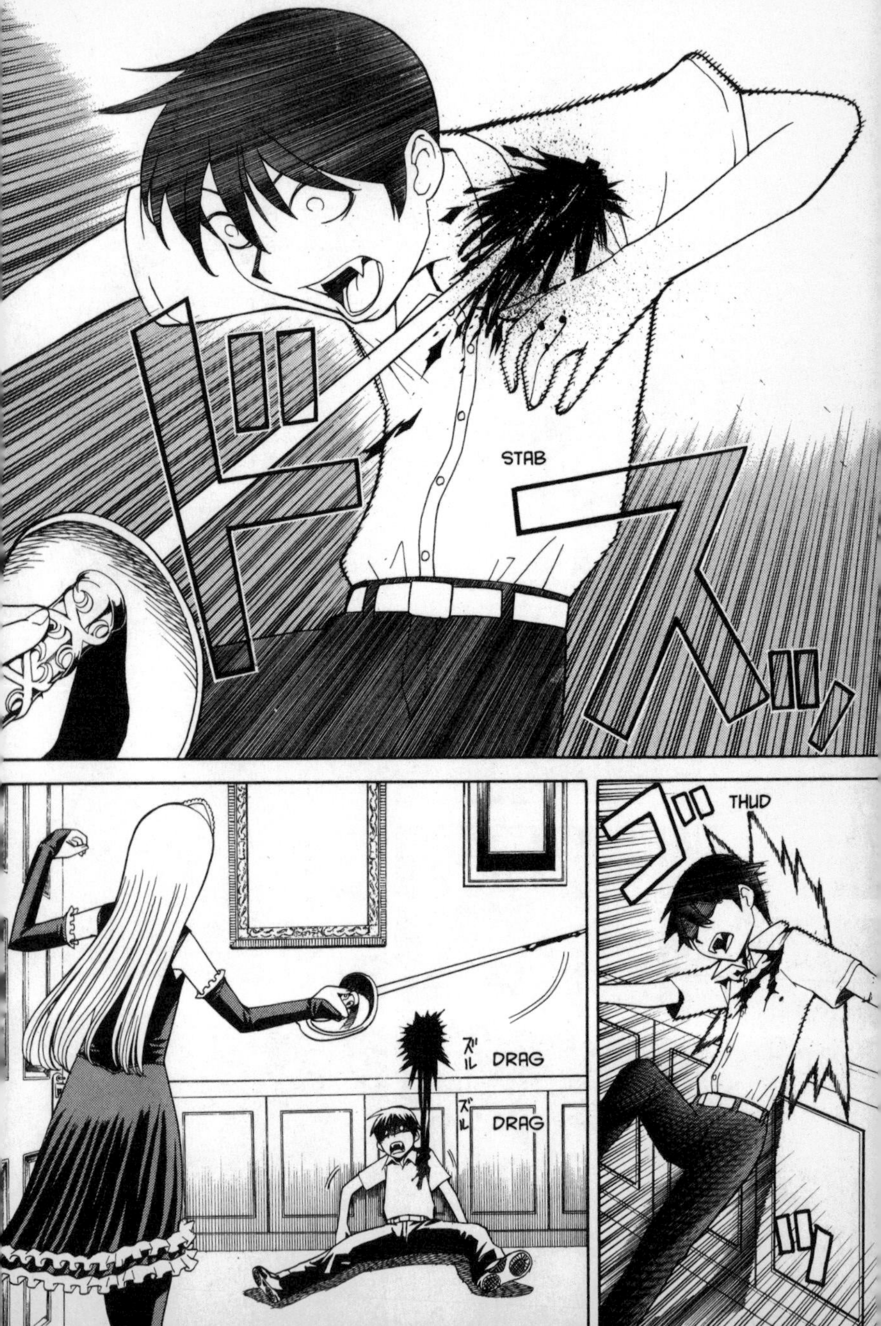
ドスッ
STAB
ゴッ
THUD
ズル
DRAG
ズル
DRAG

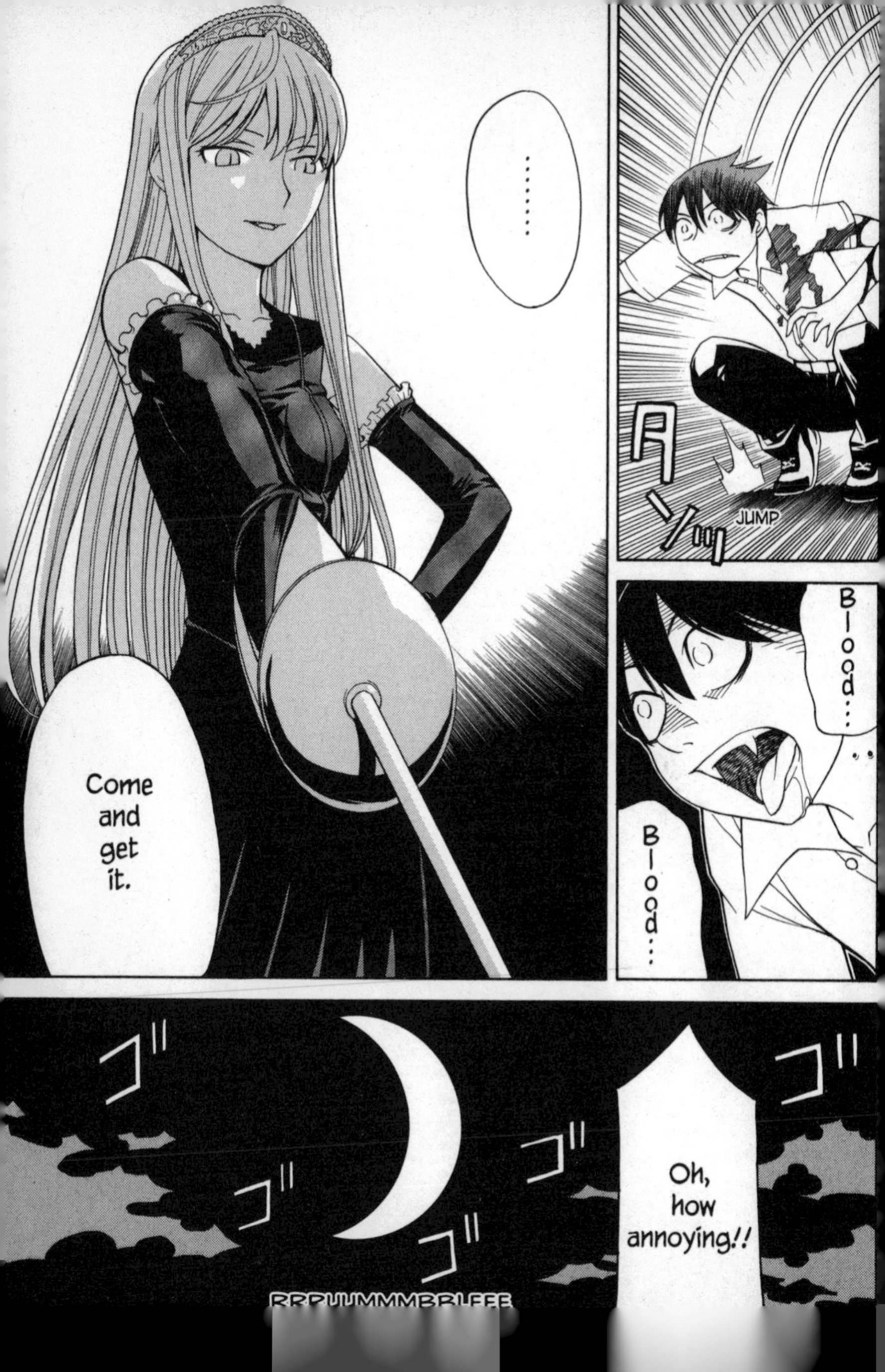
JUMP
Blood...
Blood...
......
Come and get it.
Oh, how annoying!!

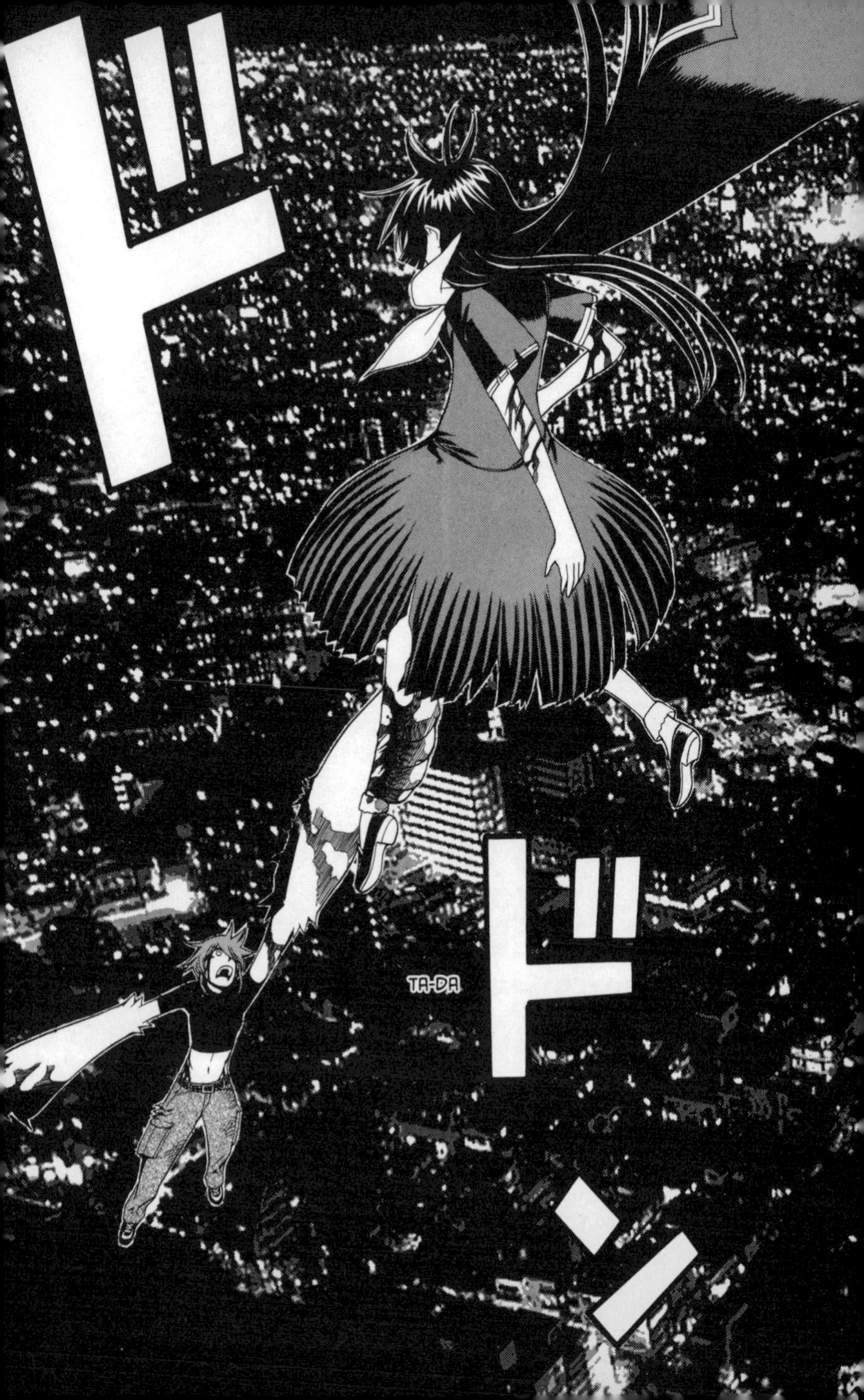
ド
TA-DA
ドン

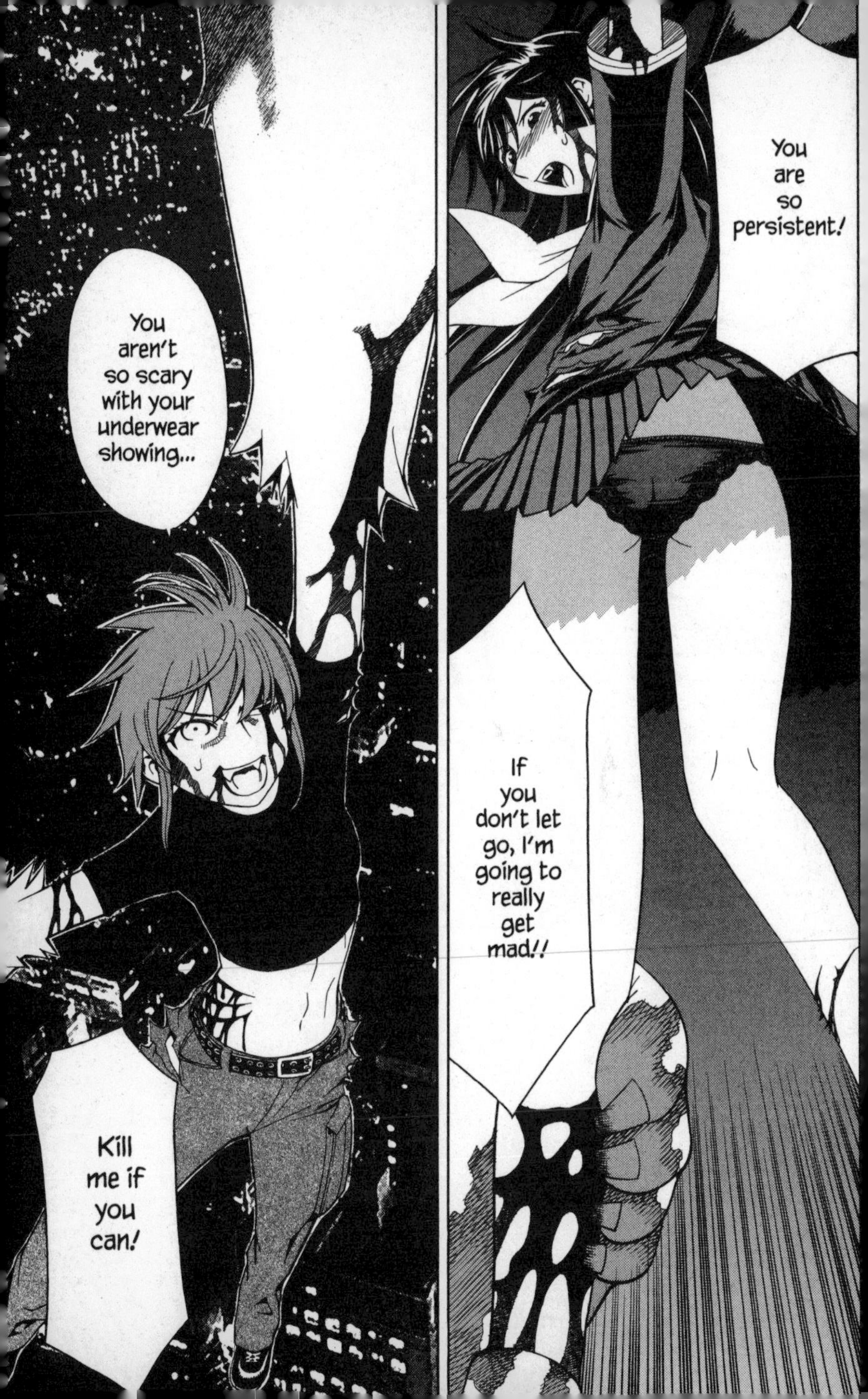
You are so persistent!
If you don't let go, I'm going to really get mad!!
You aren't so scary with your underwear showing...
Kill me if you can!

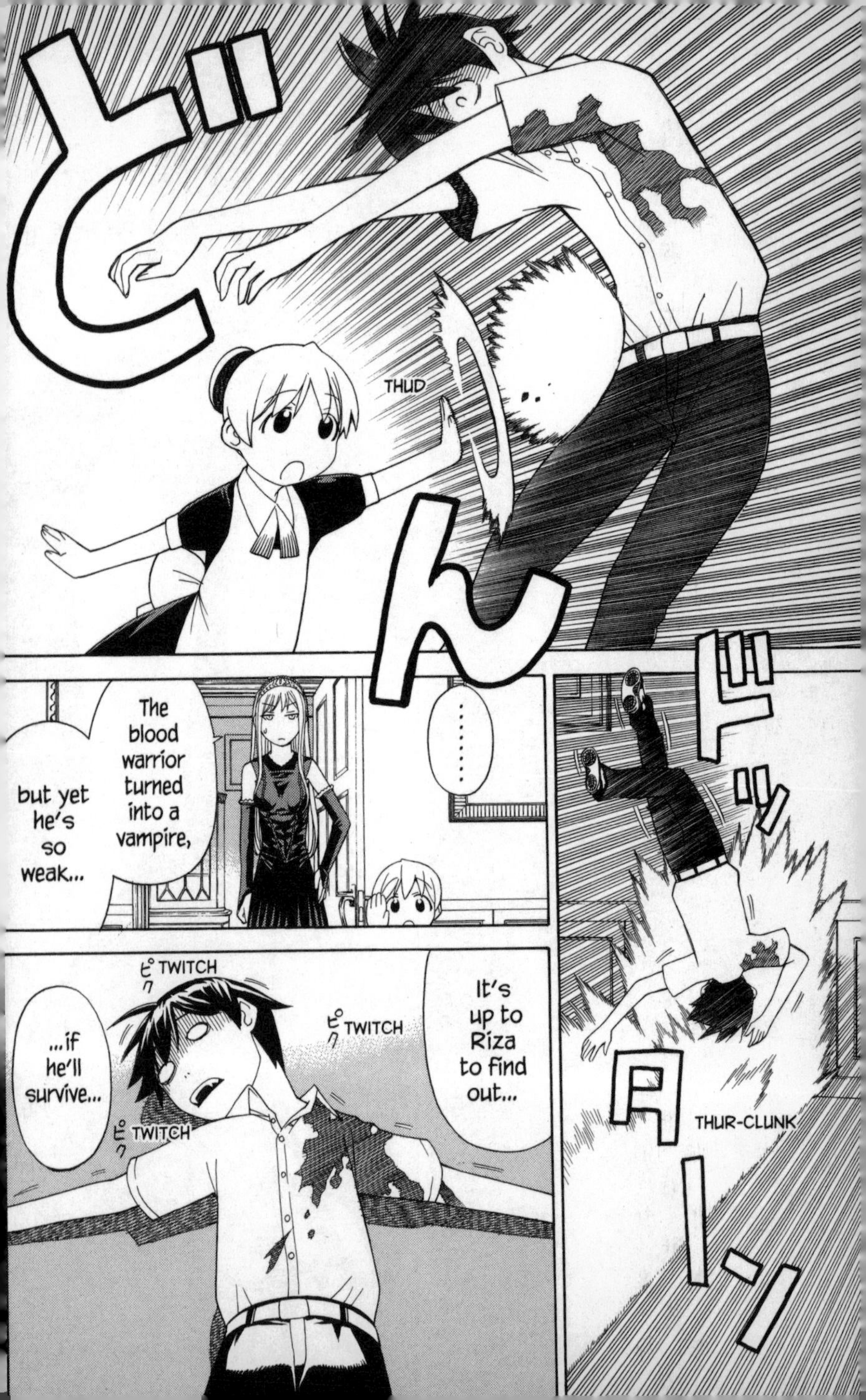
THUD
THUR-CLUNK
. . . . . .
The blood warrior turned into a vampire,
but yet he's so weak...
It's up to Riza to find out...
...if he'll survive...
TWITCH
TWITCH
TWITCH

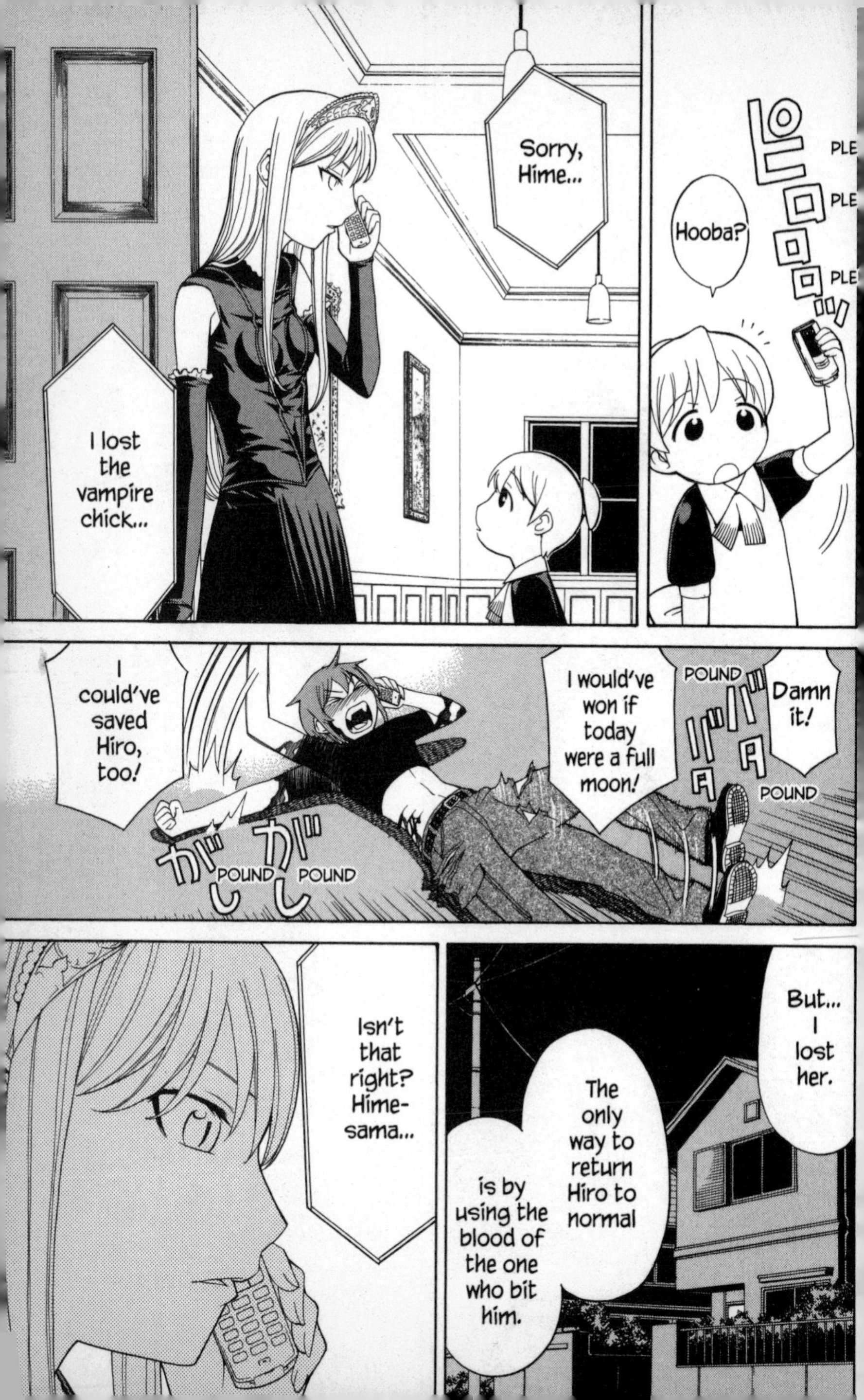
PLE
PLE
PLE
Hooba?
Sorry, Hime...
I lost the vampire chick...
POUND
Damn it!
POUND
I would've won if today were a full moon!
I could've saved Hiro, too!
POUND
POUND
But... I lost her.
The only way to return Hiro to normal
is by using the blood of the one who bit him.
Isn't that right? Hime-sama...

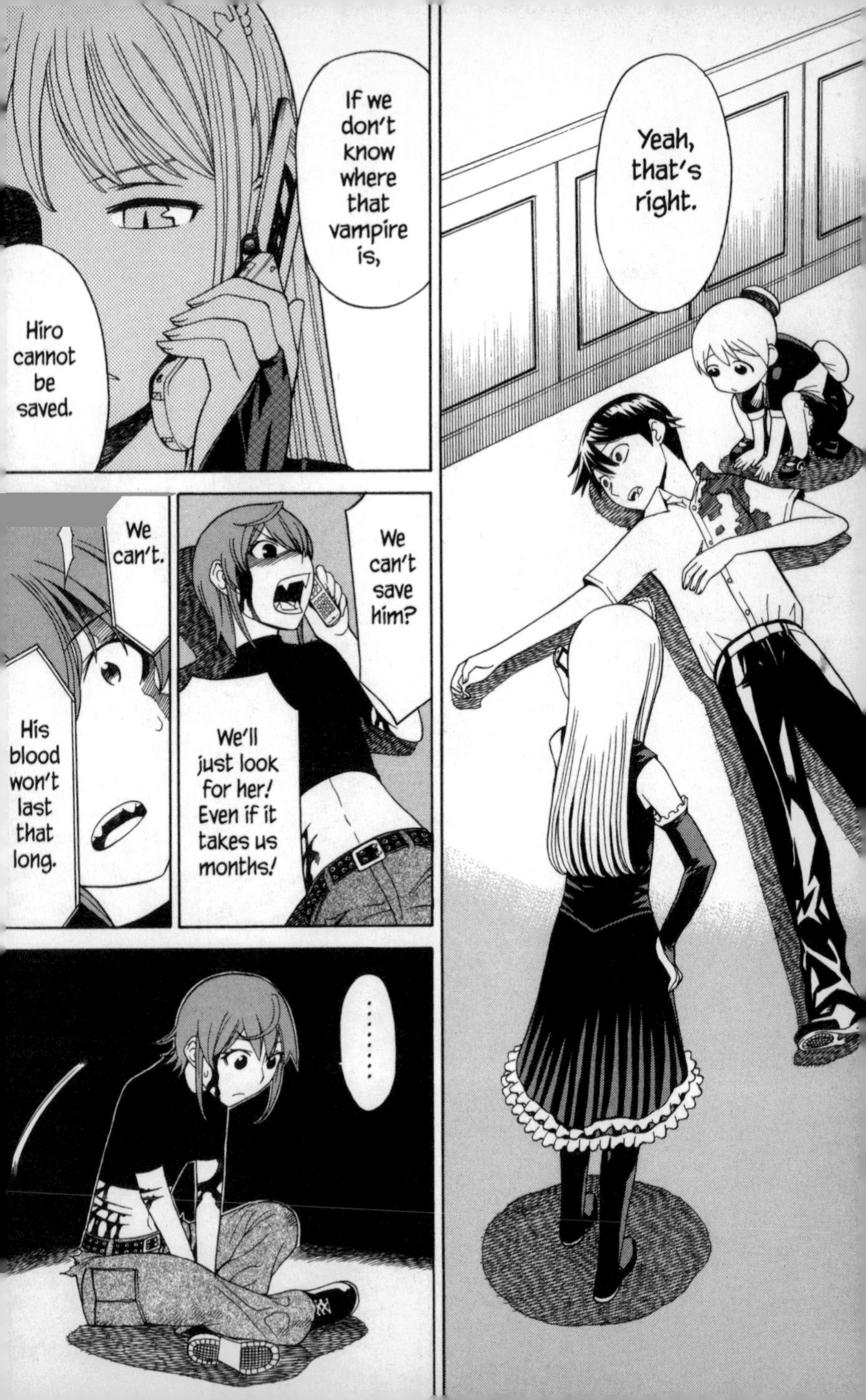
Yeah, that's right.
If we don't know where that vampire is,
Hiro cannot be saved.
We can't save him?
We'll just look for her! Even if it takes us months!
We can't.
His blood won't last that long.
......

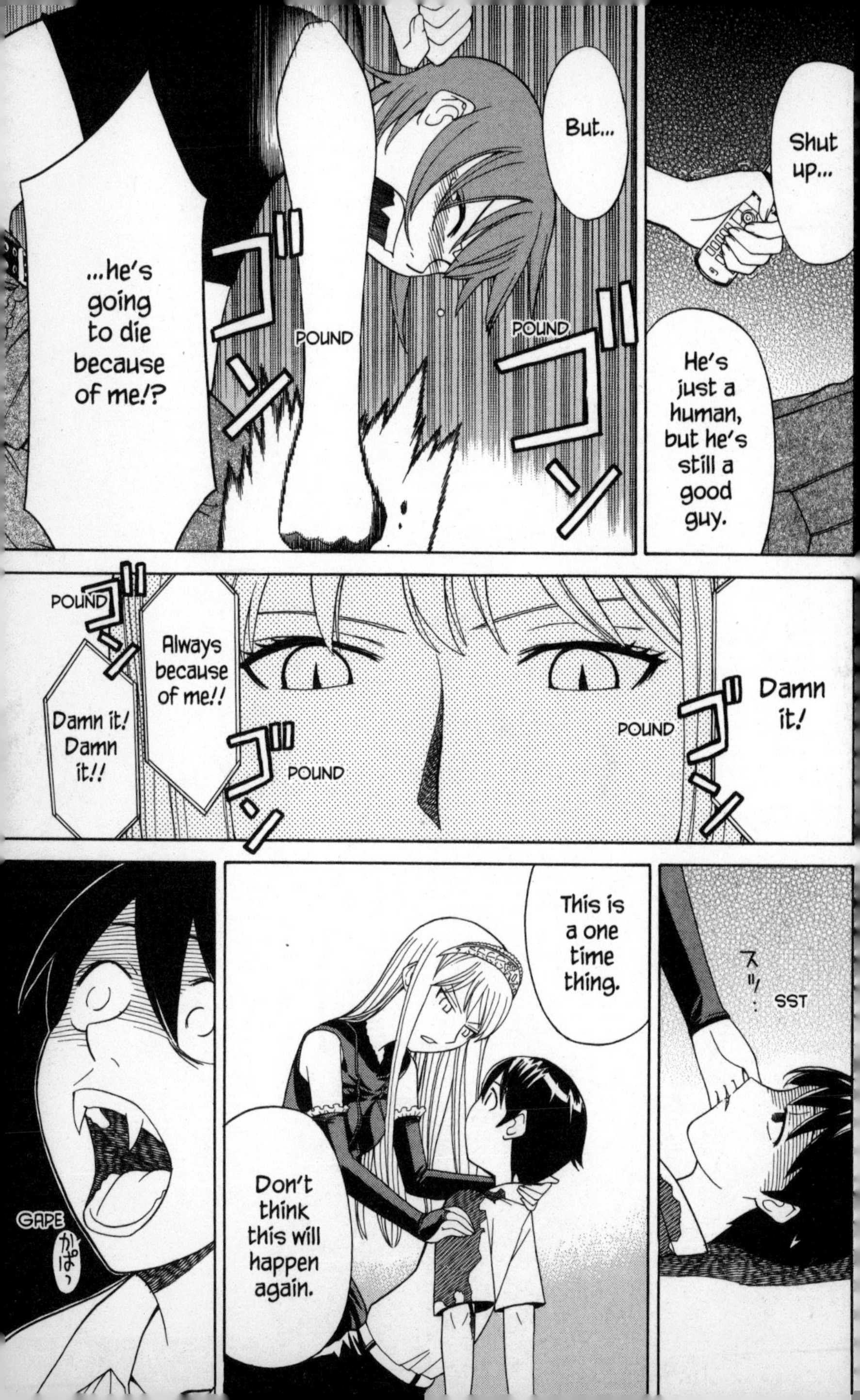
Shut up...
He's just a human, but he's still a good guy.
But...
POUND
POUND
...he's going to die because of me!?
Damn it!
POUND
POUND
Always because of me!!
POUND
Damn it! Damn it!!
スッ
SST
This is a one time thing.
Don't think this will happen again.
GAPE
かぱっ

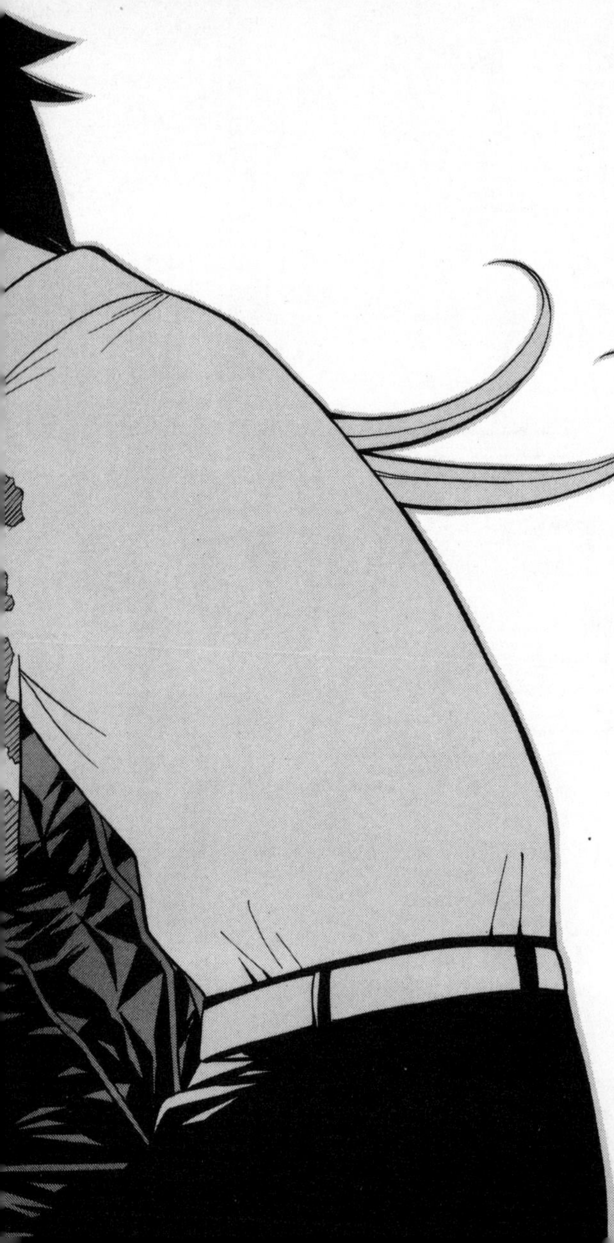

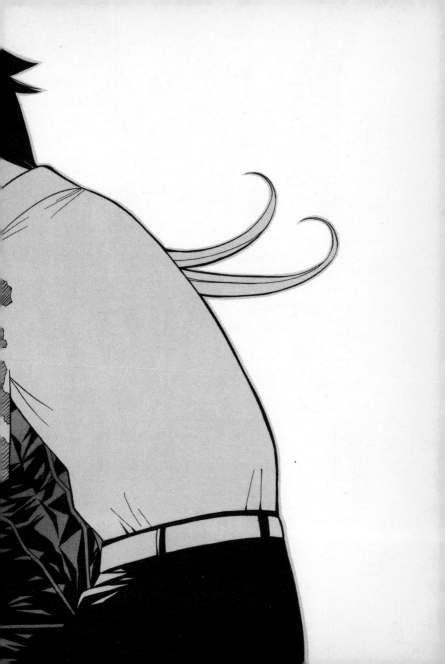

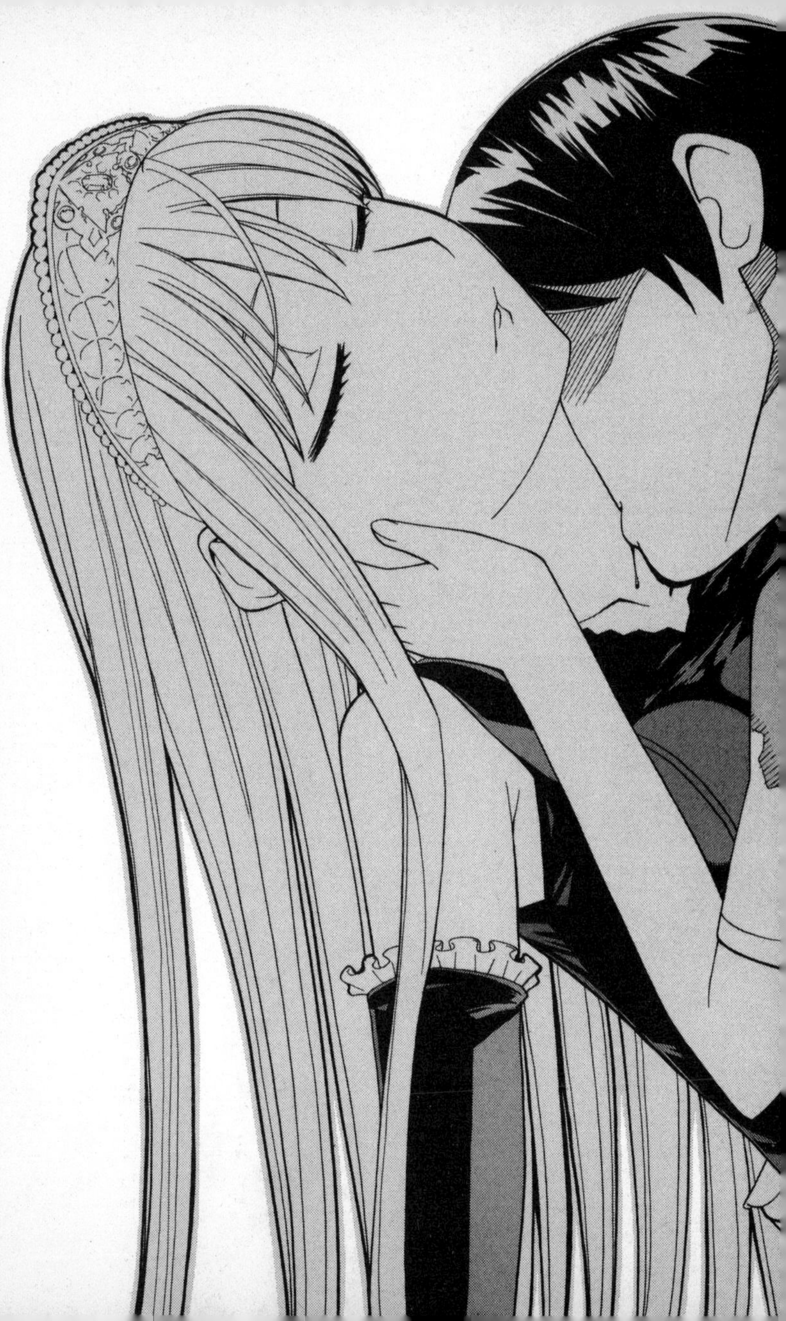

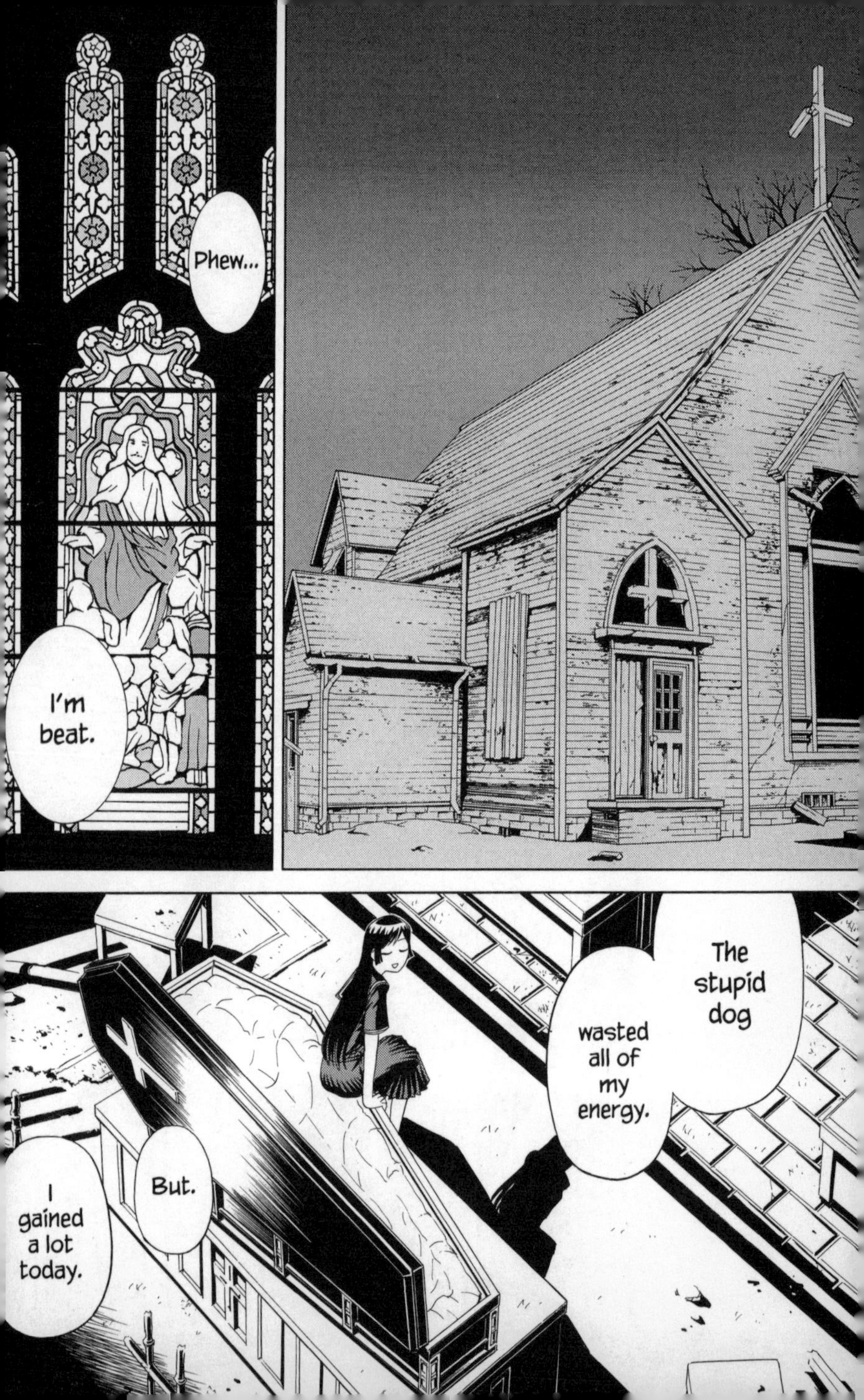
Phew...
I'm beat.
The stupid dog
wasted all of my energy.
But.
I gained a lot today.

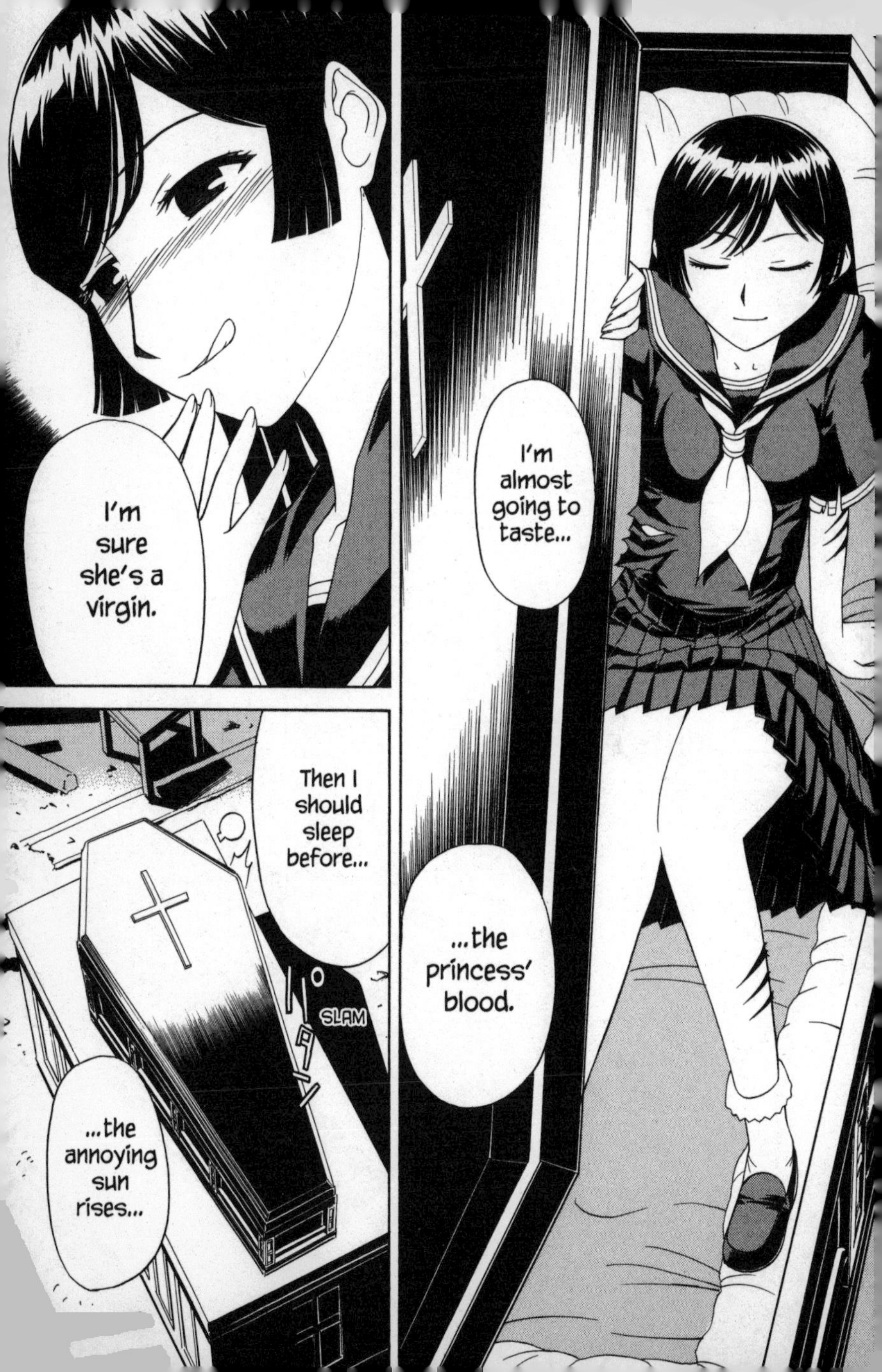
I'm almost going to taste...
...the princess' blood.
I'm sure she's a virgin.
Then I should sleep before...
SLAM
...the annoying sun rises...

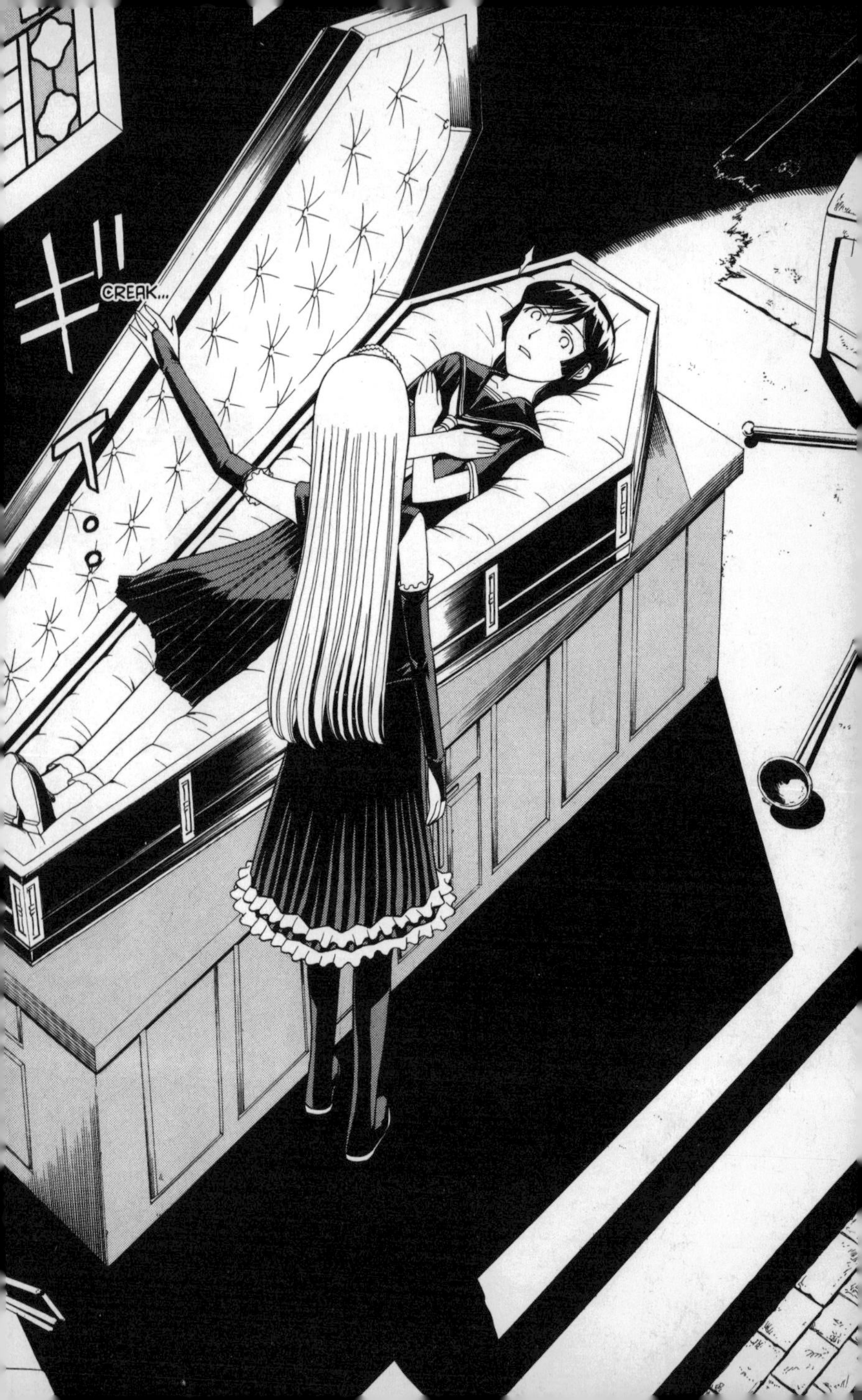
CREAK...

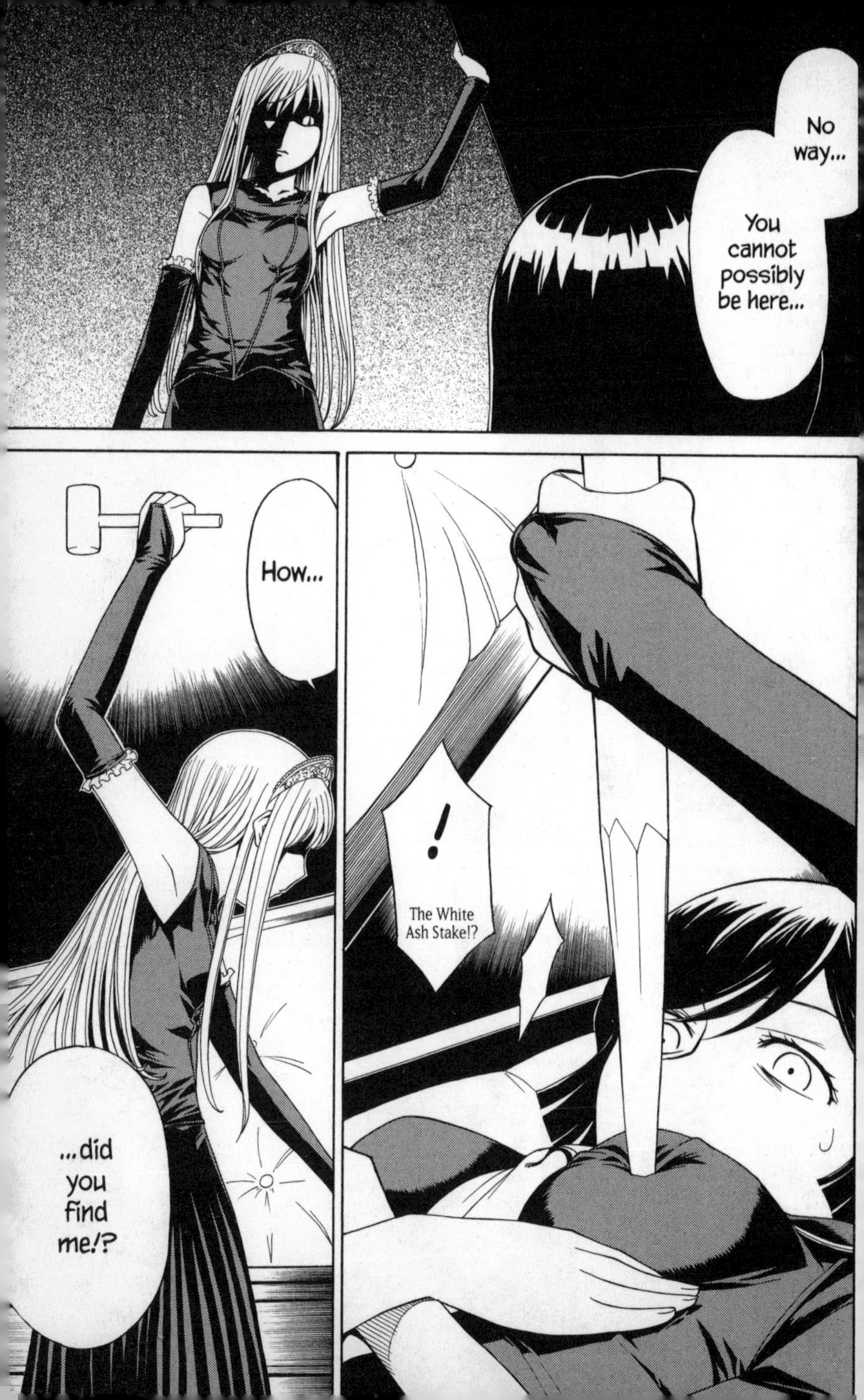
No way...
You cannot possibly be here...
!
The White Ash Stake!?
How...
...did you find me!?

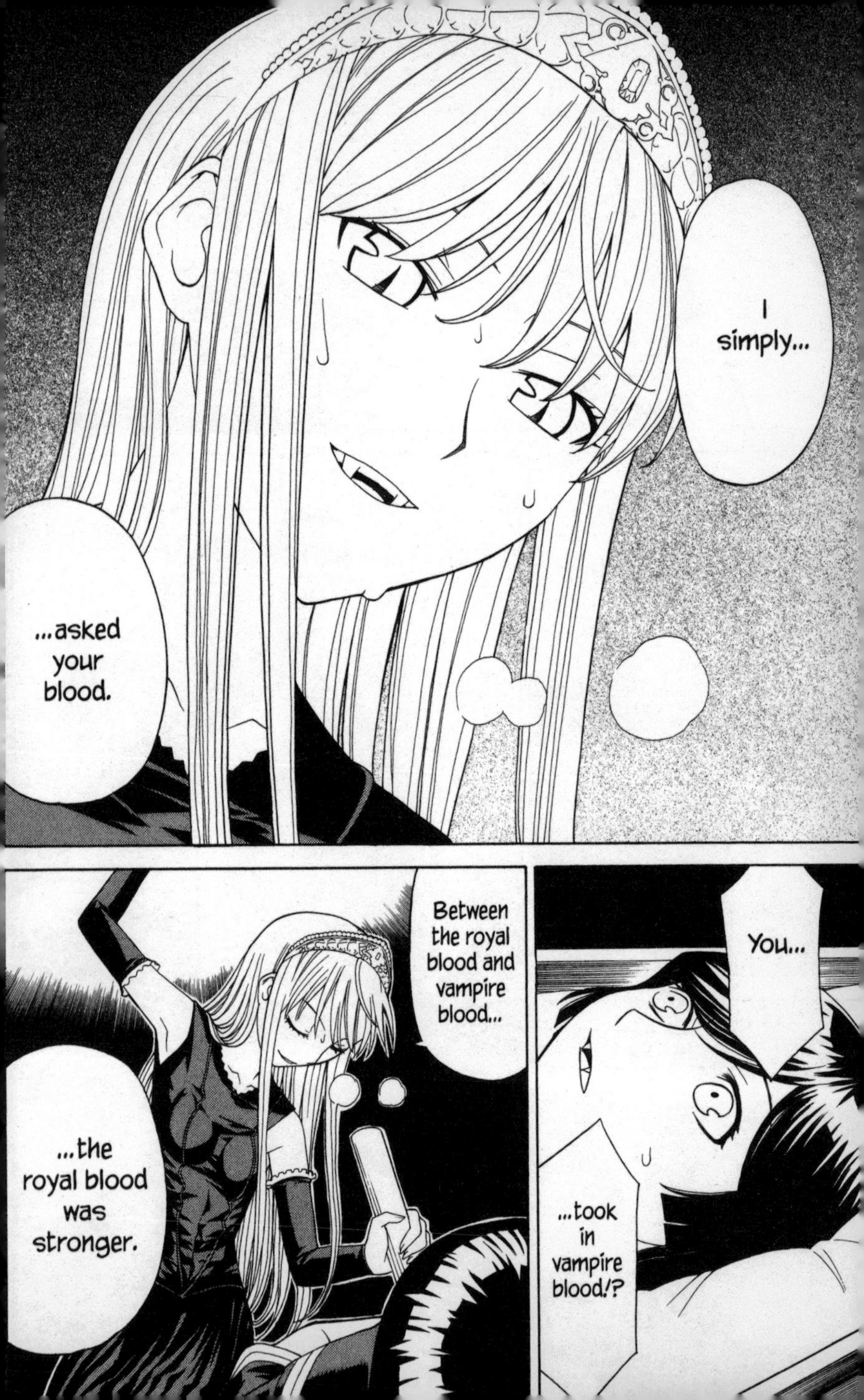
I simply...
...asked your blood.
You...
...took in vampire blood!?
Between the royal blood and vampire blood...
...the royal blood was stronger.

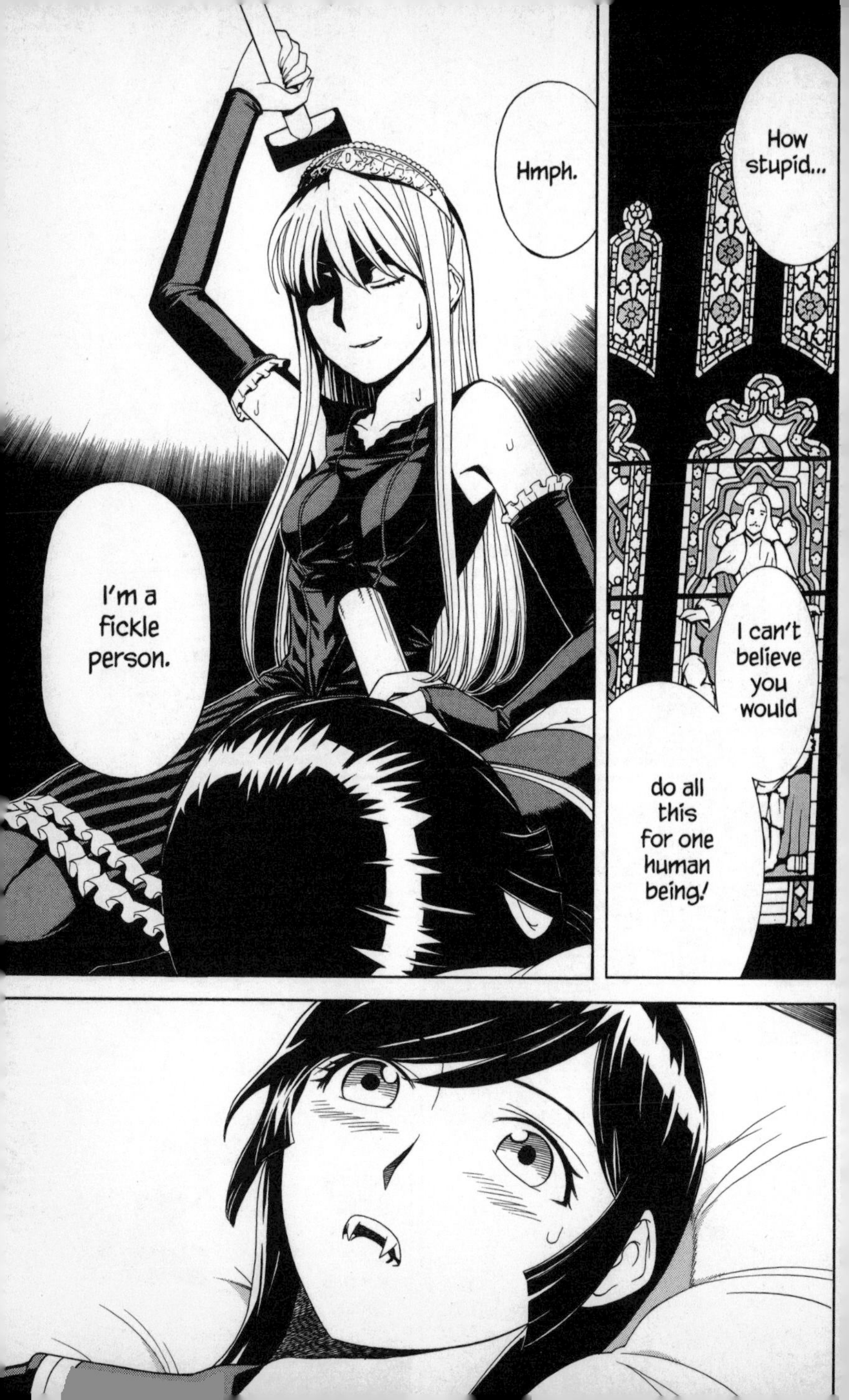
How stupid...
I can't believe you would
do all this for one human being!
Hmph.
I'm a fickle person.

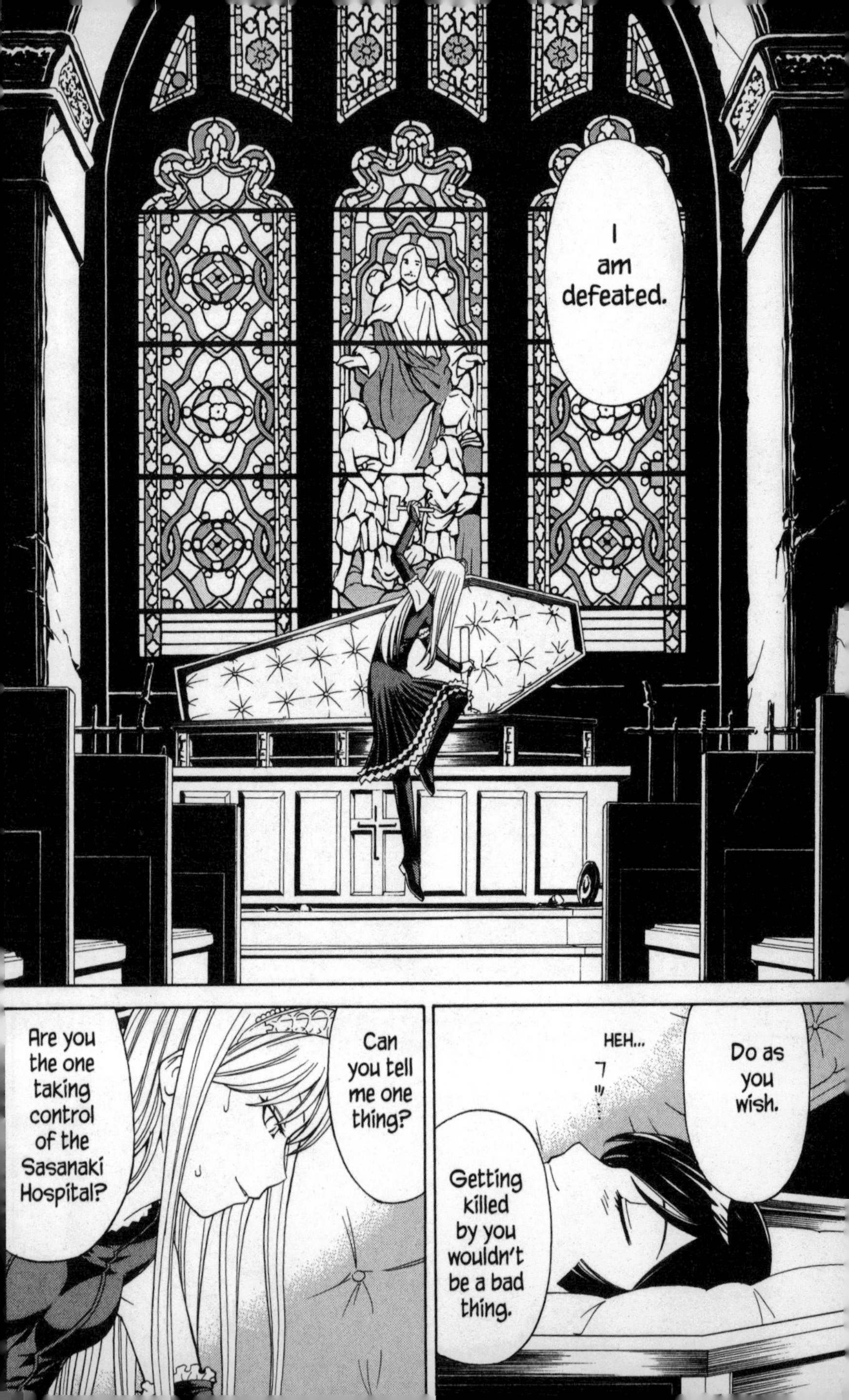
I am defeated.
Do as you wish.
HEH...
フッ...
Getting killed by you wouldn't be a bad thing.
Can you tell me one thing?
Are you the one taking control of the Sasanaki Hospital?

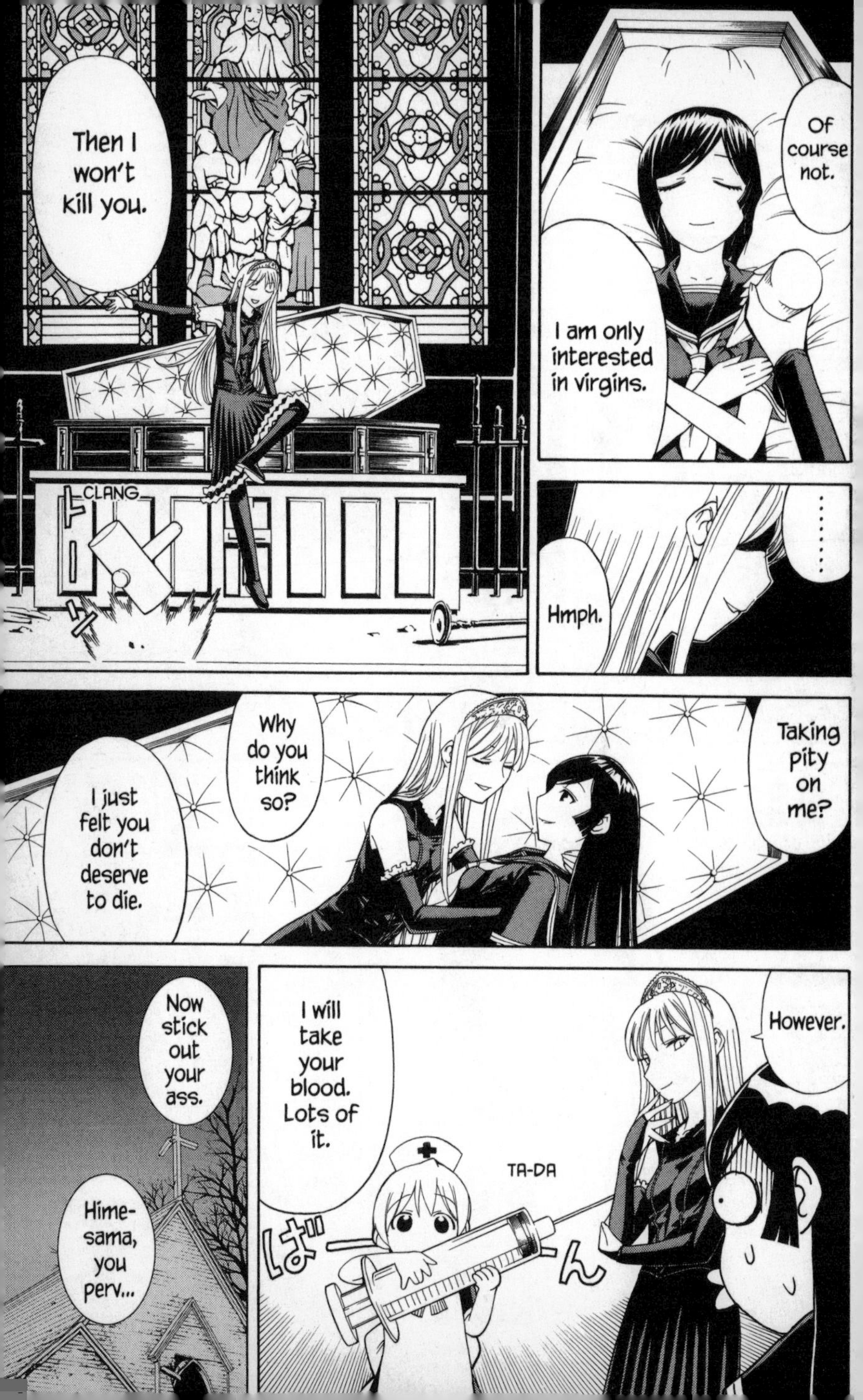
Of course not.
I am only interested in virgins.
……
Hmph.
Then I won't kill you.
CLANG
Taking pity on me?
Why do you think so?
I just felt you don't deserve to die.
However.
I will take your blood. Lots of it.
TA-DA
ばーん
Now stick out your ass.
Hime-sama, you perv...

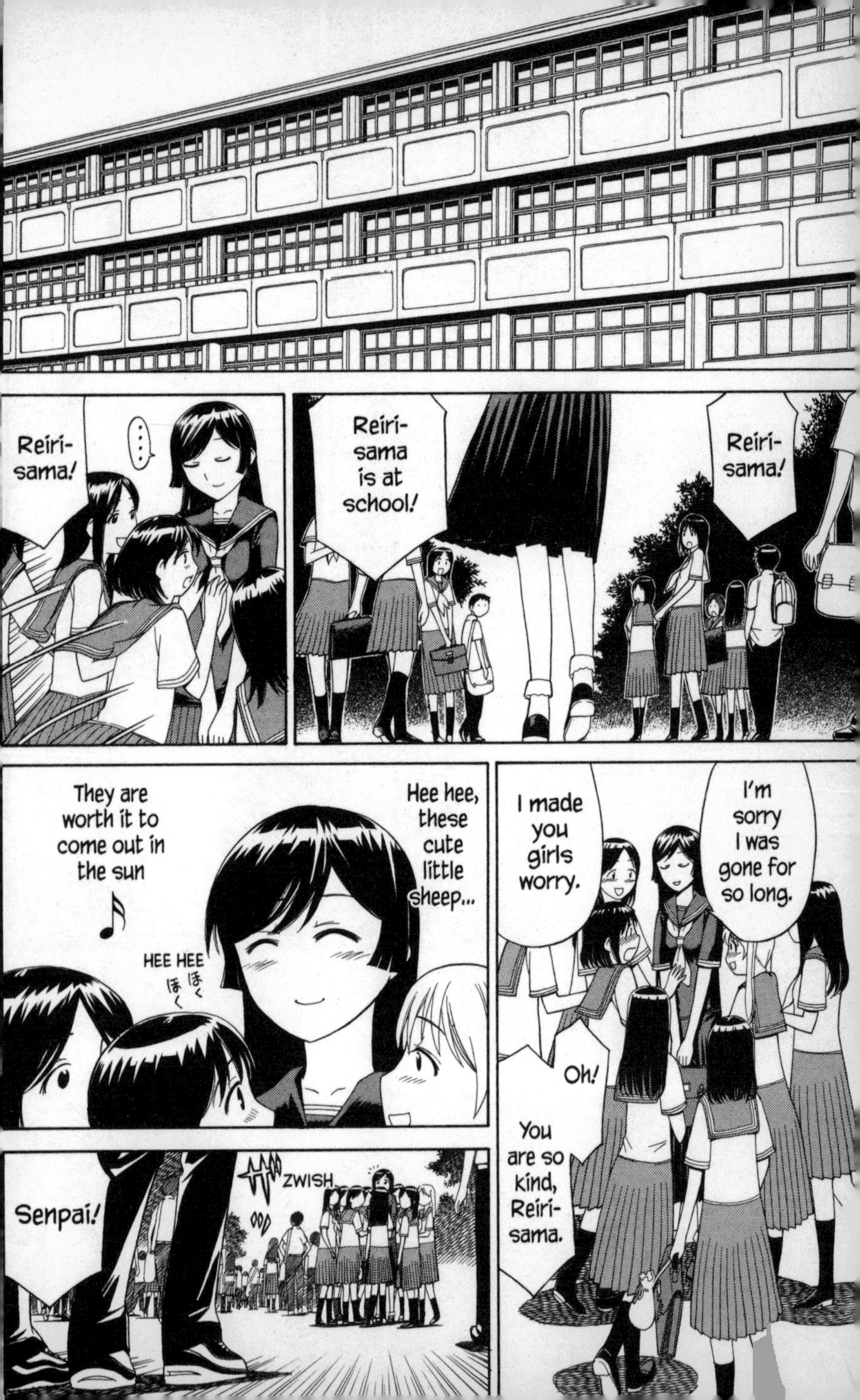
Reiri-sama!
Reiri-sama is at school!
Reiri-sama!
...
I'm sorry I was gone for so long.
I made you girls worry.
Oh!
You are so kind, Reiri-sama.
Hee hee, these cute little sheep...
They are worth it to come out in the sun ♪
HEE HEE
ほくほく
ZWISH
Senpai!

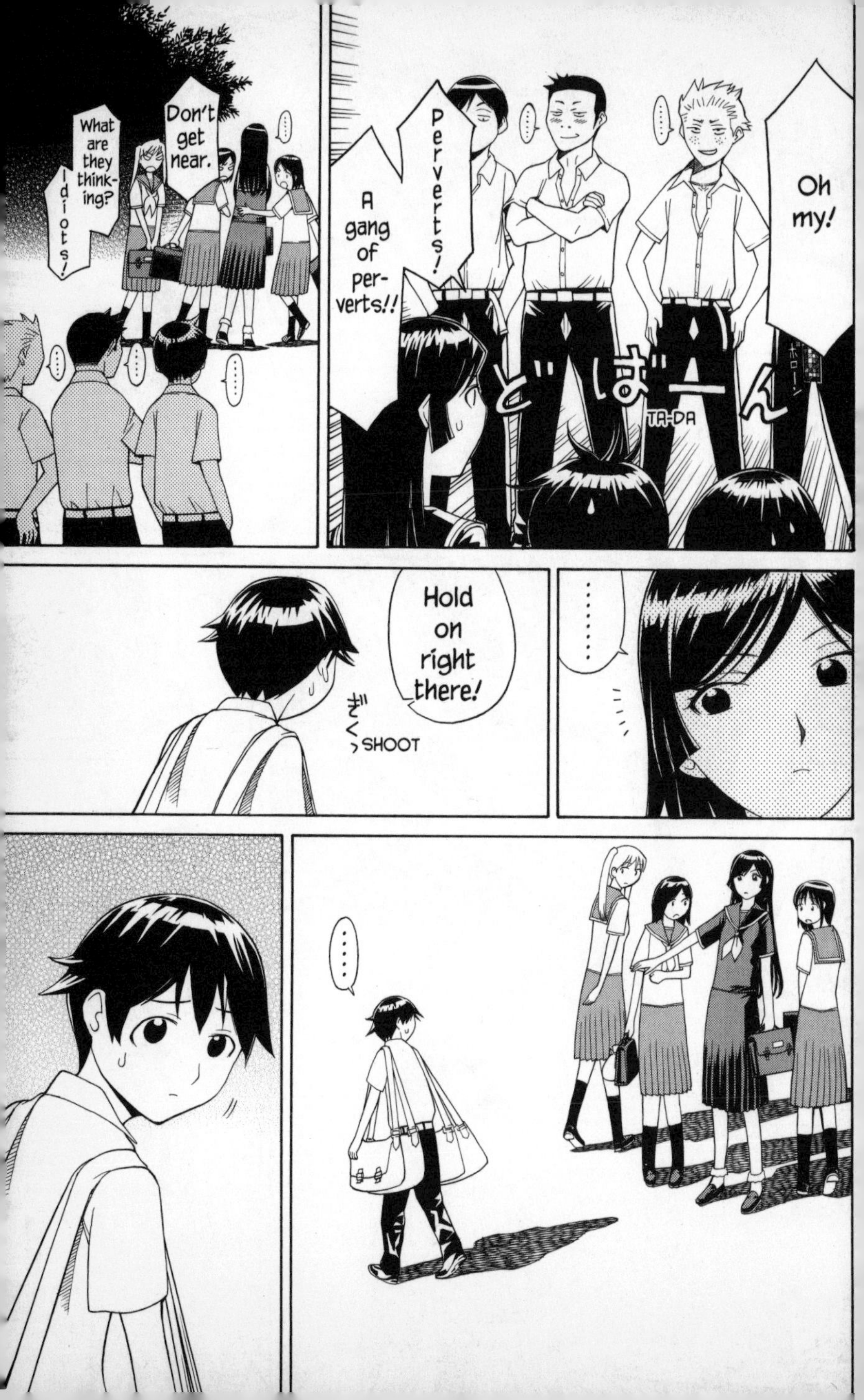
Oh my!
......
......
Perverts!
A gang of perverts!!
どばーん
TA-DA
ボローン
Don't get near.
What are they thinking?
Idiots!
......
......
......
......
......
Hold on right there!
ぞくっ
SHOOT
......

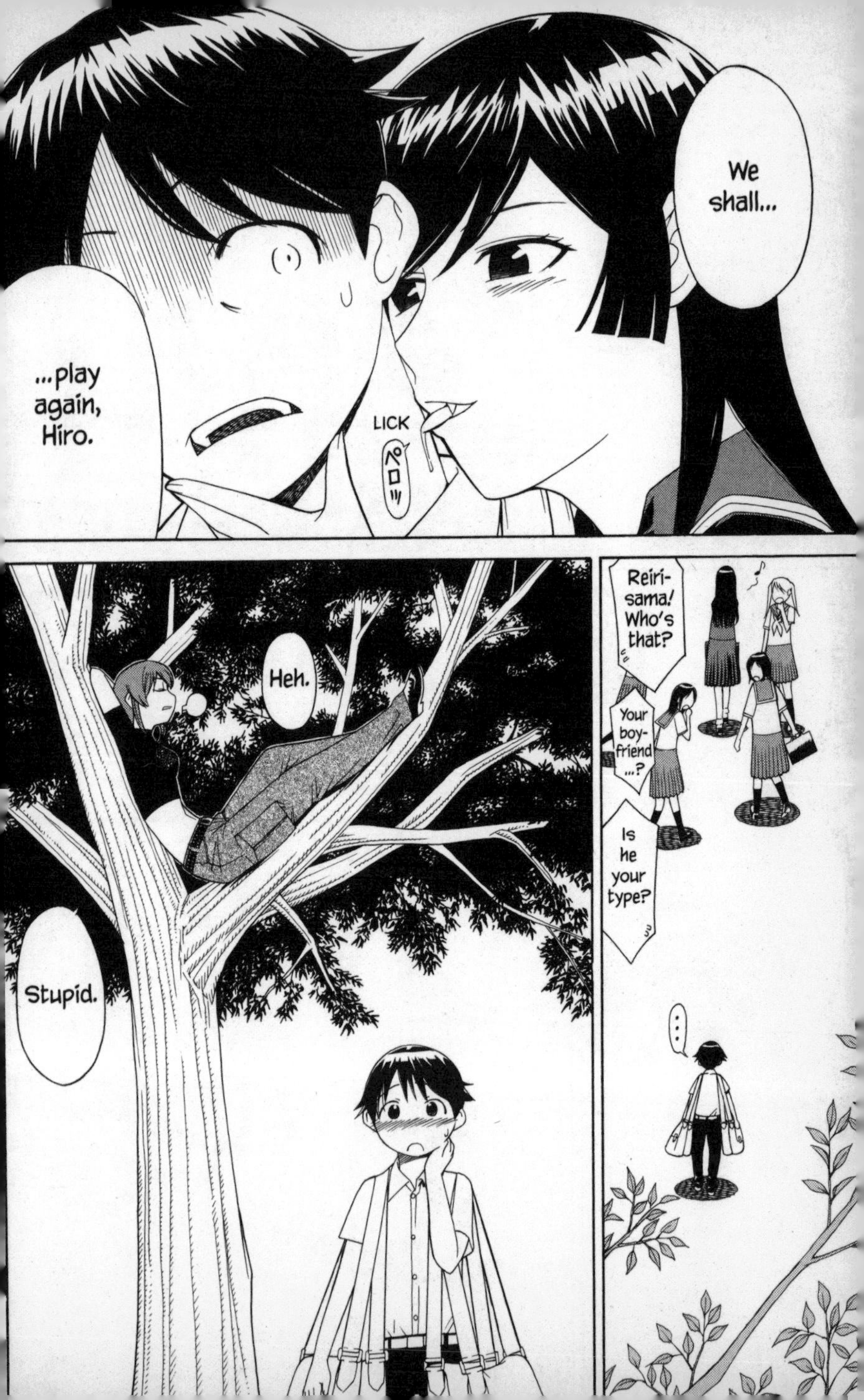
We shall...
...play again, Hiro.
LICK
ペロッ
Reiri-sama! Who's that?
Your boy-friend...?
Is he your type?
...
Heh.
Stupid.

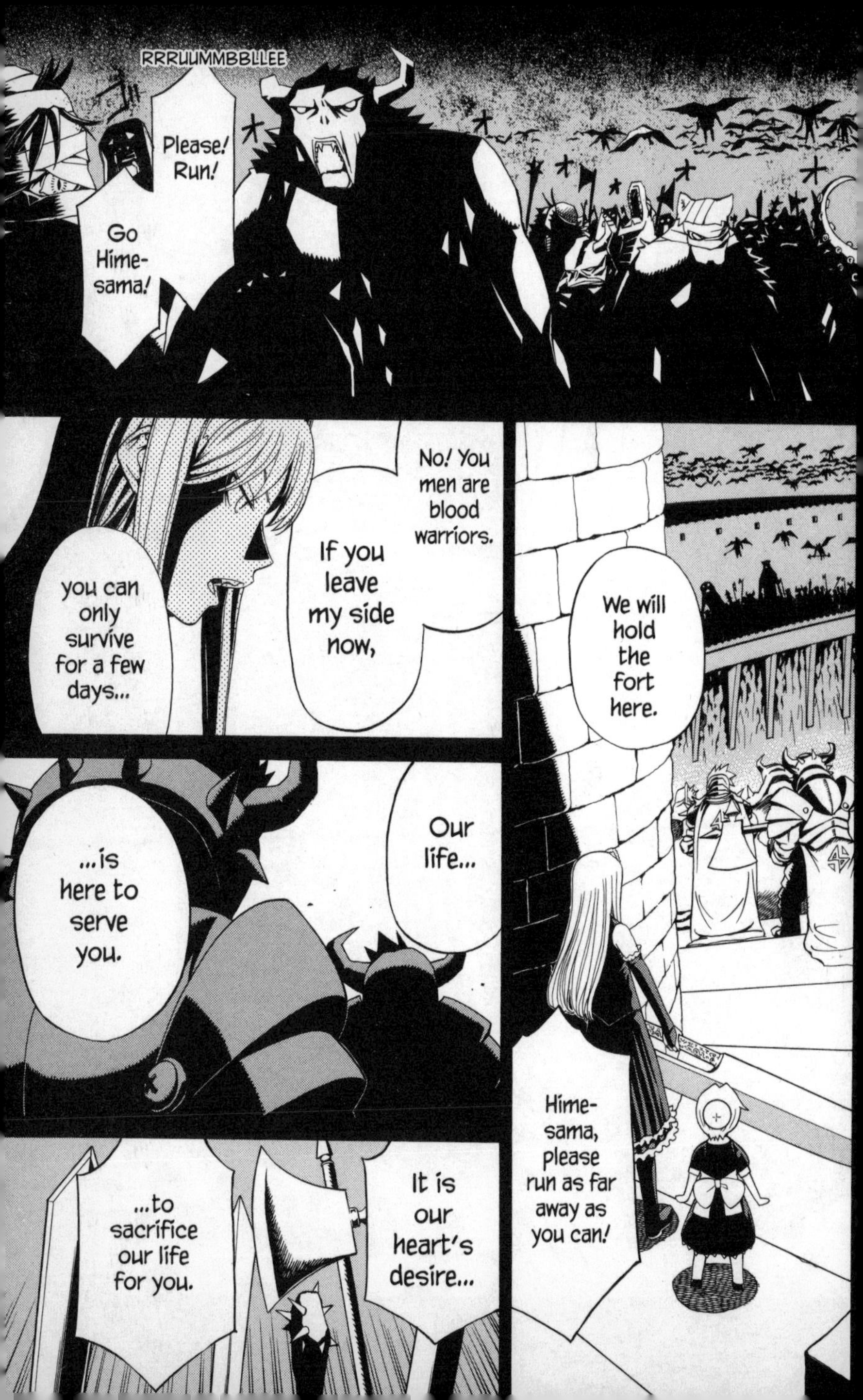
RRRUUMMBBLLEE
Please! Run!
Go Hime-sama!
We will hold the fort here.
Hime-sama, please run as far away as you can!
No! You men are blood warriors.
If you leave my side now,
you can only survive for a few days...
Our life...
...is here to serve you.
It is our heart's desire...
...to sacrifice our life for you.

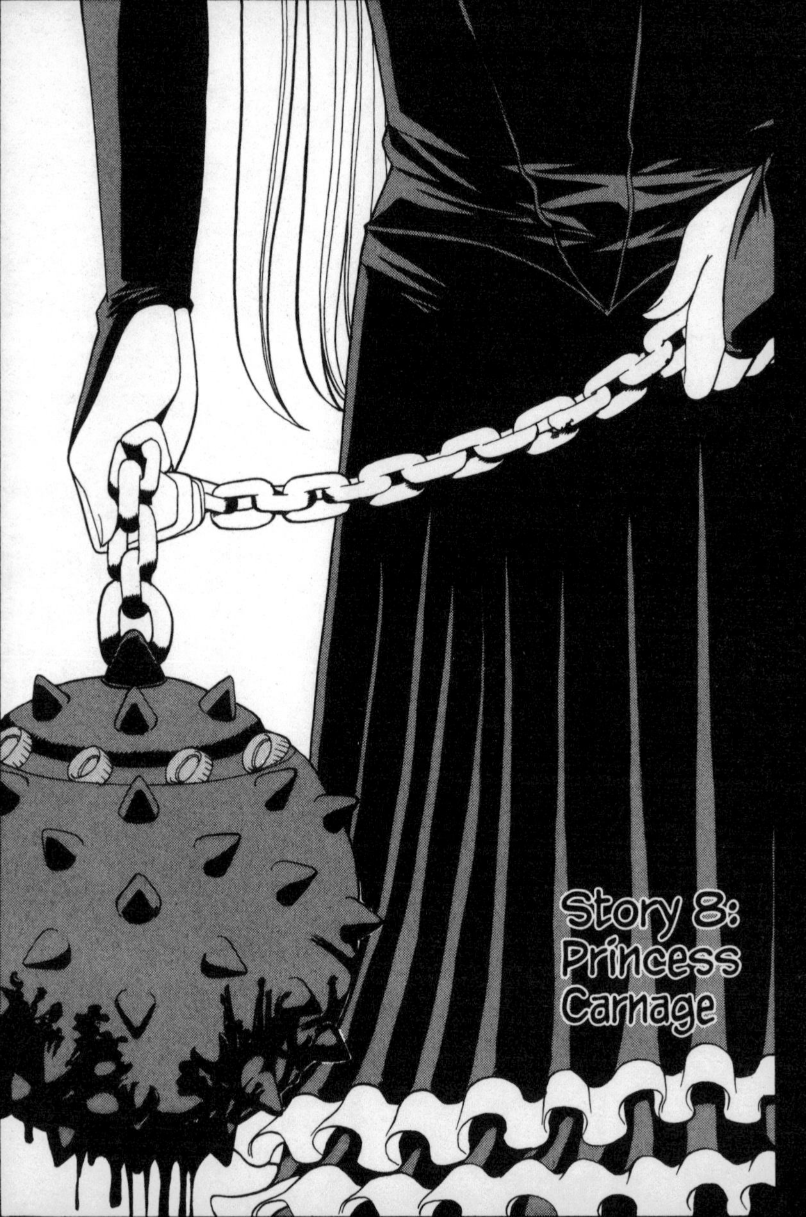
Story 8:
Princess
Carnage

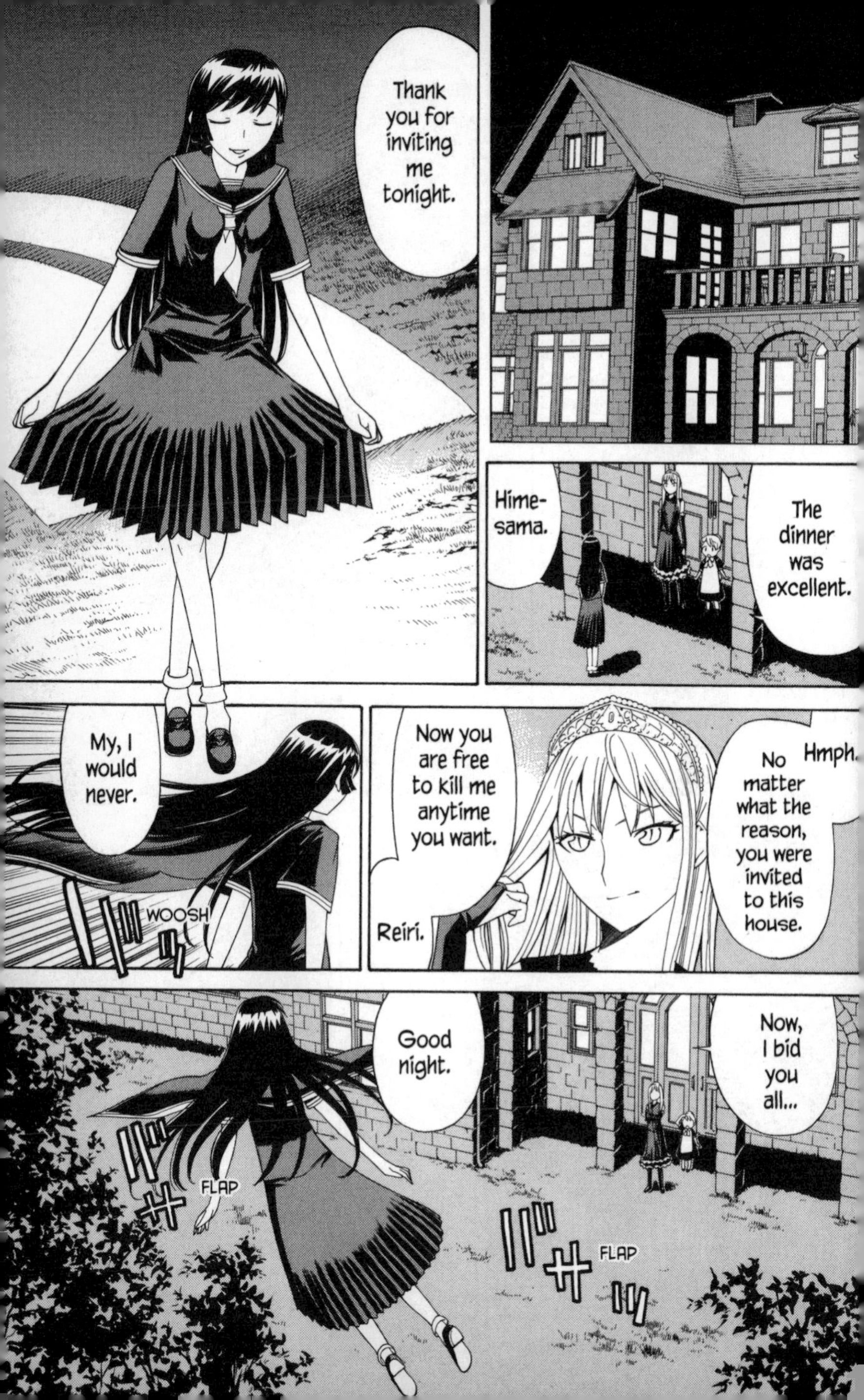
The dinner was excellent.
Hime-sama.
Thank you for inviting me tonight.
Hmph.
No matter what the reason, you were invited to this house.
Now you are free to kill me anytime you want.
Reiri.
My, I would never.
WOOSH
Now, I bid you all...
Good night.
FLAP
FLAP

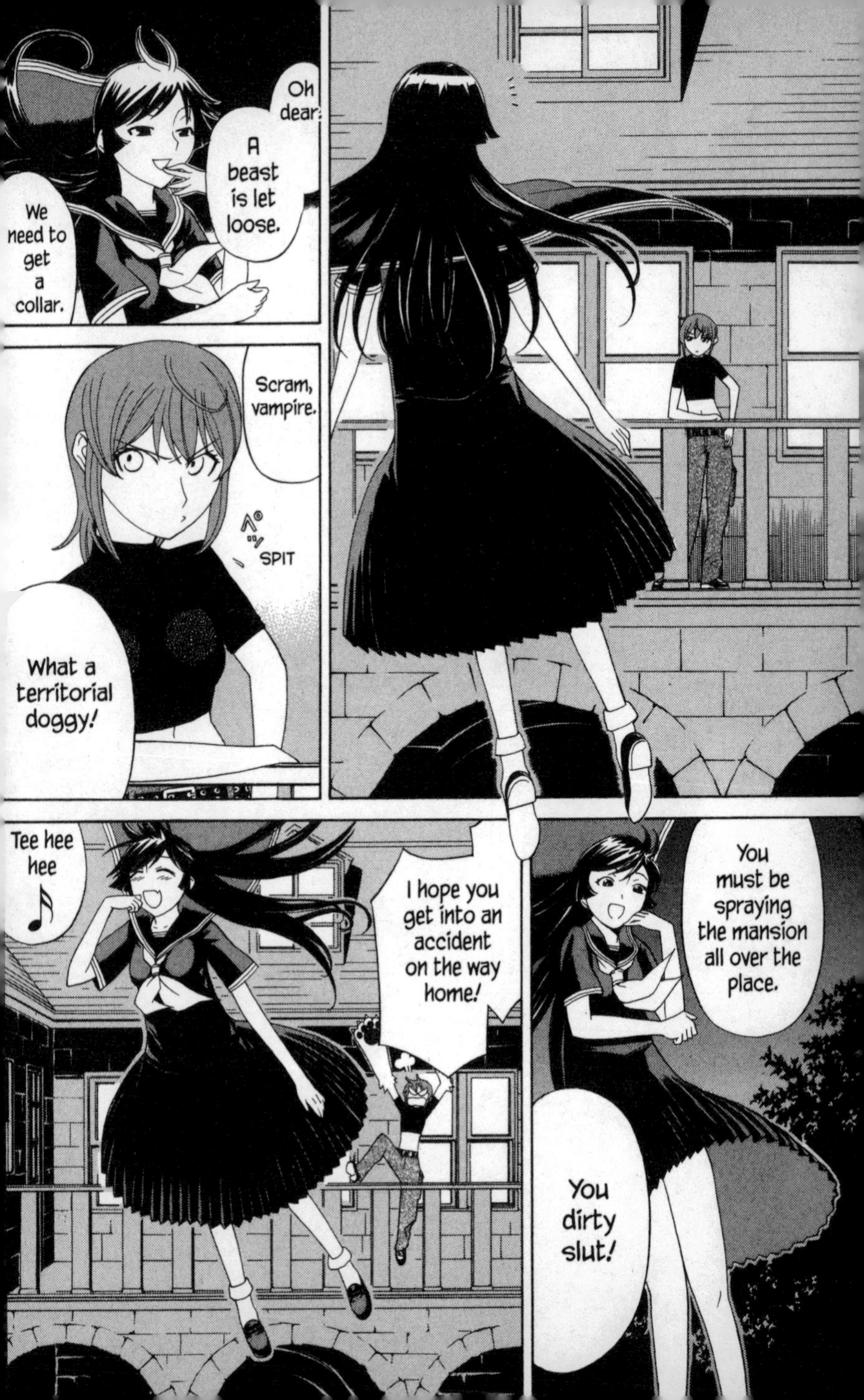
Oh dear.
A beast is let loose.
We need to get a collar.
Scram, vampire.
SPIT
What a territorial doggy!
You must be spraying the mansion all over the place.
You dirty slut!
I hope you get into an accident on the way home!
Tee hee hee ♪

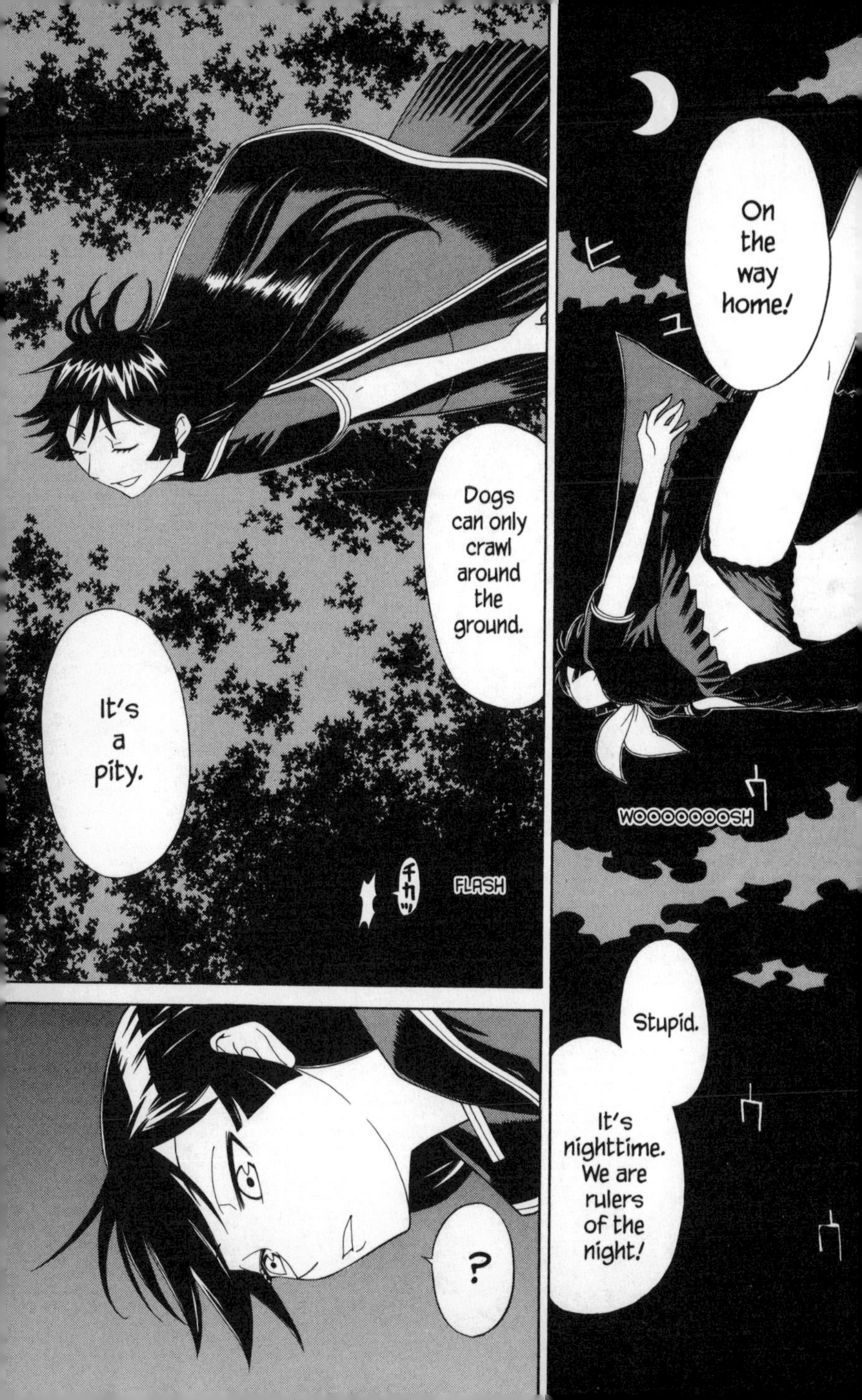
On the way home!
WOOOOOOOOSH
Stupid.
It's nighttime. We are rulers of the night!
Dogs can only crawl around the ground.
It's a pity.
FLASH
?

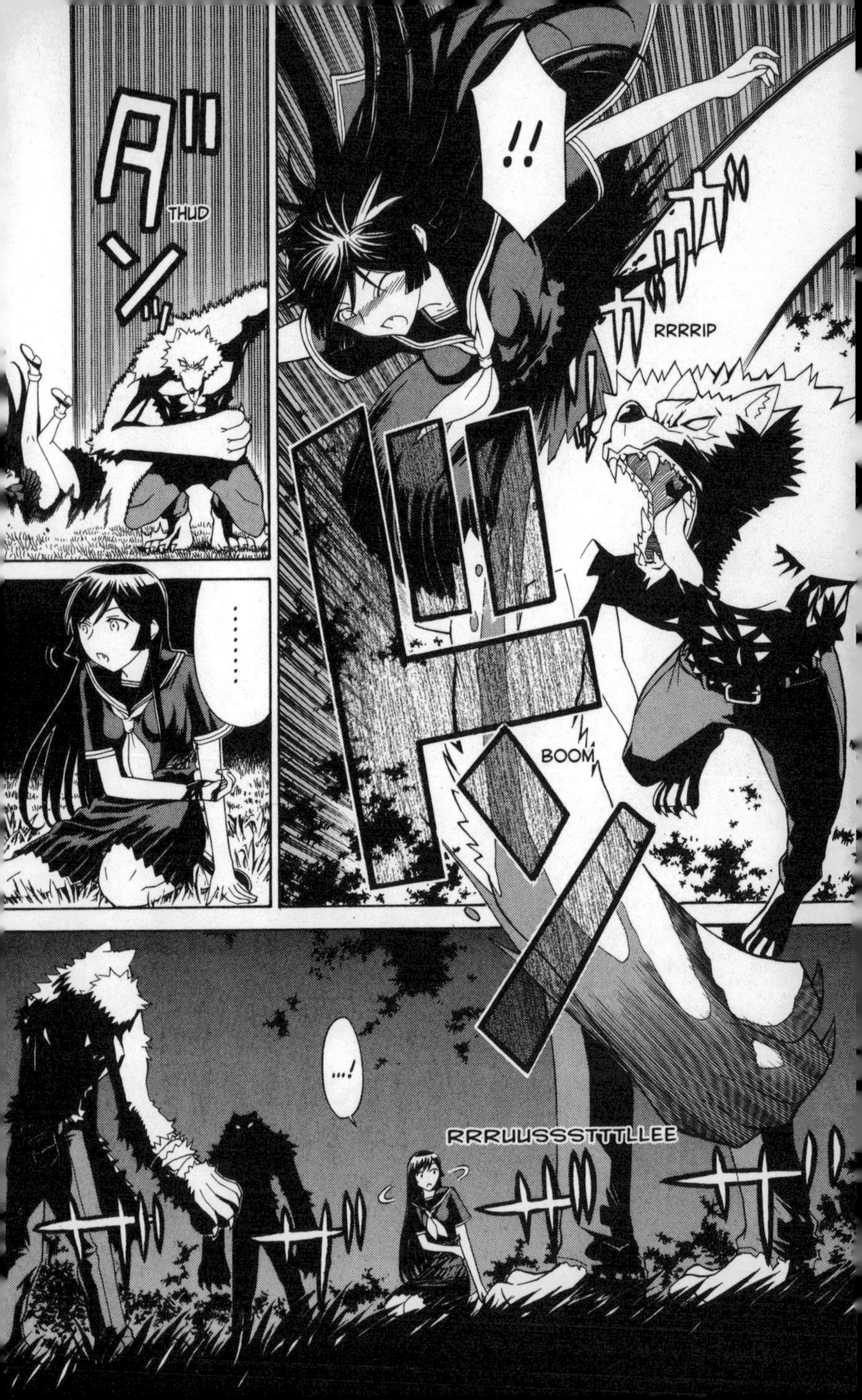
!!
RRRRIP
BOOM
THUD
......
...!
RRRUUSSSTTTLLEE

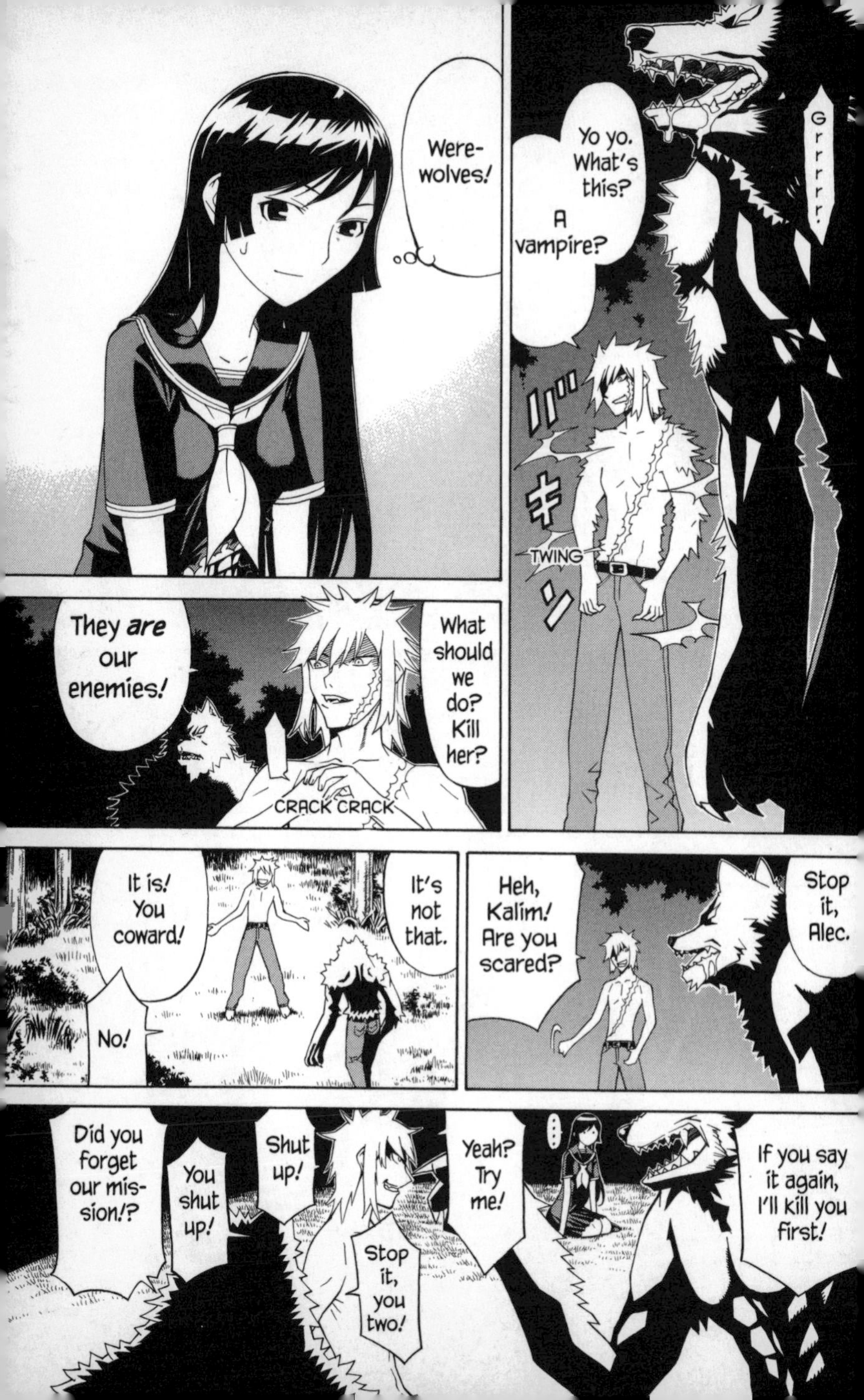
Grrrrr.
Yo yo. What's this? A vampire?
TWING
Were-wolves!
What should we do? Kill her?
They are our enemies!
CRACK CRACK
Stop it, Alec.
Heh, Kalim! Are you scared?
It's not that.
It is! You coward!
No!
If you say it again, I'll kill you first!
...
Yeah? Try me!
Shut up!
Stop it, you two!
You shut up!
Did you forget our mis-sion!?

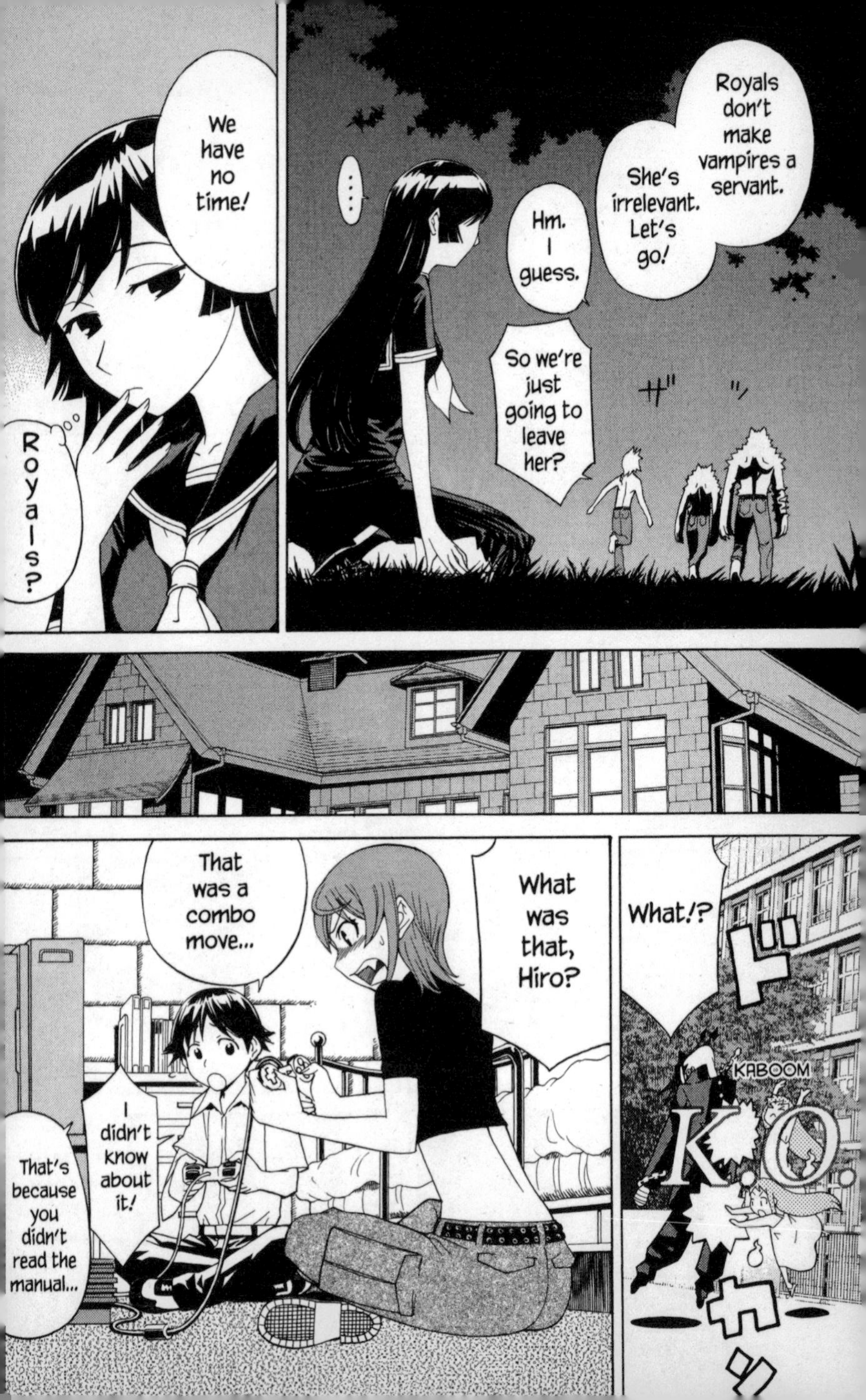
Royals don't make vampires a servant.
She's irrelevant. Let's go!
Hm. I guess.
...
So we're just going to leave her?
We have no time!
Royals?
What!?
KABOOM
K.O.
What was that, Hiro?
That was a combo move...
I didn't know about it!
That's because you didn't read the manual...

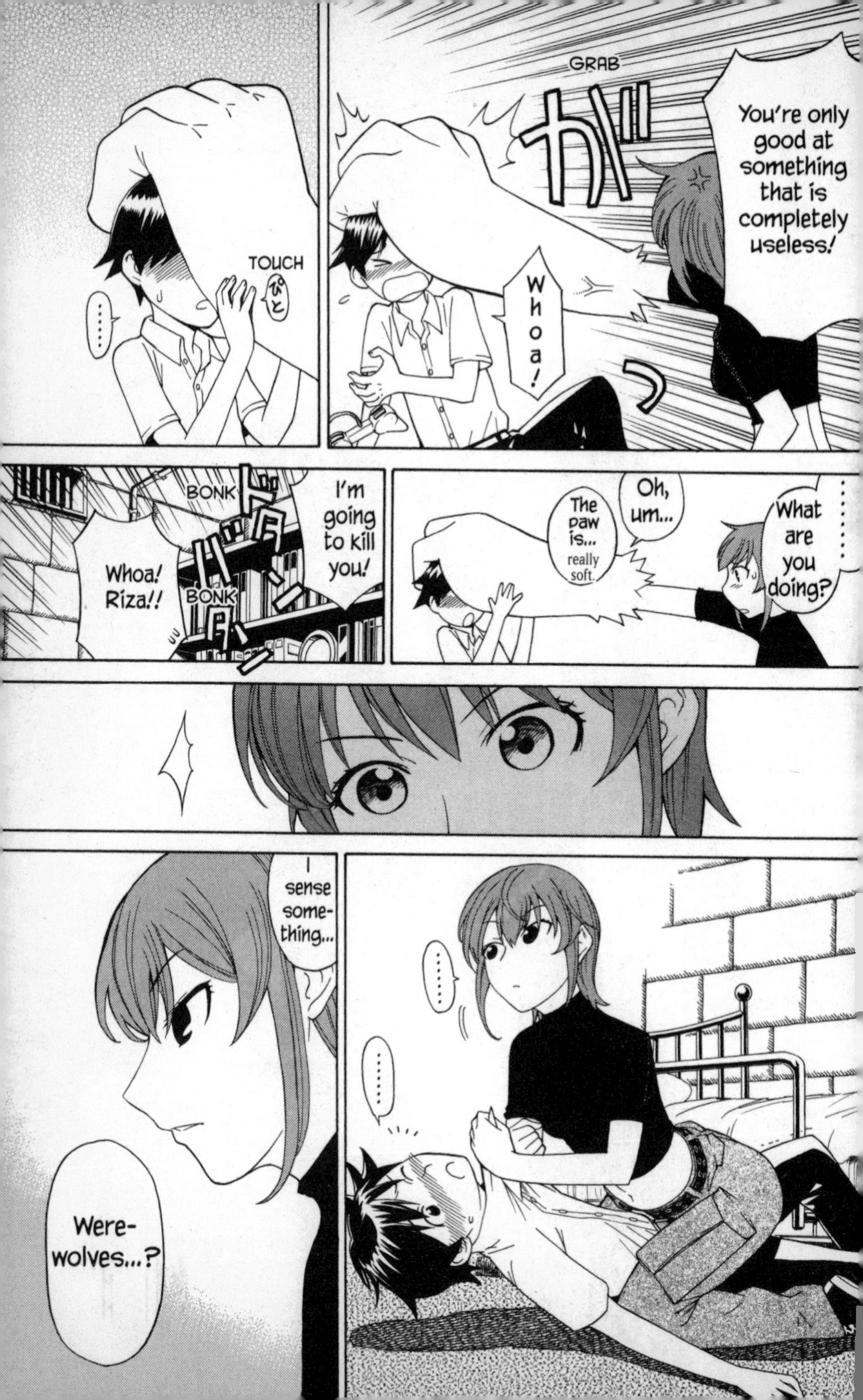
GRAB
You're only good at something that is completely useless!
Whoa!
TOUCH
......
......
What are you doing?
Oh, um...
The paw is... really soft.
I'm going to kill you!
BONK
BONK
Whoa! Riza!!
......
......
I sense some-thing...
Were-wolves...?

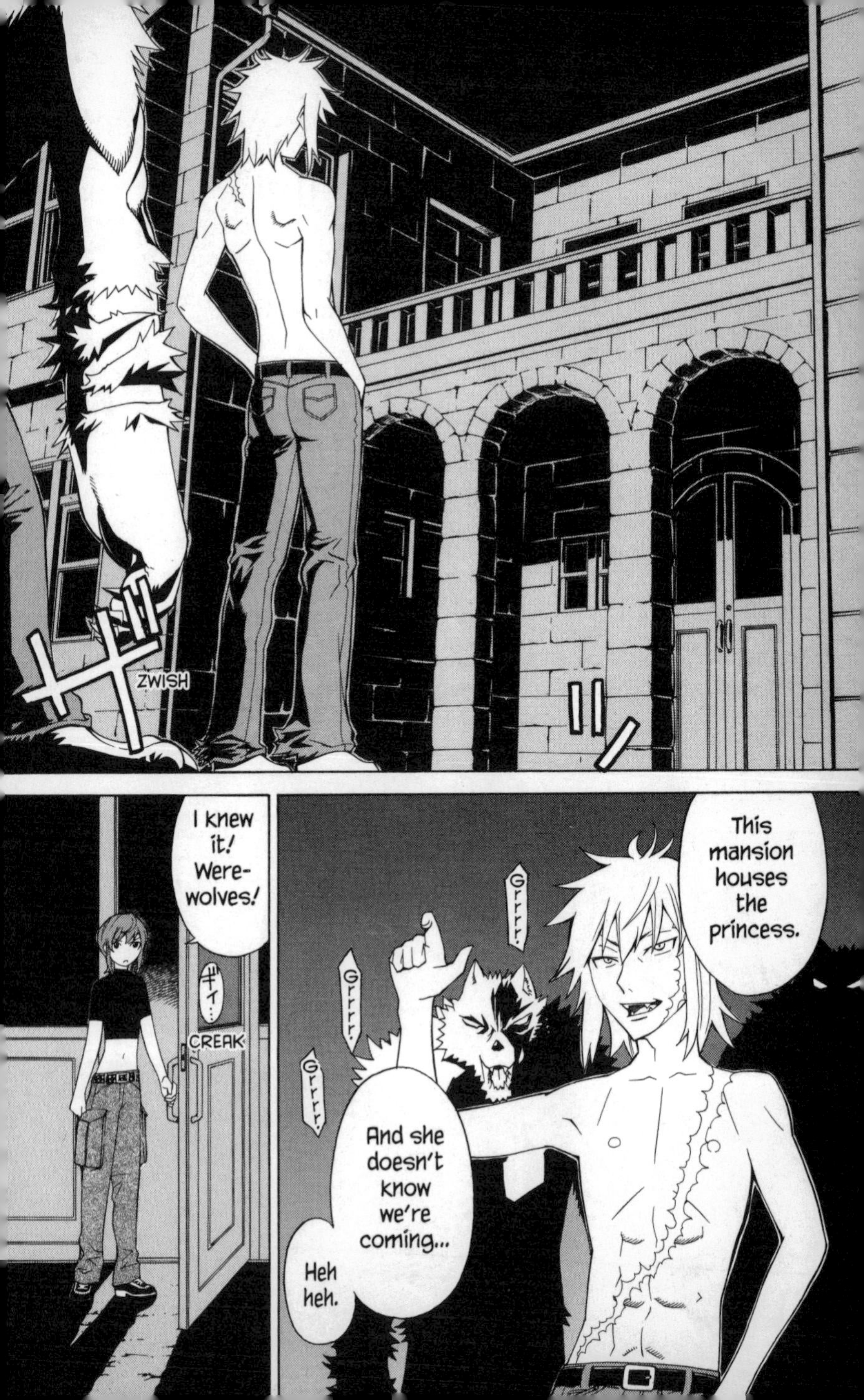
ZWISH
This mansion houses the princess.
Grrr.
Grrrr.
Grrrr.
And she doesn't know we're coming...
Heh heh.
I knew it! Were-wolves!
ギィ…
CREAK

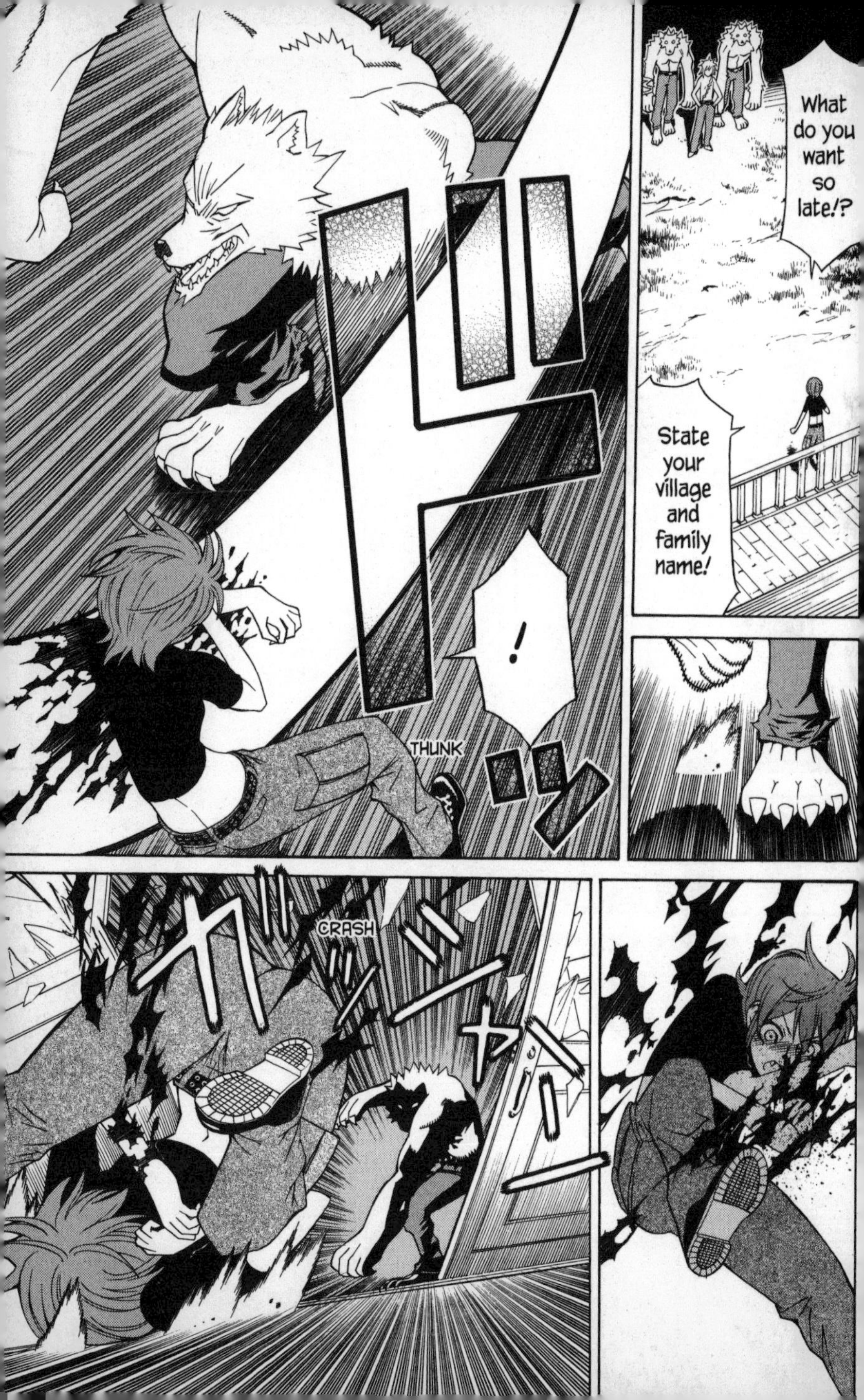
What do you want so late!?
State your village and family name!
!
THUNK
CRASH

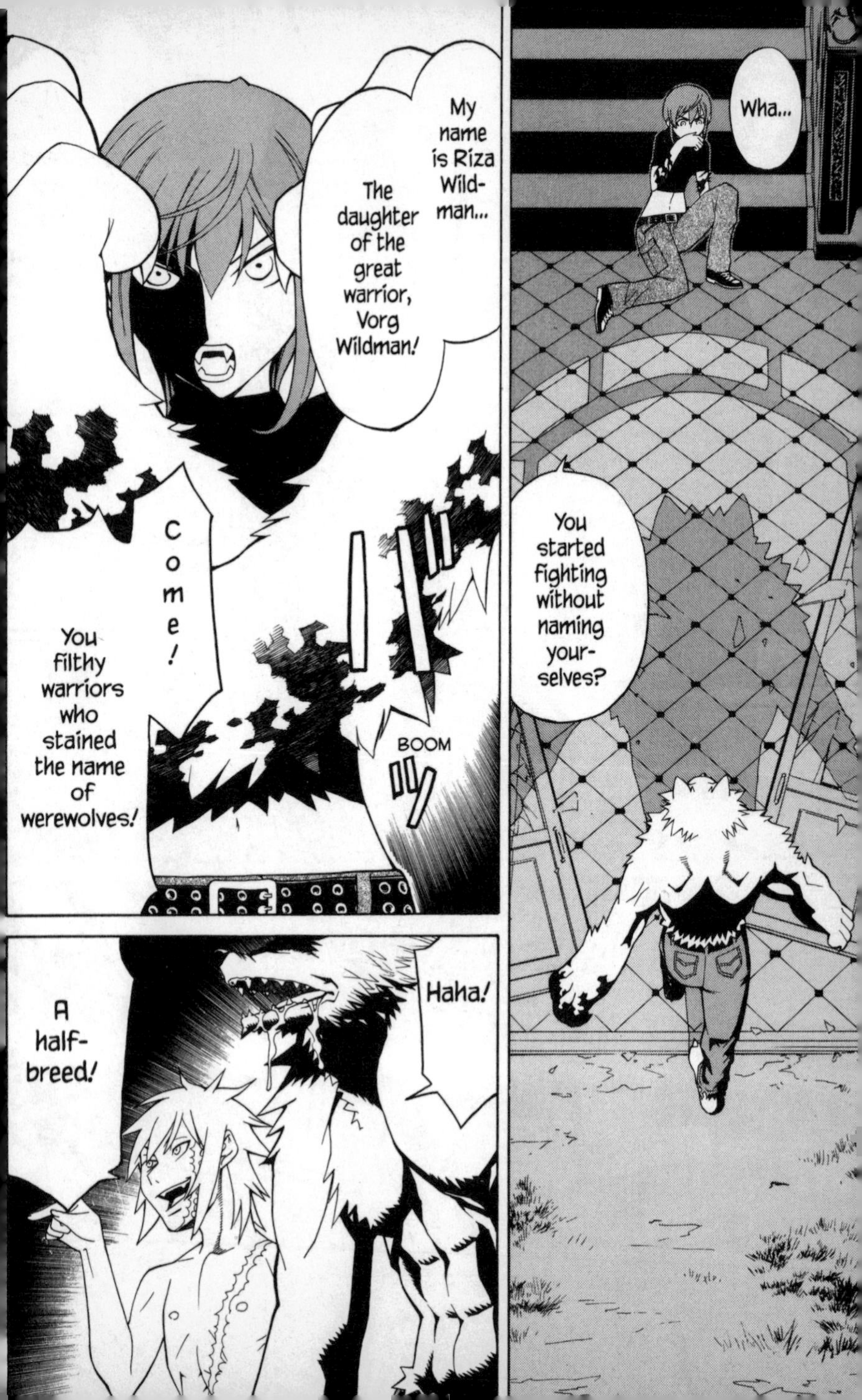
Wha...
You started fighting without naming yourselves?
My name is Riza Wildman...
The daughter of the great warrior, Vorg Wildman!
Come!
You filthy warriors who stained the name of werewolves!
BOOM
Haha!
A half-breed!

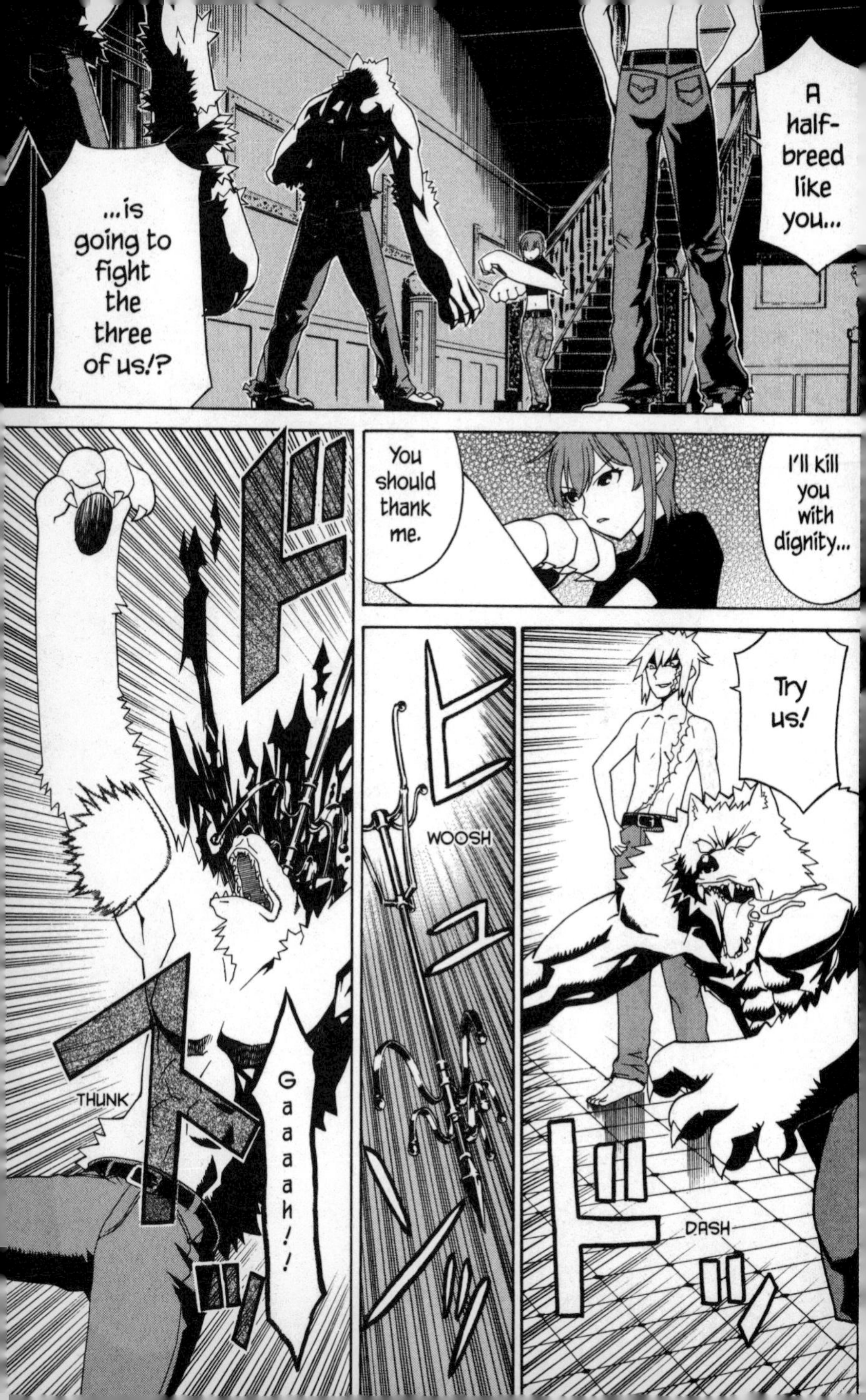
A half-breed like you...
...is going to fight the three of us!?
I'll kill you with dignity...
You should thank me.
Try us!
DASH
WOOSH
Gaaaaah!!
THUNK

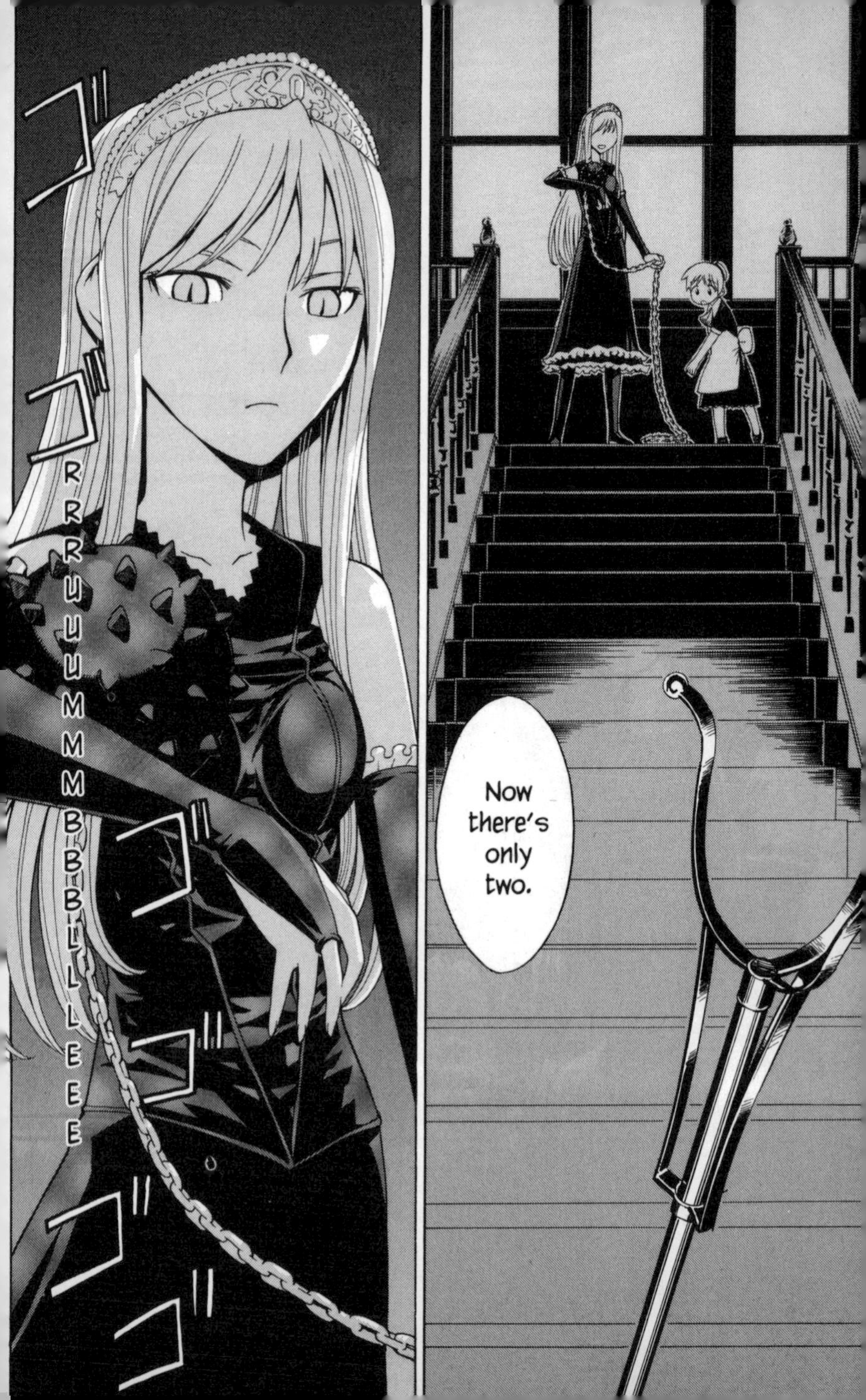
Now there's only two.
RRRUUUMMMBBBLLLEEE

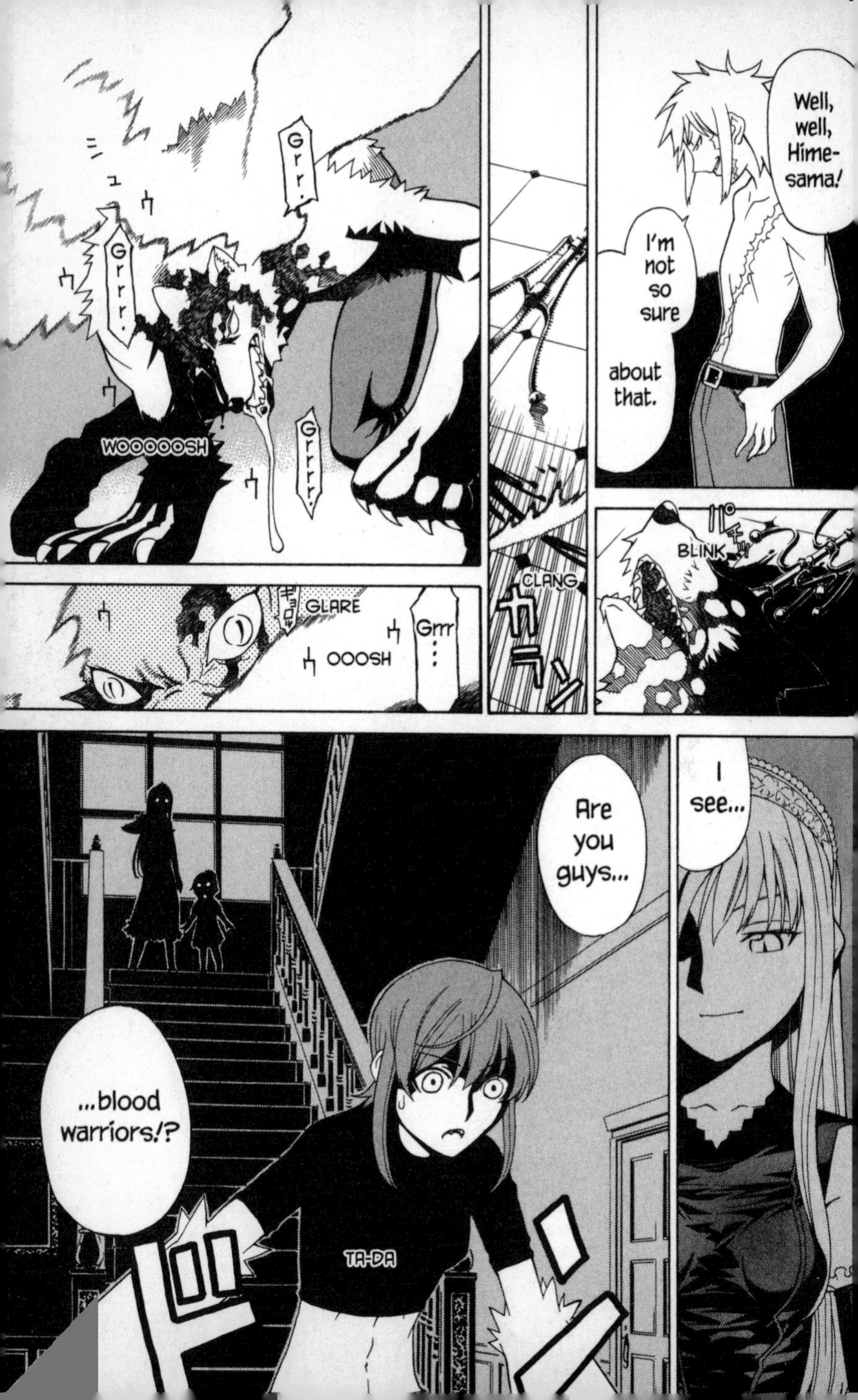

Well, well, Hime-sama!
I'm not so sure about that.
BLINK
CLANG
Grr.
Grrr.
WOOOOOSH
Grrrr.
GLARE
Grrr...
OOOSH
I see...
Are you guys...
...blood warriors!?
TA-DA

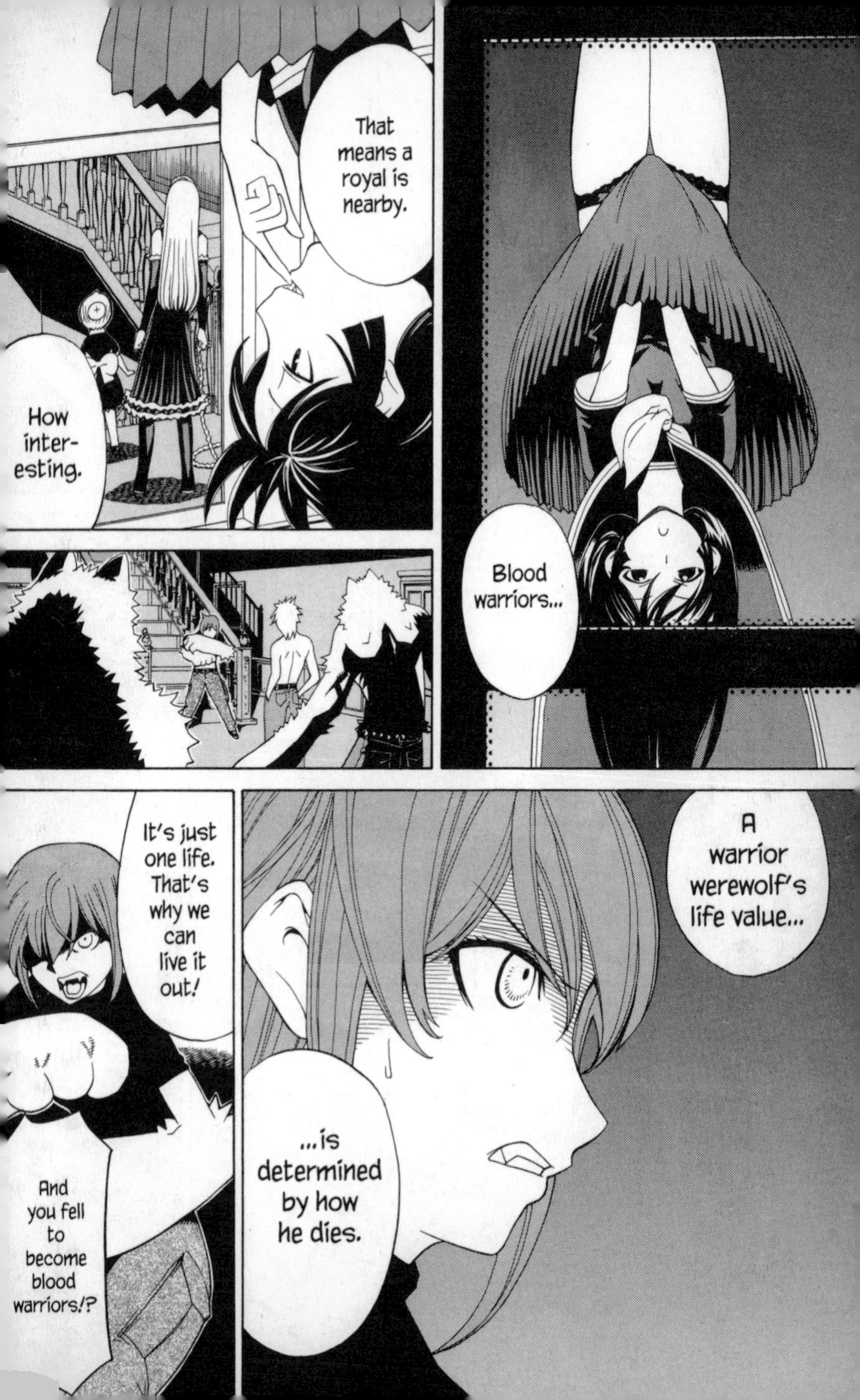
Blood warriors...
That means a royal is nearby.
How interesting.
A warrior werewolf's life value...
...is determined by how he dies.
It's just one life. That's why we can live it out!
And you fell to become blood warriors!?

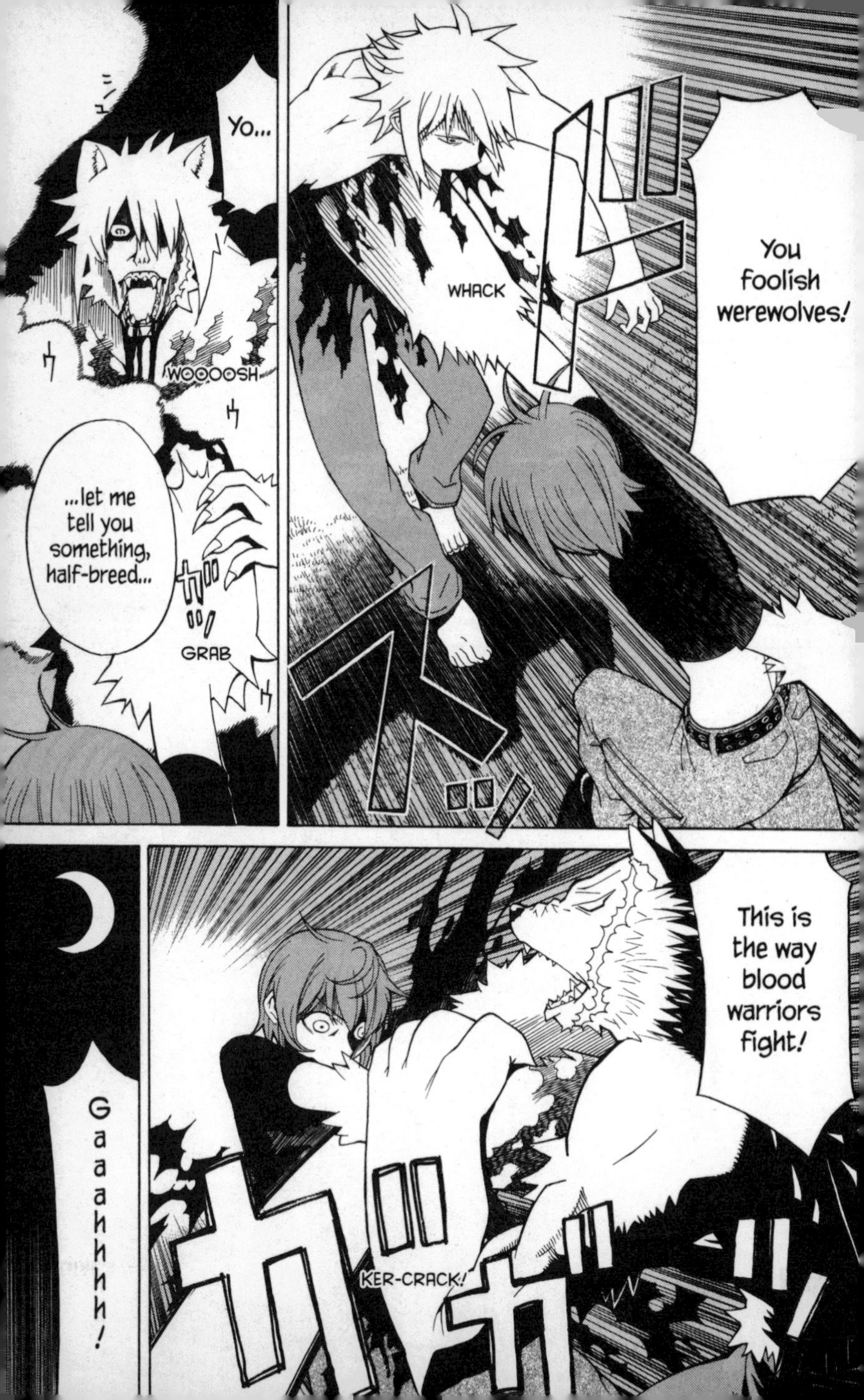
You foolish werewolves!
WHACK
Yo...
WOOOOSH
...let me tell you something, half-breed...
GRAB
This is the way blood warriors fight!
KER-CRACK!
Gaaahhhhh!

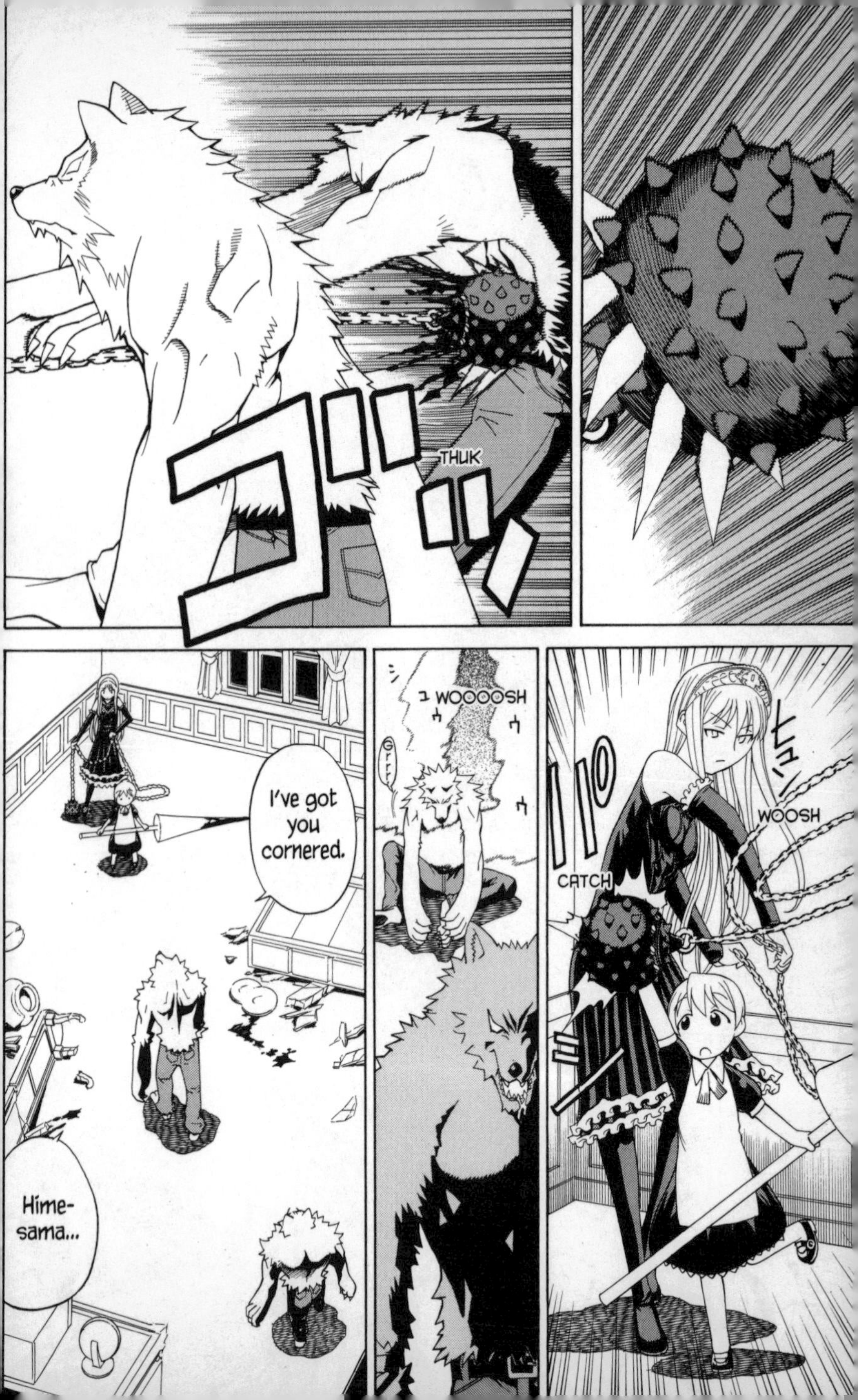

ゴッ
THUK
WOOSH
CATCH
WOOOOSH
I've got you cornered.
Hime-sama...

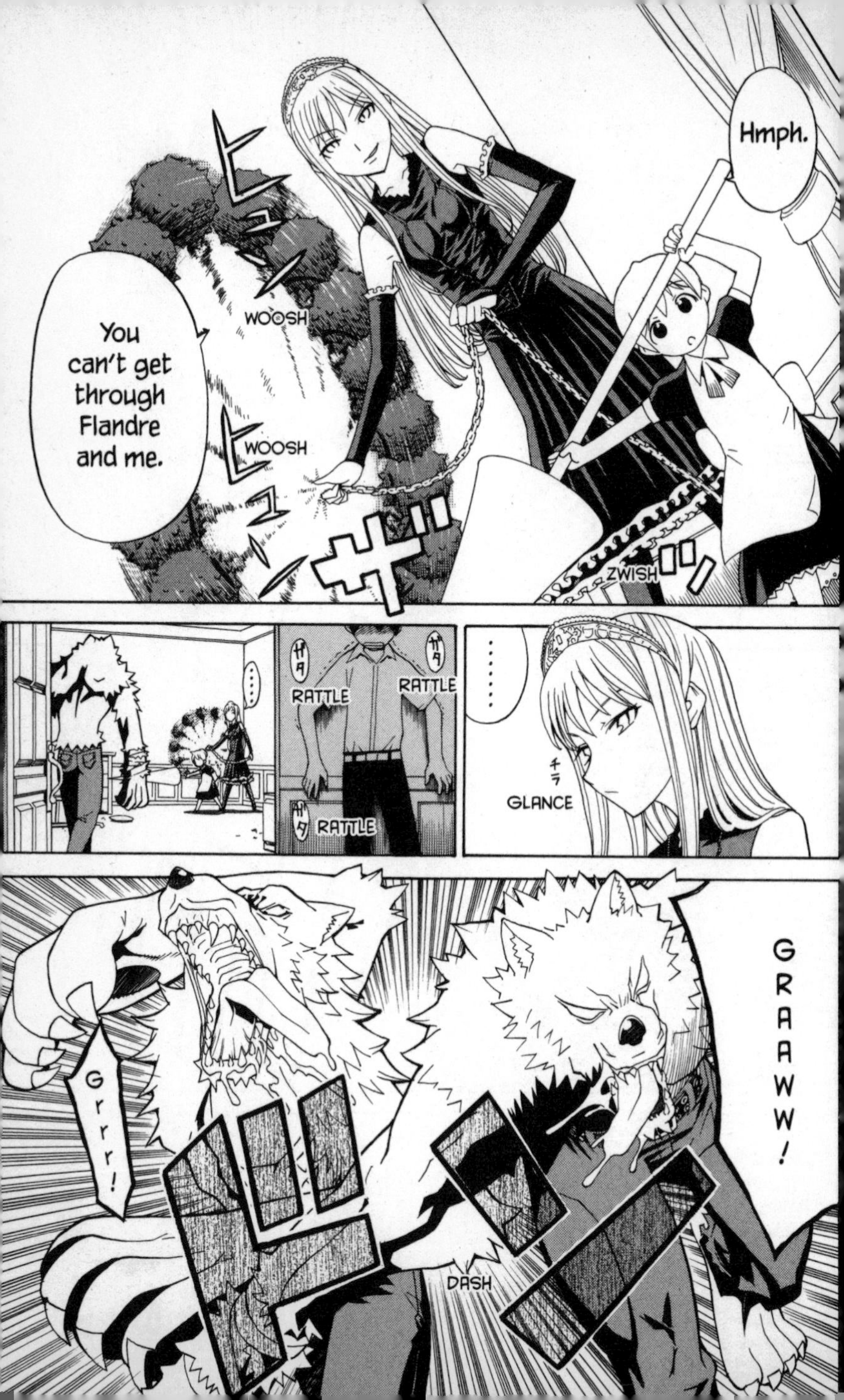

Hmph.
You can't get through Flandre and me.
WOOSH
WOOSH
ZWISH
......
チラ
GLANCE
ガタ
RATTLE
ガタ
RATTLE
ガタ
RATTLE
.....
GRAAWW!
Grrr!
DASH

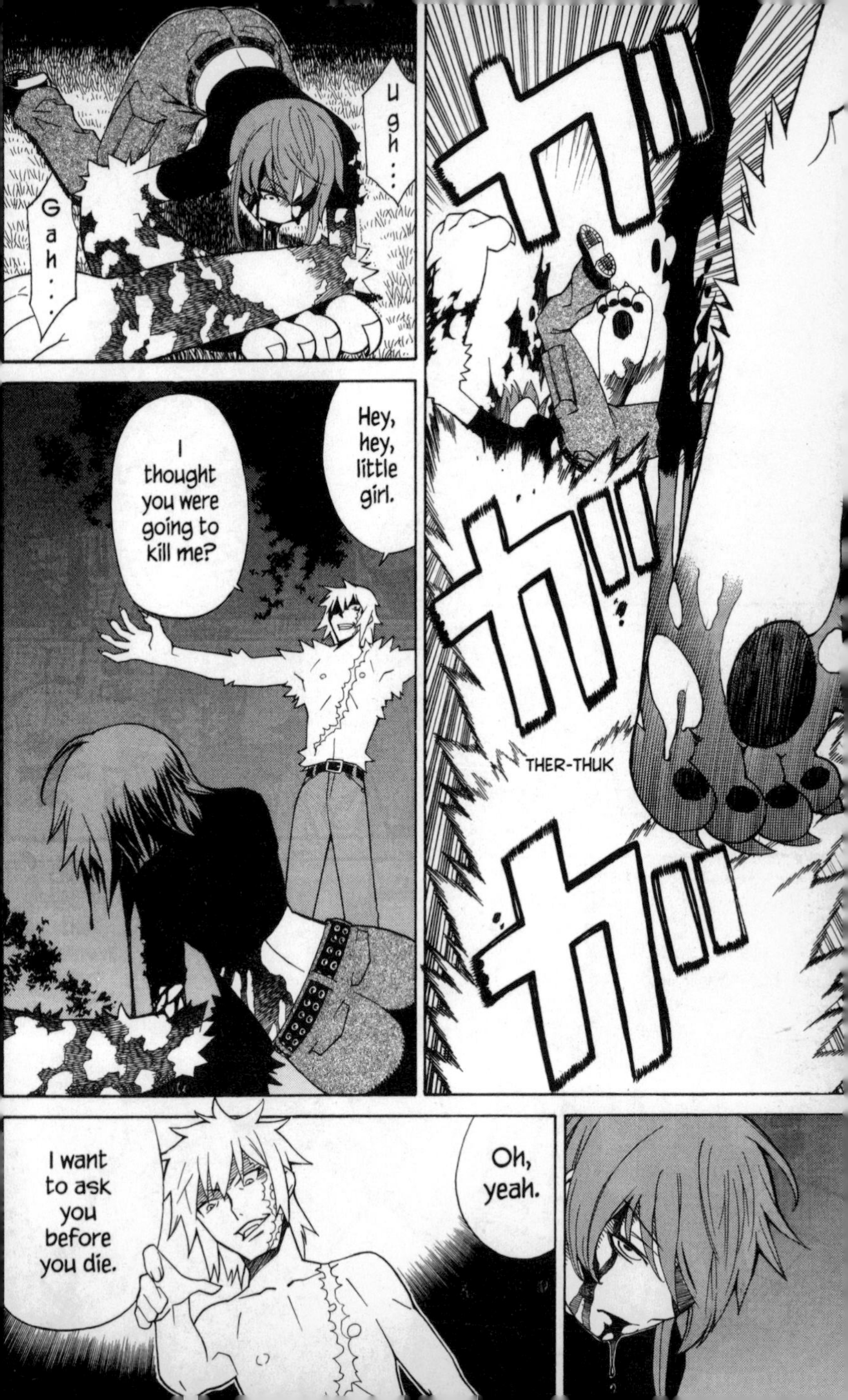
THER-THUK
Ugh...
Gah...
Hey, hey, little girl.
I thought you were going to kill me?
Oh, yeah.
I want to ask you before you die.

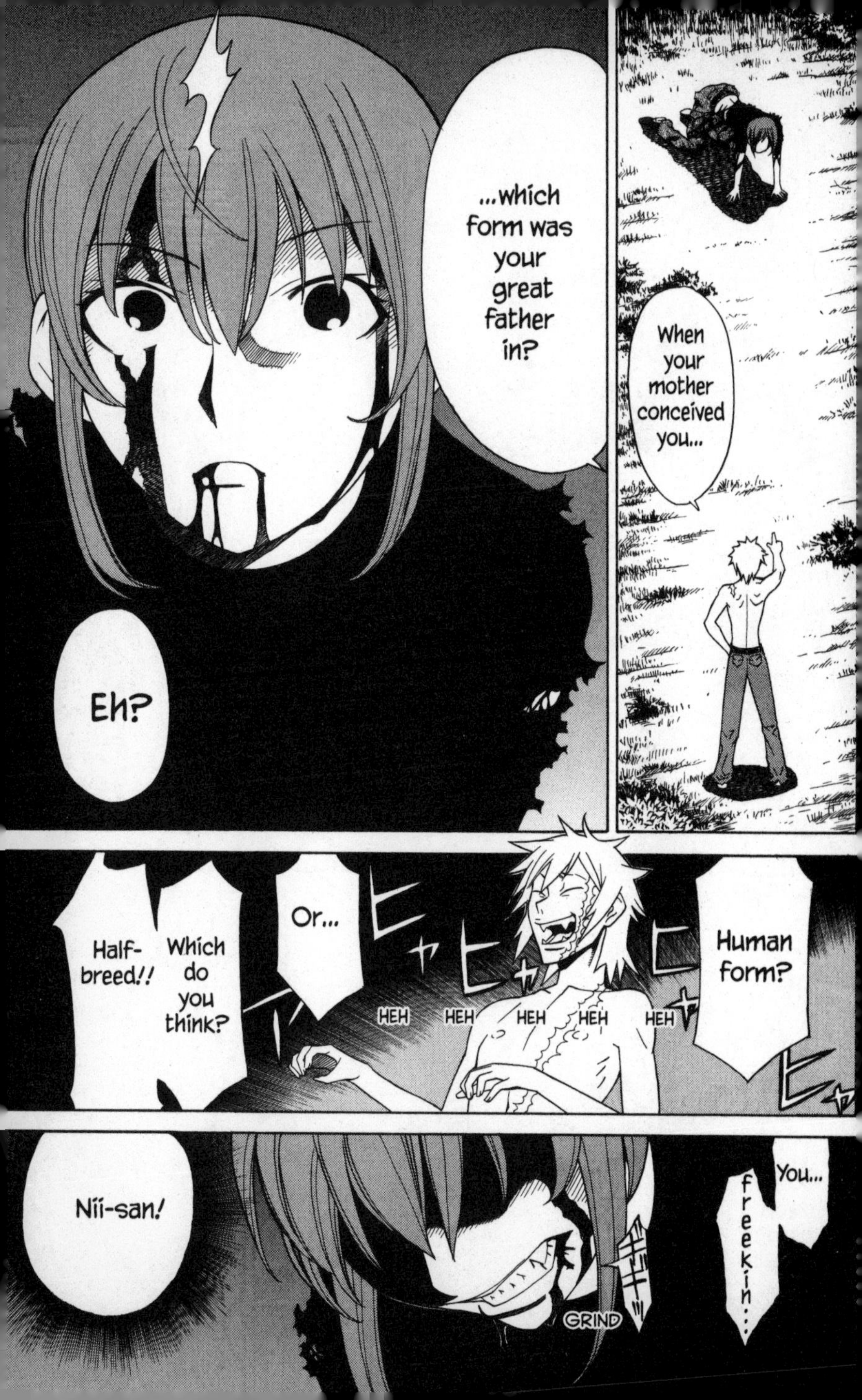
When your mother conceived you...
...which form was your great father in?
Eh?
Human form?
HEH HEH HEH HEH HEH
Or...
Which do you think?
Half-breed!!
You...
freekin...
GRIND
Nii-san!

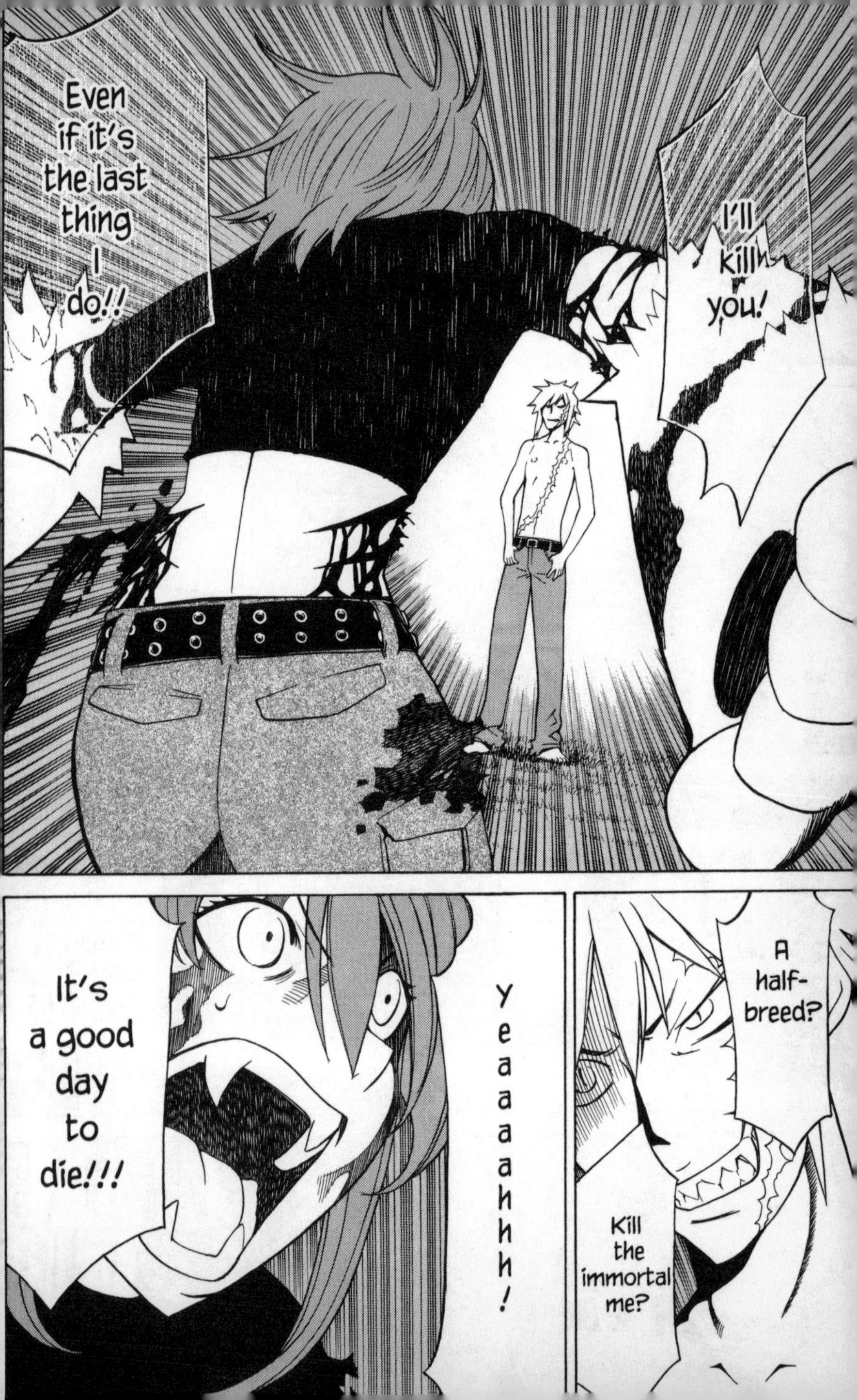
I'll kill you!
Even if it's the last thing I do!!
A half-breed?
Kill the immortal me?
Yeaaaaahhh!
It's a good day to die!!!

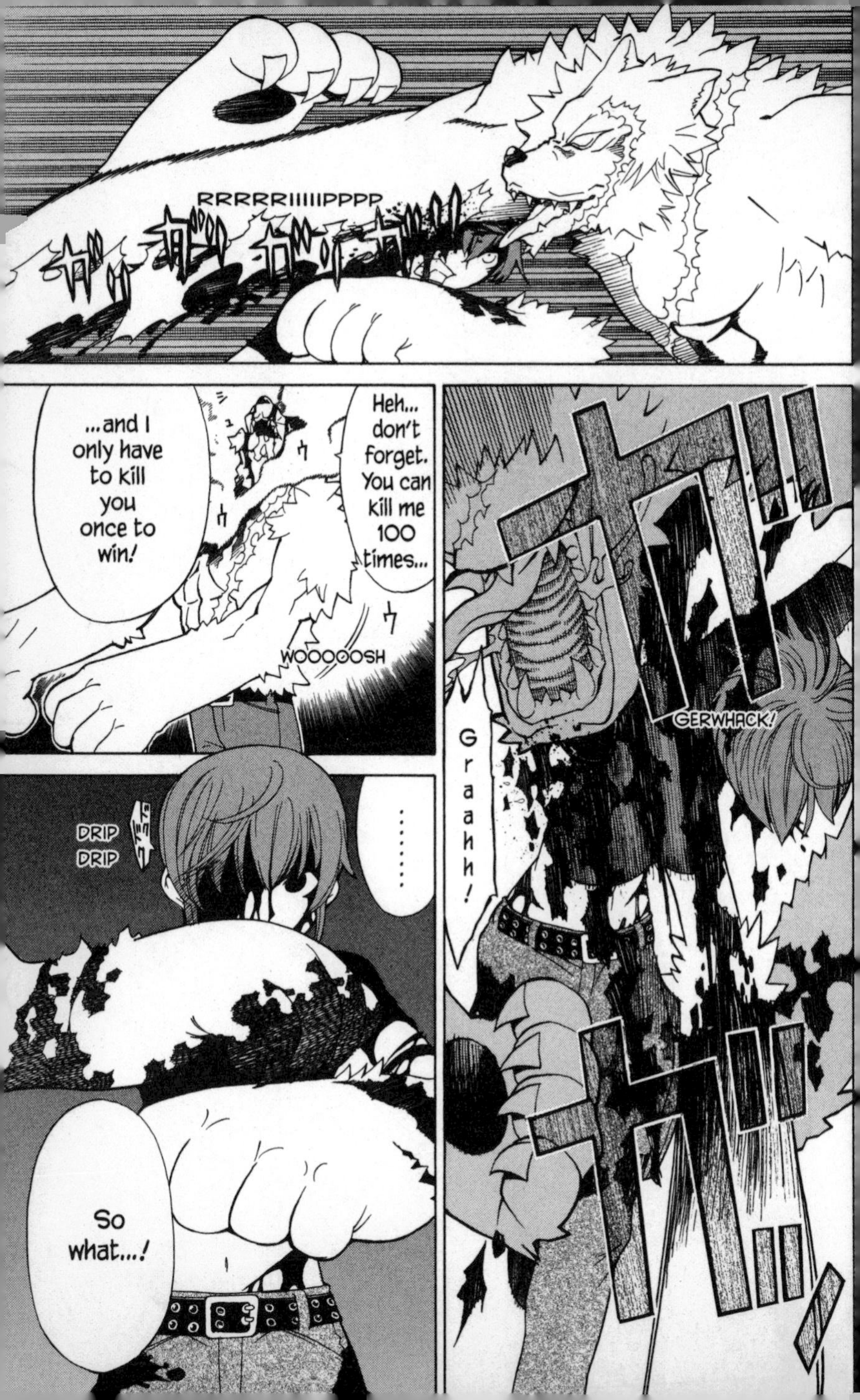
RRRRRIIIIIPPPP
GERWHACK!
Graahh!
Heh... don't forget. You can kill me 100 times...
...and I only have to kill you once to win!
WOOOOOSH
....
DRIP DRIP
So what...!

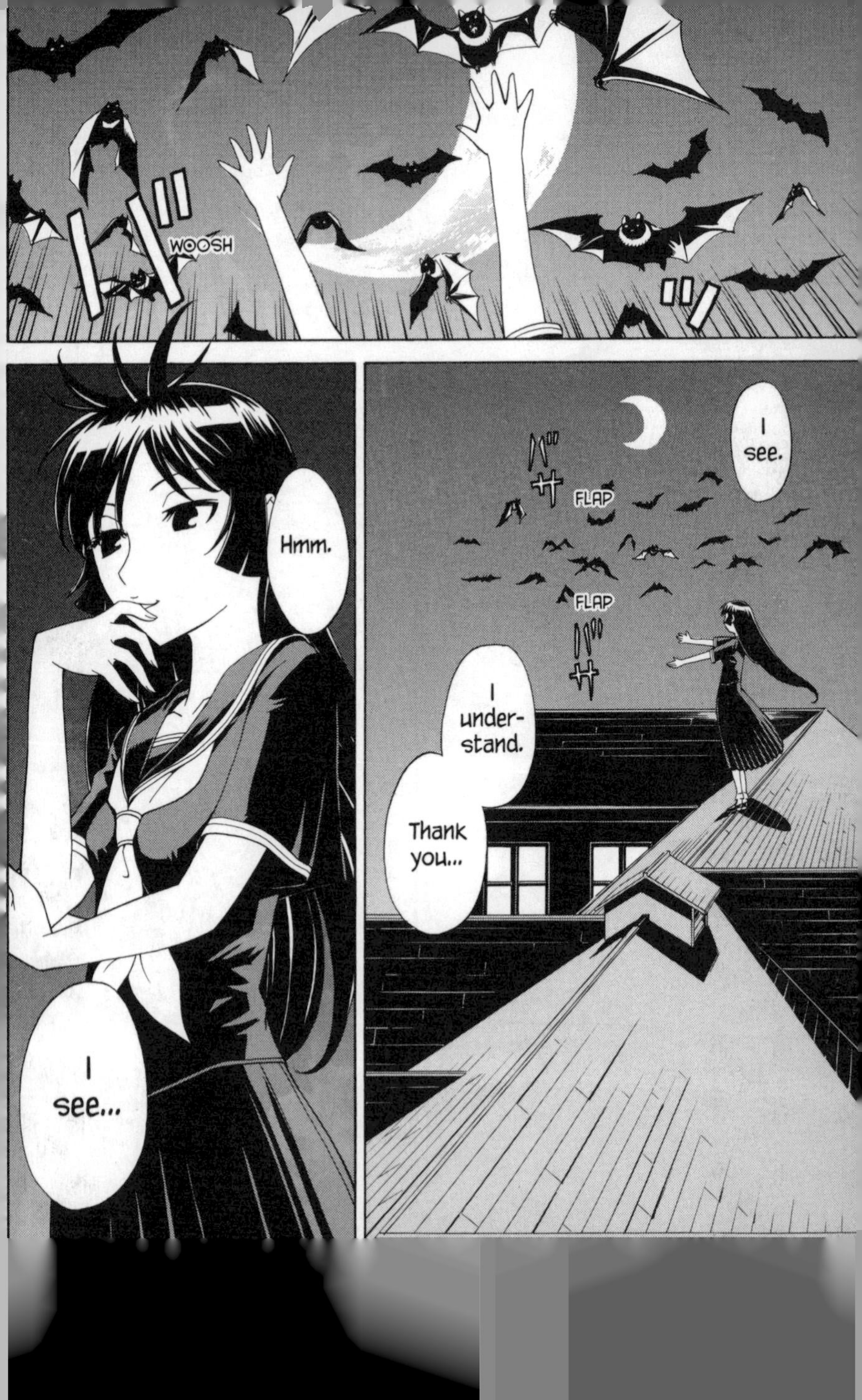
WOOSH
I see.
FLAP
FLAP
I understand.
Thank you...
Hmm.
I see...

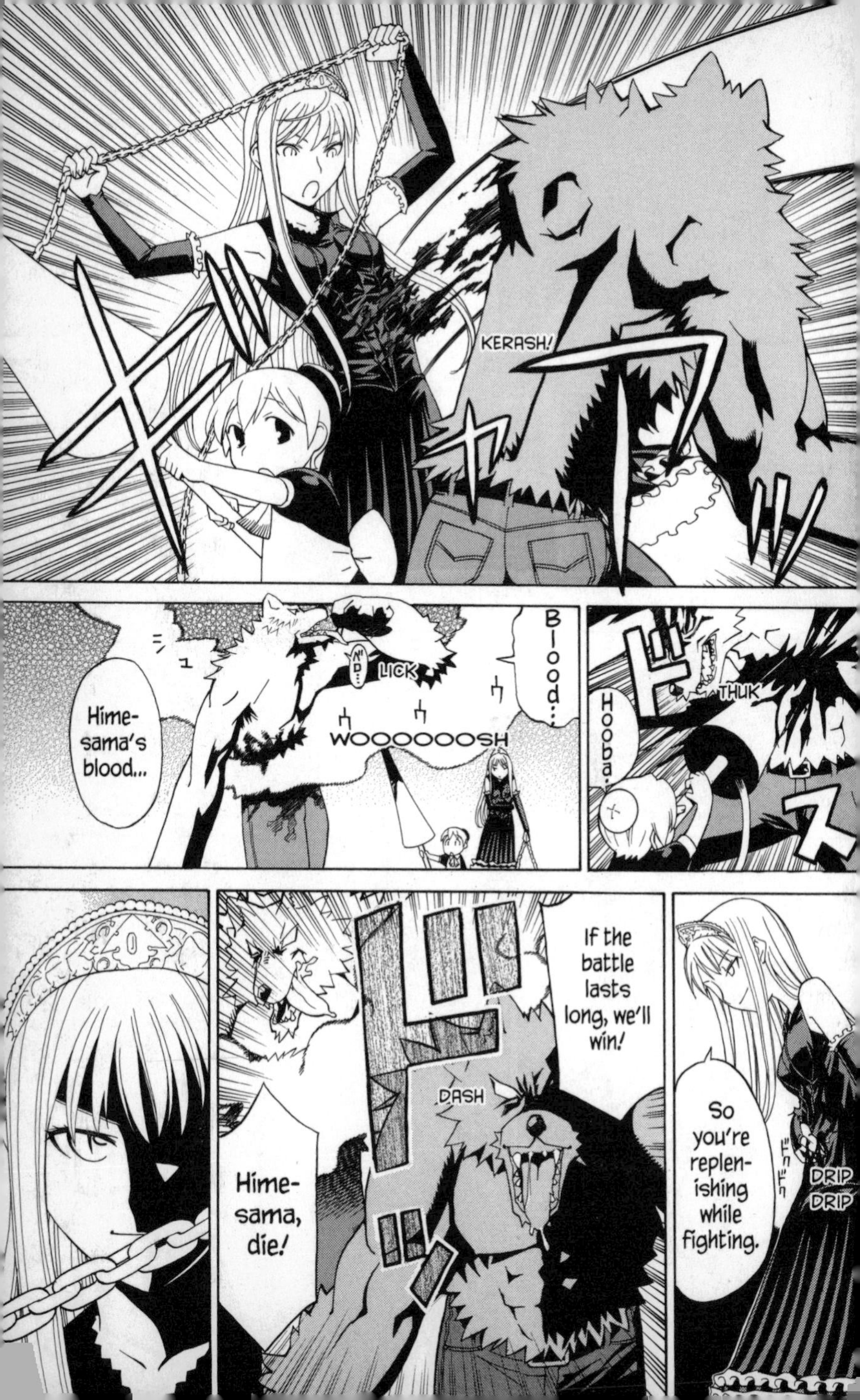
KERASH!
Hooba...
THUK
Blood...
LICK
WOOOOOOOSH
Hime-sama's blood...
So you're replen-ishing while fighting.
DRIP DRIP
If the battle lasts long, we'll win!
DASH
Hime-sama, die!

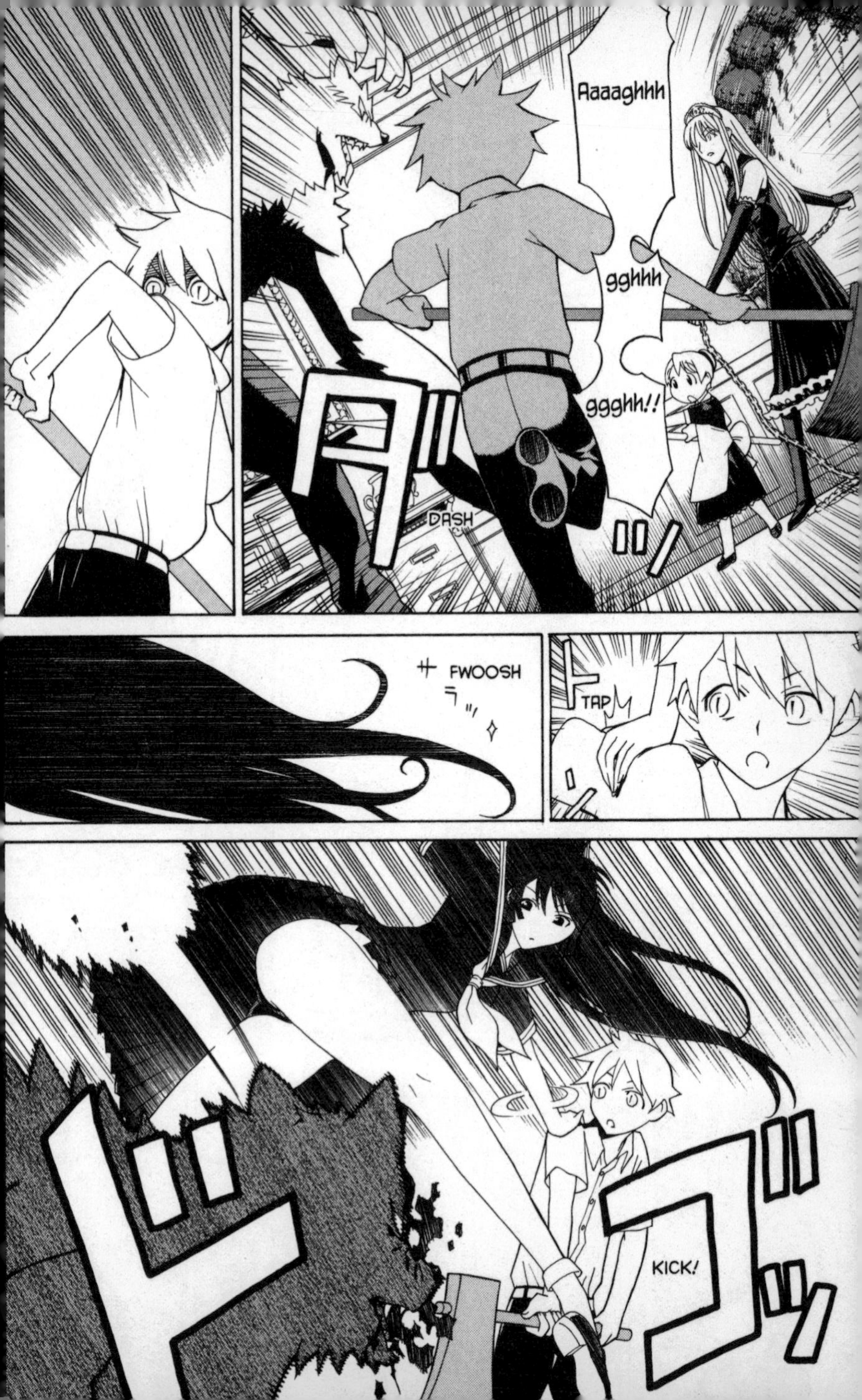
Aaaaghhh
gghhh
ggghh!!
DASH
TAP
FWOOSH
KICK!

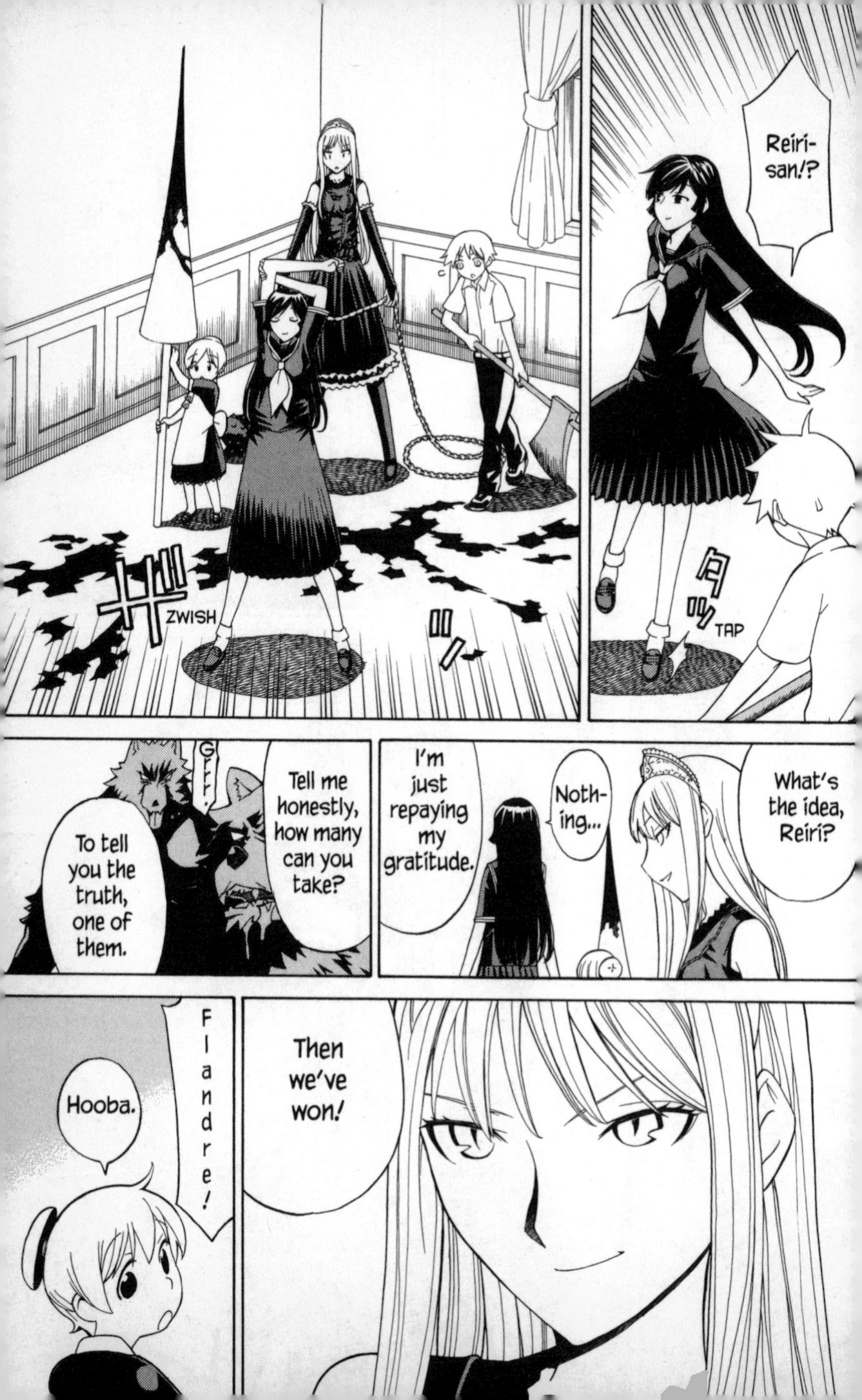
Reiri-san!?
TAP
ZWISH
What's the idea, Reiri?
Noth-ing...
I'm just repaying my gratitude.
Tell me honestly, how many can you take?
Grrr!
To tell you the truth, one of them.
Then we've won!
Flandre!
Hooba.

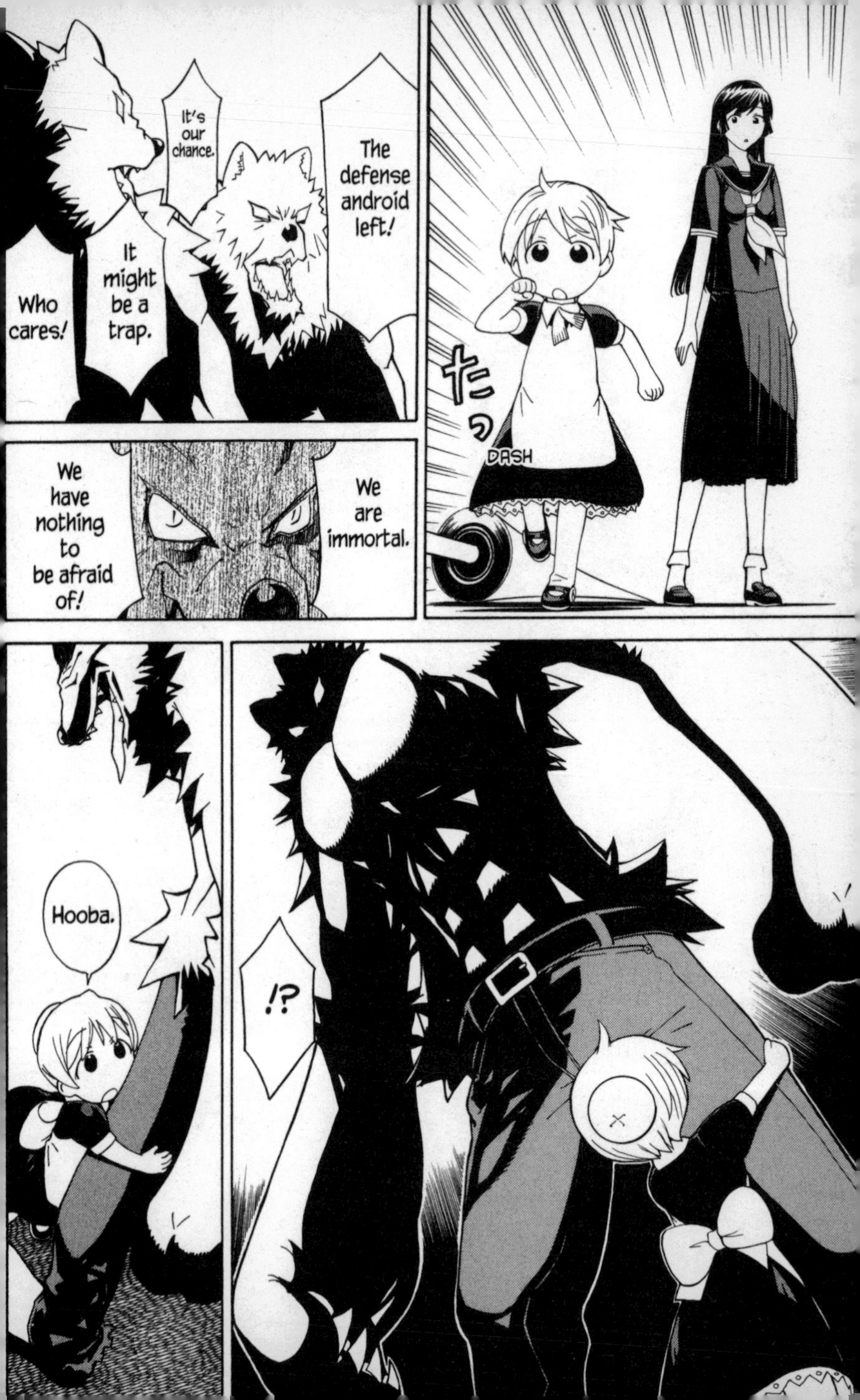
たっ
DASH
The defense android left!
It's our chance.
It might be a trap.
Who cares!
We are immortal.
We have nothing to be afraid of!
!?
Hooba.

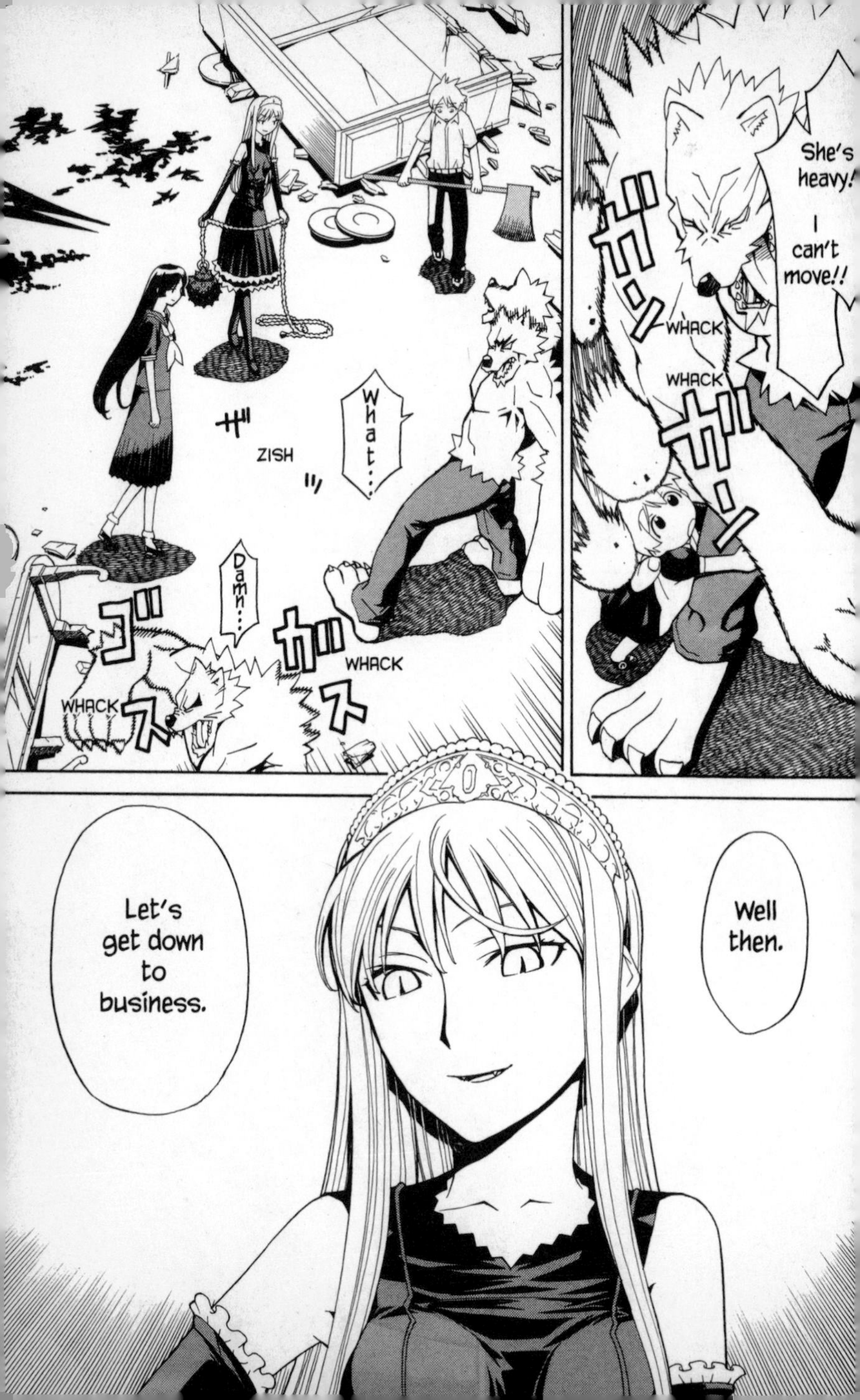
She's heavy!
I can't move!!
WHACK
WHACK
What...
ザ ッ
ZISH
Damn...
ガス
WHACK
ゴス
WHACK
Well then.
Let's get down to business.

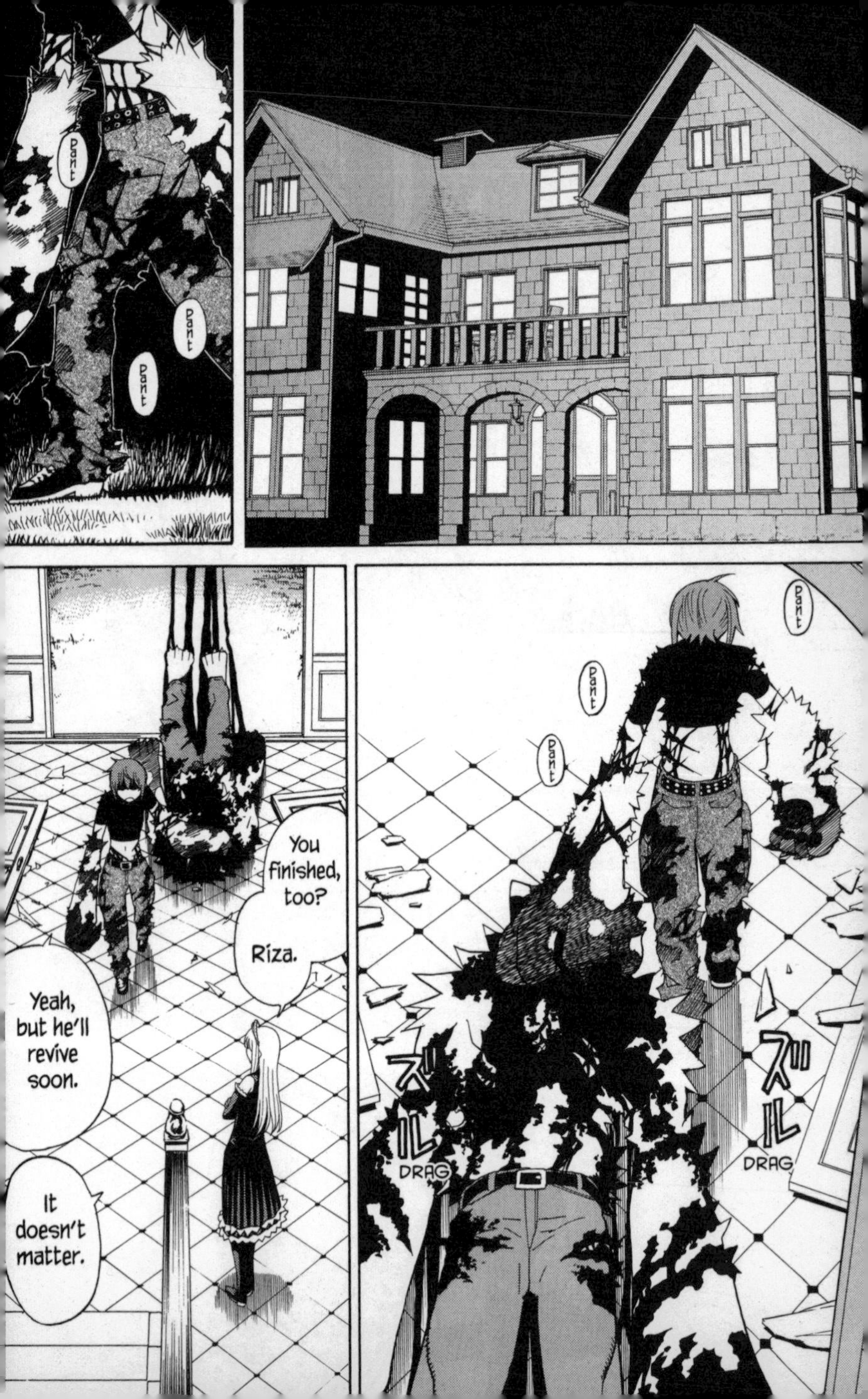
pant
pant
pant
pant
pant
pant
ズル
DRAG
ズル
DRAG
You finished, too?
Riza.
Yeah, but he'll revive soon.
It doesn't matter.

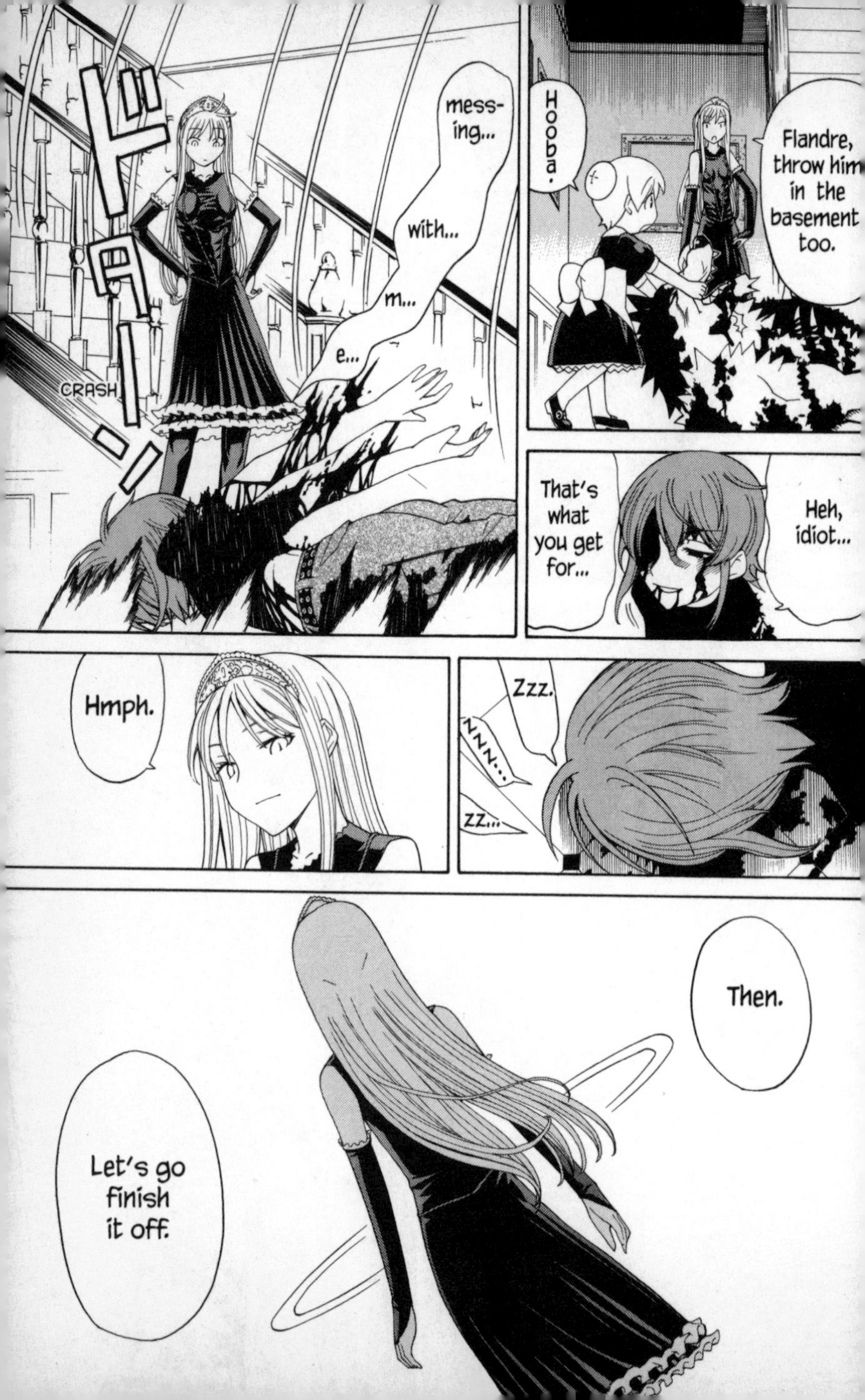
Flandre, throw him in the basement too.
Hooba.
Heh, idiot...
That's what you get for...
messing...
with...
m...
e...
CRASH
Zzz.
Nnn...
zz...
Hmph.
Then.
Let's go finish it off.

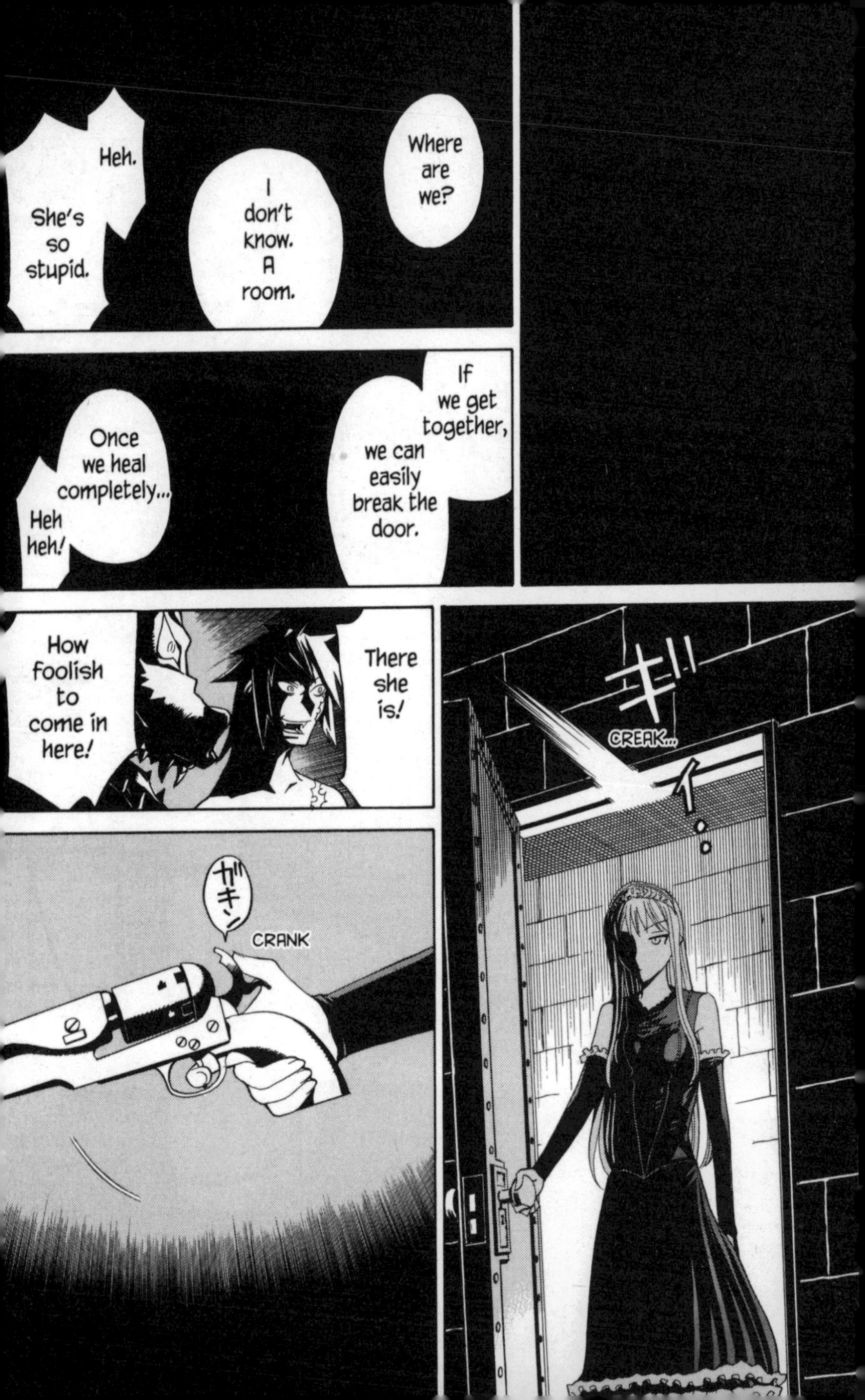
Where are we?
I don't know. A room.
Heh.
She's so stupid.
If we get together, we can easily break the door.
Once we heal completely...
Heh heh!
ギィ
CREAK...
There she is!
How foolish to come in here!
ガキン
CRANK

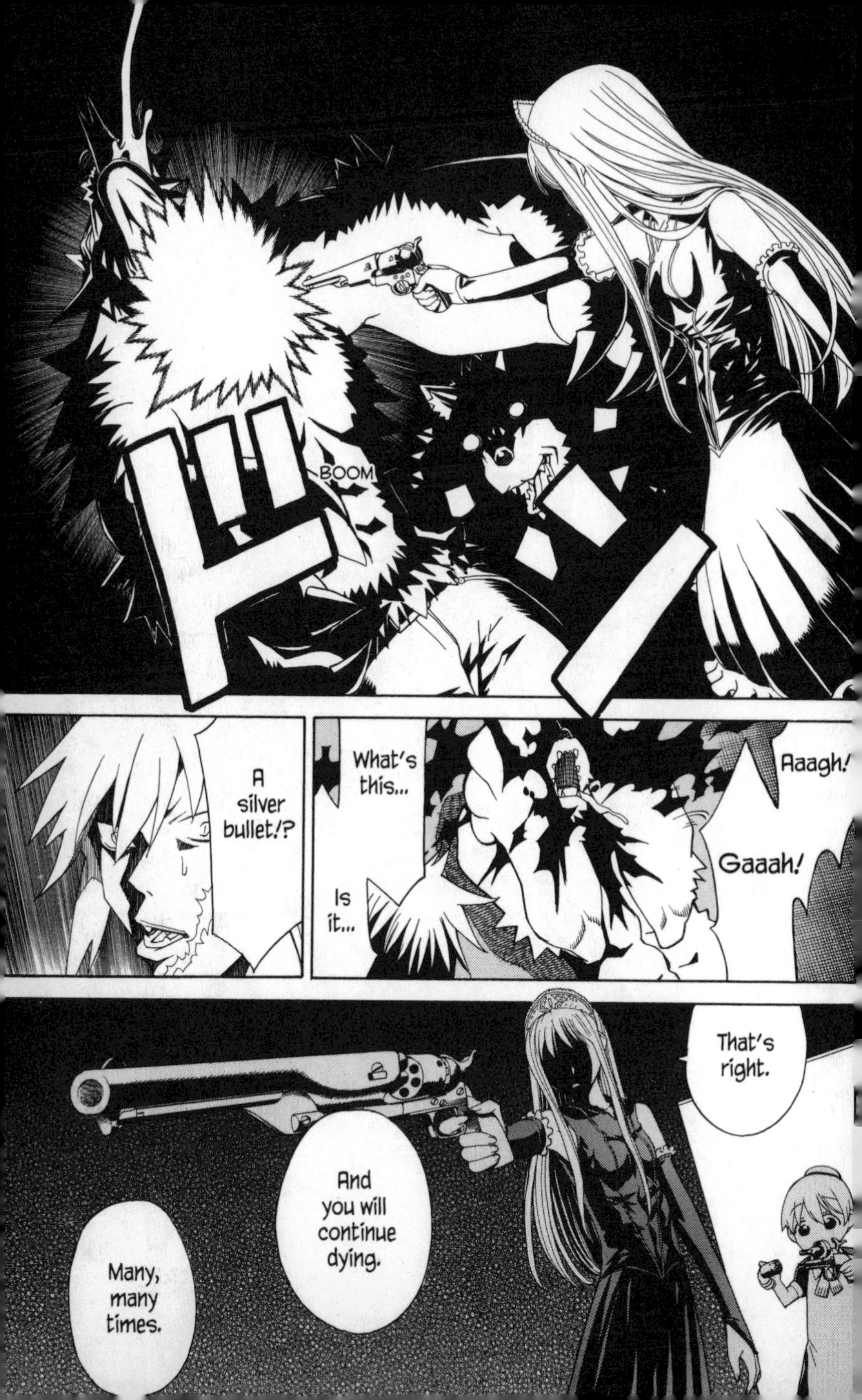
BOOM
Aaagh!
What's this...
Gaaah!
Is it...
A silver bullet!?
That's right.
And you will continue dying.
Many, many times.

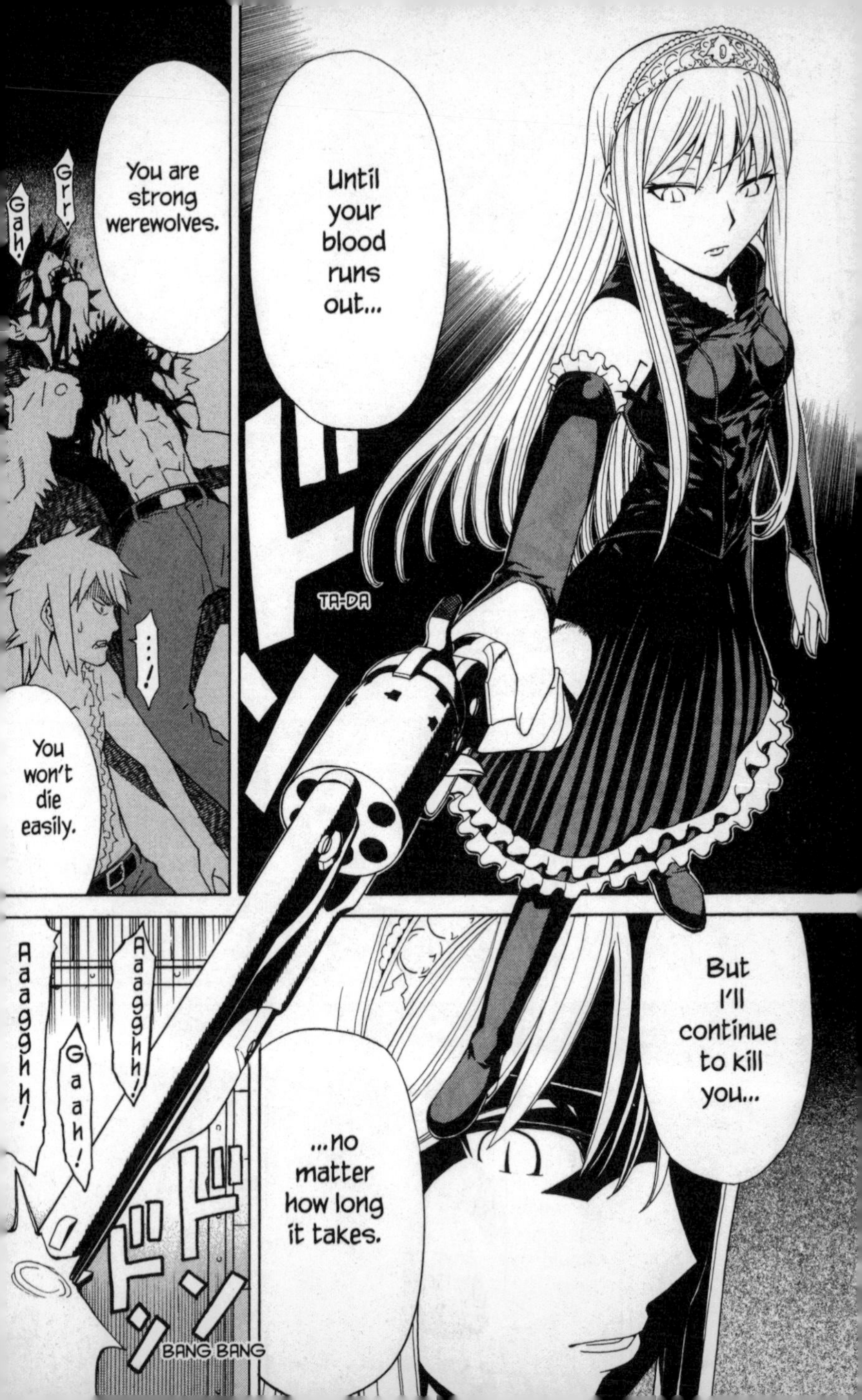
Until your blood runs out...
TA-DA
You are strong werewolves.
Grr.
Gah.
...!
You won't die easily.
But I'll continue to kill you...
...no matter how long it takes.
Aaagghh!
Gaah!
Aaagghh!
BANG BANG

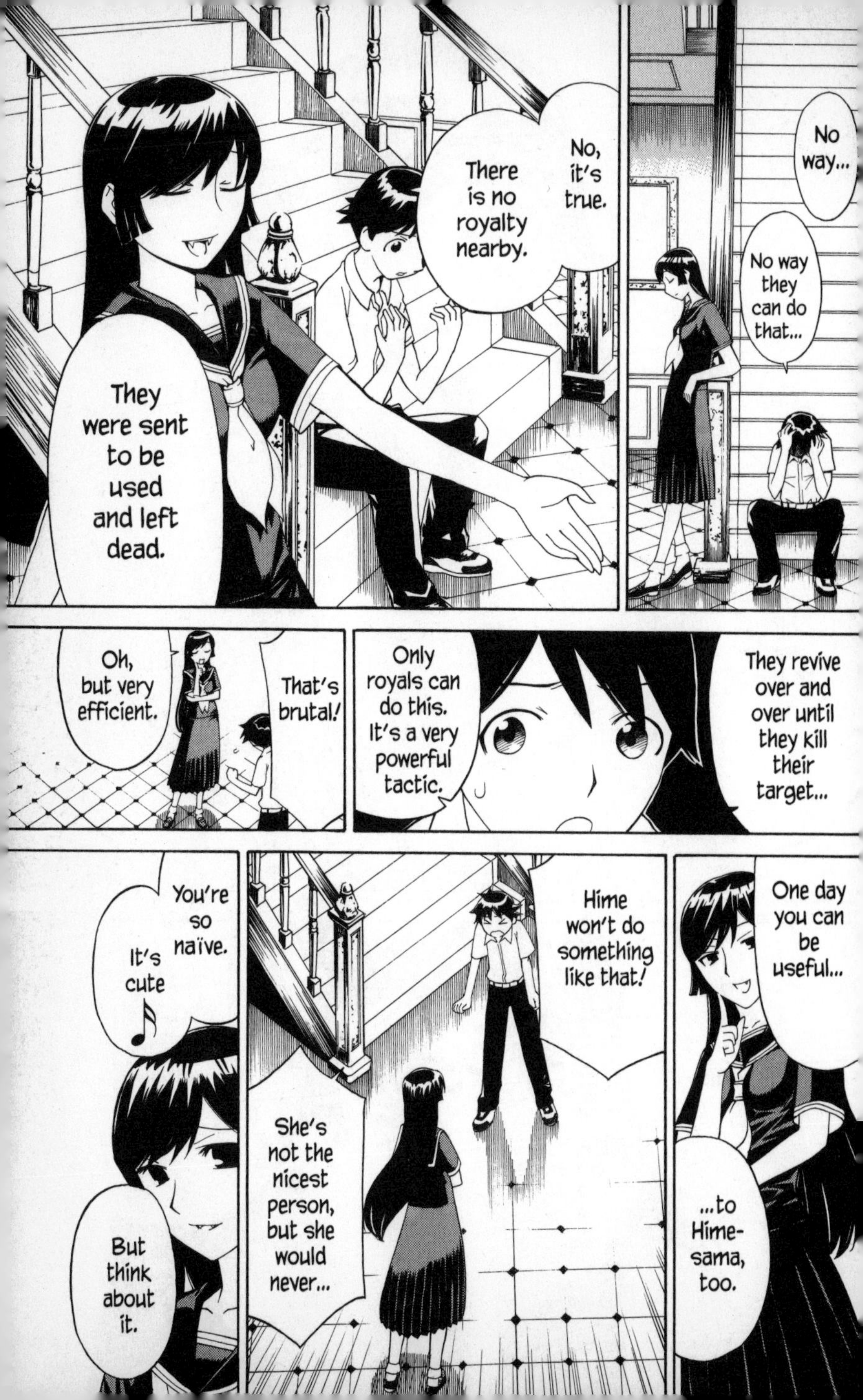
No way...
No way they can do that...
No, it's true.
There is no royalty nearby.
They were sent to be used and left dead.
They revive over and over until they kill their target...
Only royals can do this. It's a very powerful tactic.
That's brutal!
Oh, but very efficient.
One day you can be useful...
...to Hime-sama, too.
Hime won't do something like that!
She's not the nicest person, but she would never...
You're so naïve.
It's cute ♪
But think about it.

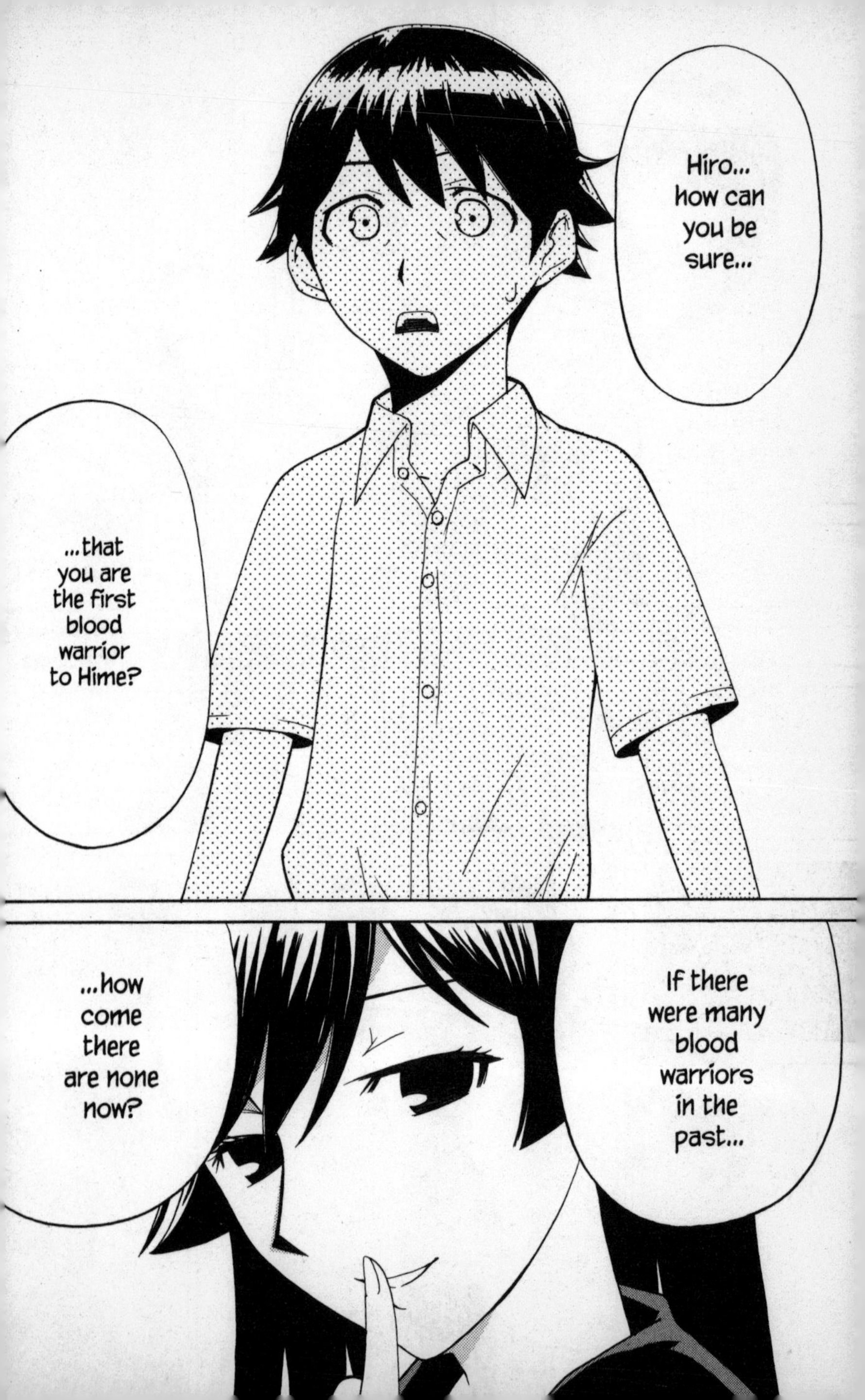
Hiro... how can you be sure...
...that you are the first blood warrior to Hime?
If there were many blood warriors in the past...
...how come there are none now?

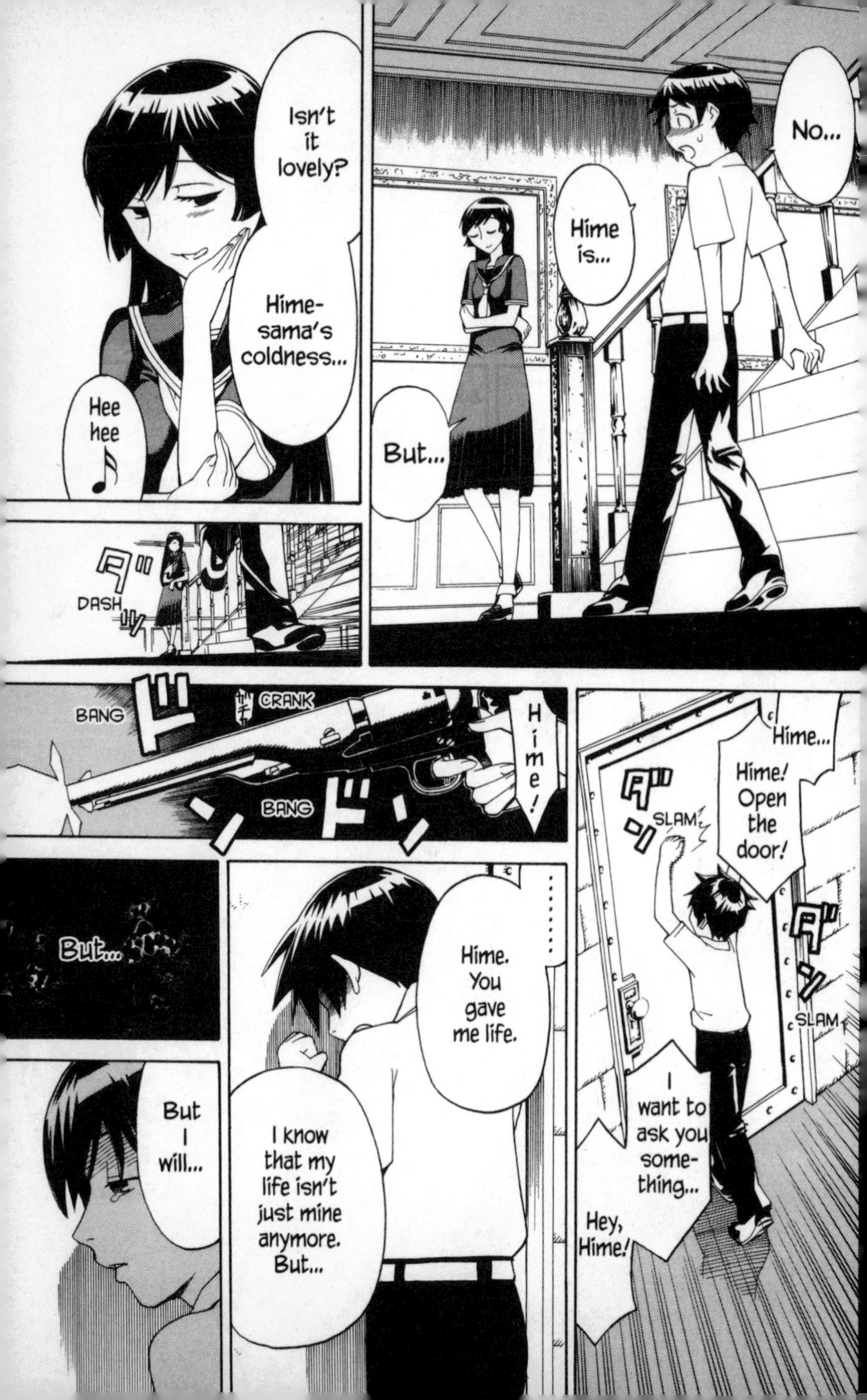
No...
Hime is...
But...
Isn't it lovely?
Hime-sama's coldness...
Hee hee ♪
DASH
Hime...
Hime! Open the door!
SLAM
SLAM
I want to ask you some-thing...
Hey, Hime!
BANG
CRANK
Hime!
BANG
......
Hime. You gave me life.
I know that my life isn't just mine anymore. But...
But...
But I will...

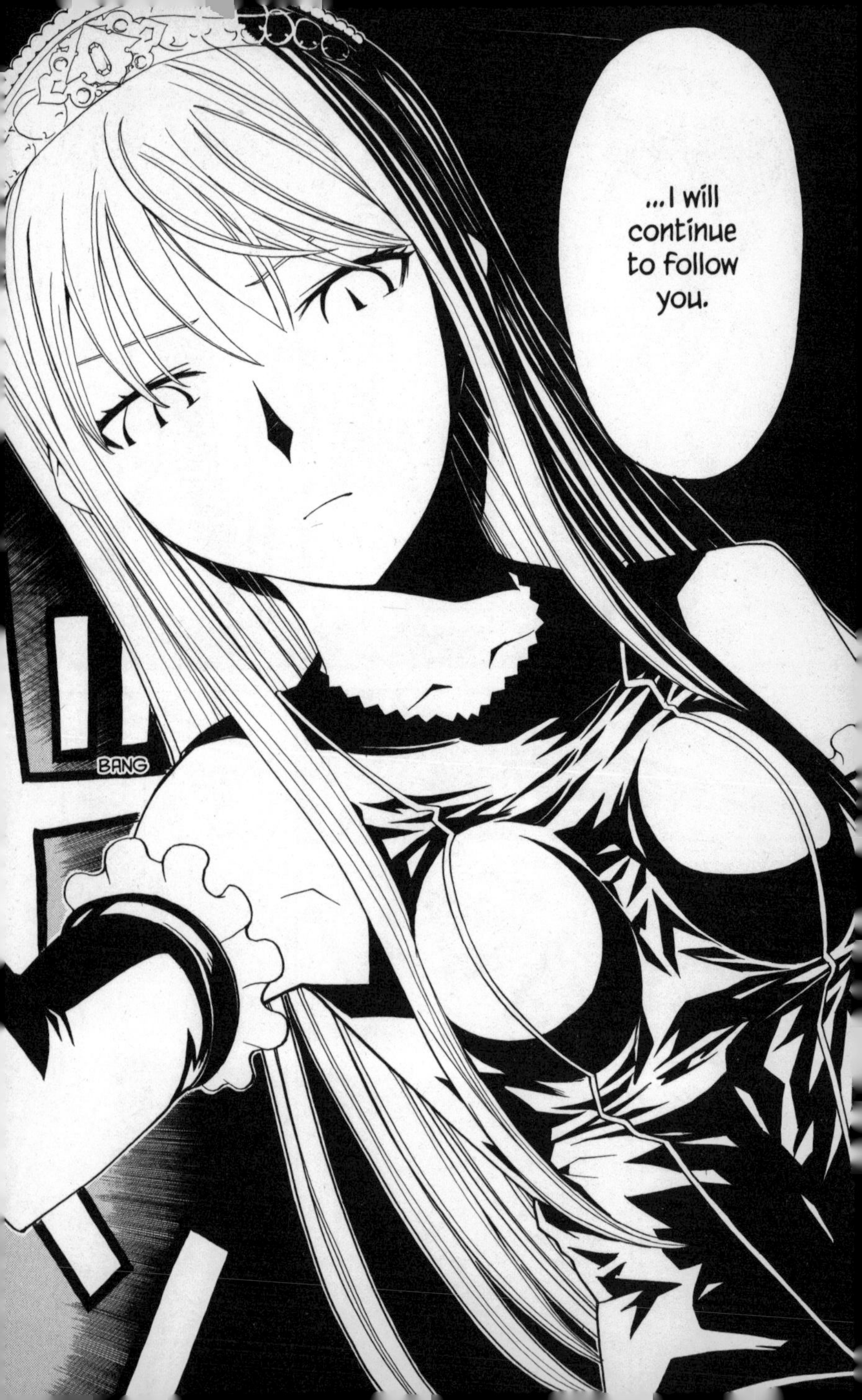
...I will continue to follow you.
BANG

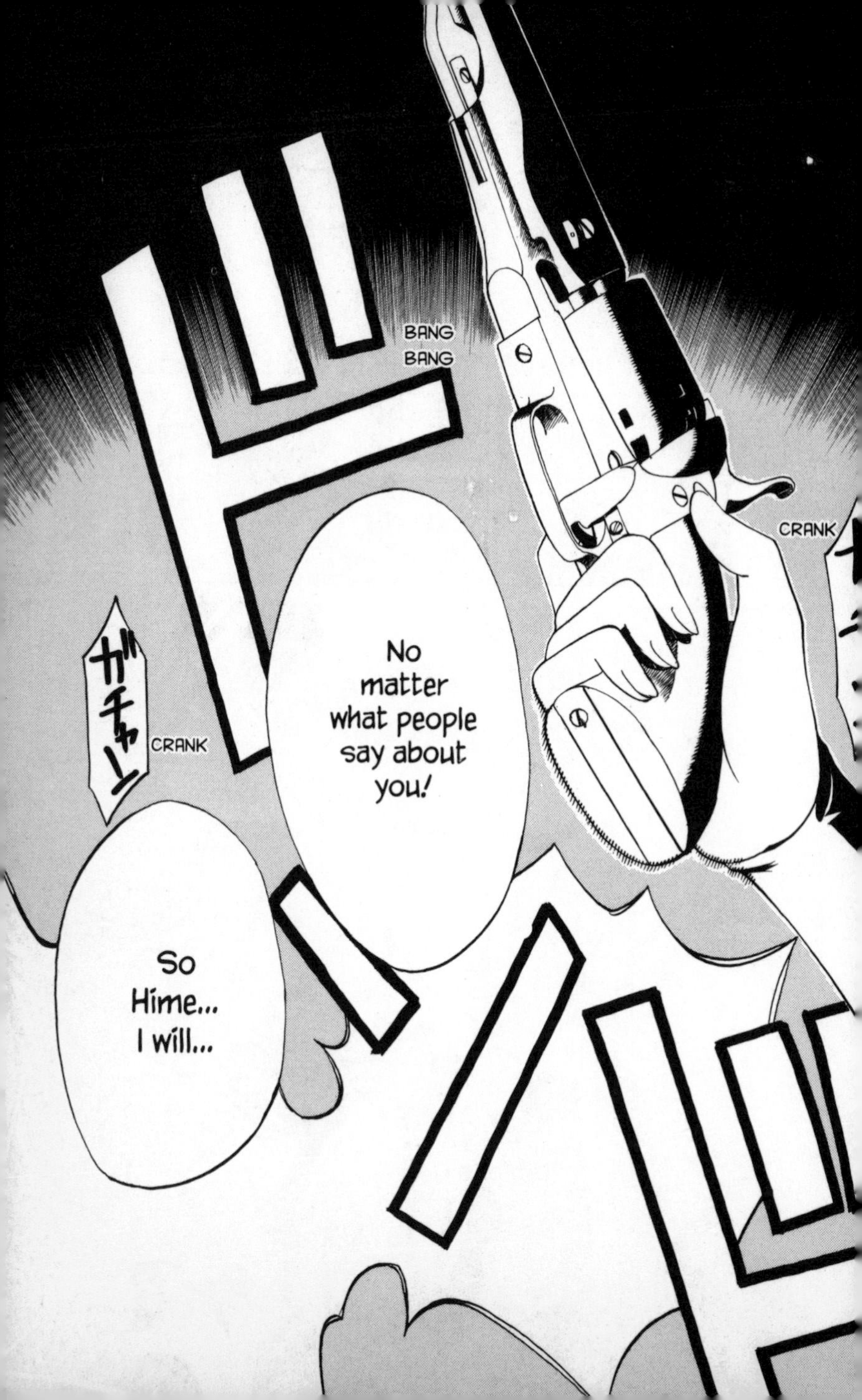
CRANK
BANG
BANG
No matter what people say about you!
ガチャン
CRANK
So Hime... I will...

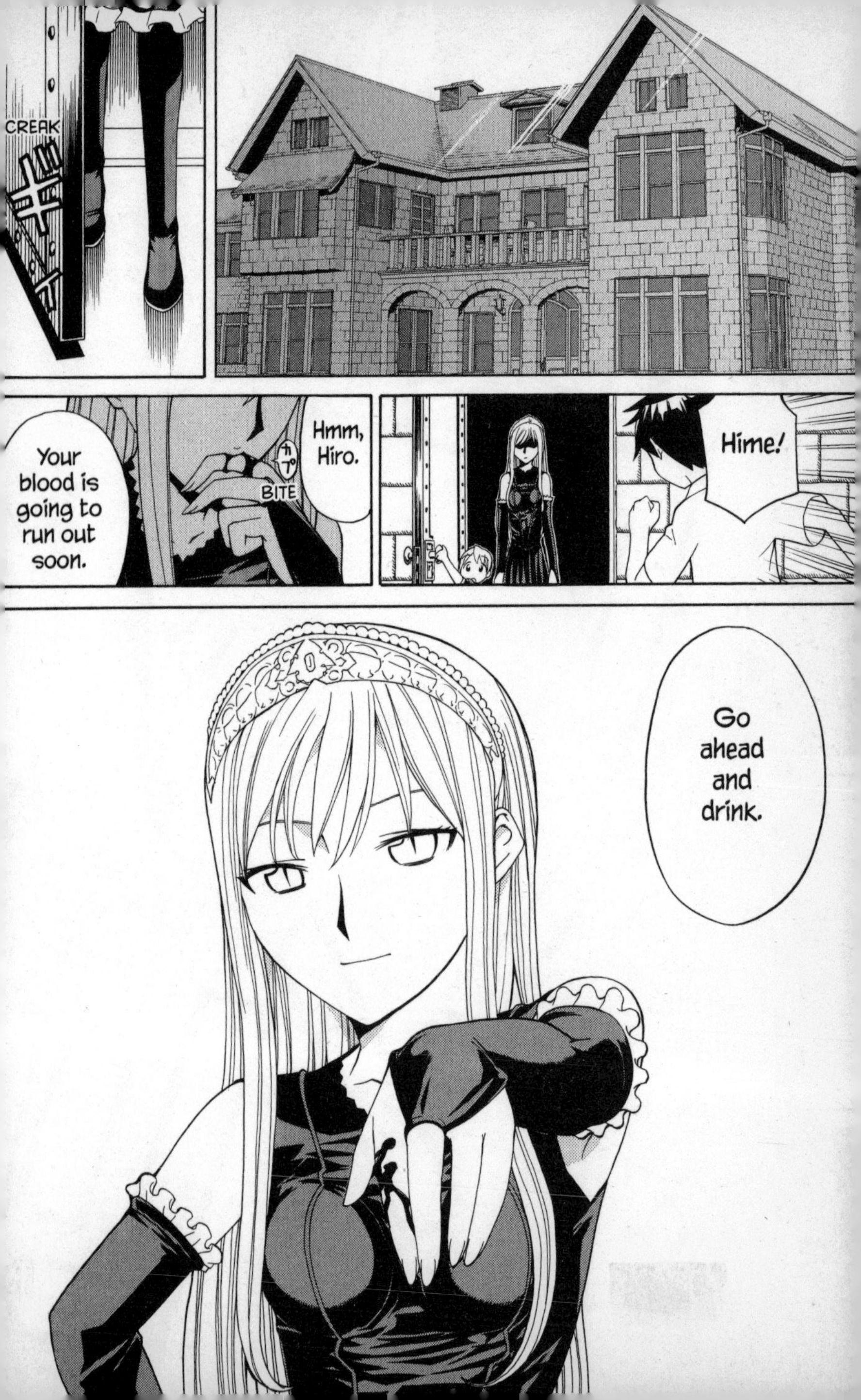
CREAK
Hime!
Hmm, Hiro.
BITE
Your blood is going to run out soon.
Go ahead and drink.

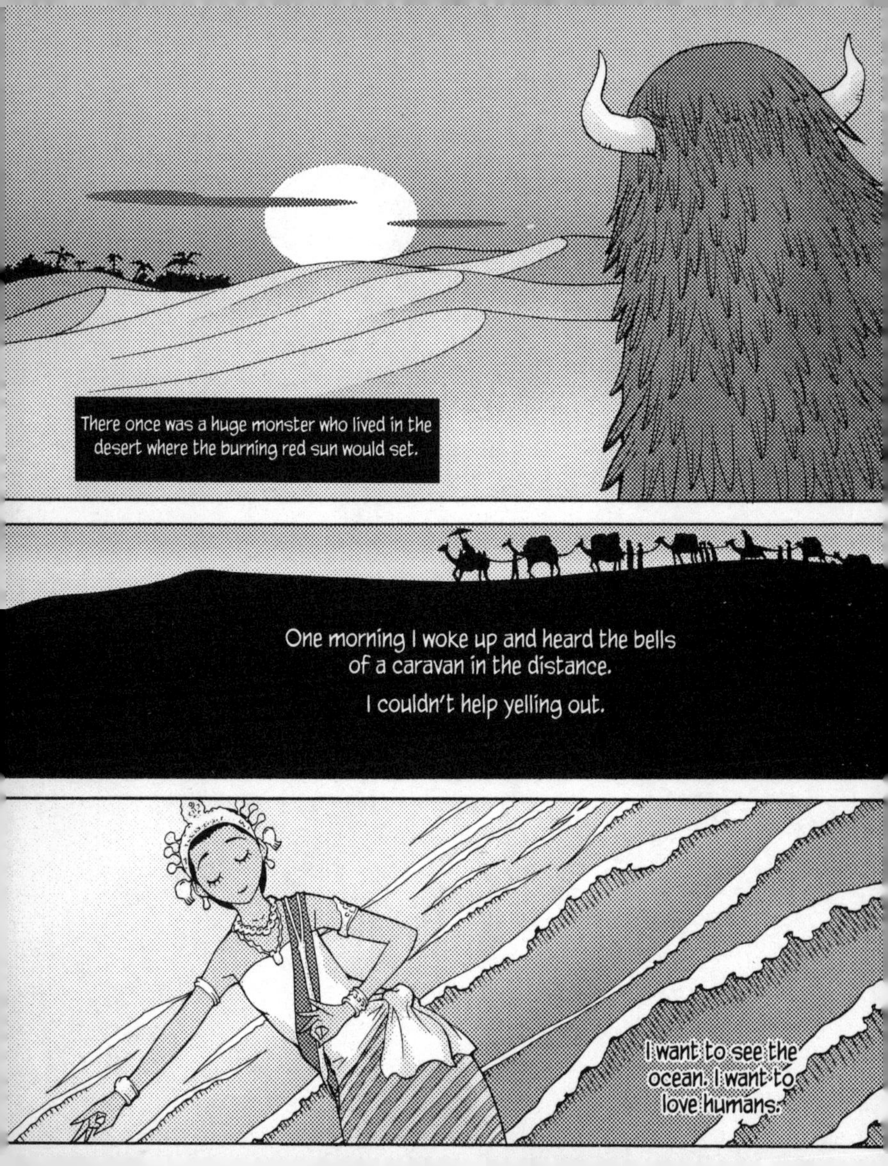
There once was a huge monster who lived in the desert where the burning red sun would set.
One morning I woke up and heard the bells of a caravan in the distance.
I couldn't help yelling out.
I want to see the ocean. I want to love humans.

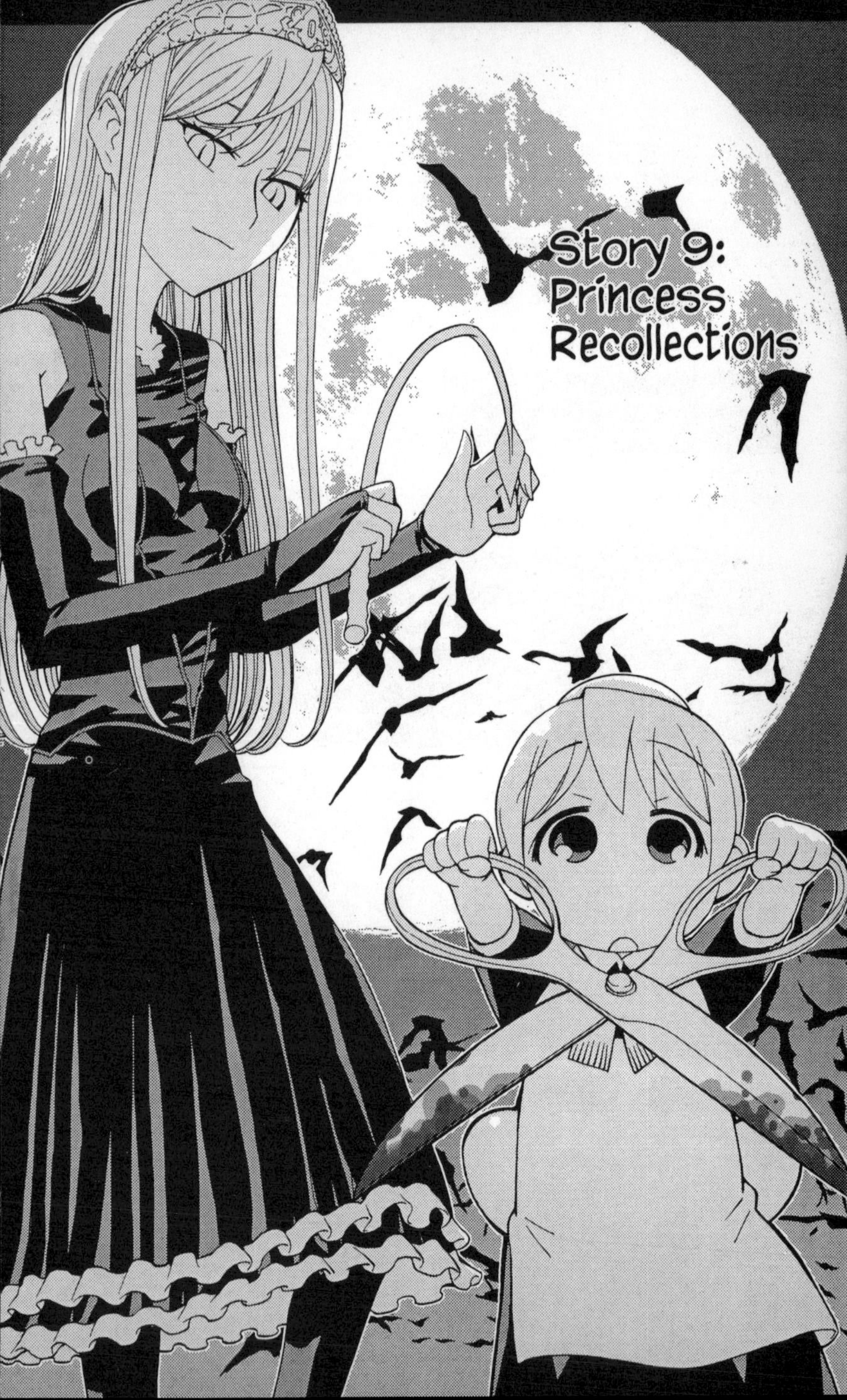
Story 9:
Princess
Recollections

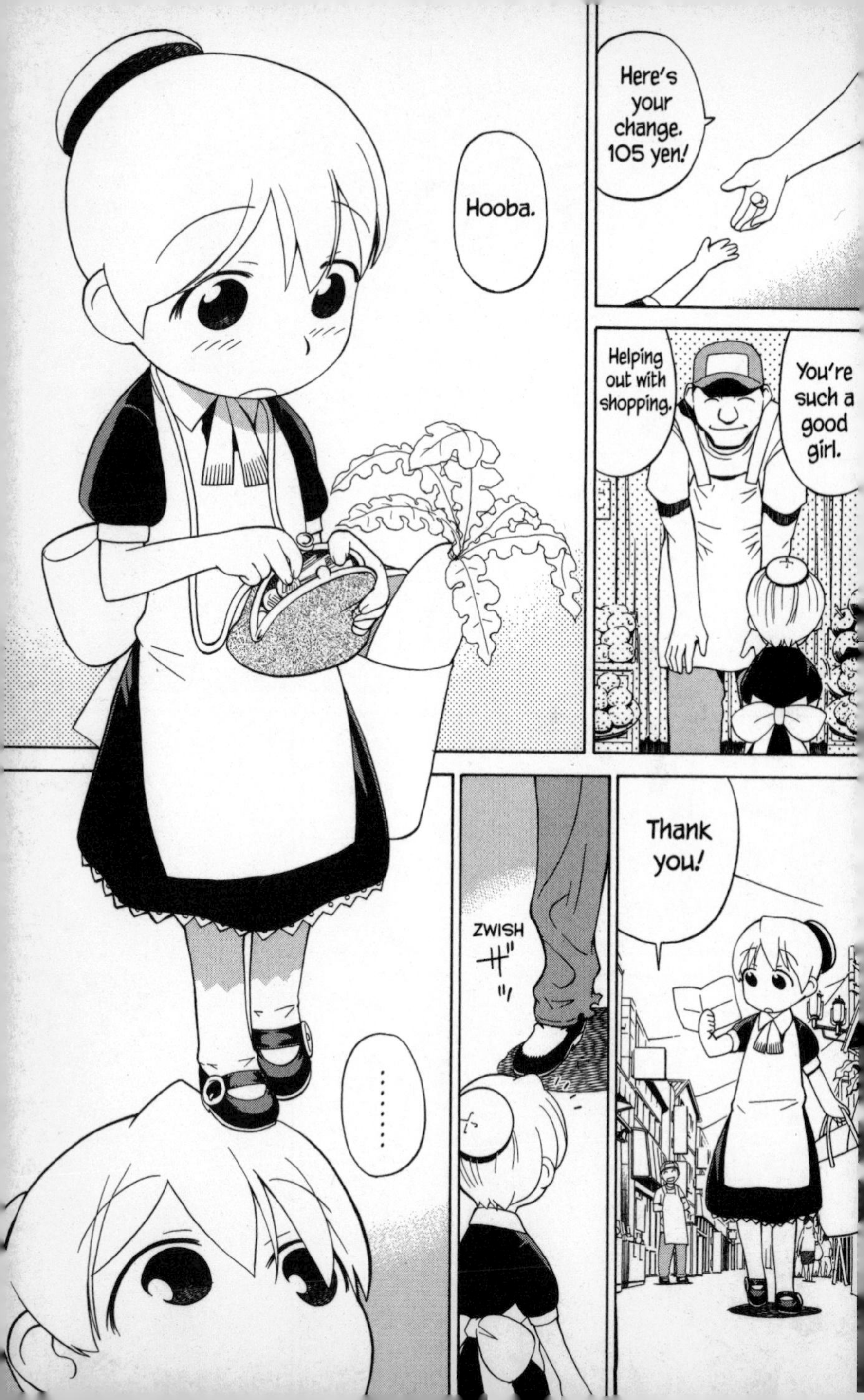
Here's your change. 105 yen!
You're such a good girl.
Helping out with shopping.
Hooba.
Thank you!
ZWISH
......

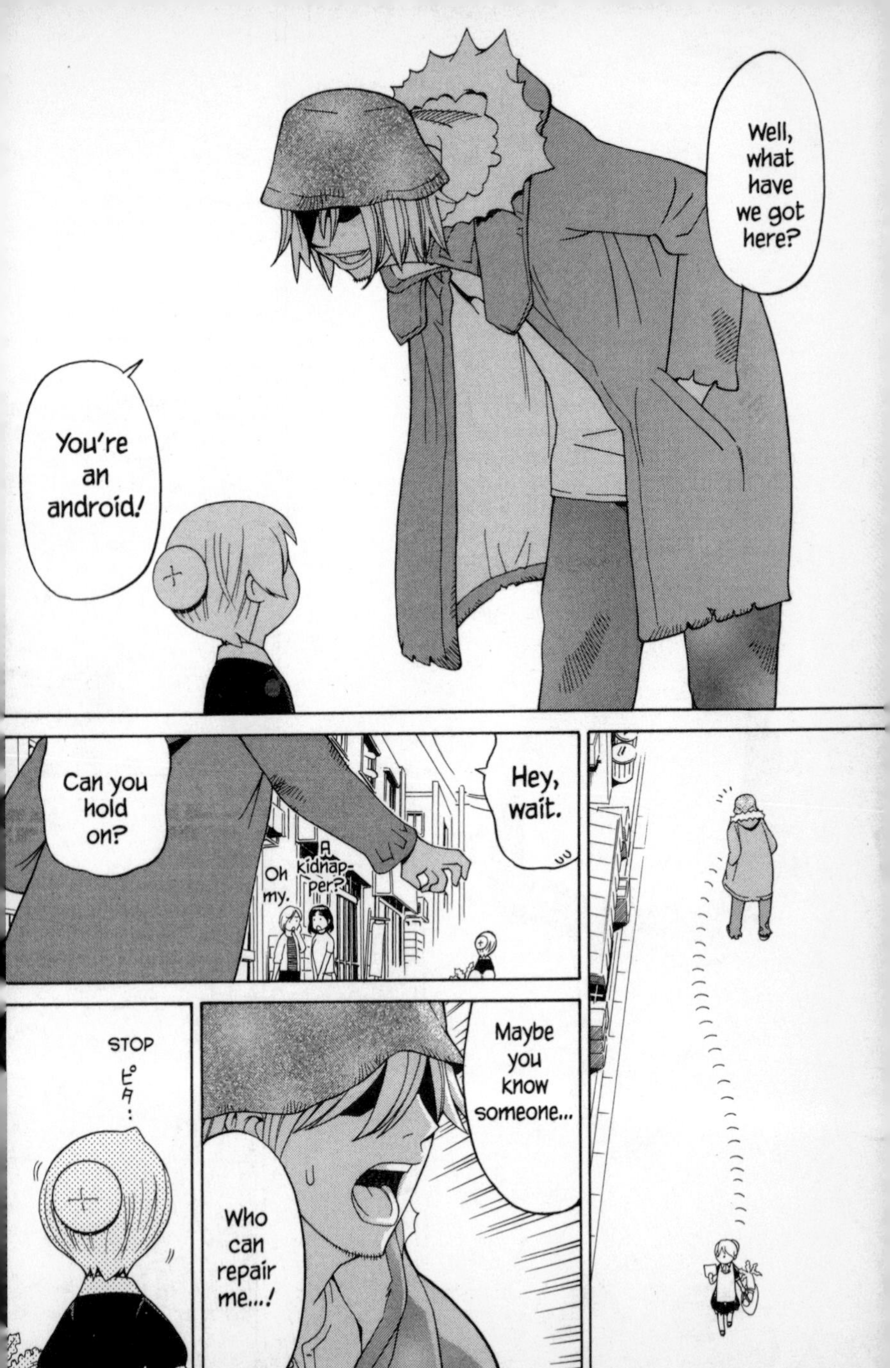
Well, what have we got here?
You're an android!
Hey, wait.
Can you hold on?
A kidnap-per?
Oh my.
Maybe you know someone...
Who can repair me...!
STOP
ピタ…

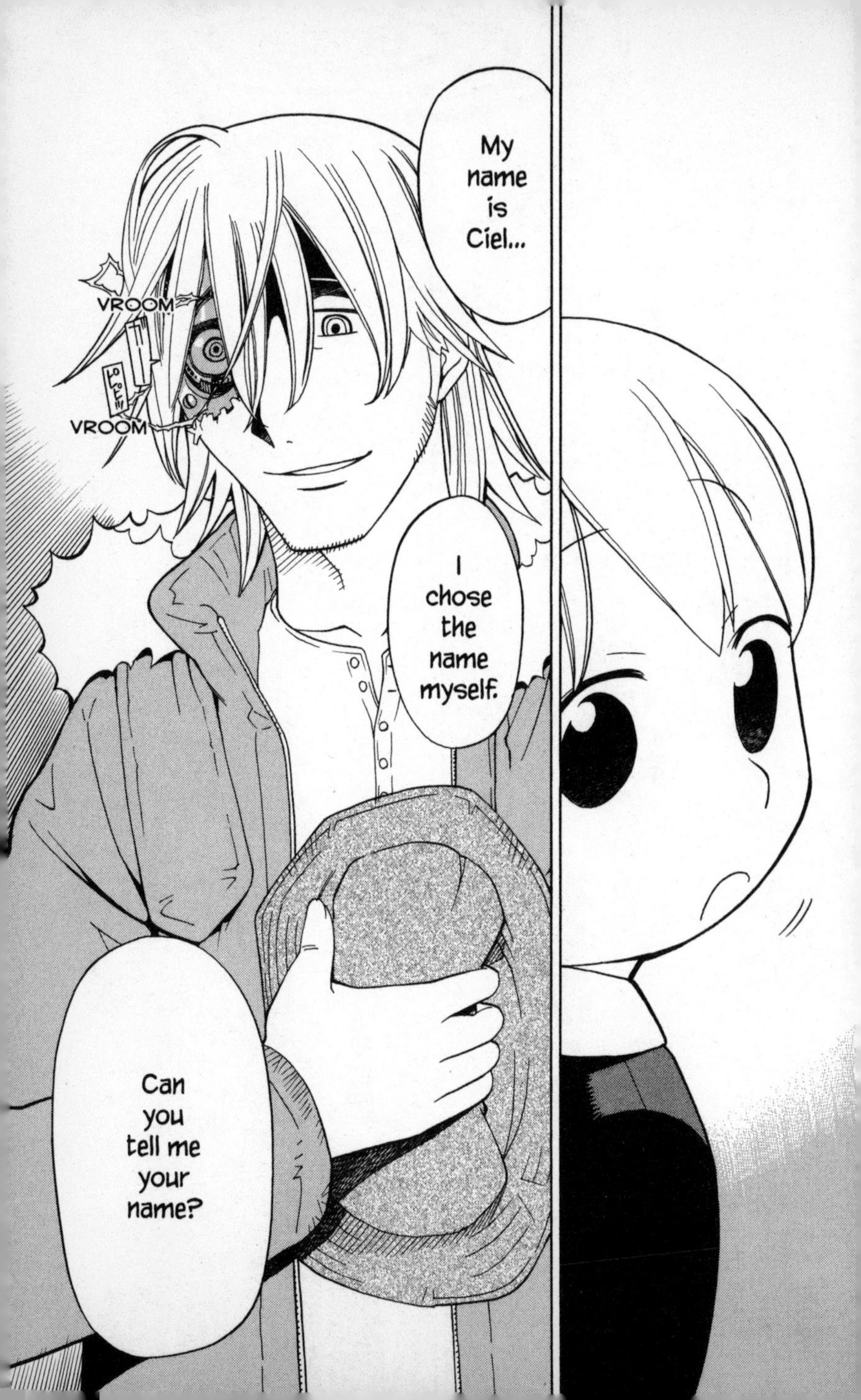
My name is Ciel...
VROOM
VROOM
I chose the name myself.
Can you tell me your name?

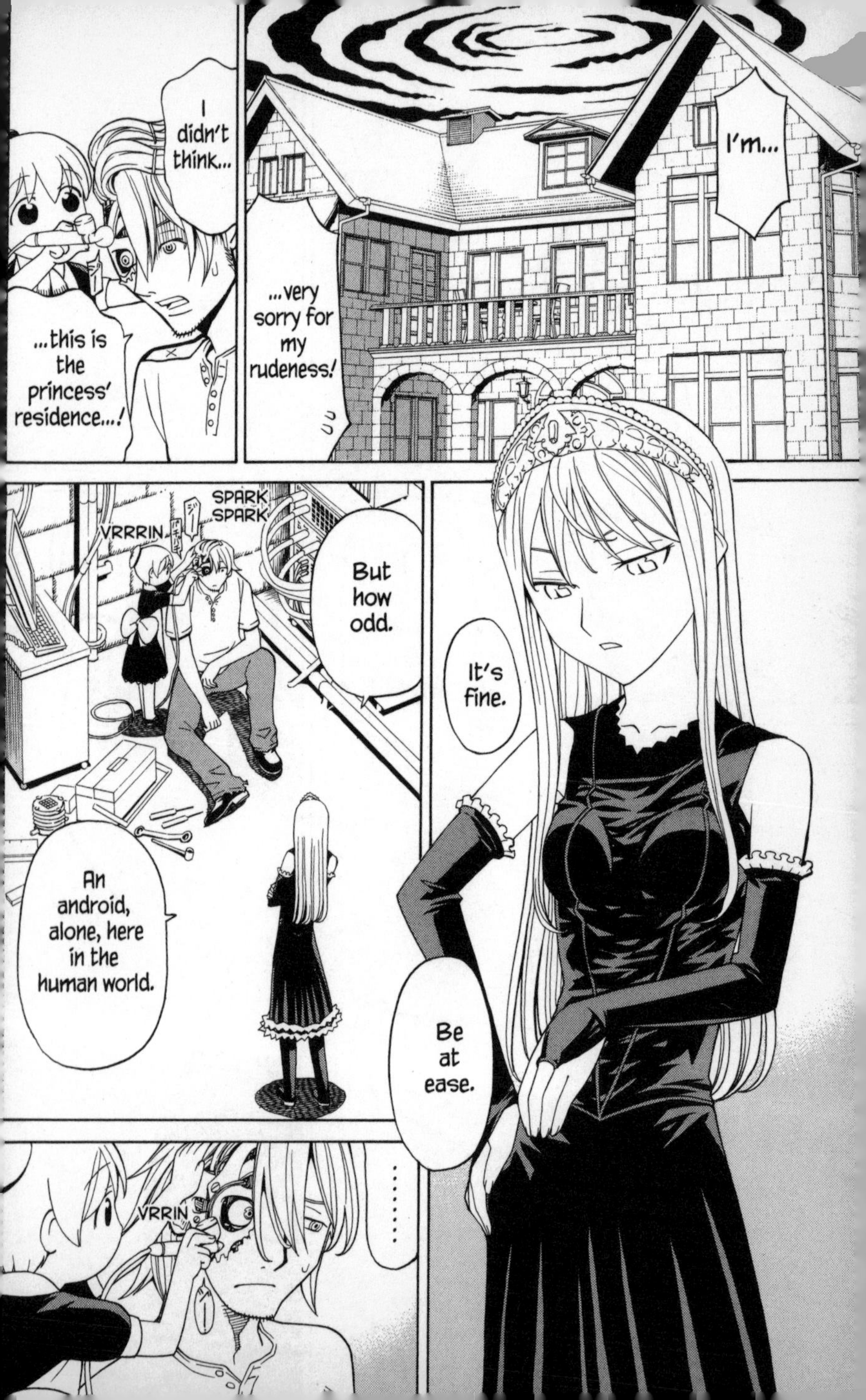
I'm...
...very sorry for my rudeness!
I didn't think...
...this is the princess' residence...!
It's fine.
Be at ease.
SPARK SPARK
VRRRIN
But how odd.
An android, alone, here in the human world.
VRRIN
......

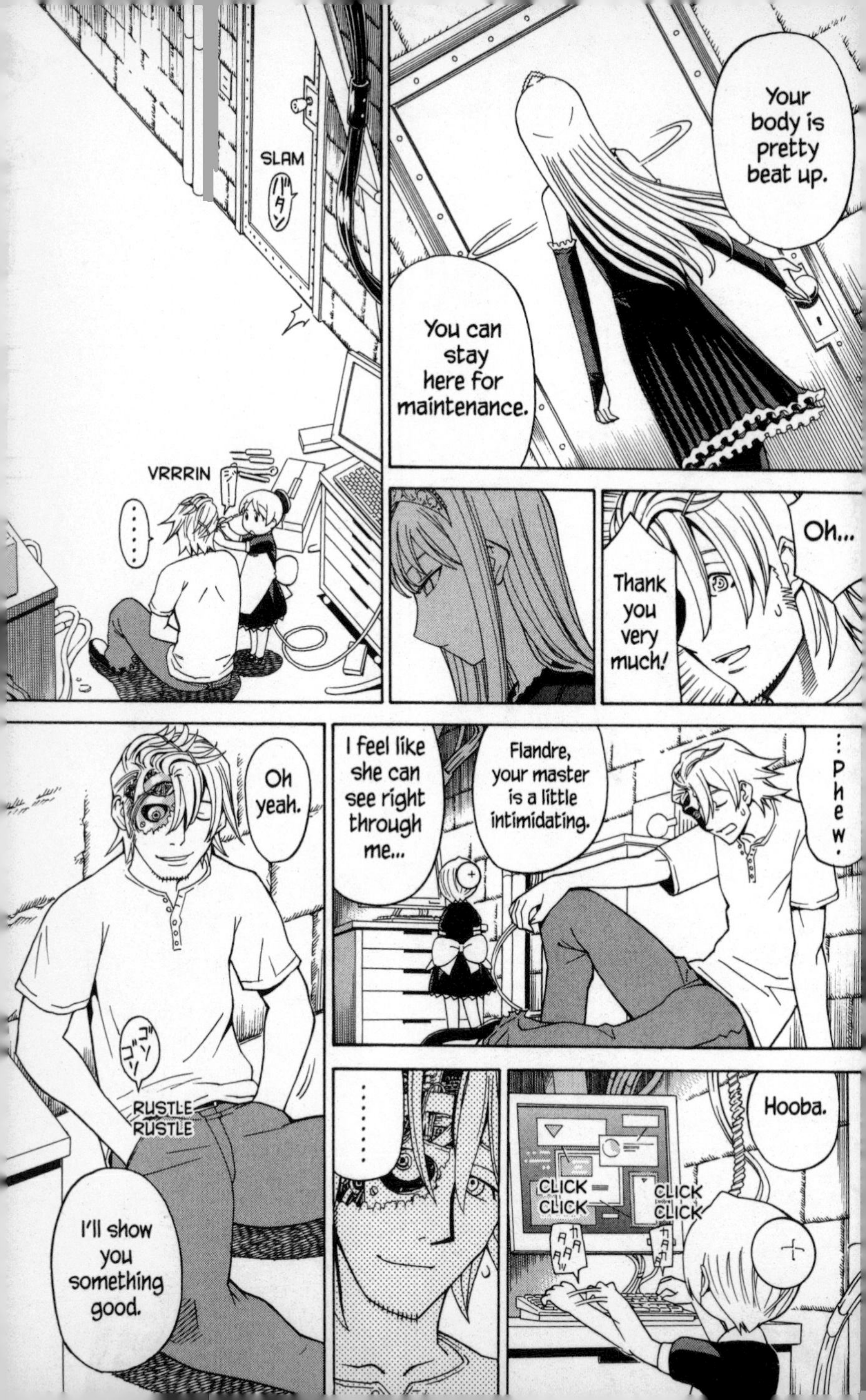
Your body is pretty beat up.
You can stay here for maintenance.
Oh...
Thank you very much!
SLAM
バタン
VRRRIN
......
...Phew.
Flandre, your master is a little intimidating.
I feel like she can see right through me...
Hooba.
CLICK CLICK
CLICK CLICK
......
Oh yeah.
ゴソゴソ
RUSTLE RUSTLE
I'll show you something good.

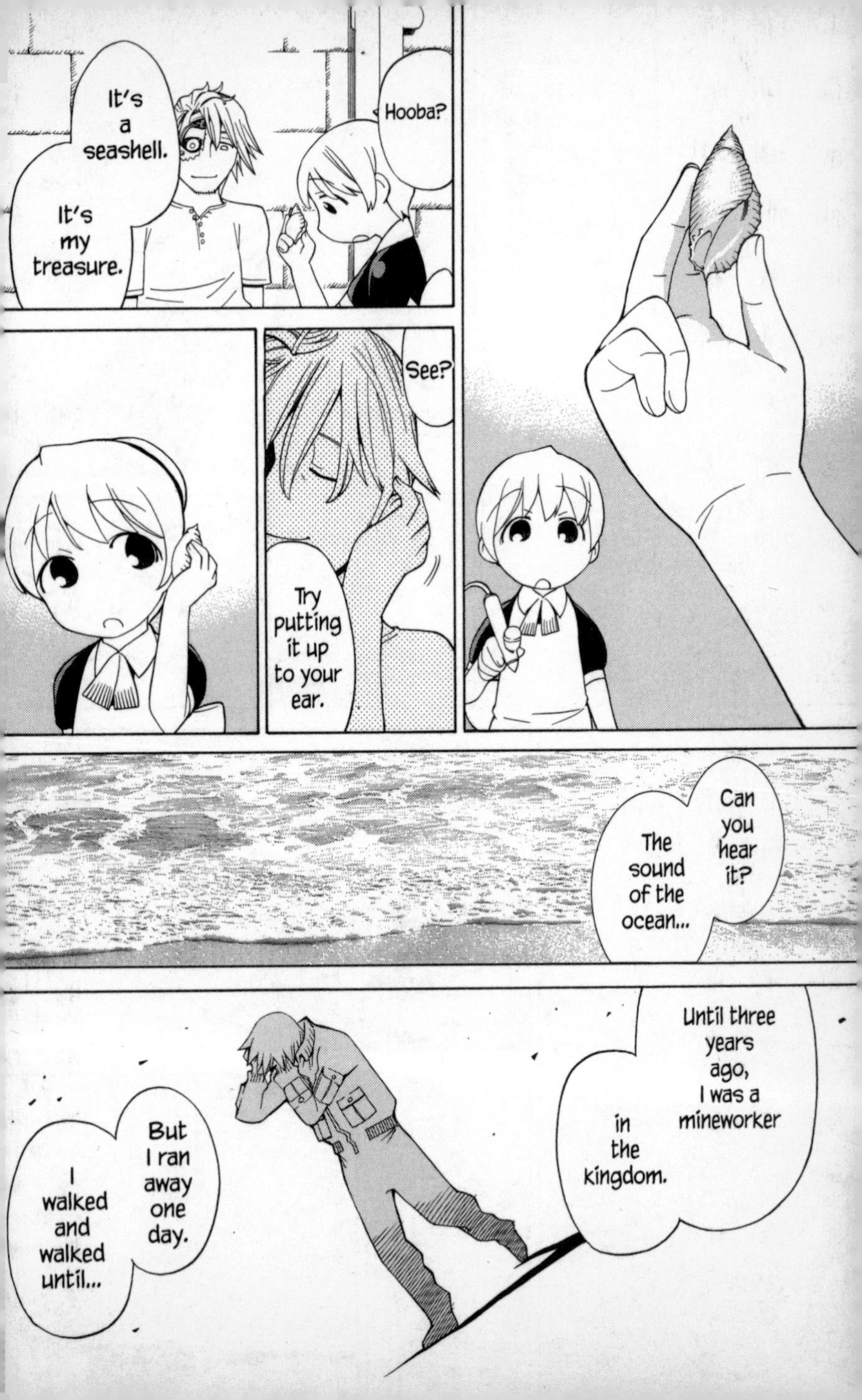
Hooba?
It's a seashell.
It's my treasure.
See?
Try putting it up to your ear.
Can you hear it?
The sound of the ocean...
Until three years ago, I was a mineworker
in the kingdom.
But I ran away one day.
I walked and walked until...

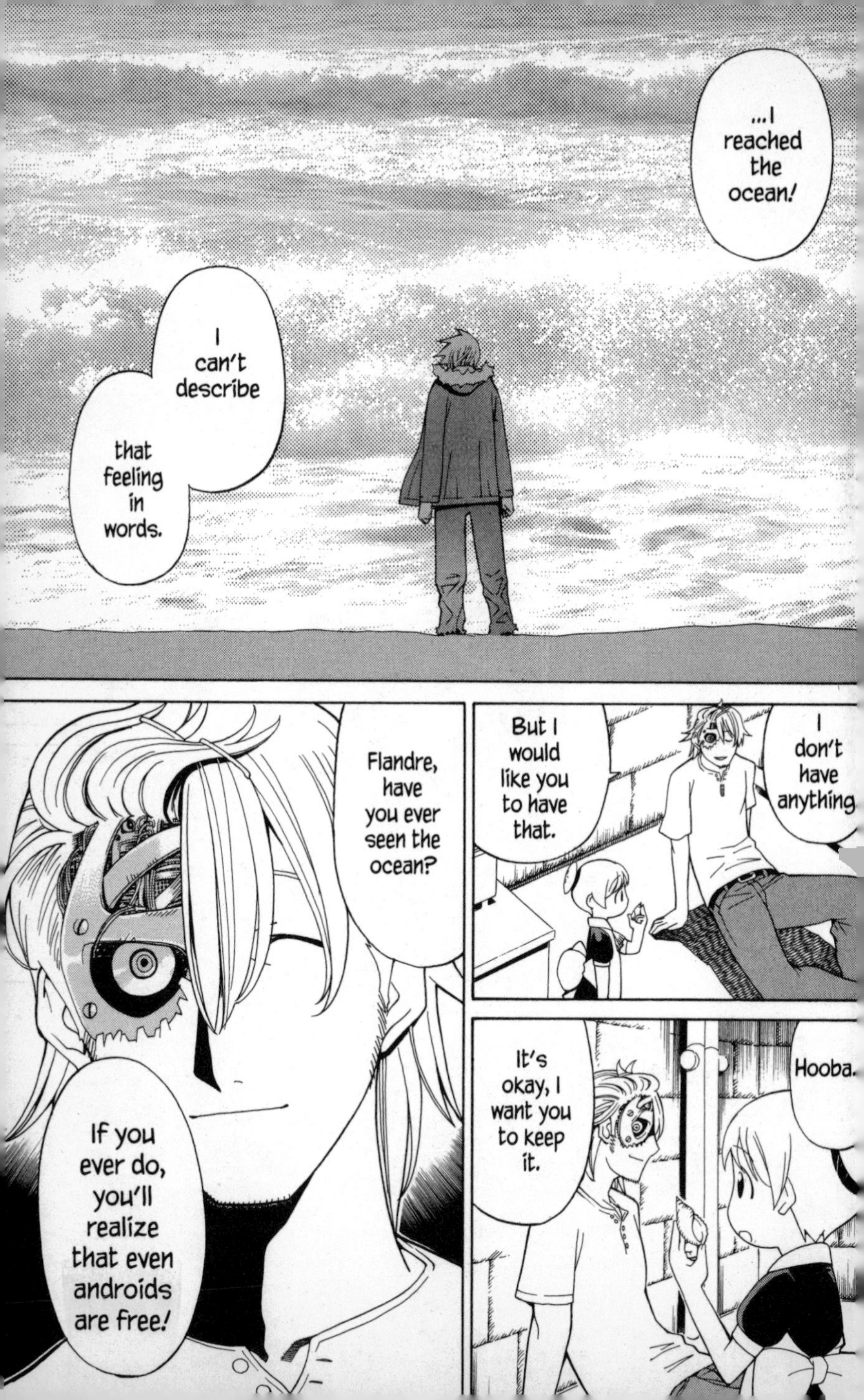
...I reached the ocean!
I can't describe that feeling in words.
I don't have anything
But I would like you to have that.
Hooba.
It's okay, I want you to keep it.
Flandre, have you ever seen the ocean?
If you ever do, you'll realize that even androids are free!

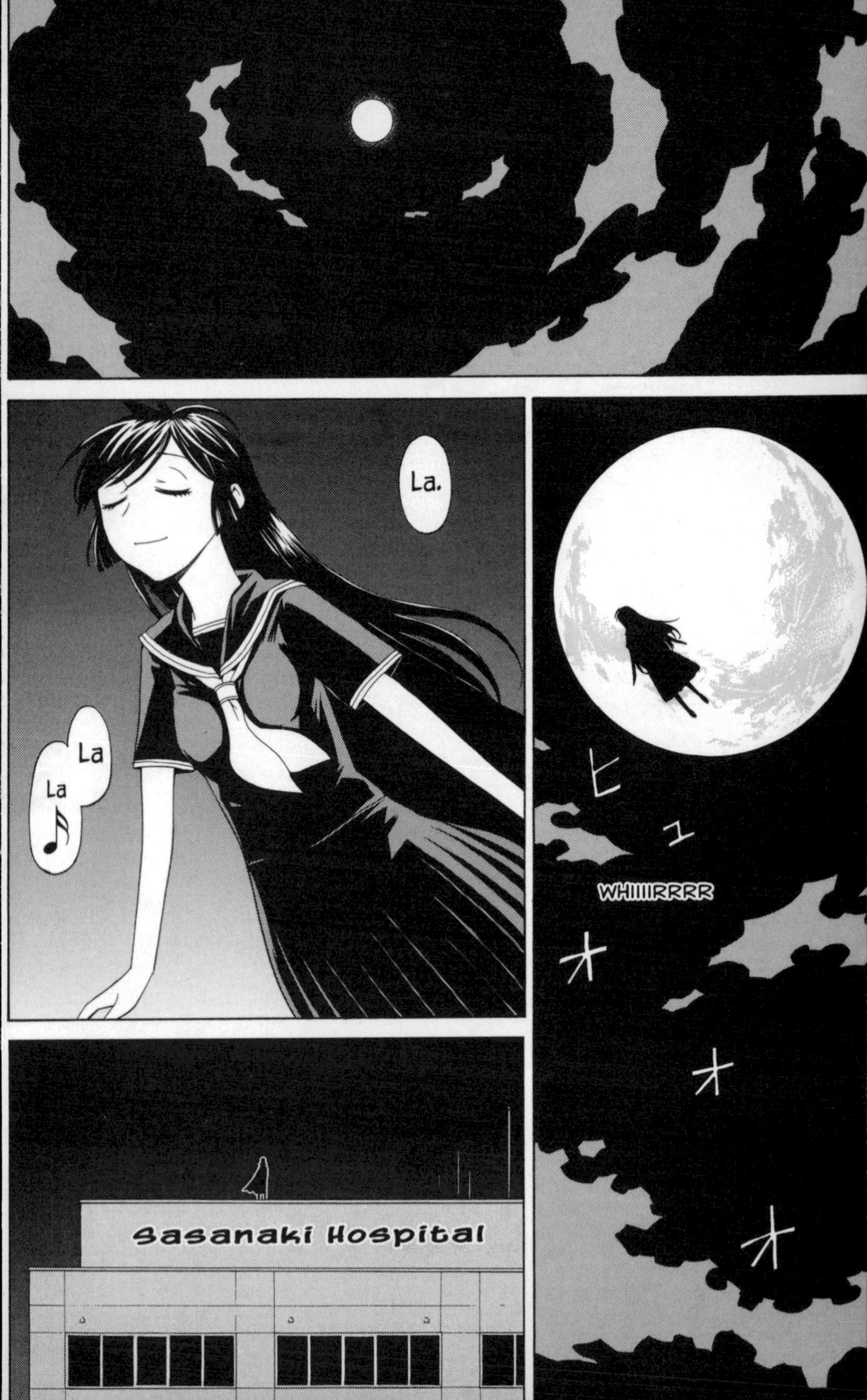
ヒュオオオ
WHIIIIRRRR
La.
La La ♪
Sasanaki Hospital

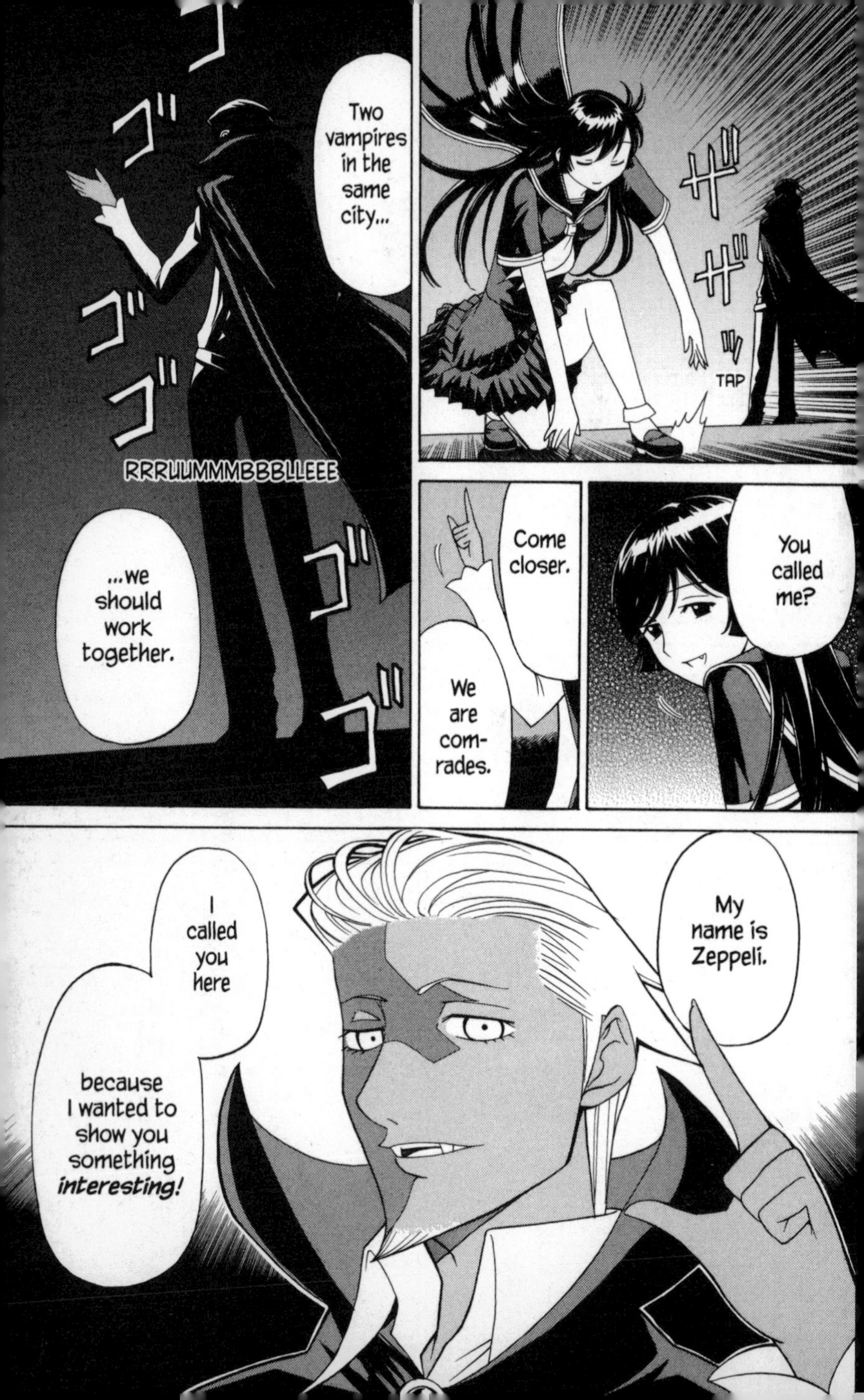
TAP
You called me?
Come closer.
We are comrades.
Two vampires in the same city...
RRRUUMMMBBBLLEEE
...we should work together.
My name is Zeppeli.
I called you here
because I wanted to show you something *interesting!*

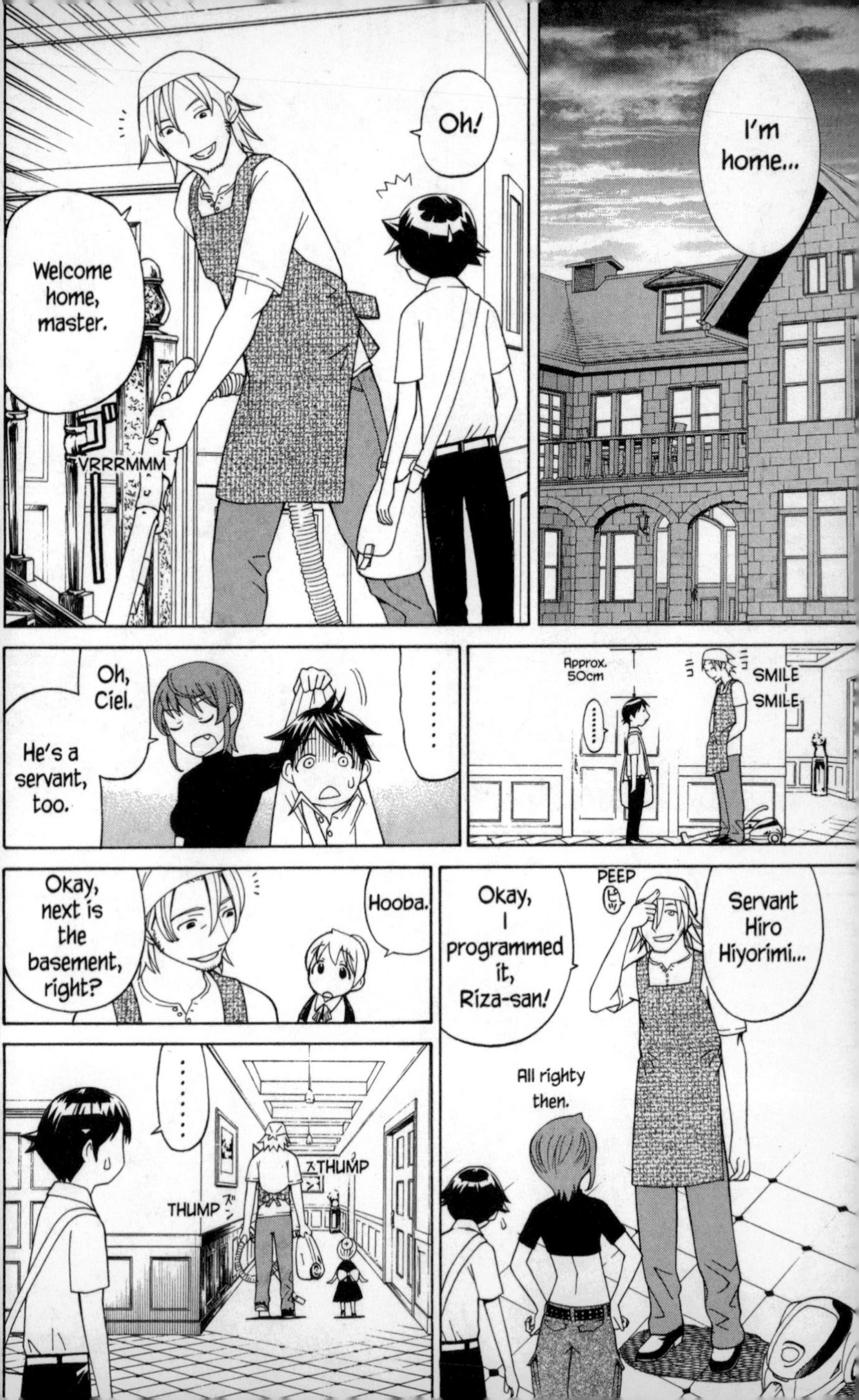
I'm home...
Oh!
Welcome home, master.
VRRRMMM
Approx. 50cm
......
SMILE SMILE
......
Oh, Ciel.
He's a servant, too.
Servant Hiro Hiyorimi...
PEEP
Okay, I programmed it, Riza-san!
All righty then.
Hooba.
Okay, next is the basement, right?
......
THUMP
THUMP

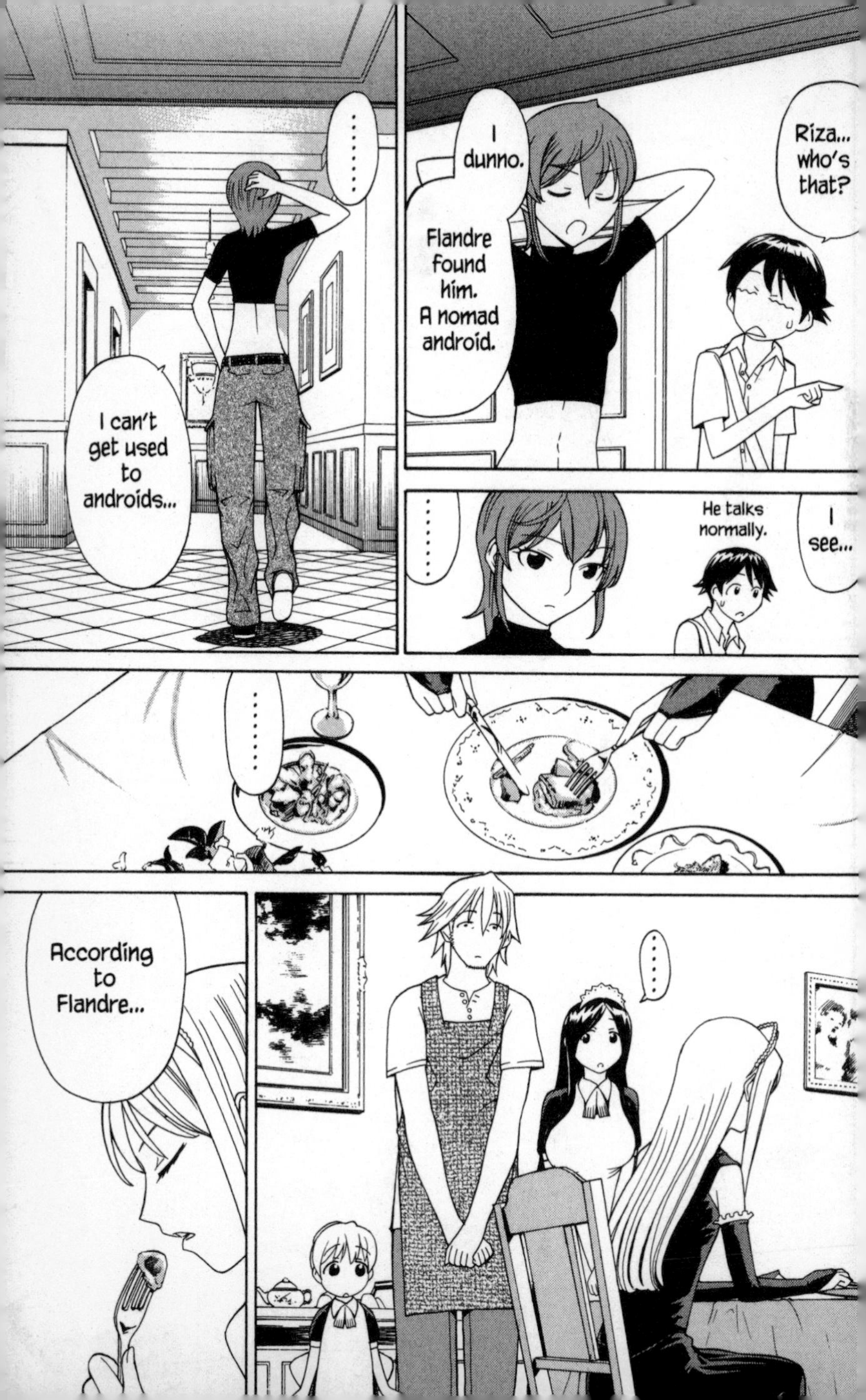
Riza... who's that?
I dunno.
Flandre found him. A nomad android.
I see...
He talks normally.
......
......
I can't get used to androids...
......
...
According to Flandre...

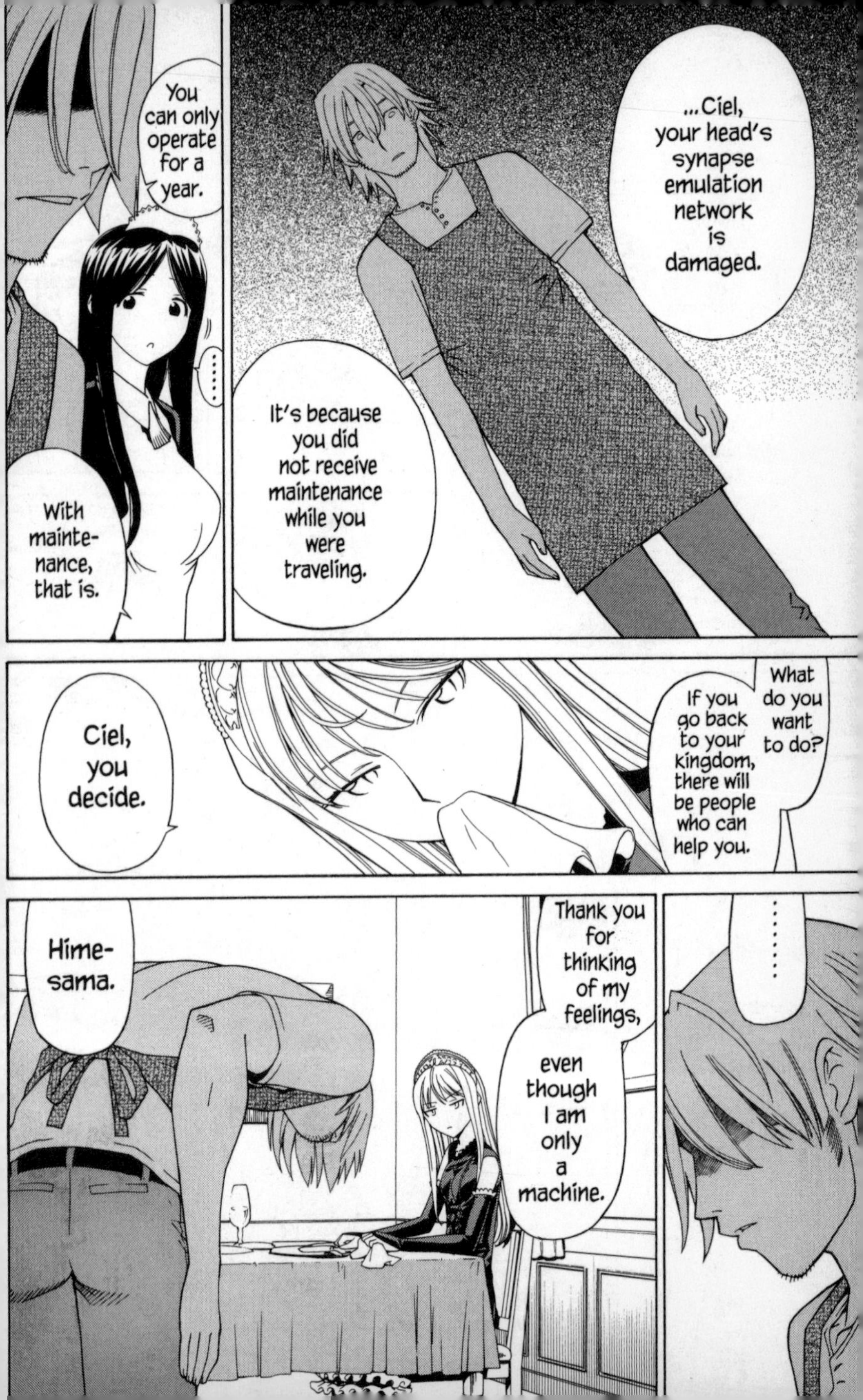
...Ciel, your head's synapse emulation network is damaged.
It's because you did not receive maintenance while you were traveling.
You can only operate for a year.
......
With mainte-nance, that is.
What do you want to do?
If you go back to your kingdom, there will be people who can help you.
Ciel, you decide.
......
Thank you for thinking of my feelings,
even though I am only a machine.
Hime-sama.

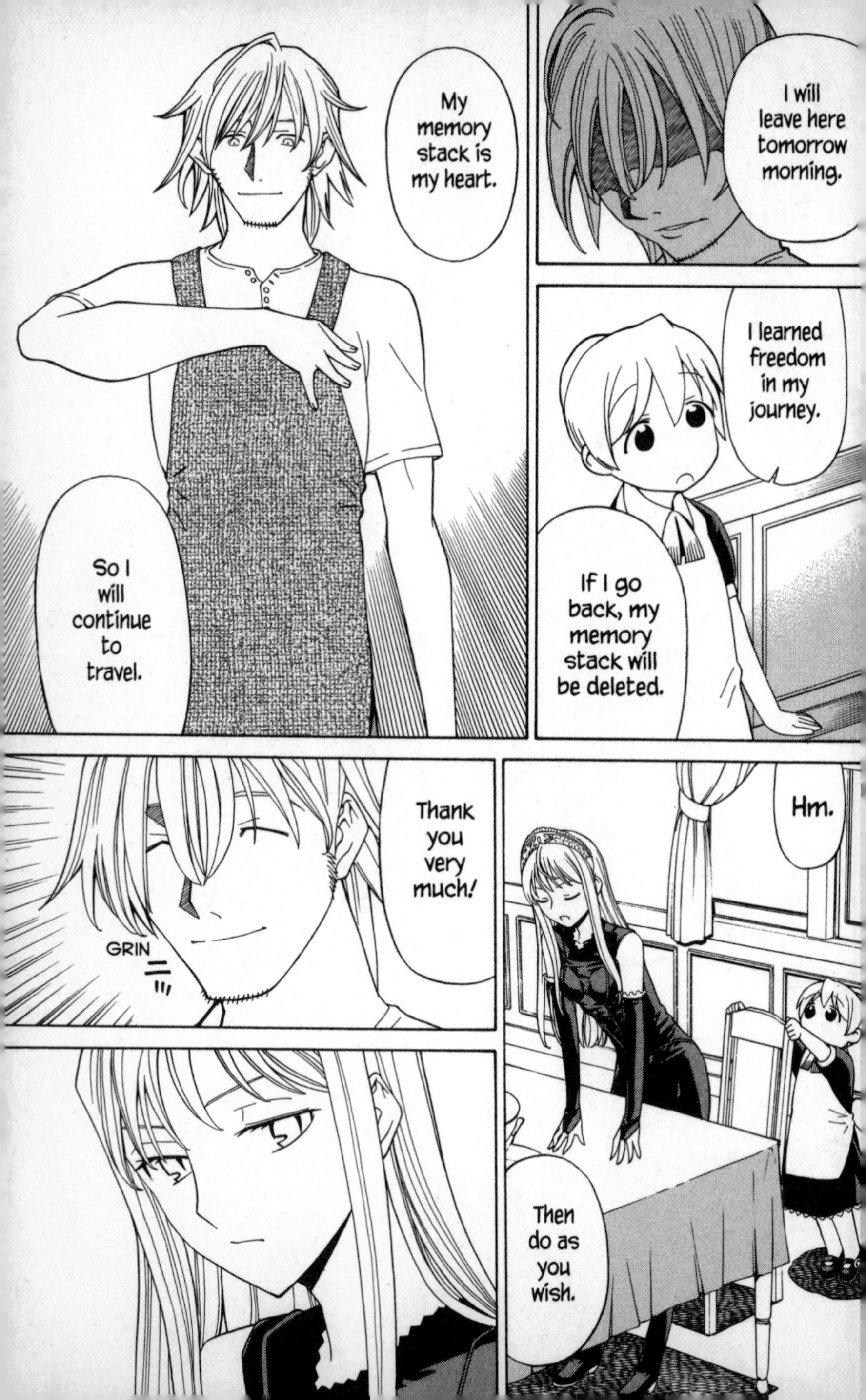
I will leave here tomorrow morning.
I learned freedom in my journey.
If I go back, my memory stack will be deleted.
My memory stack is my heart.
So I will continue to travel.
Hm.
Then do as you wish.
Thank you very much!
GRIN

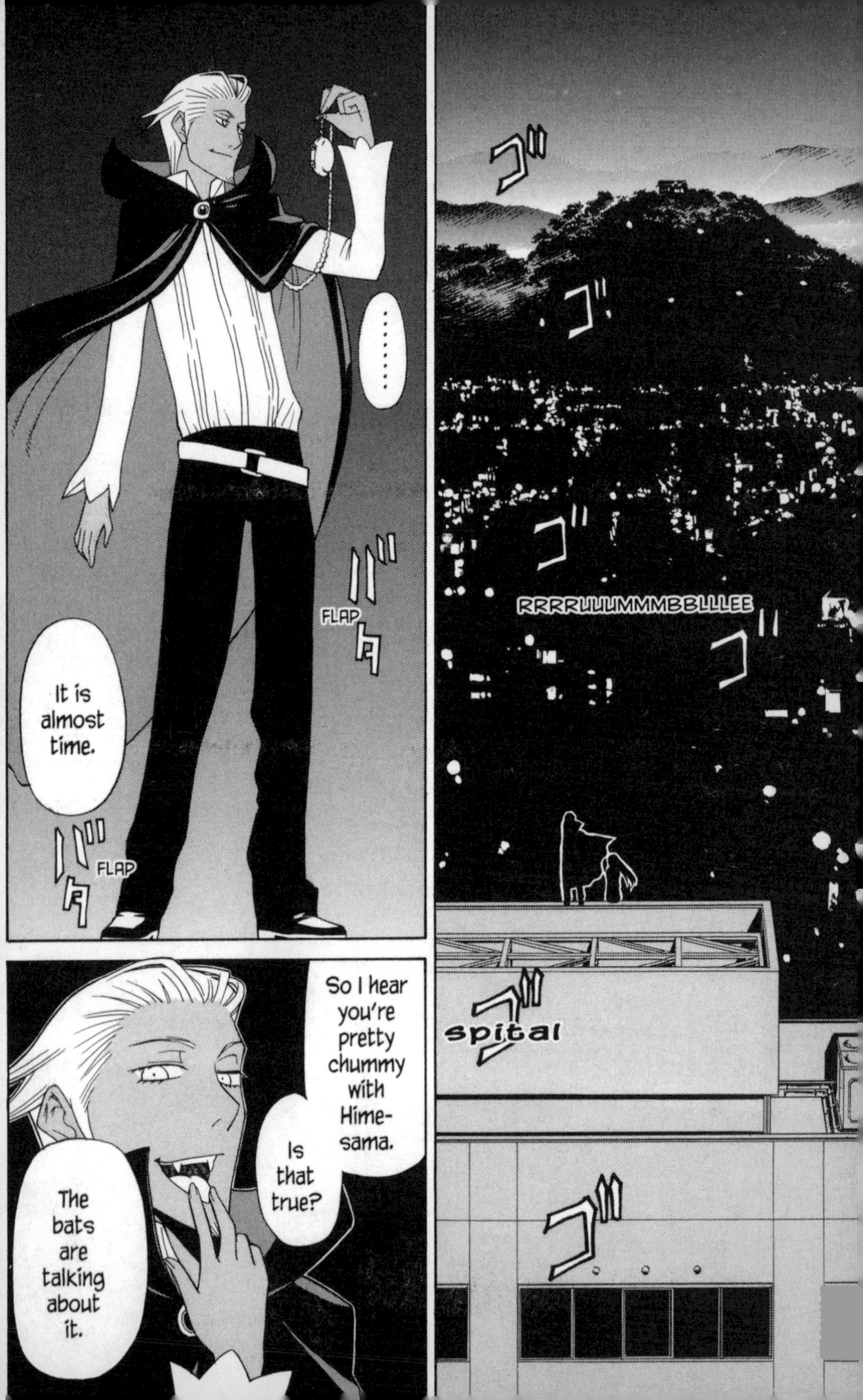
RRRRUUUMMMBBLLLEE
spital
......
It is almost time.
FLAP
FLAP
So I hear you're pretty chummy with Hime-sama.
Is that true?
The bats are talking about it.

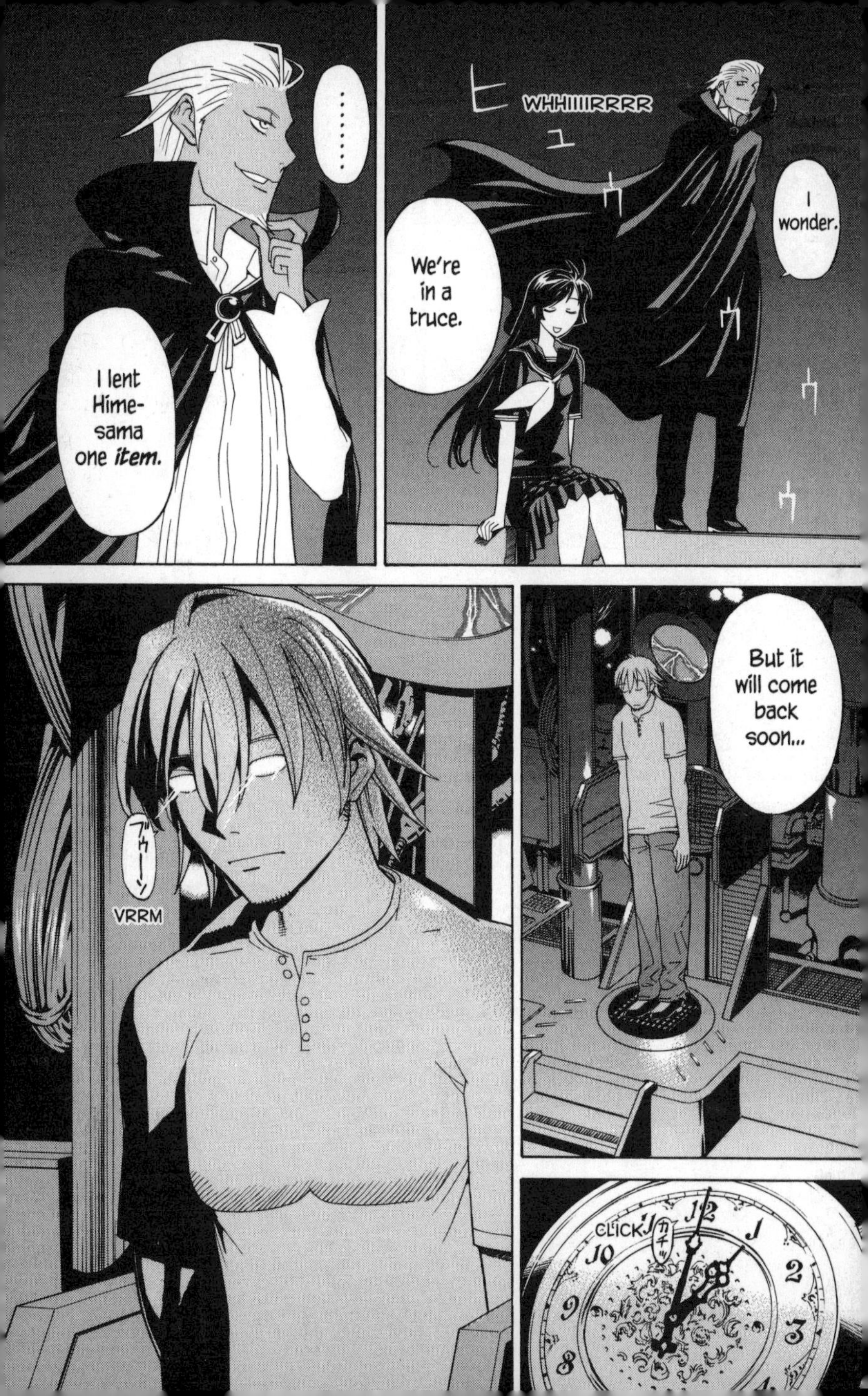
ヒュ
WHHIIIIRRRR
I wonder.
We're in a truce.
……
I lent Hime-sama one *item.*
But it will come back soon...
CLICK
カチッ
ブゥーン
VRRM

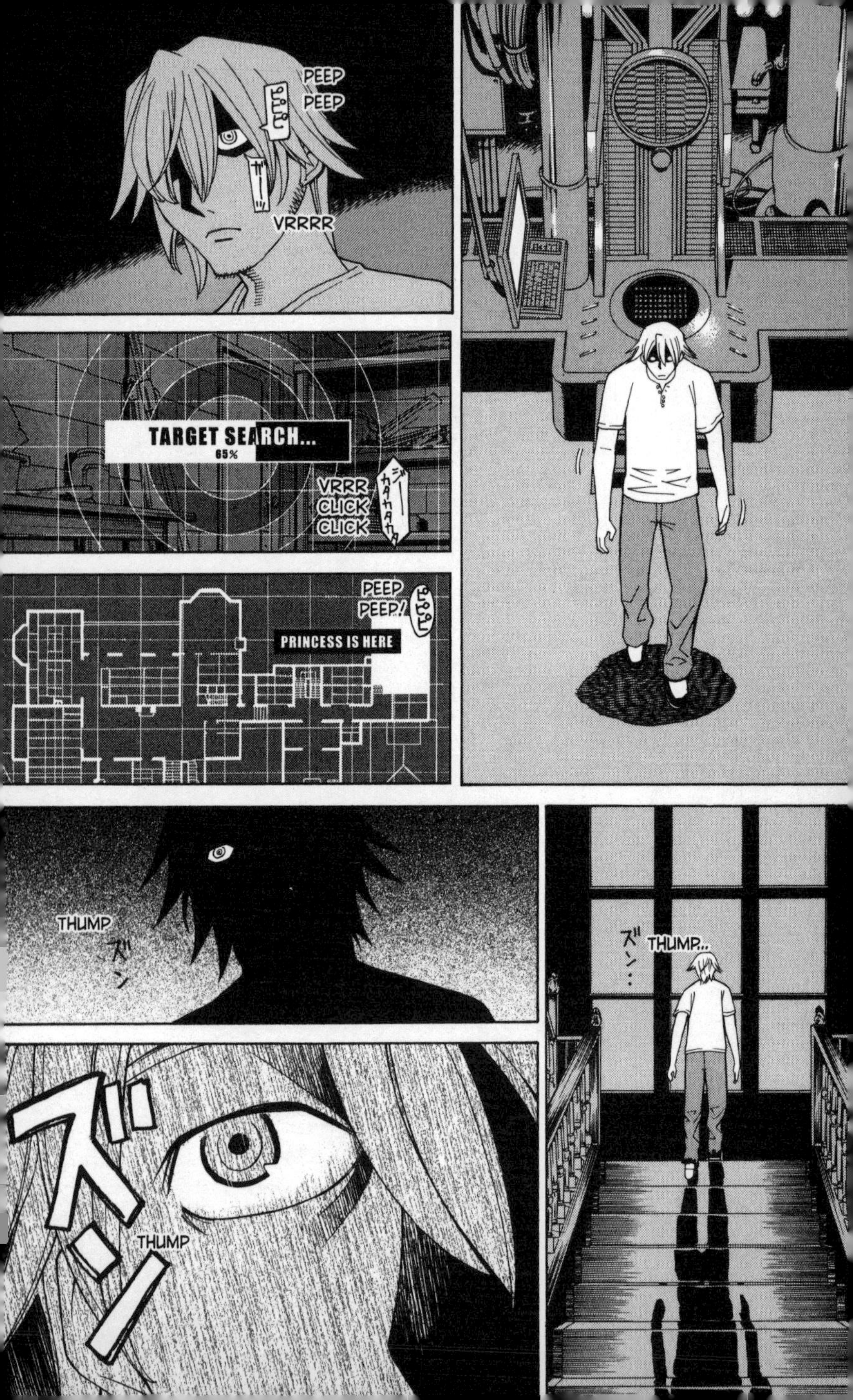
PEEP
PEEP
ピピピ
ガーッ
VRRRR
TARGET SEARCH...
65%
VRRR
CLICK
CLICK
ジーカタカタカタ
PEEP
PEEP!
ピピピ
PRINCESS IS HERE
ズン・・
THUMP...
THUMP
ズン
ズン
THUMP

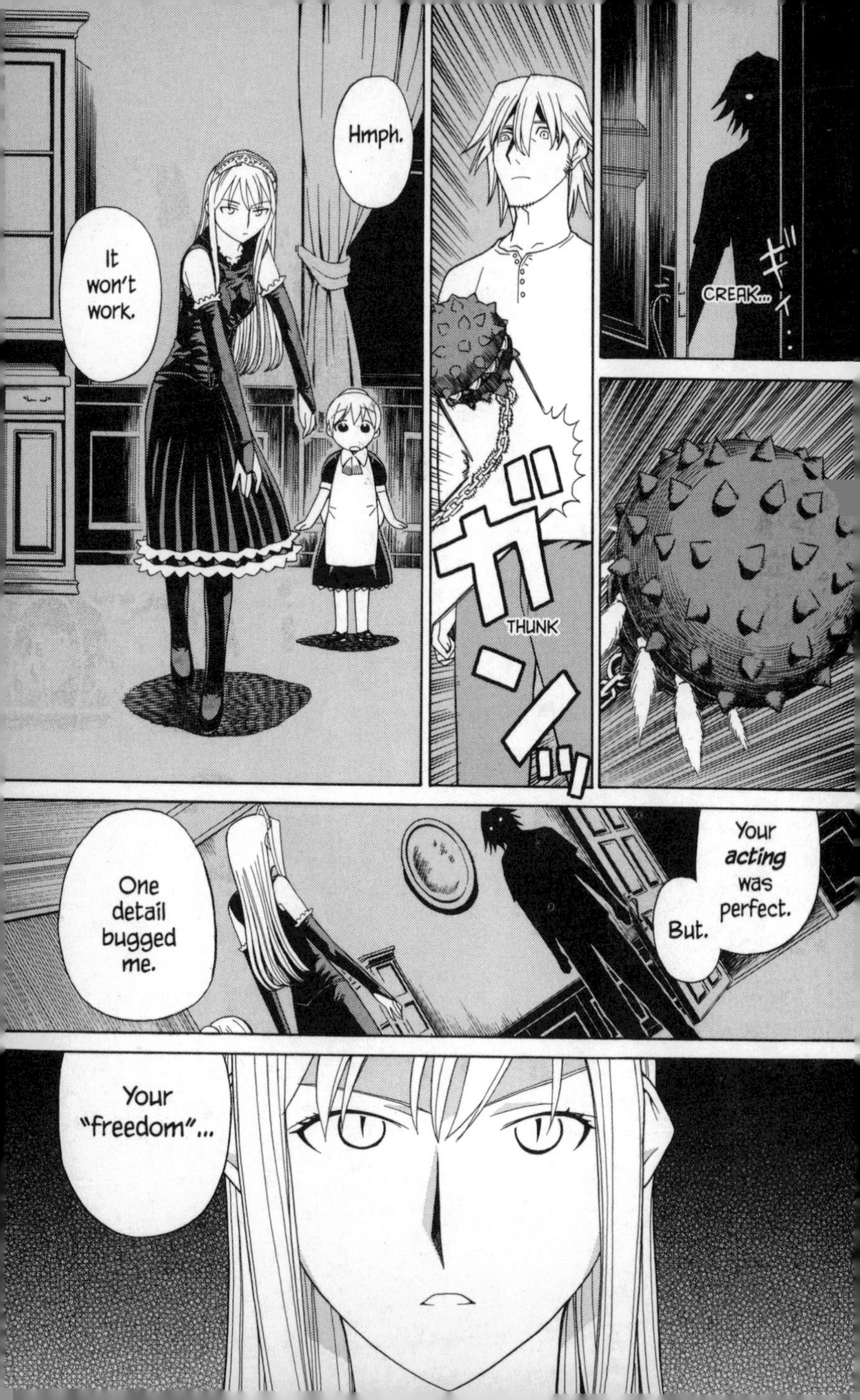
ギィ…
CREAK...
ガンッ
THUNK
Hmph.
It won't work.
Your *acting* was perfect.
But.
One detail bugged me.
Your "freedom"...

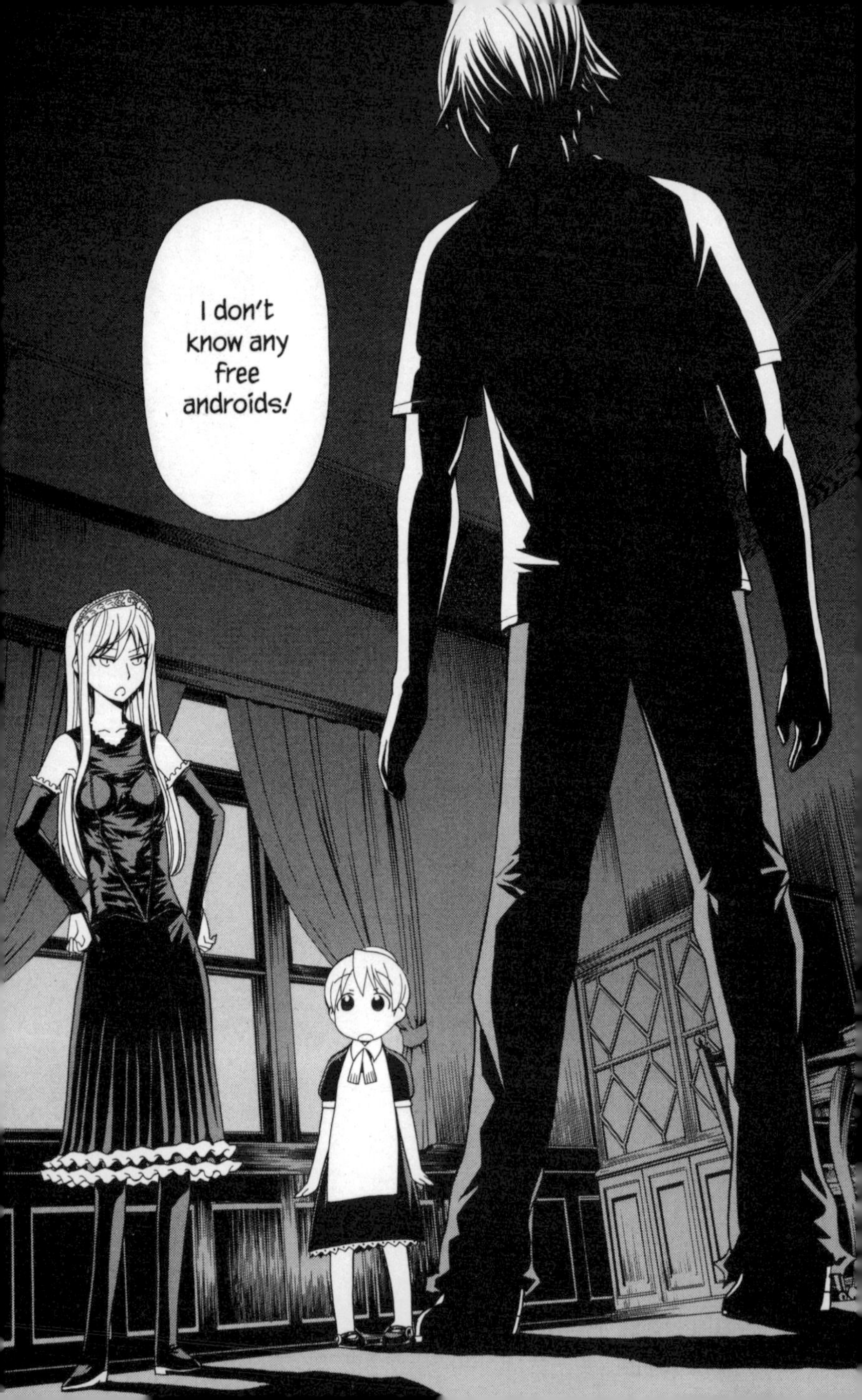
I don't know any free androids!

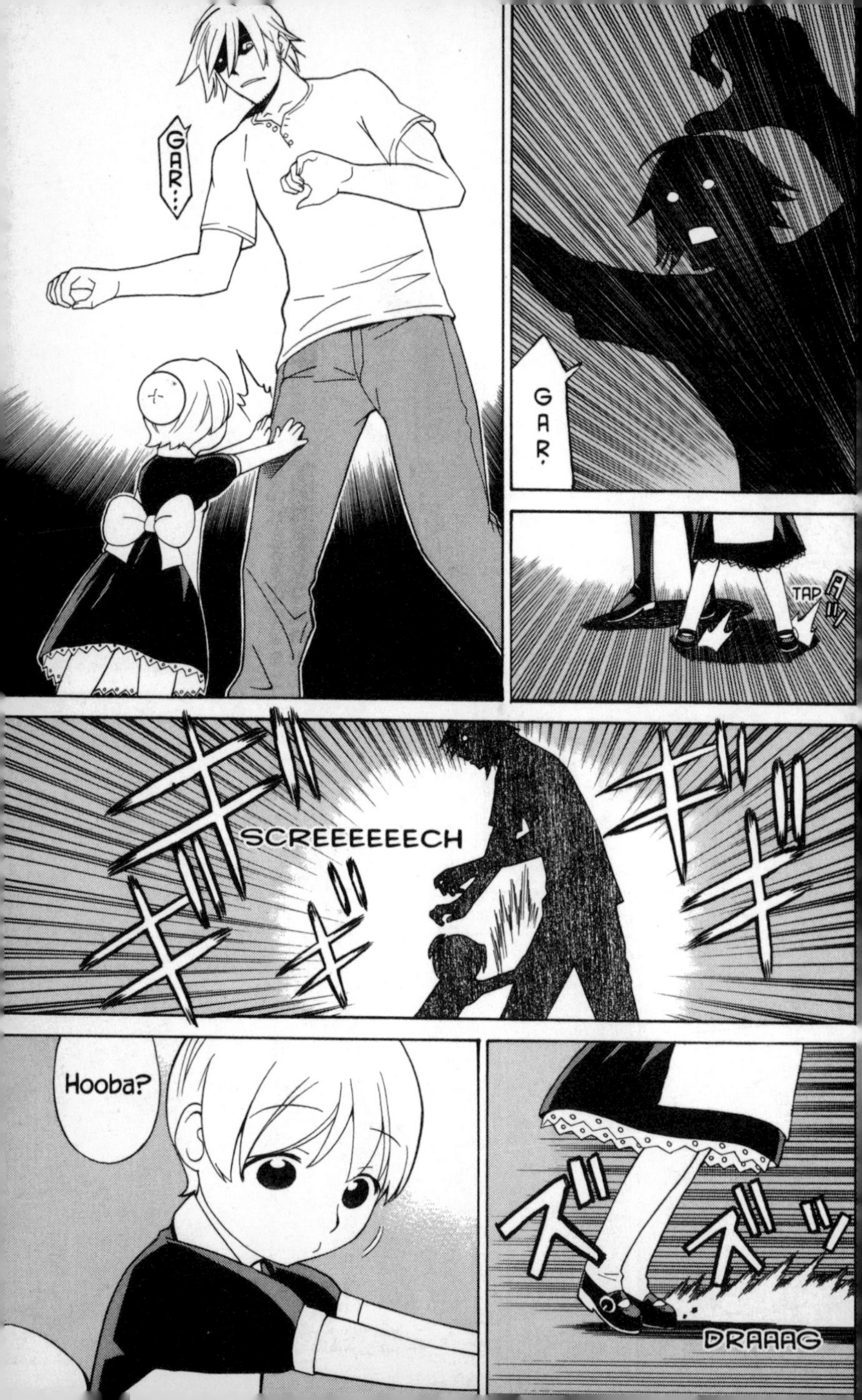
GAR.
TAP
GAR...
SCREEEEEECH
DRAAAG
Hooba?

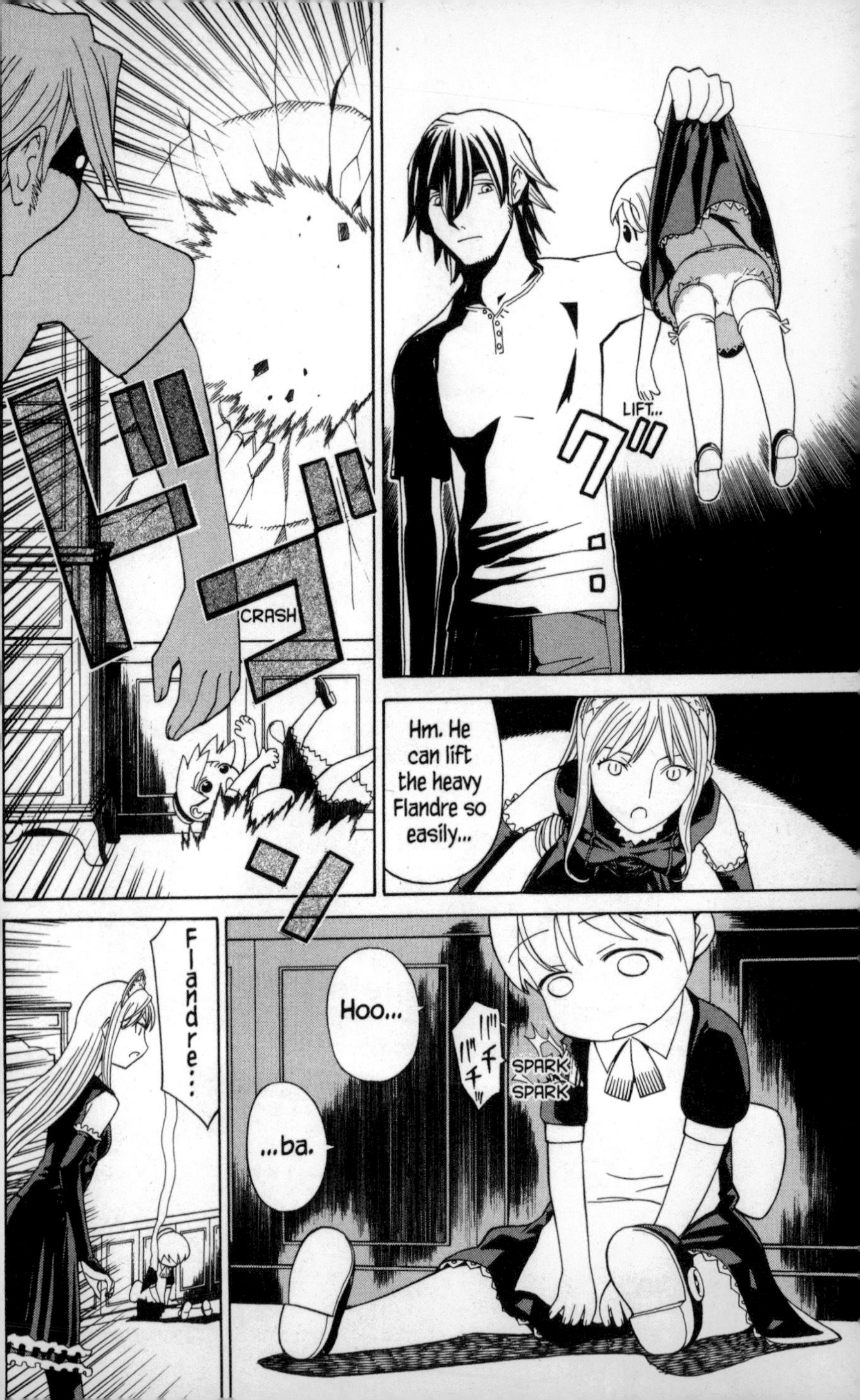
LIFT...
Hm. He can lift the heavy Flandre so easily...
CRASH
Hoo...
...ba.
SPARK SPARK
Flandre...

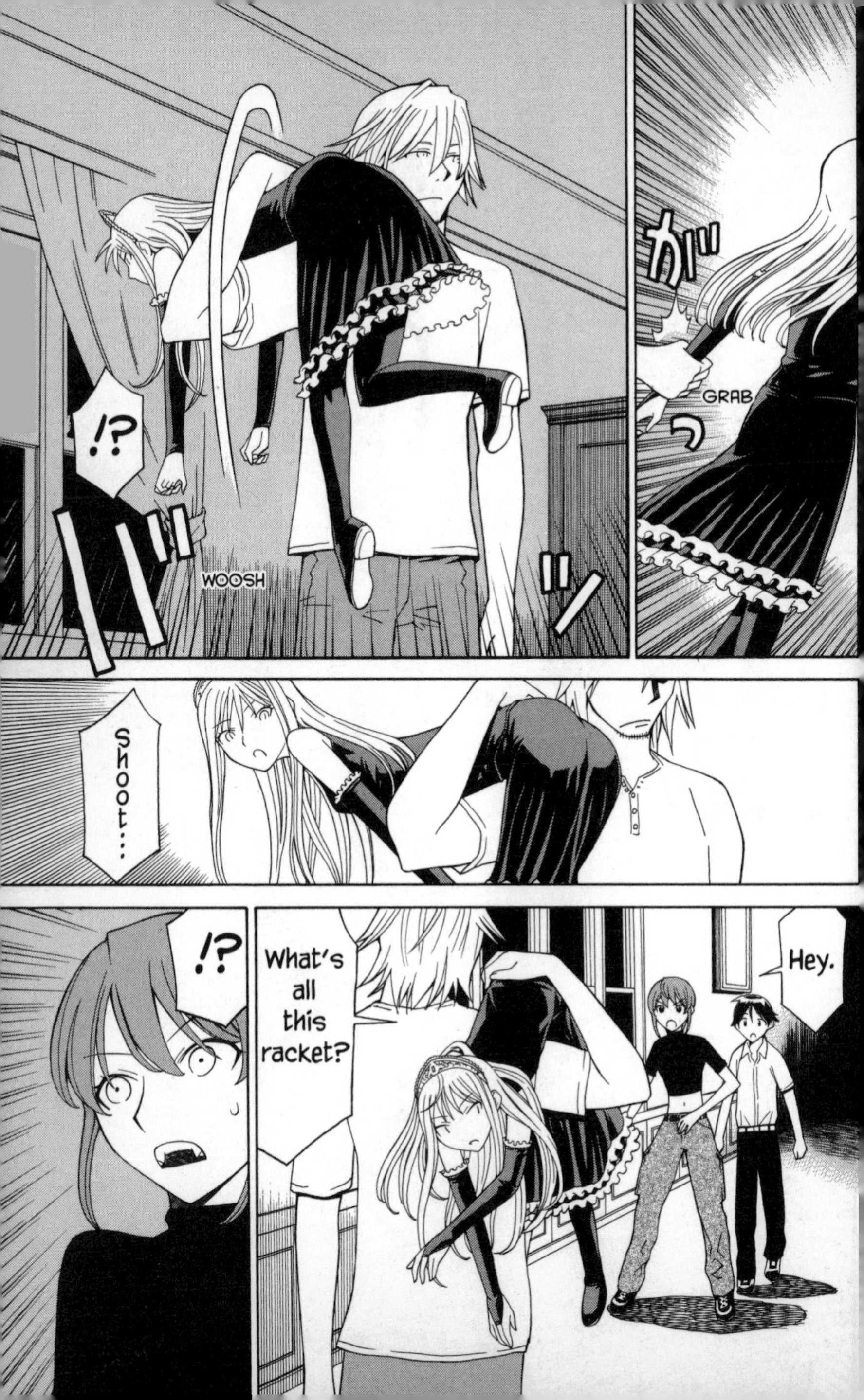
GRAB
!?
WOOSH
Shoot...
Hey.
What's all this racket?
!?

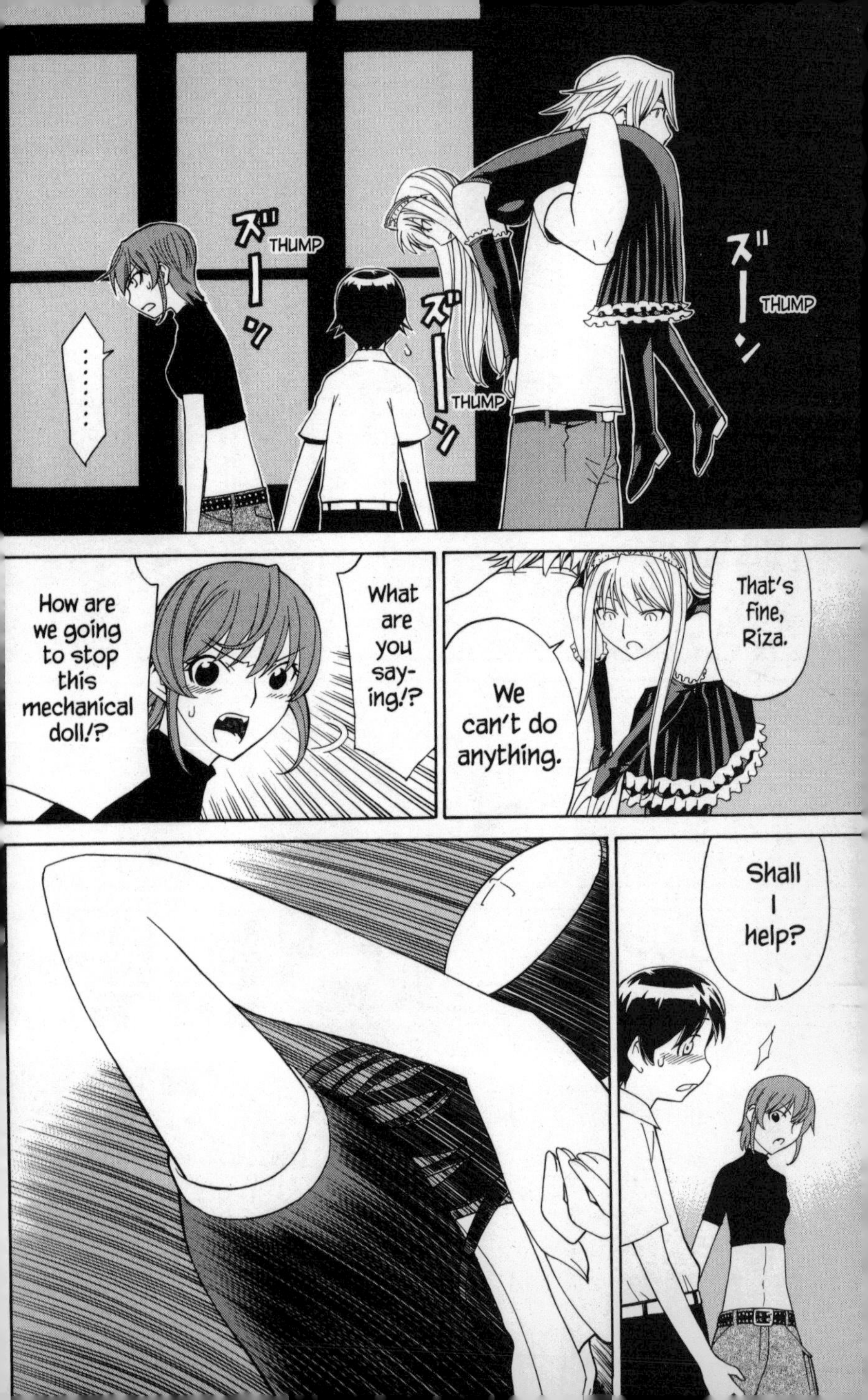
ズーン
THUMP
ズーッ
THUMP
ズーッ
THUMP
......
That's fine, Riza.
We can't do anything.
What are you say-ing!?
How are we going to stop this mechanical doll!?
Shall I help?

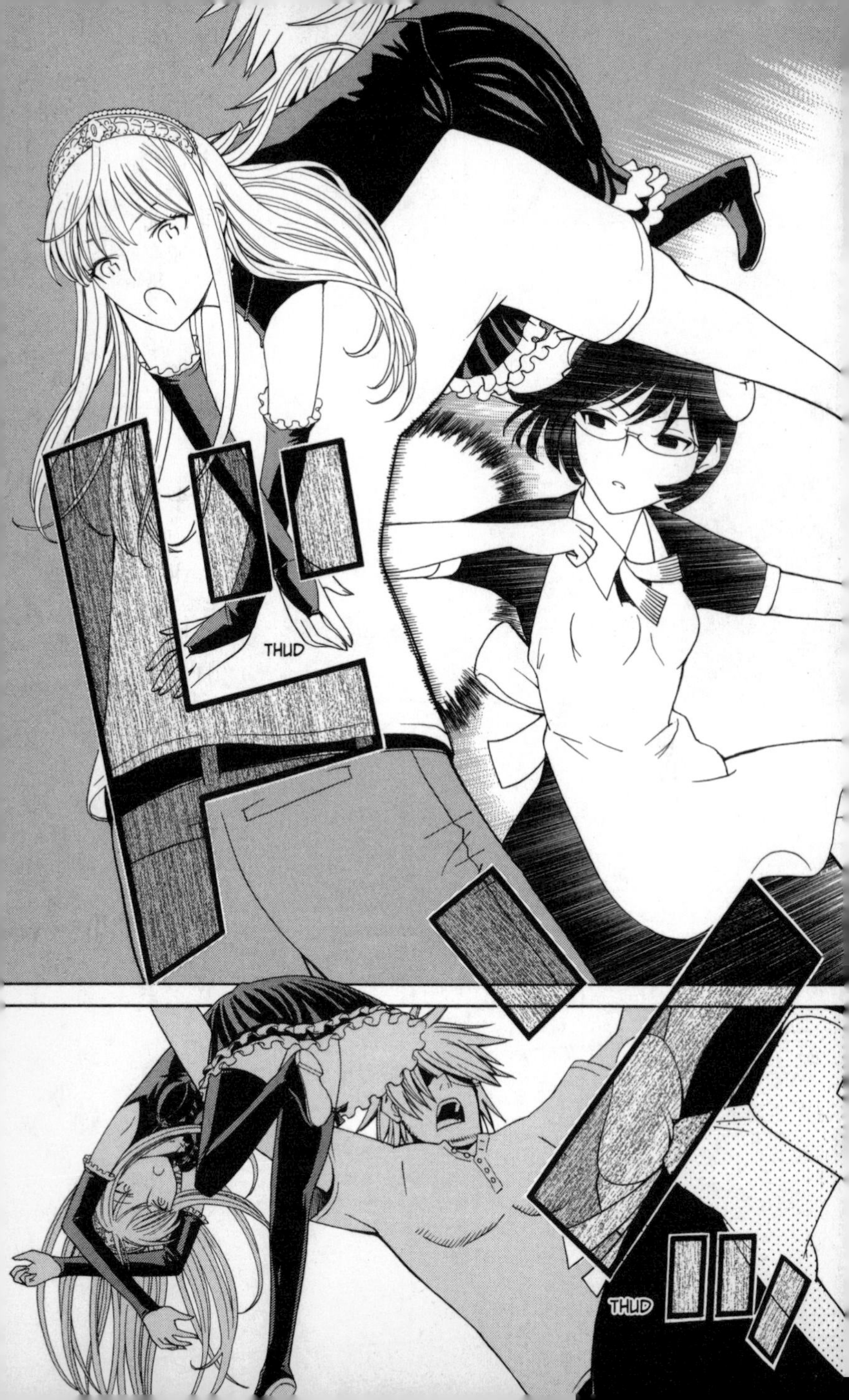
THUD
THUD

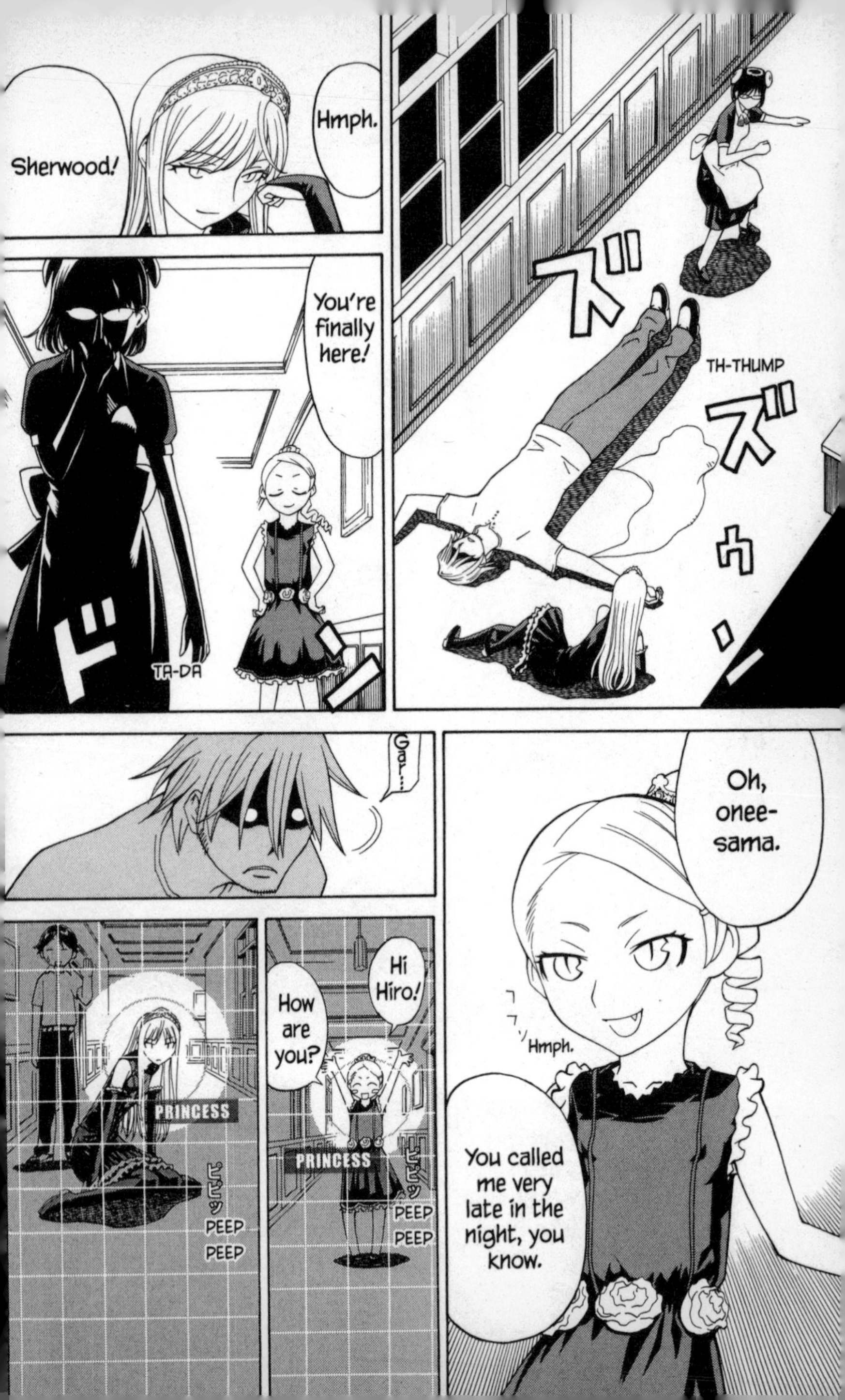

ズ
TH-THUMP
ズウ
Hmph.
Sherwood!
You're finally here!
TA-DA
ド
Oh, onee-sama.
Hmph.
You called me very late in the night, you know.
Gar....
Hi Hiro!
How are you?
PRINCESS
ピピッ
PEEP PEEP
PRINCESS
ピピッ
PEEP PEEP

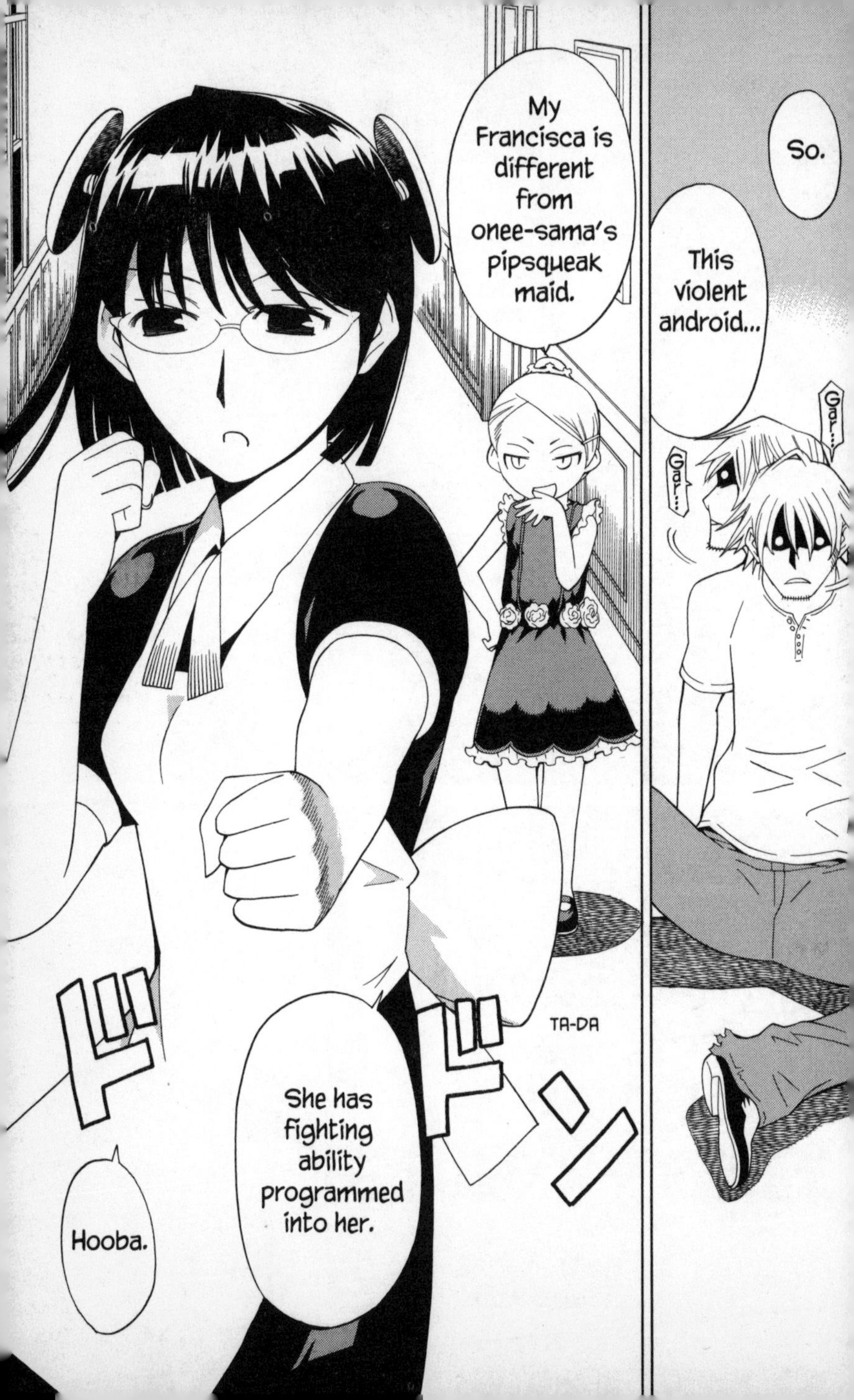
So.
This violent android...
Gar...
Gar...
My Francisca is different from onee-sama's pipsqueak maid.
She has fighting ability programmed into her.
TA-DA
Hooba.

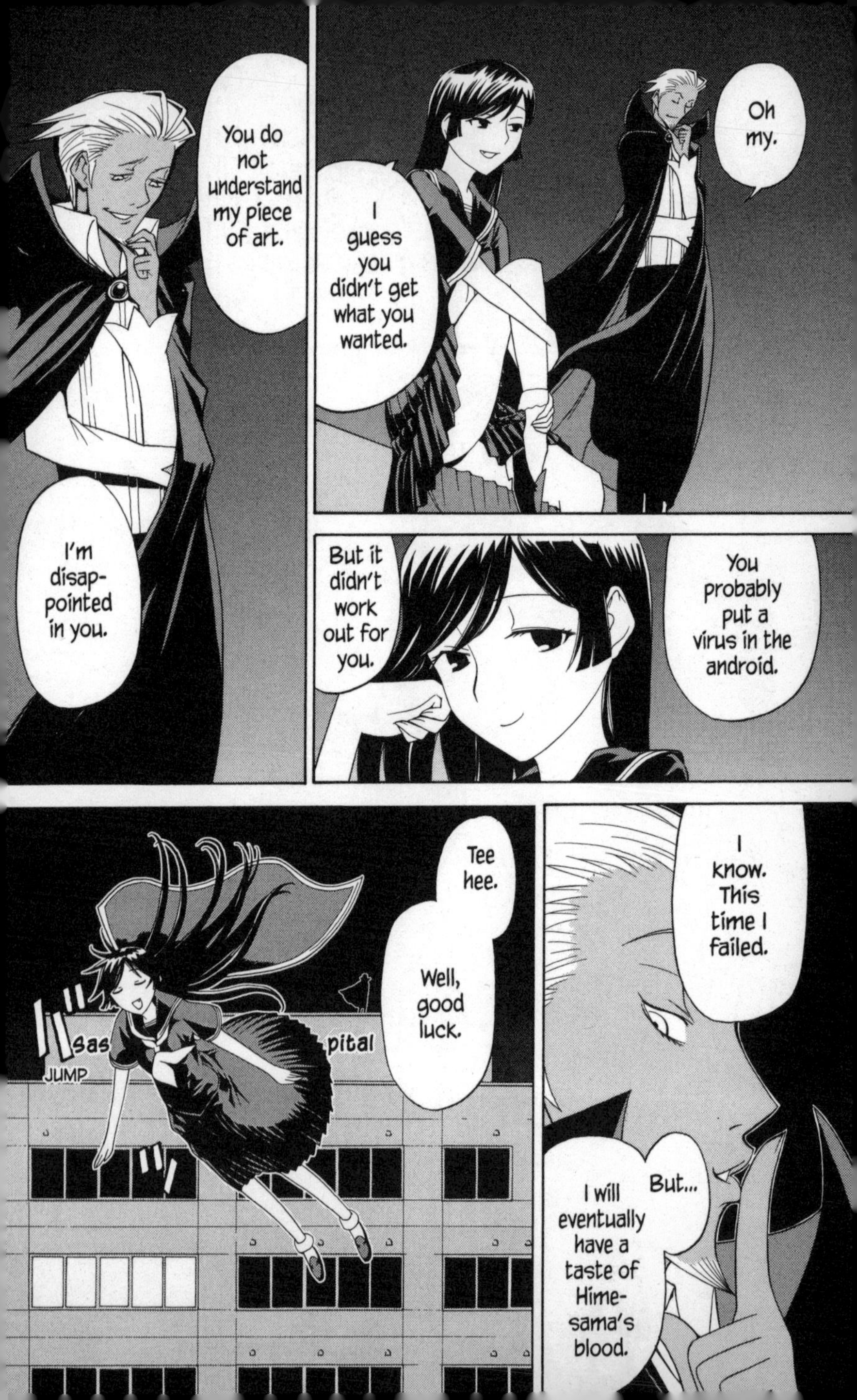

Oh my.
I guess you didn't get what you wanted.
You probably put a virus in the android.
But it didn't work out for you.
You do not understand my piece of art.
I'm disap-pointed in you.
I know. This time I failed.
But...
I will eventually have a taste of Hime-sama's blood.
Tee hee.
Well, good luck.
sas
pital
JUMP

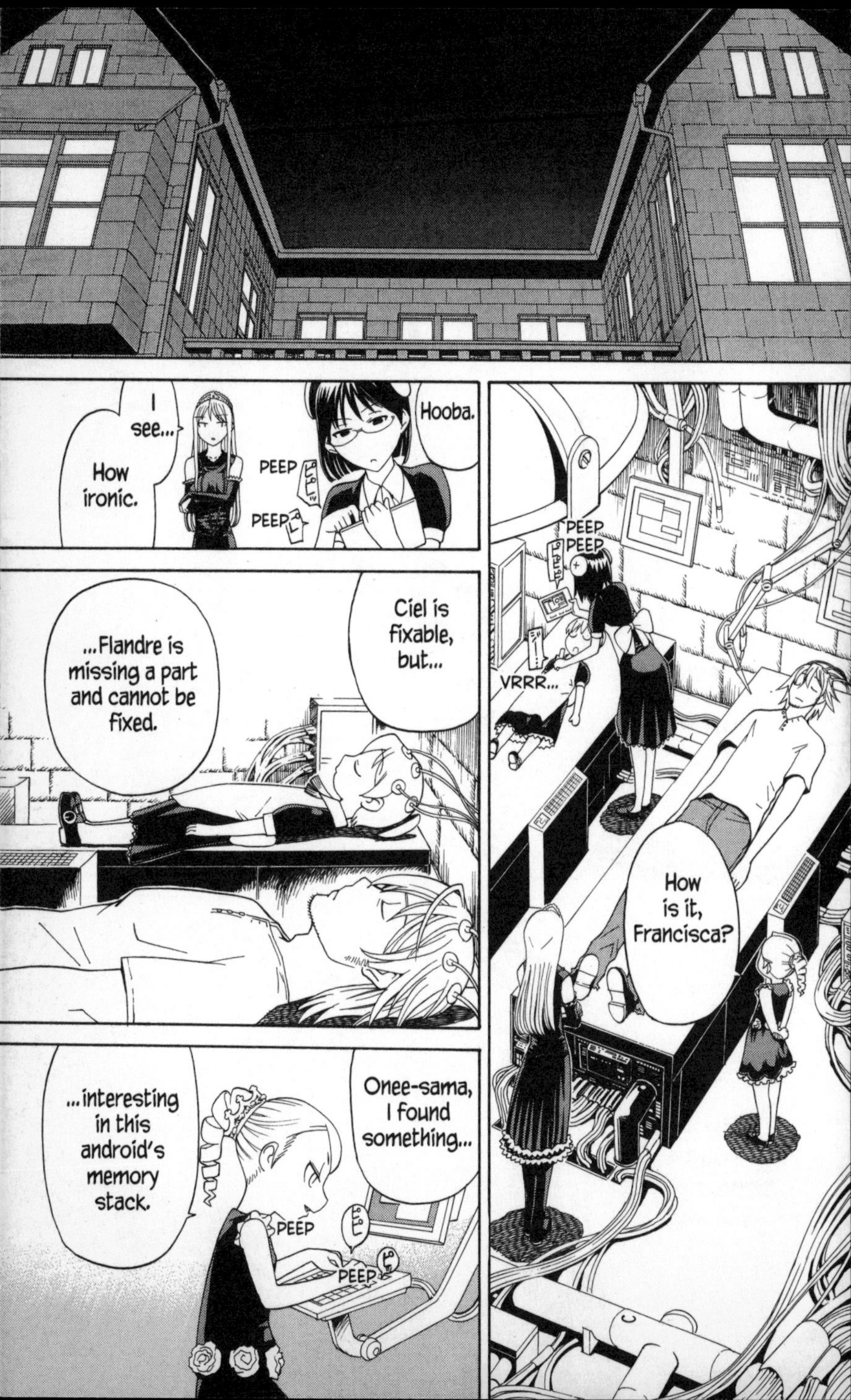
PEEP
PEEP
VRRR...
How is it, Francisca?
Hooba.
PEEP
PEEP
I see...
How ironic.
Ciel is fixable, but...
...Flandre is missing a part and cannot be fixed.
Onee-sama, I found something...
...interesting in this android's memory stack.
PEEP
PEEP

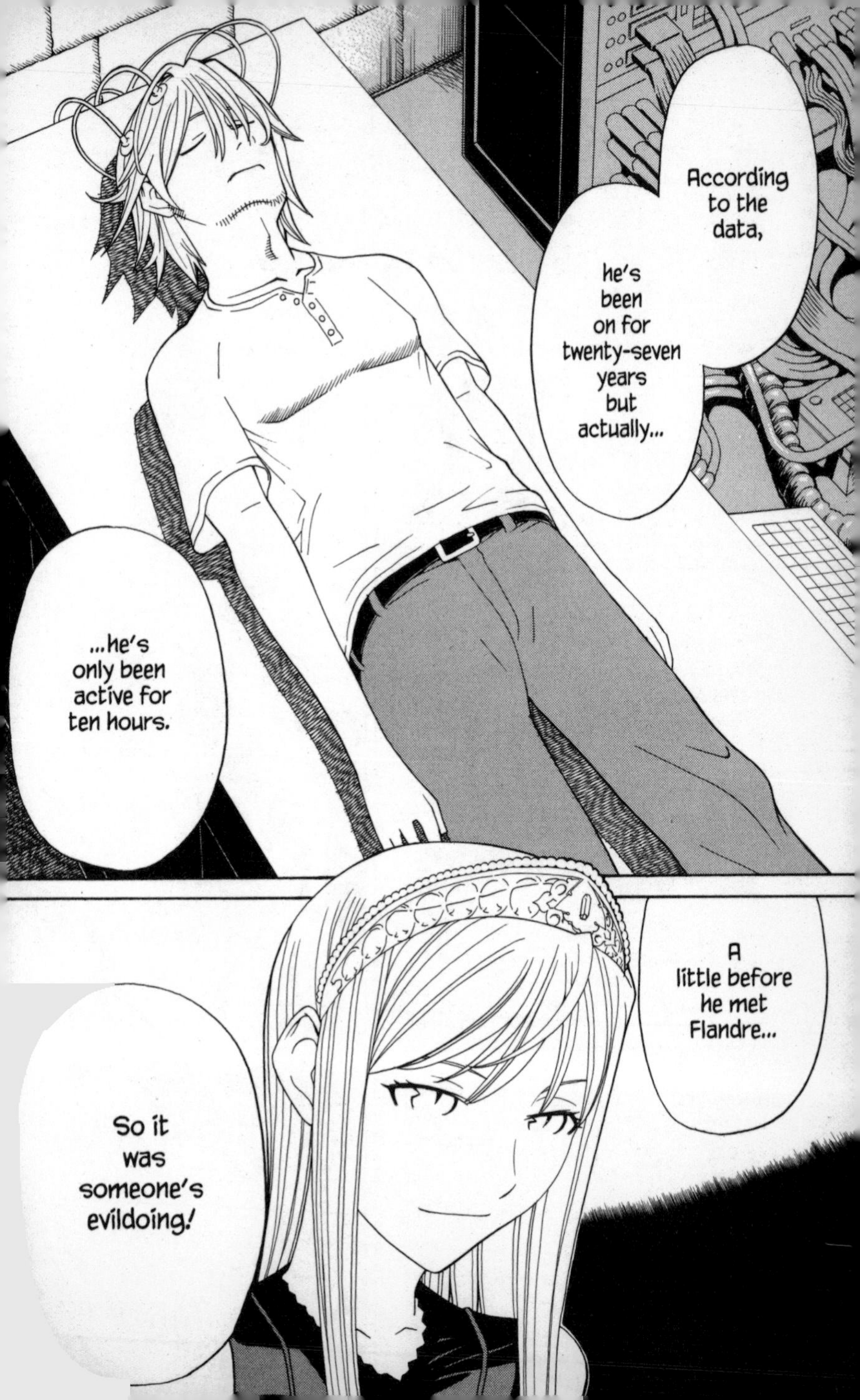
According to the data,
he's been on for twenty-seven years but actually...
...he's only been active for ten hours.
A little before he met Flandre...
So it was someone's evildoing!

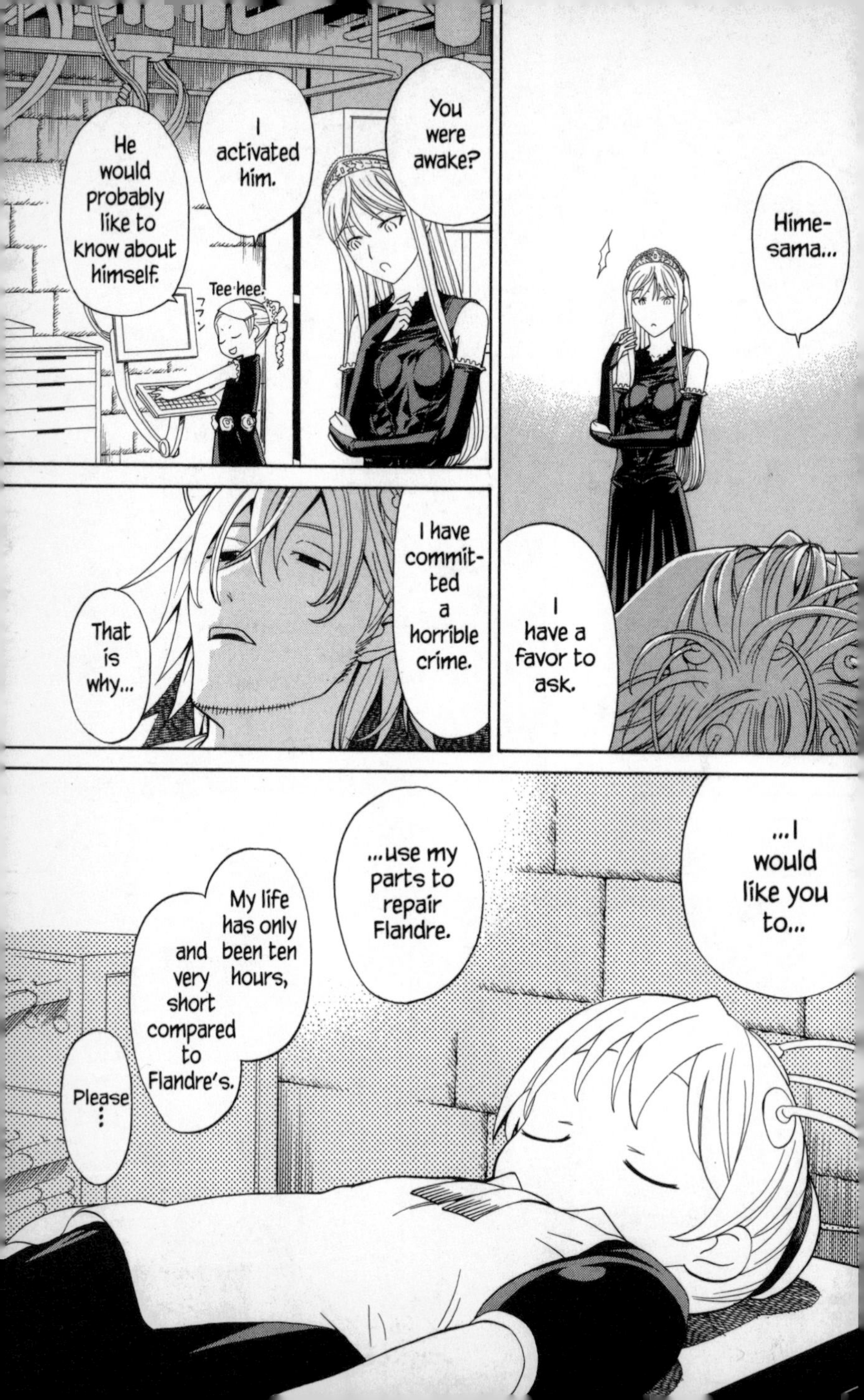
Hime-sama...
You were awake?
I activated him.
He would probably like to know about himself.
Tee hee.
I have a favor to ask.
I have committed a horrible crime.
That is why...
...I would like you to...
...use my parts to repair Flandre.
My life has only been ten hours,
and very short compared to Flandre's.
Please...

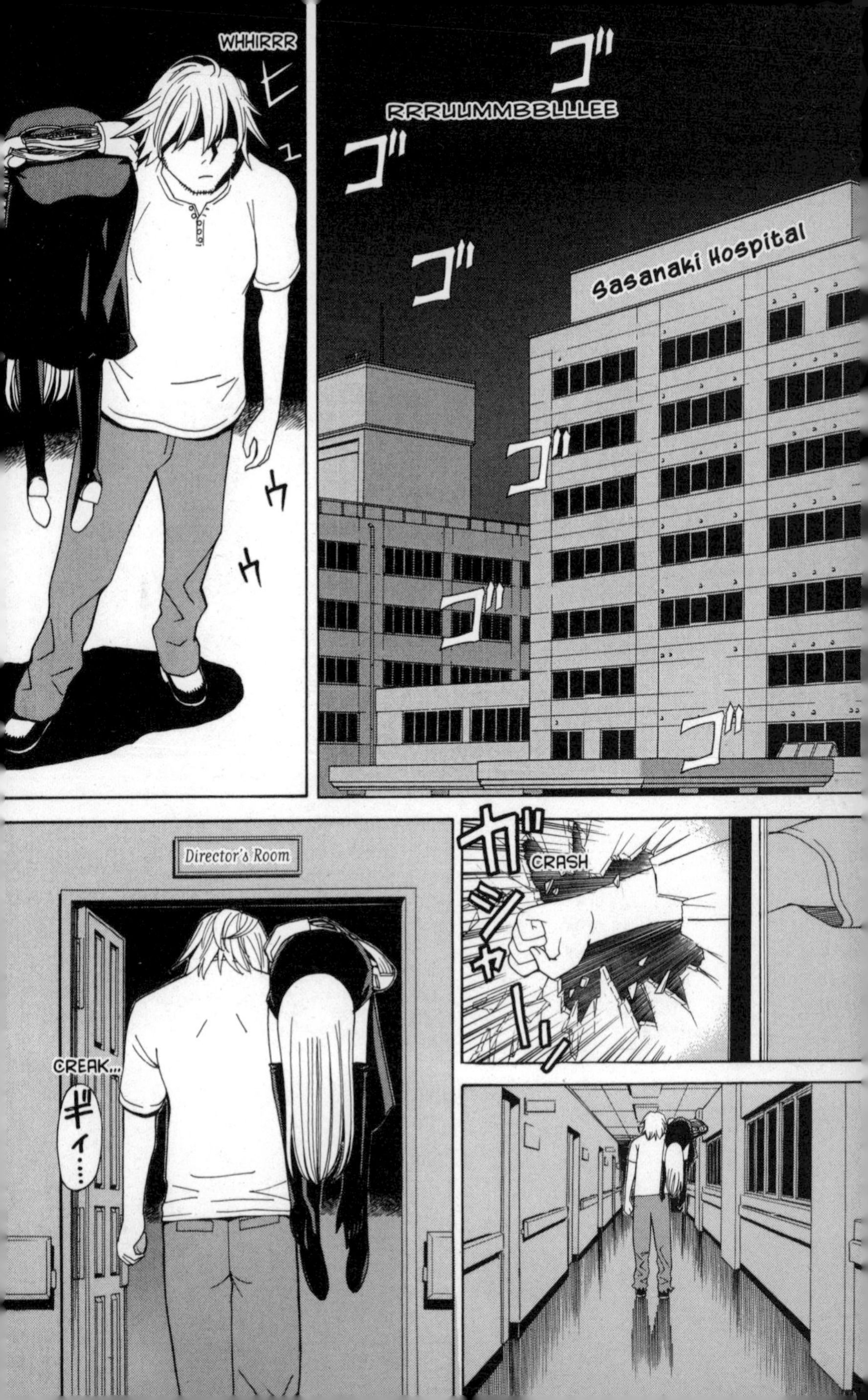

ゴ
RRRUUMMBBLLLLEE
ゴ
ゴ
ゴ
ゴ
ゴ
Sasanaki Hospital
WHHIRRR
ヒュ
ウ
ウ
ガシャーン
CRASH
Director's Room
CREAK...
ギィ……

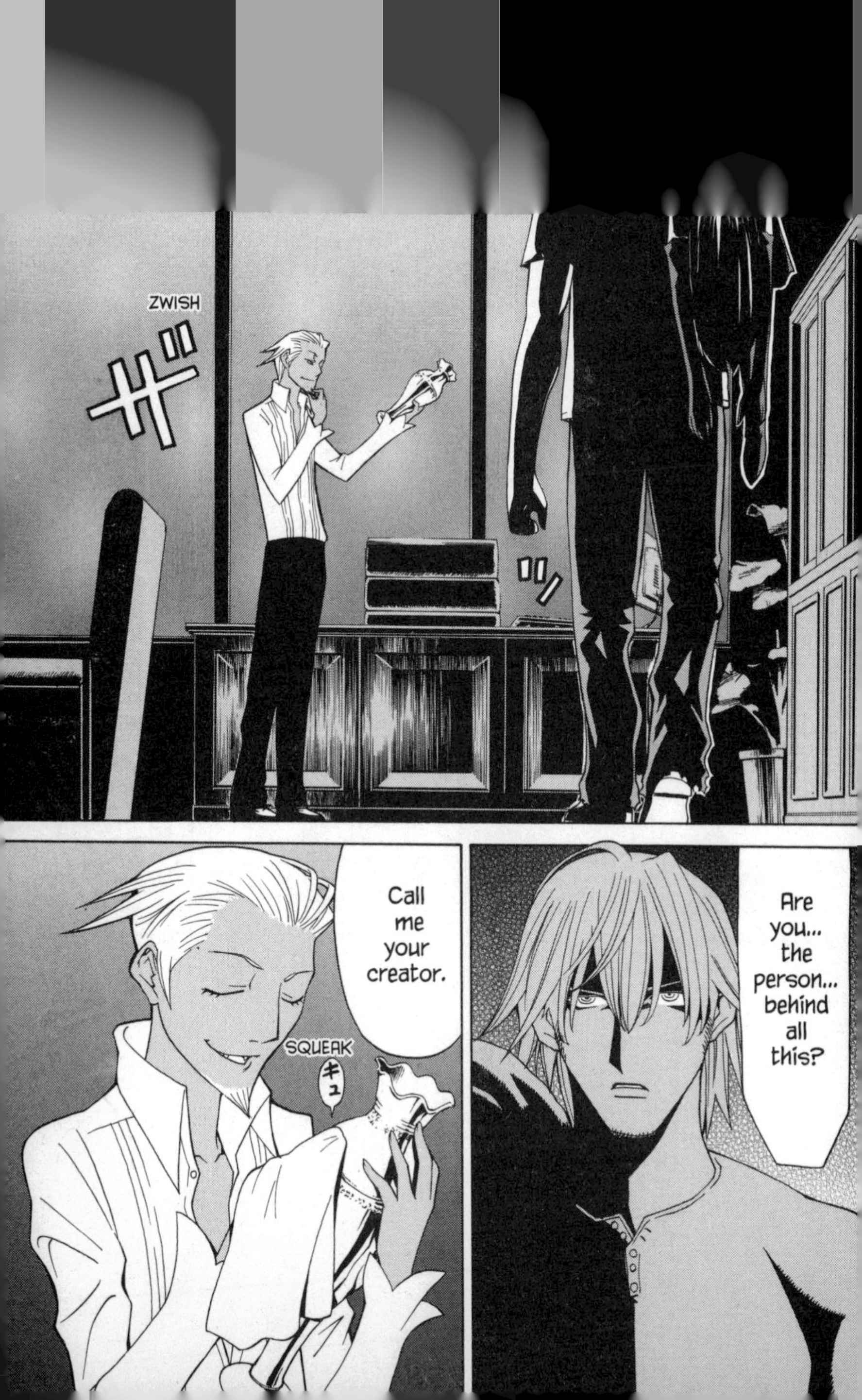
ZWISH
Are you... the person... behind all this?
Call me your creator.
SQUEAK
キュ

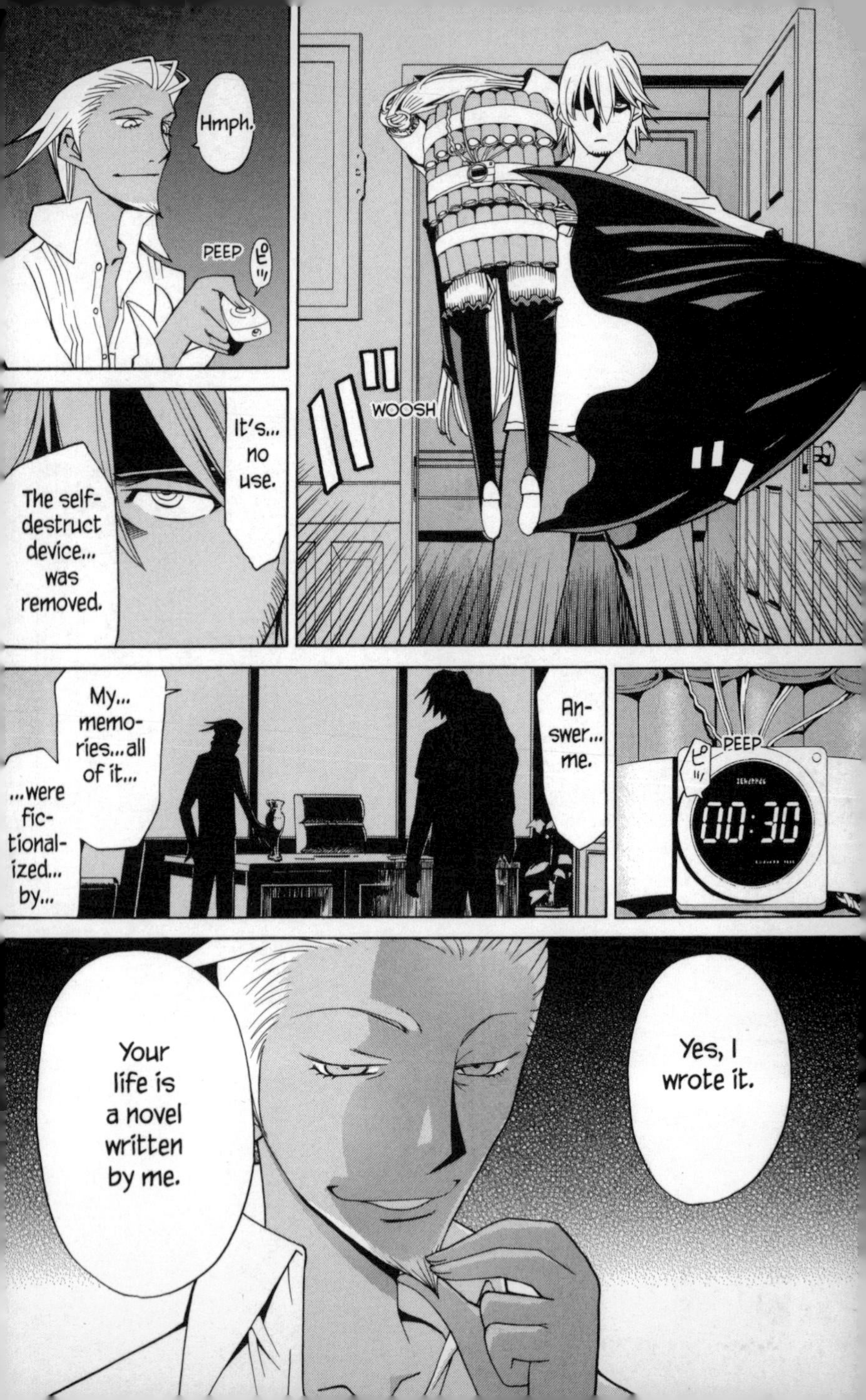
WOOSH
Hmph.
PEEP
ピッ
It's... no use.
The self-destruct device... was removed.
PEEP
ピッ
00:30
Answer... me.
My... memories...all of it...
...were fictionalized... by...
Yes, I wrote it.
Your life is a novel written by me.

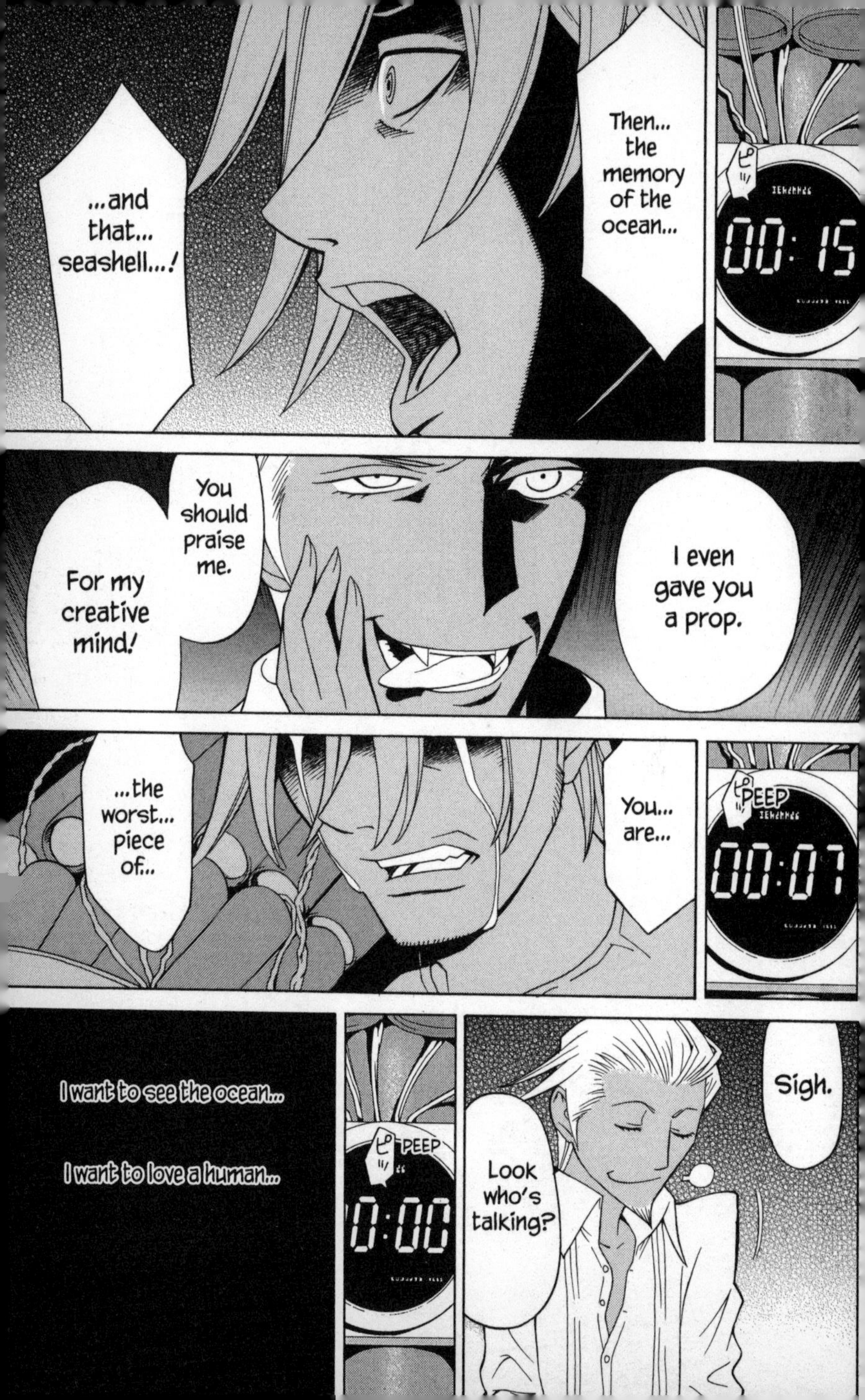

ピ
00:15
Then... the memory of the ocean...
...and that... seashell...!
I even gave you a prop.
You should praise me.
For my creative mind!
ピ PEEP
00:07
You... are...
...the worst... piece of...
Sigh.
Look who's talking?
ピ PEEP
0:00
I want to see the ocean...
I want to love a human...

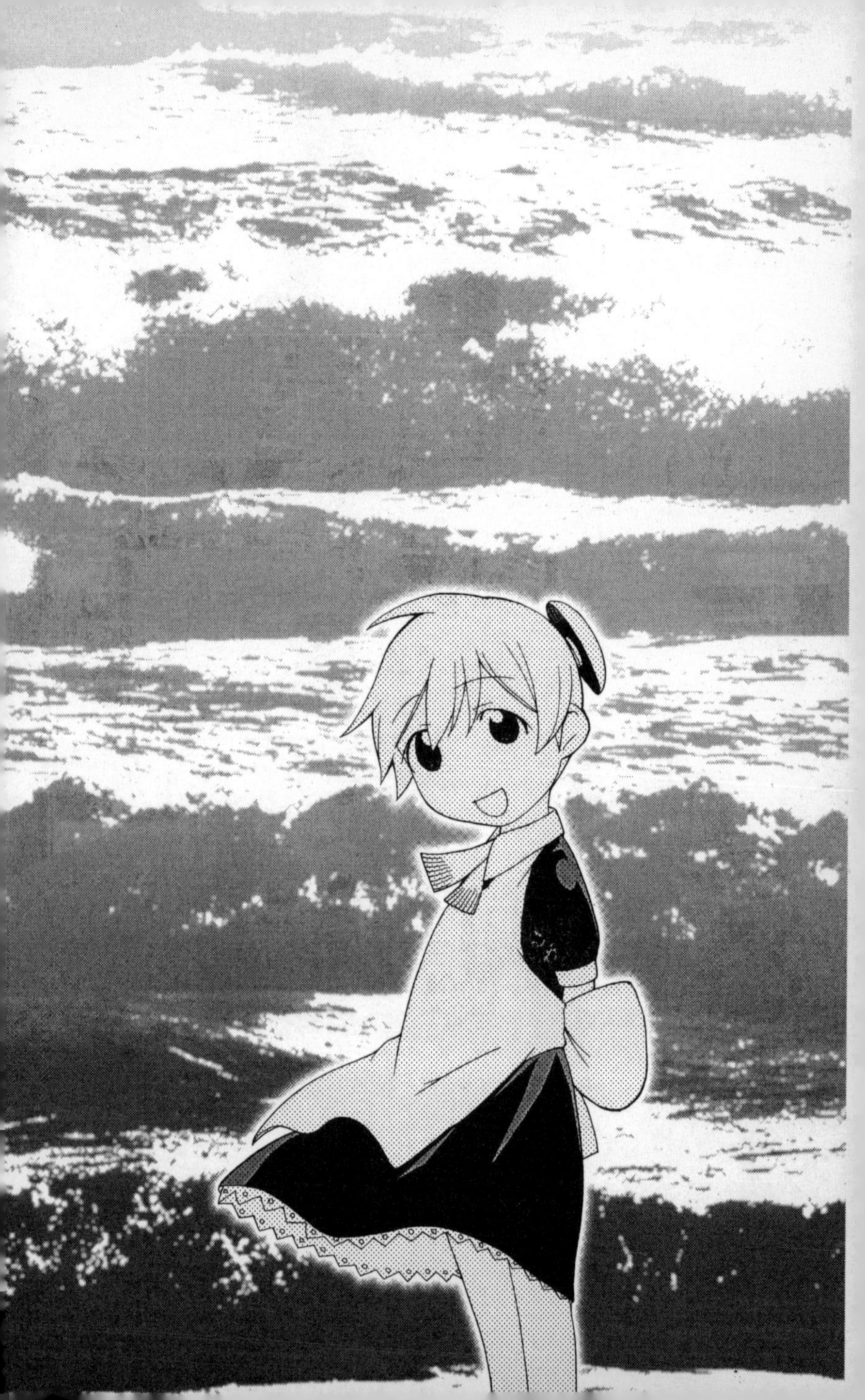

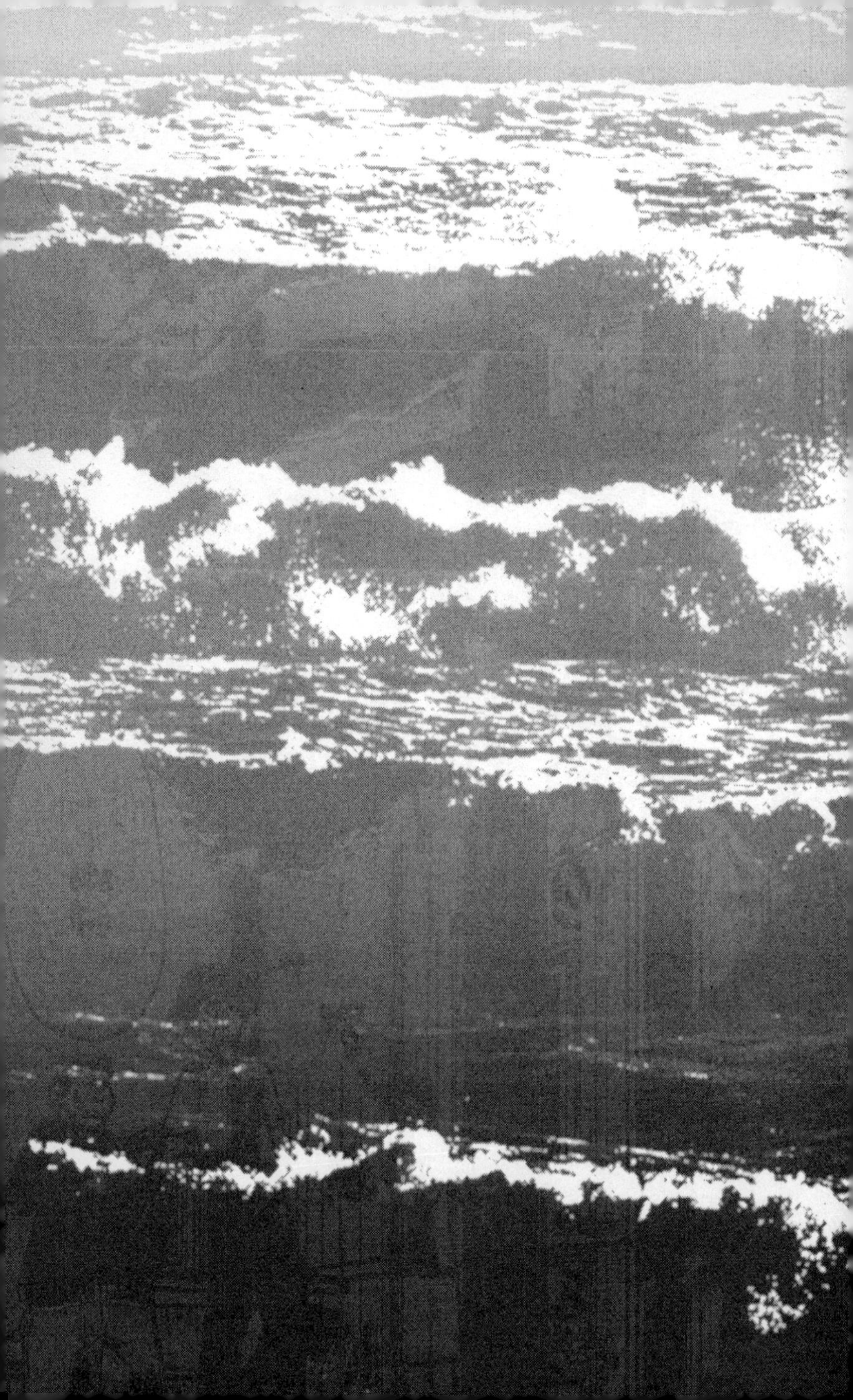

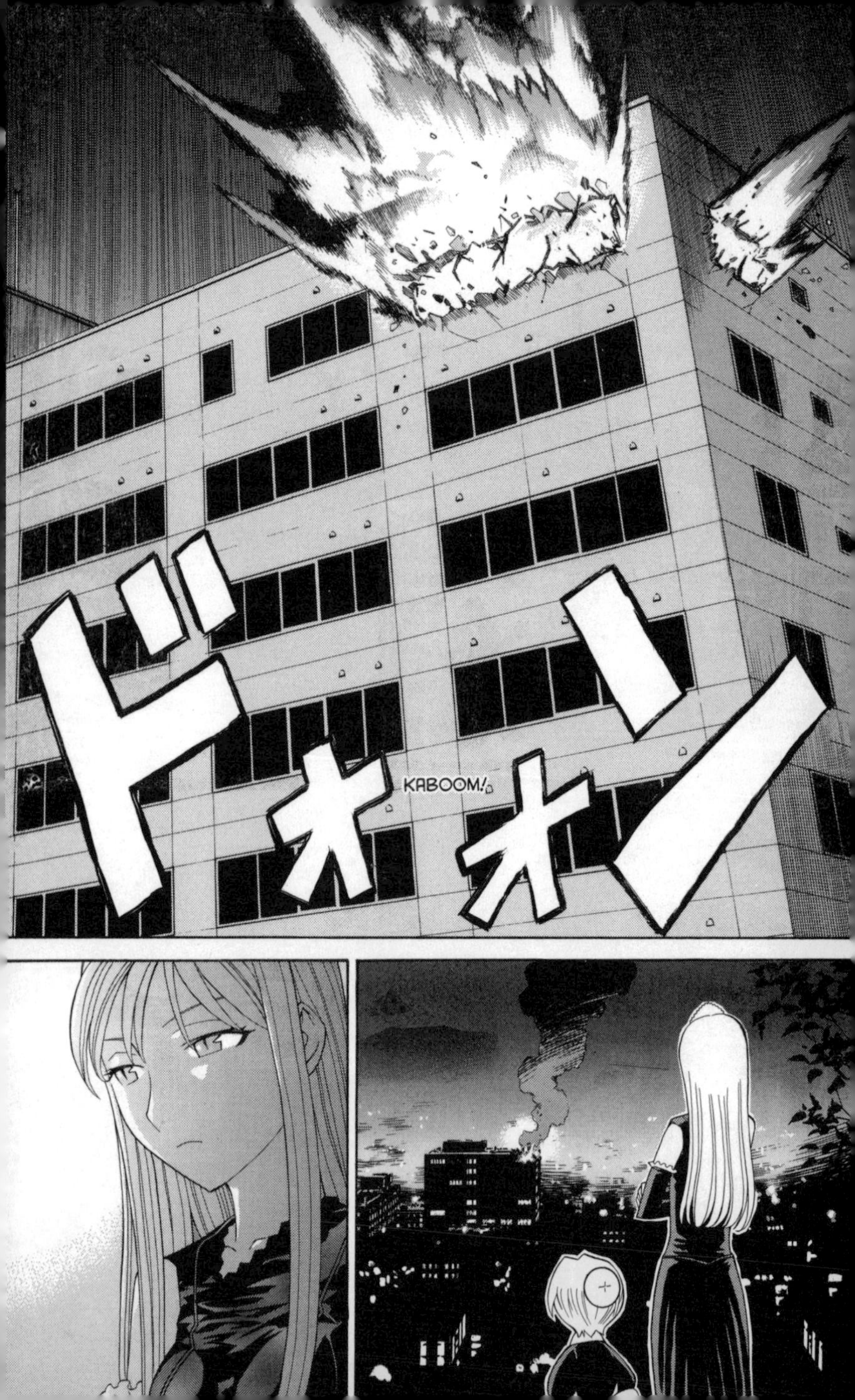
ドォォン
KABOOM!

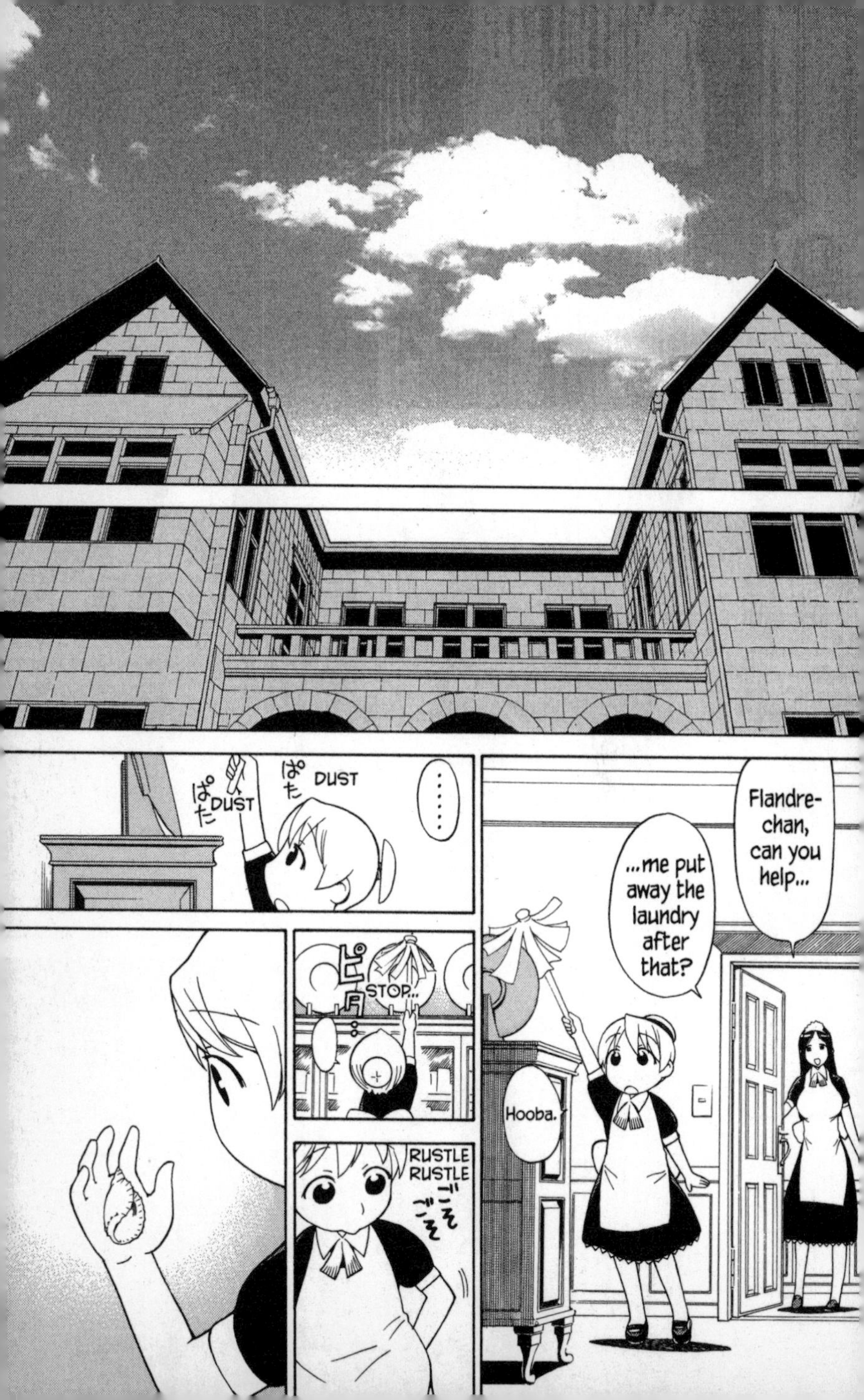

Flandre-chan, can you help...
...me put away the laundry after that?
Hooba.
......
ぱた DUST
ぱた DUST
ピタ
STOP...
RUSTLE RUSTLE
ごそごそ

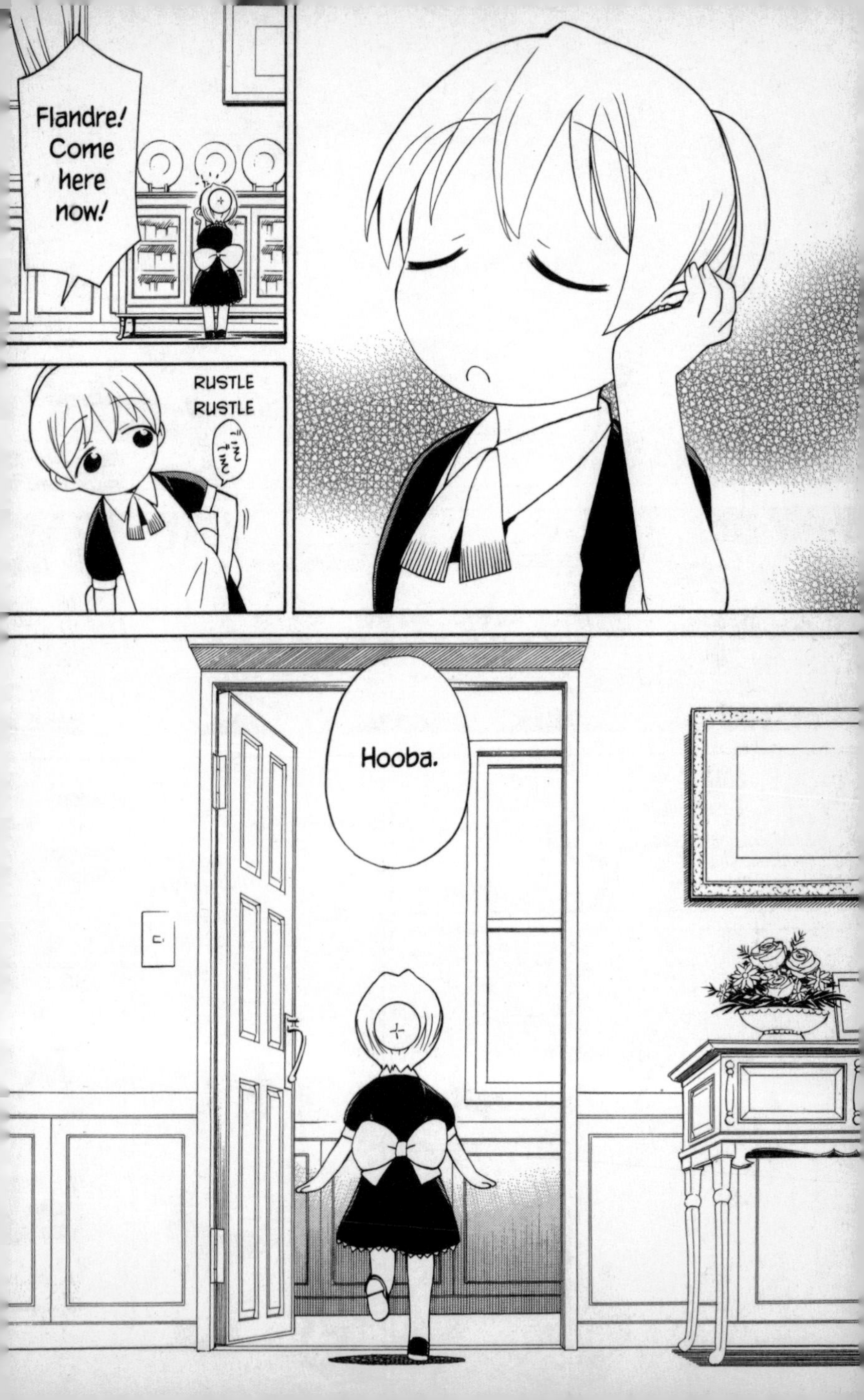
Flandre! Come here now!
RUSTLE RUSTLE
Hooba.

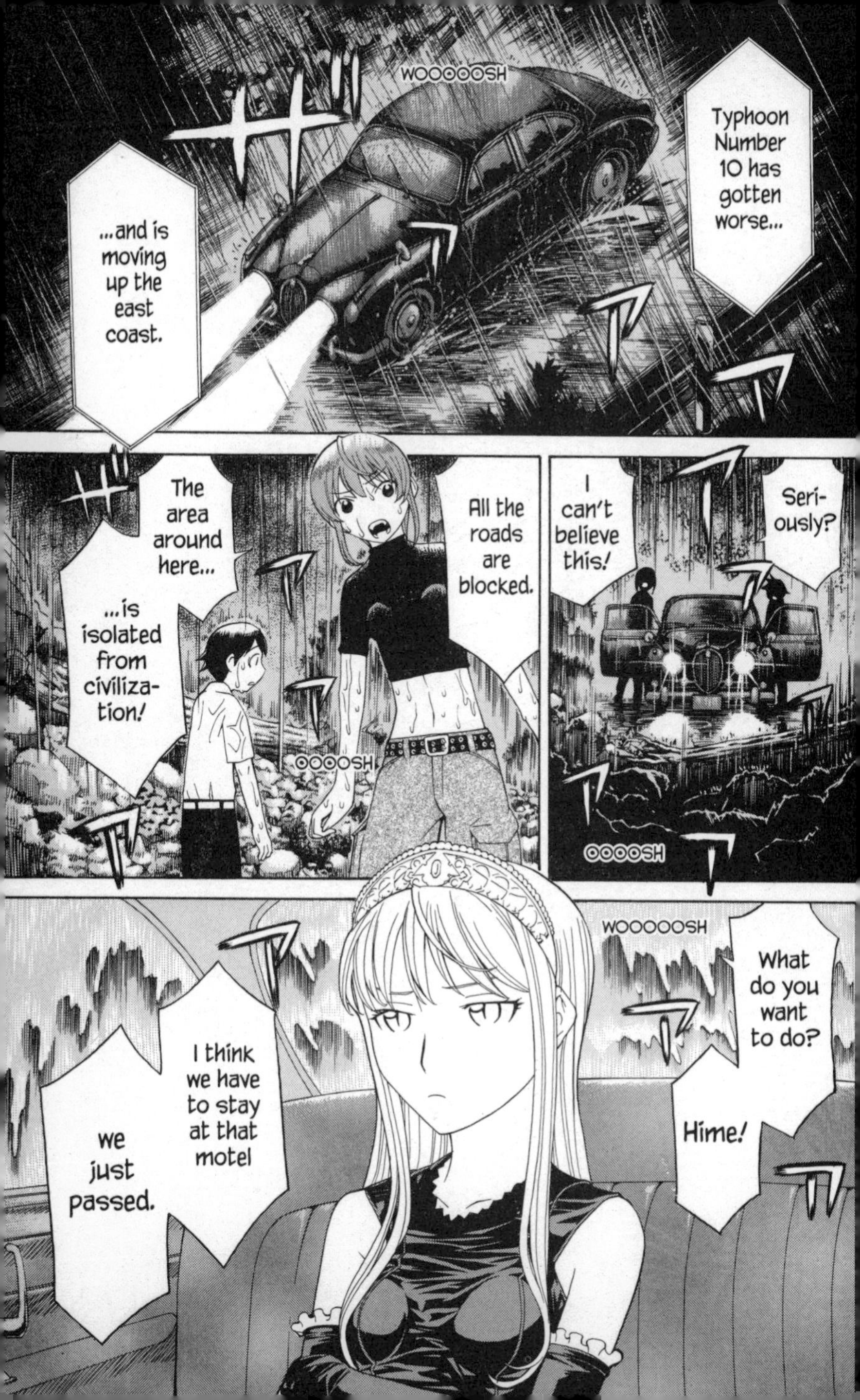
Typhoon Number 10 has gotten worse...
WOOOOOSH
...and is moving up the east coast.
Seri-ously?
I can't believe this!
OOOOSH
All the roads are blocked.
The area around here...
...is isolated from civilization!
OOOOSH
WOOOOOSH
What do you want to do?
Hime!
I think we have to stay at that motel
we just passed.

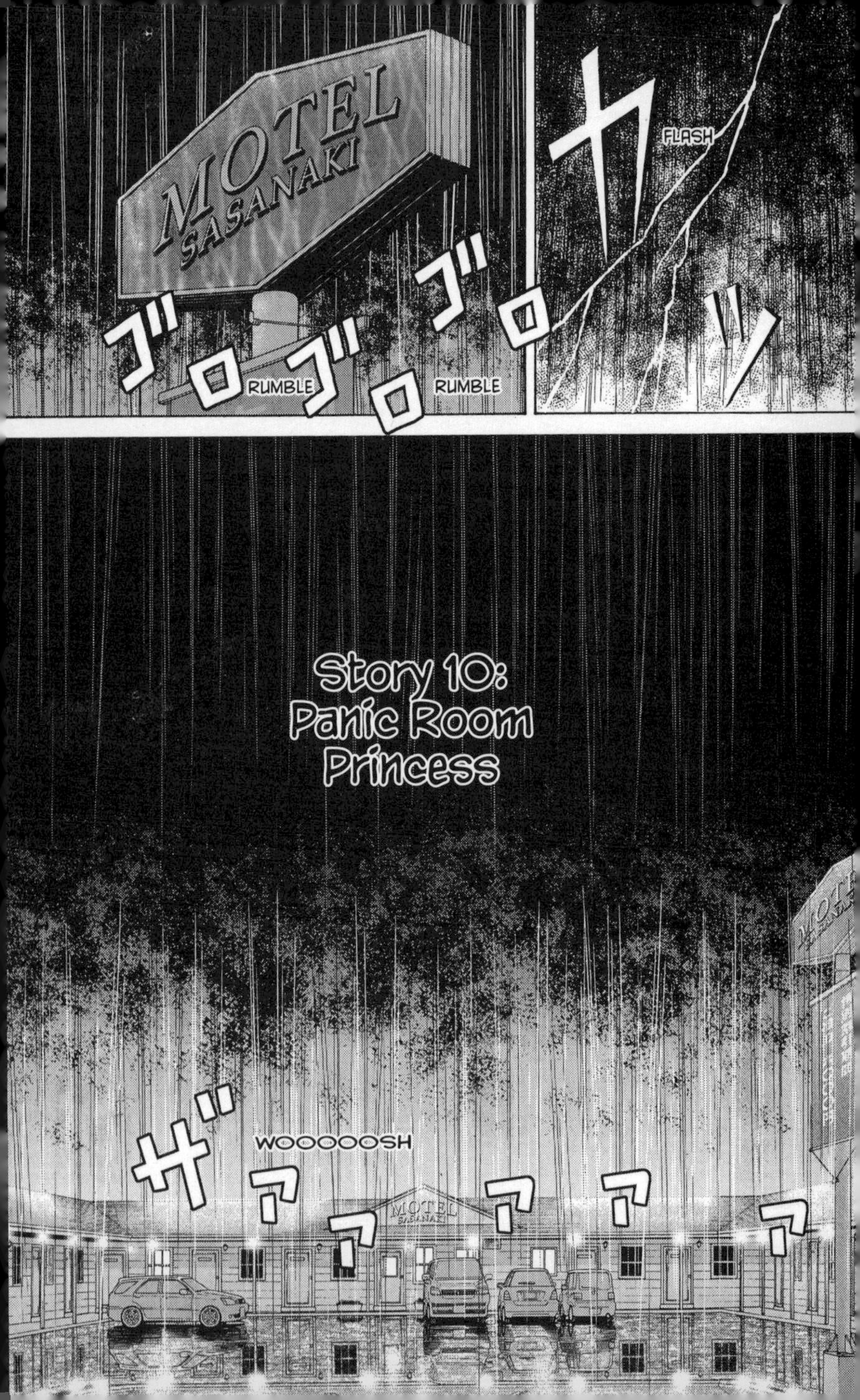
カッ
FLASH
MOTEL
SASANAKI
ゴロゴロゴロ
RUMBLE
RUMBLE
Story 10:
Panic Room
Princess
ザァァァァァ
WOOOOOSH
MOTEL
SASANAKI

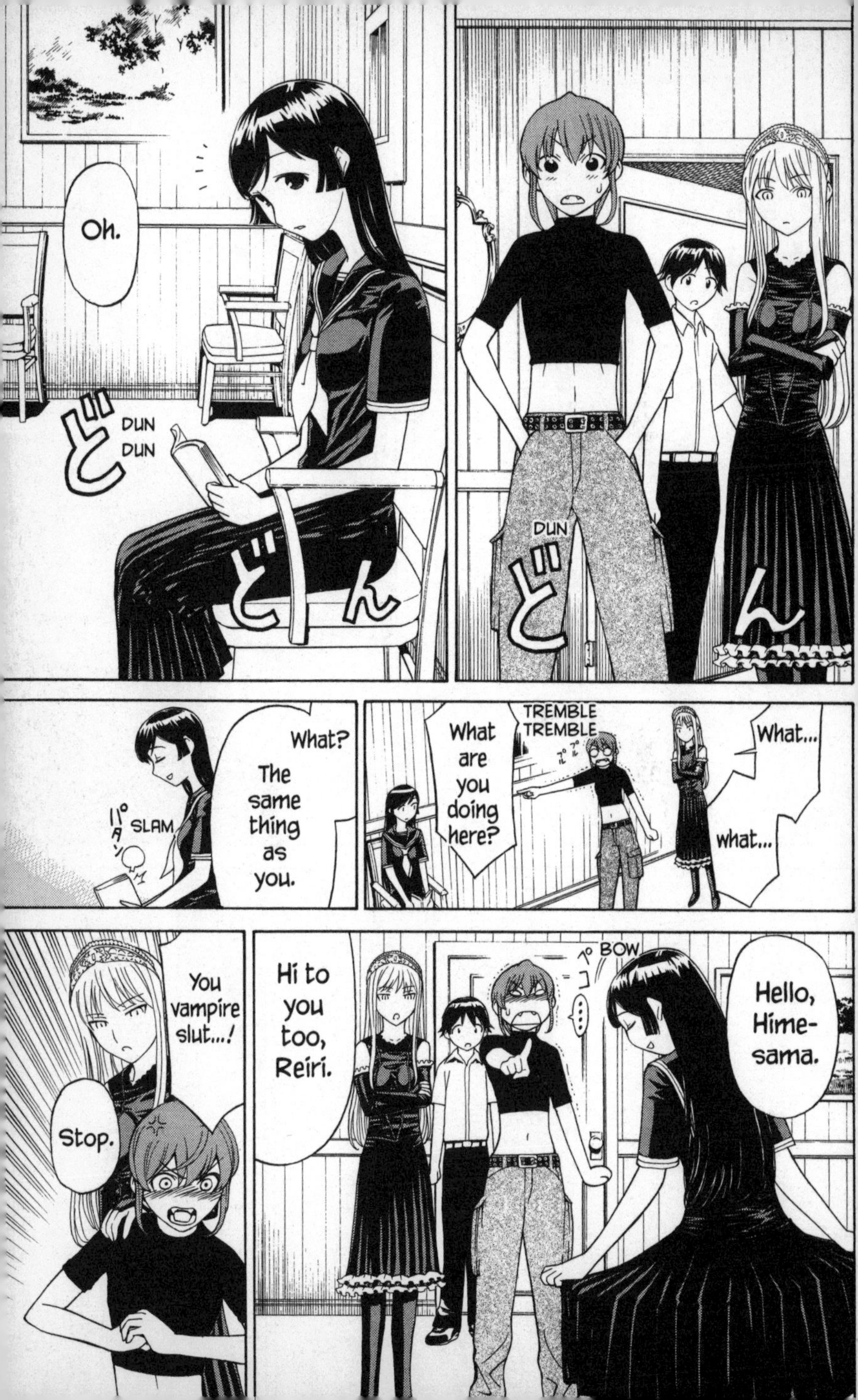
DUN
どん
Oh.
DUN DUN
どん
What...
what...
TREMBLE TREMBLE
What are you doing here?
What? The same thing as you.
SLAM
Hello, Hime-sama.
BOW
...
Hi to you too, Reiri.
You vampire slut...!
Stop.

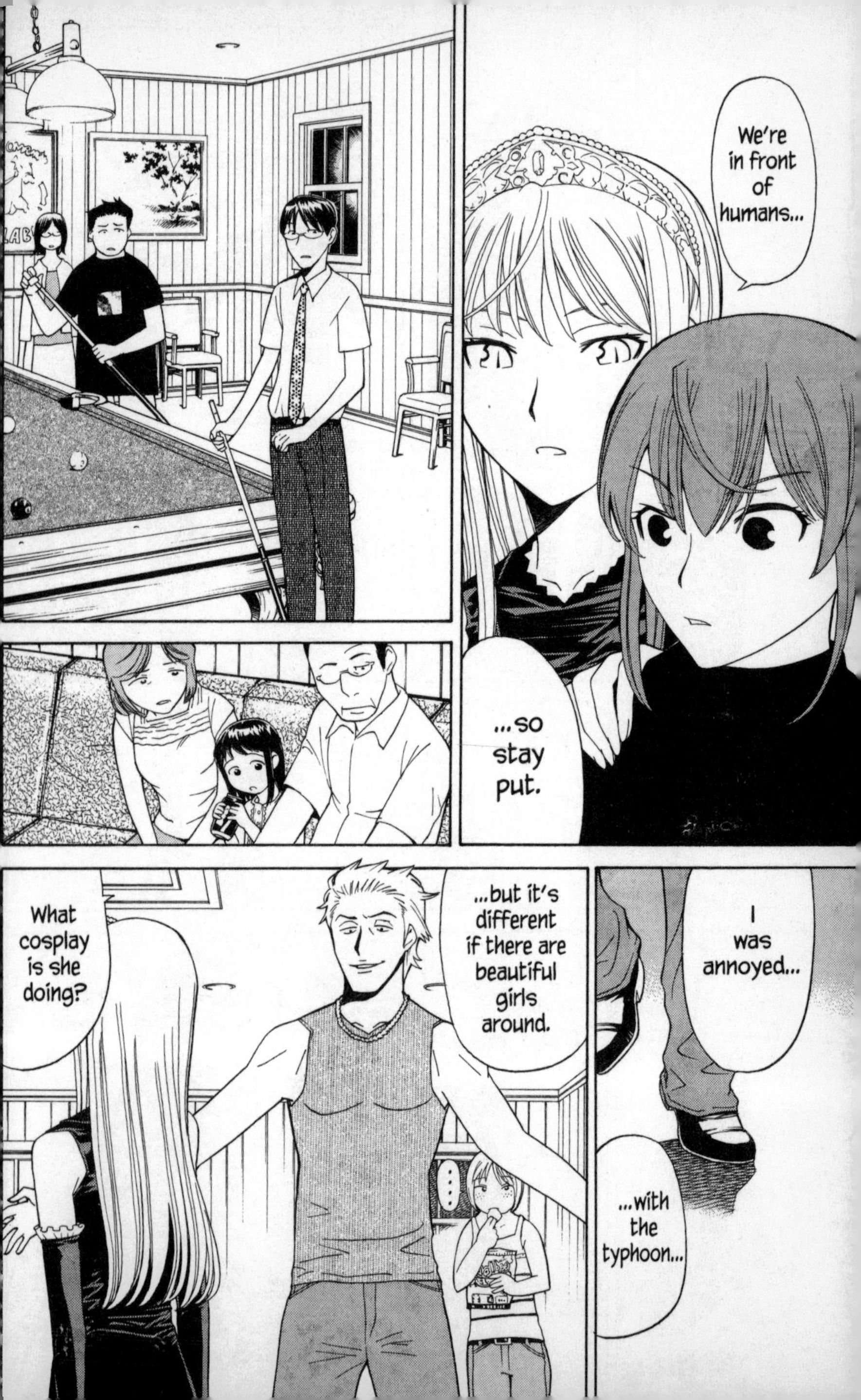
We're in front of humans...
...so stay put.
I was annoyed...
...with the typhoon...
...but it's different if there are beautiful girls around.
What cosplay is she doing?
...

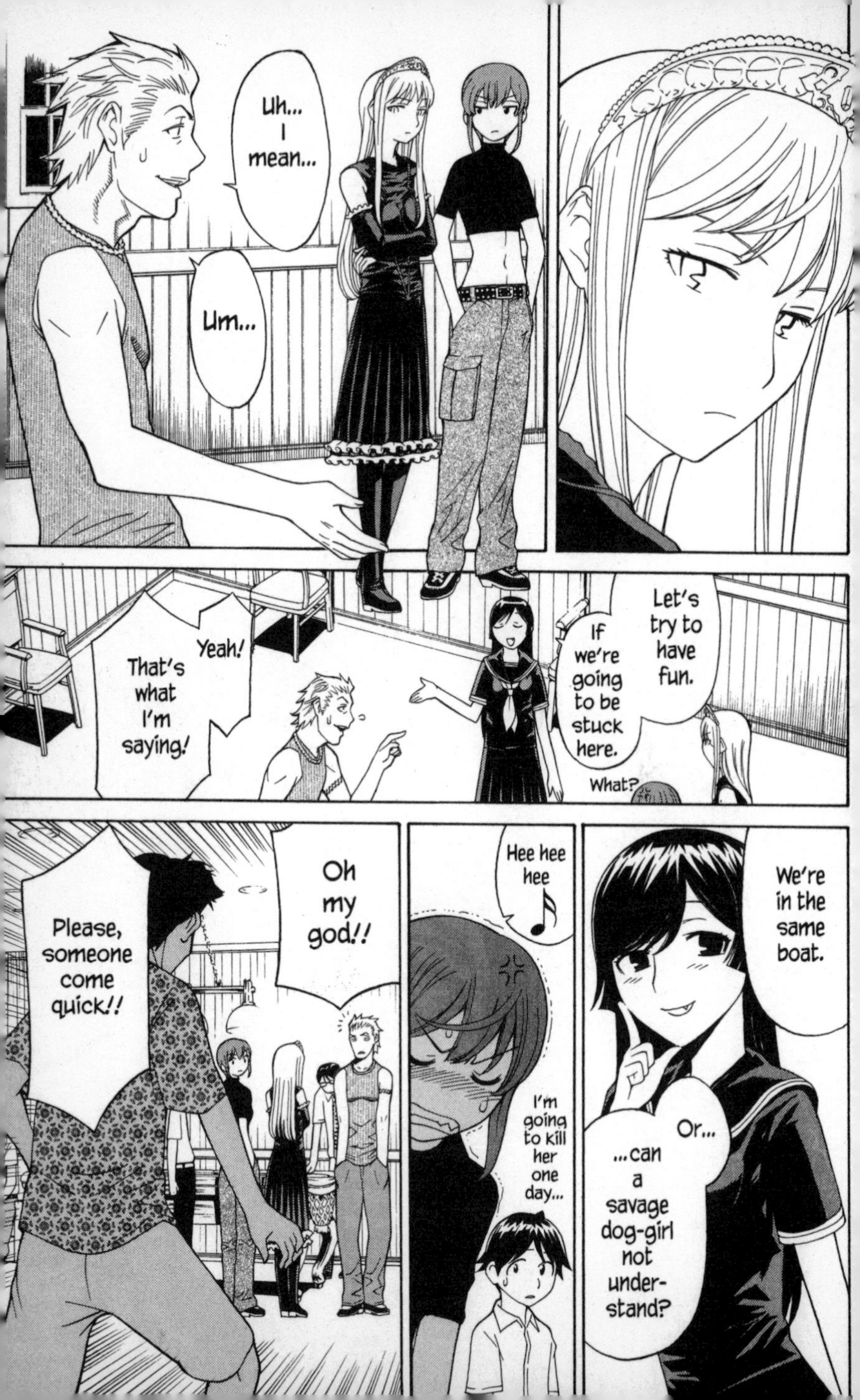
Uh... I mean...
Um...
Let's try to have fun.
If we're going to be stuck here.
What?
Yeah! That's what I'm saying!
We're in the same boat.
Or...
...can a savage dog-girl not understand?
Hee hee hee ♪
I'm going to kill her one day...
Oh my god!!
Please, someone come quick!!

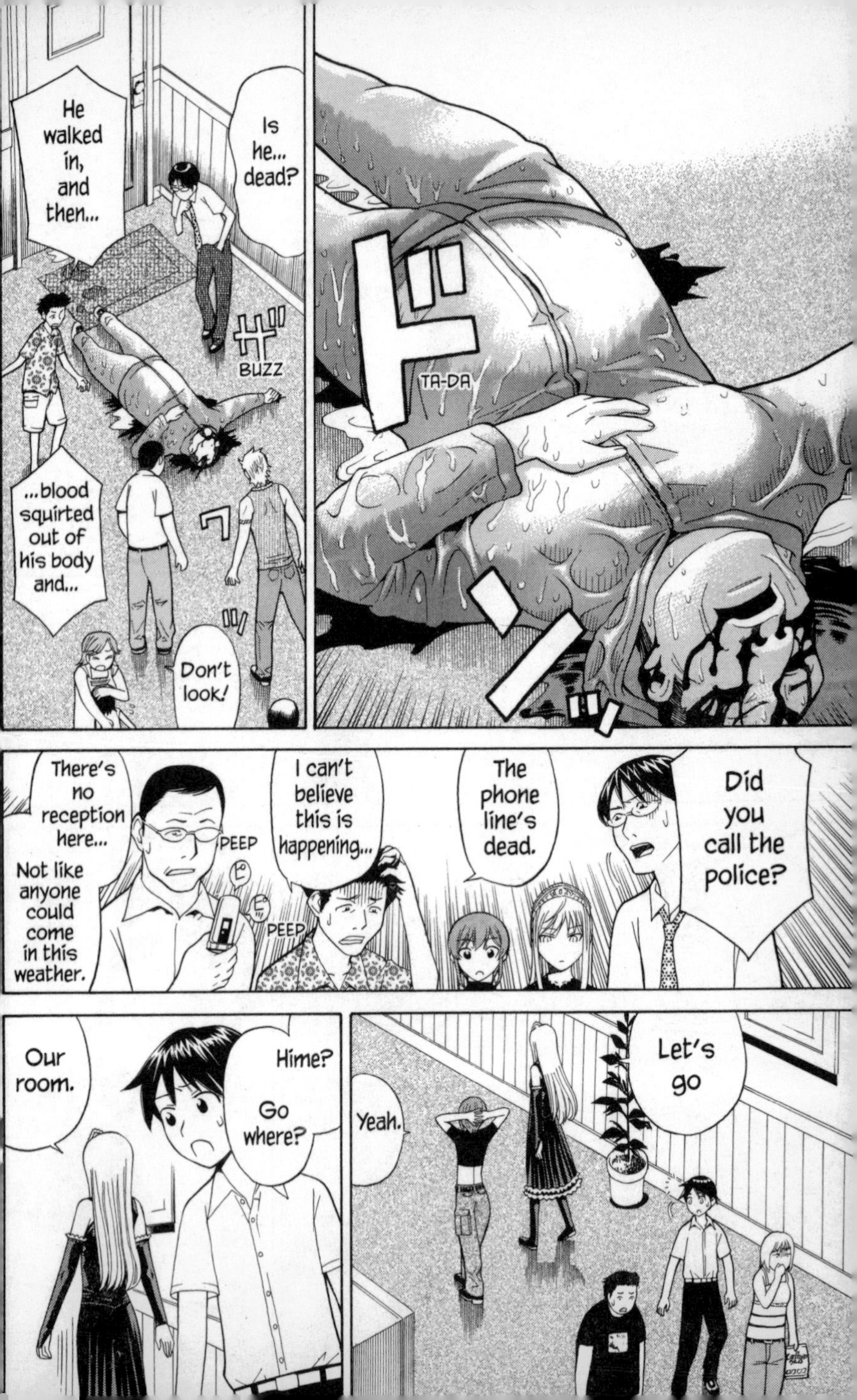
TA-DA
Is he... dead?
He walked in, and then...
BUZZ
...blood squirted out of his body and...
Don't look!
Did you call the police?
The phone line's dead.
I can't believe this is happening...
PEEP
PEEP
There's no reception here...
Not like anyone could come in this weather.
Let's go
Yeah.
Hime?
Go where?
Our room.

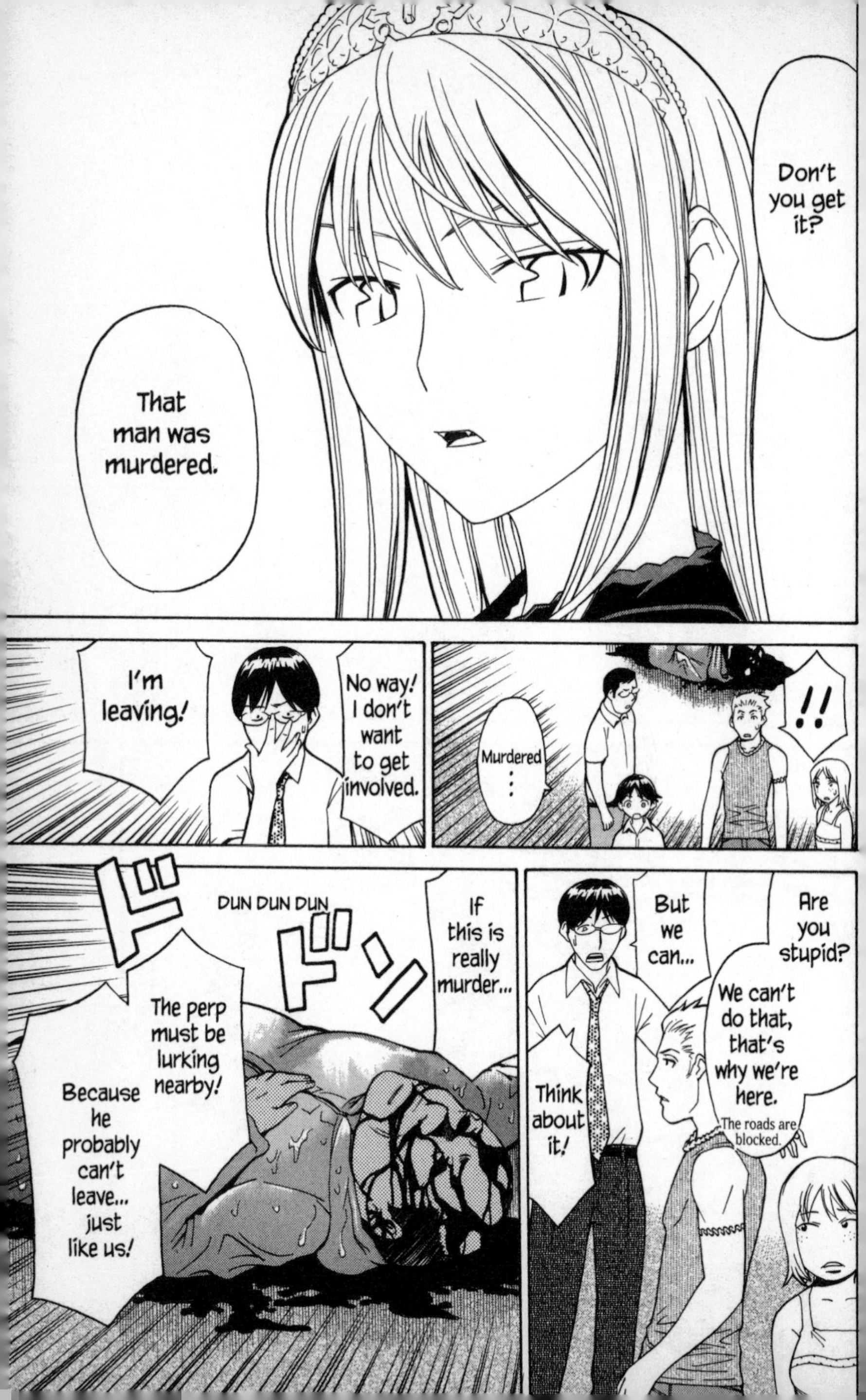
Don't you get it?
That man was murdered.
!!
Murdered...
No way! I don't want to get involved.
I'm leaving!
Are you stupid?
But we can...
We can't do that, that's why we're here.
The roads are blocked.
Think about it!
If this is really murder...
ドドン
DUN DUN DUN
The perp must be lurking nearby!
Because he probably can't leave... just like us!

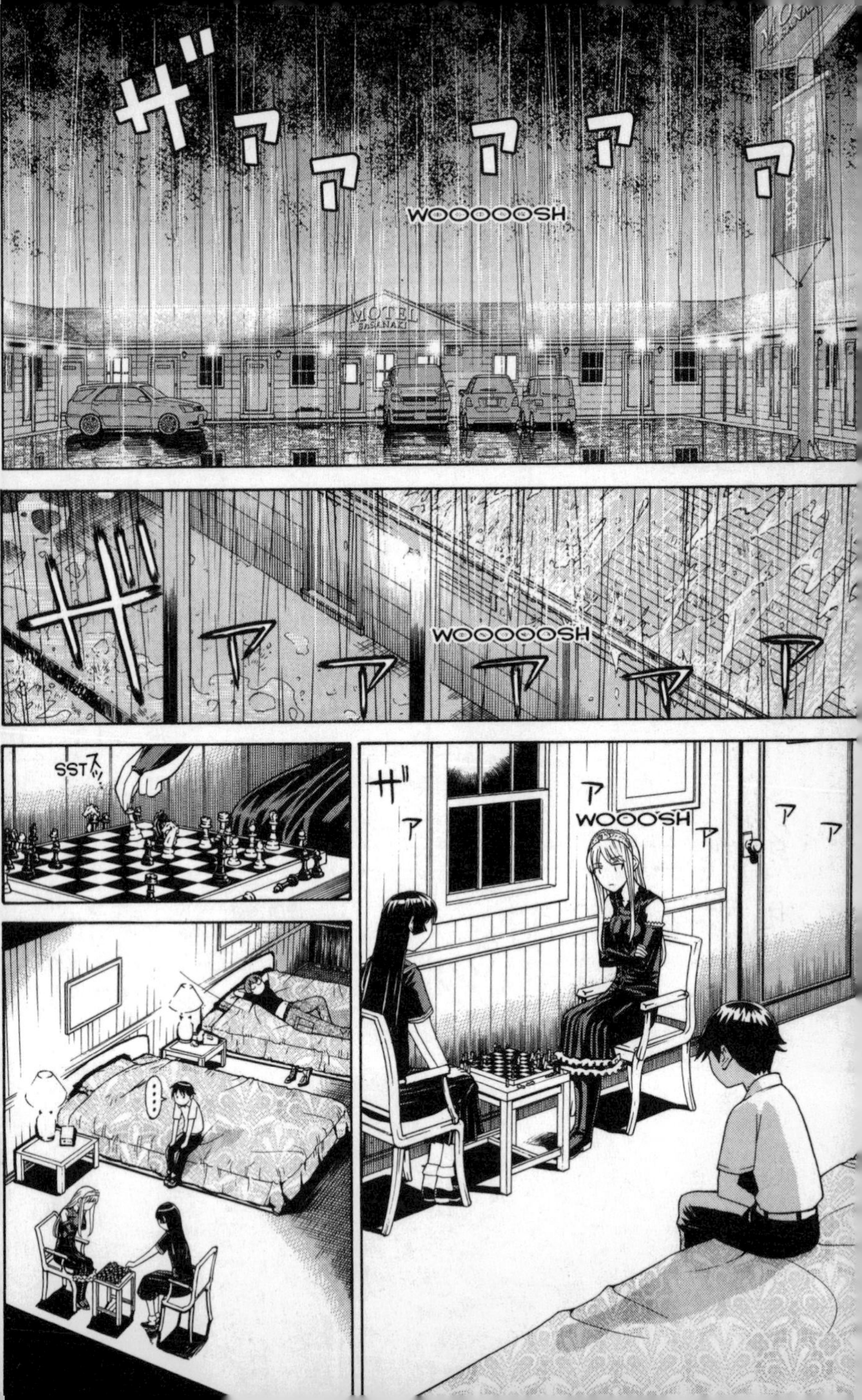

ザアアアア
WOOOOOSH
ザァァァァァ
WOOOOOSH
ザァァァァァ
WOOOSH
SST スッ
…

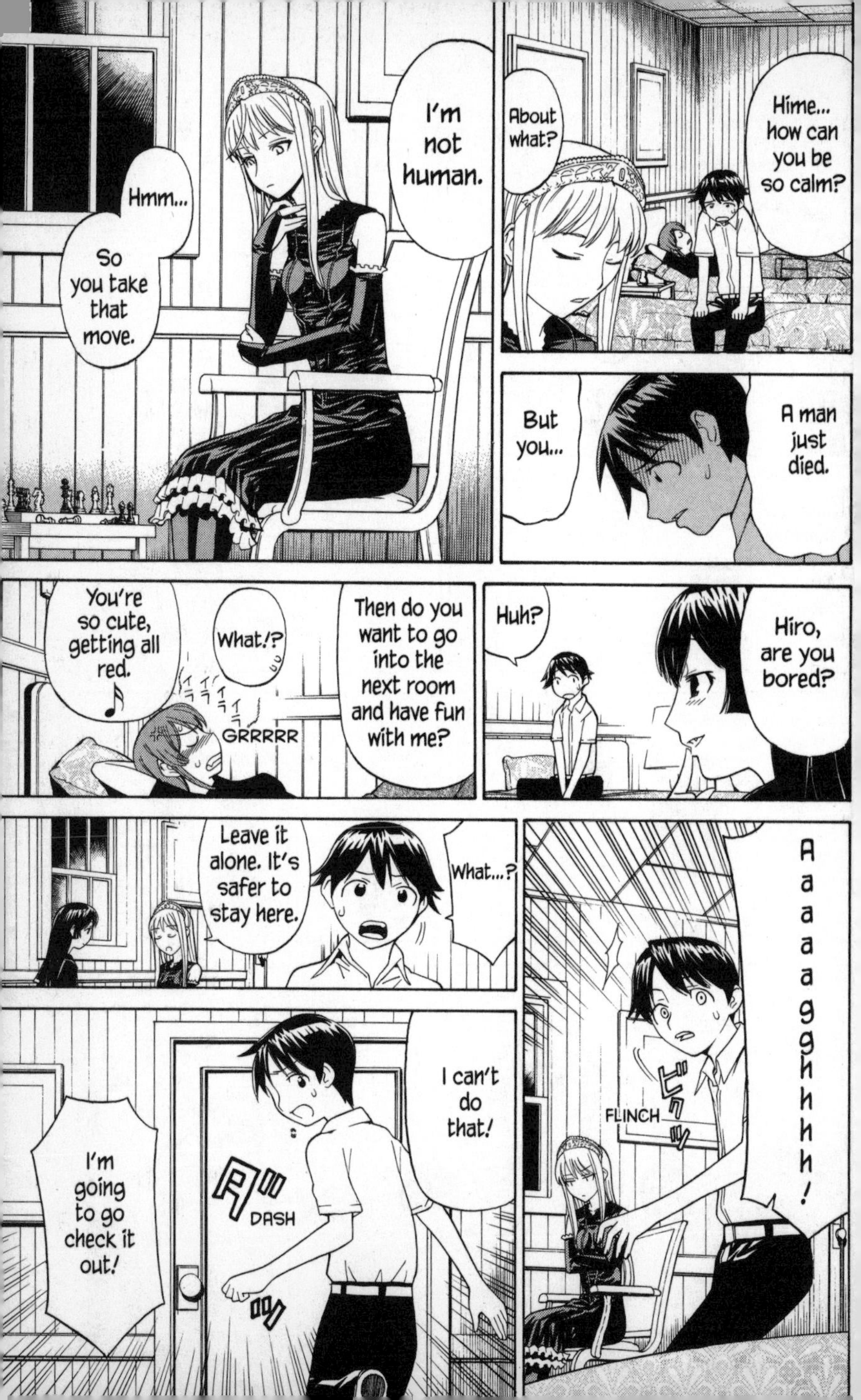
Hime... how can you be so calm?
About what?
A man just died.
But you...
I'm not human.
Hmm...
So you take that move.
Hiro, are you bored?
Huh?
Then do you want to go into the next room and have fun with me?
What!?
GRRRRR
You're so cute, getting all red. ♪
Aaaaaagghhhh!
FLINCH
What...?
Leave it alone. It's safer to stay here.
I can't do that!
DASH
I'm going to go check it out!

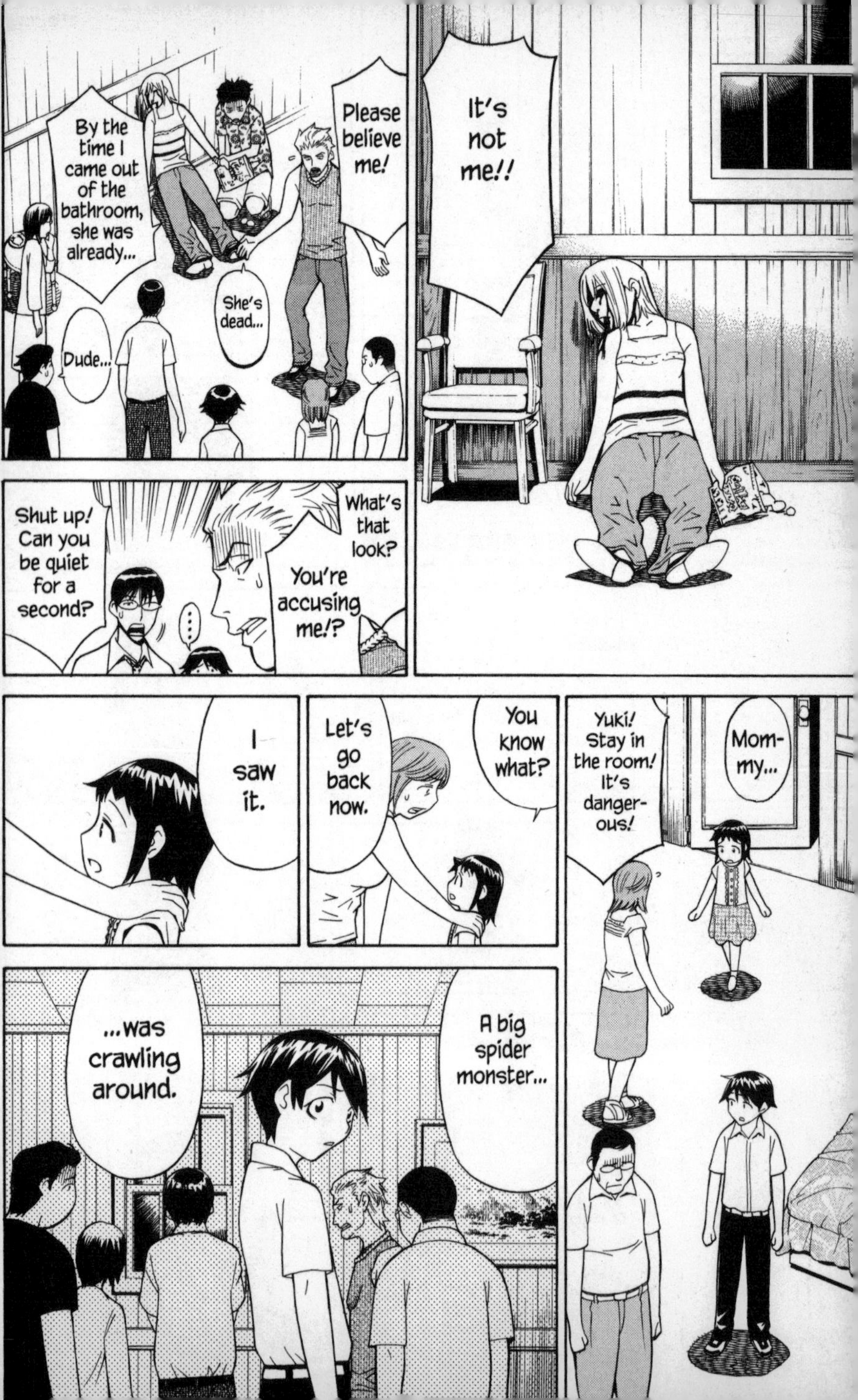

It's not me!!
Please believe me!
By the time I came out of the bathroom, she was already...
She's dead...
Dude...
What's that look?
You're accusing me!?
...
Shut up! Can you be quiet for a second?
Mom-my...
Yuki! Stay in the room! It's danger-ous!
You know what?
Let's go back now.
I— saw it.
A big spider monster...
...was crawling around.

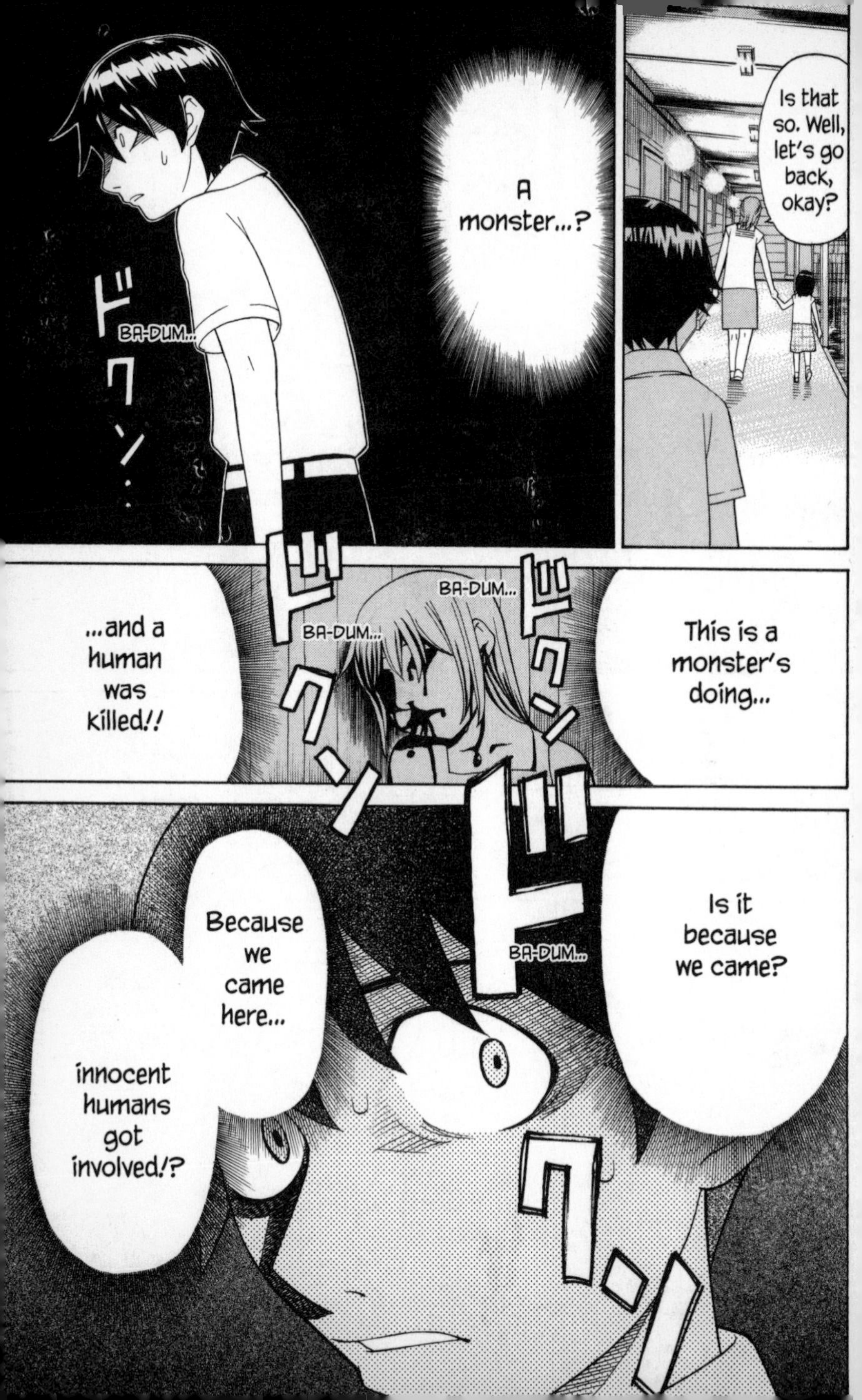
Is that so. Well, let's go back, okay?
A monster...?
ドクン…
BA-DUM...
This is a monster's doing...
ドクン
BA-DUM...
ドクン
BA-DUM...
...and a human was killed!!
Is it because we came?
ドクン
BA-DUM...
Because we came here...
innocent humans got involved!?

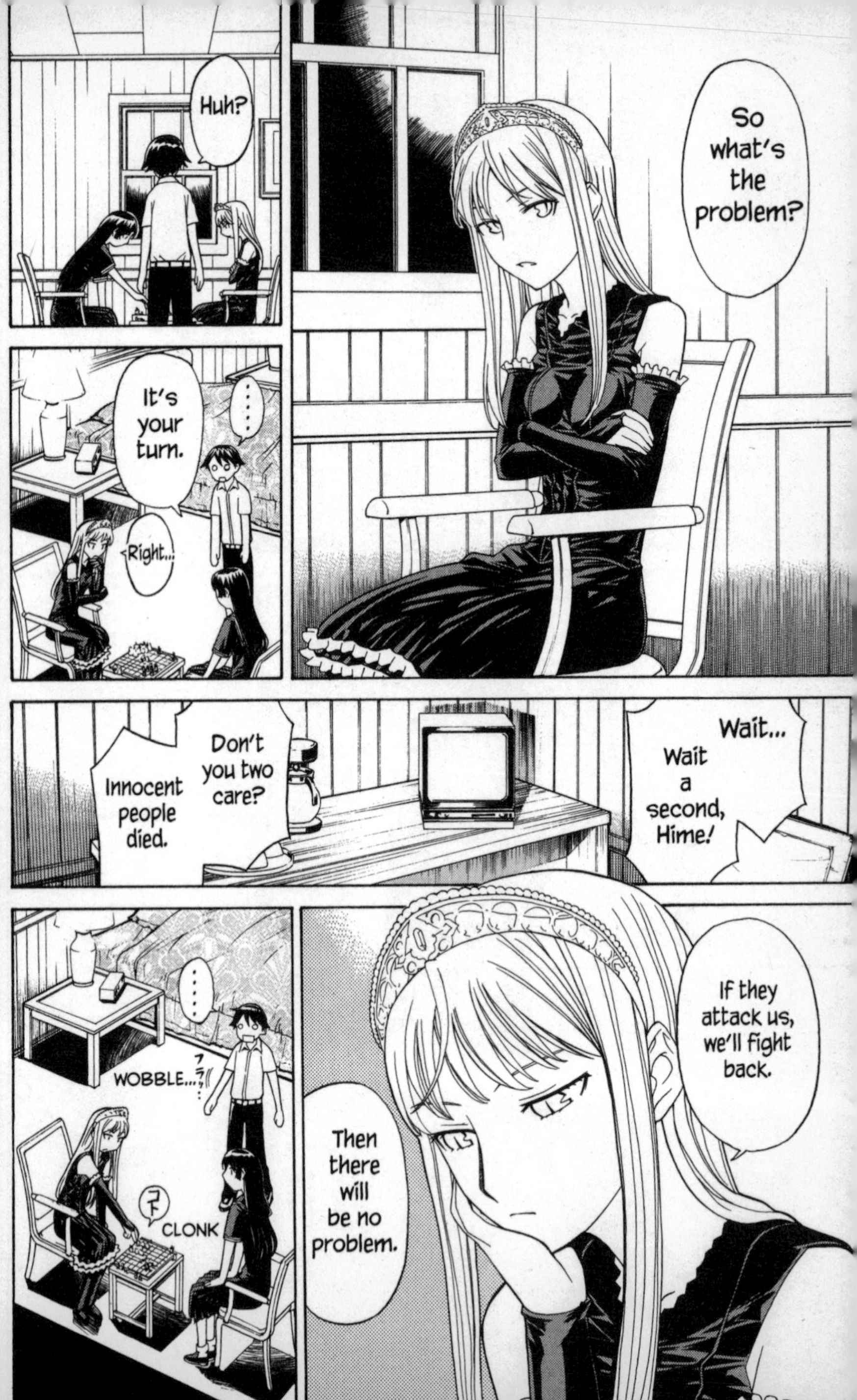
So what's the problem?
Huh?
.....
It's your turn.
Right...
Wait...
Wait a second, Hime!
Don't you two care?
Innocent people died.
If they attack us, we'll fight back.
Then there will be no problem.
.....
WOBBLE...
CLONK

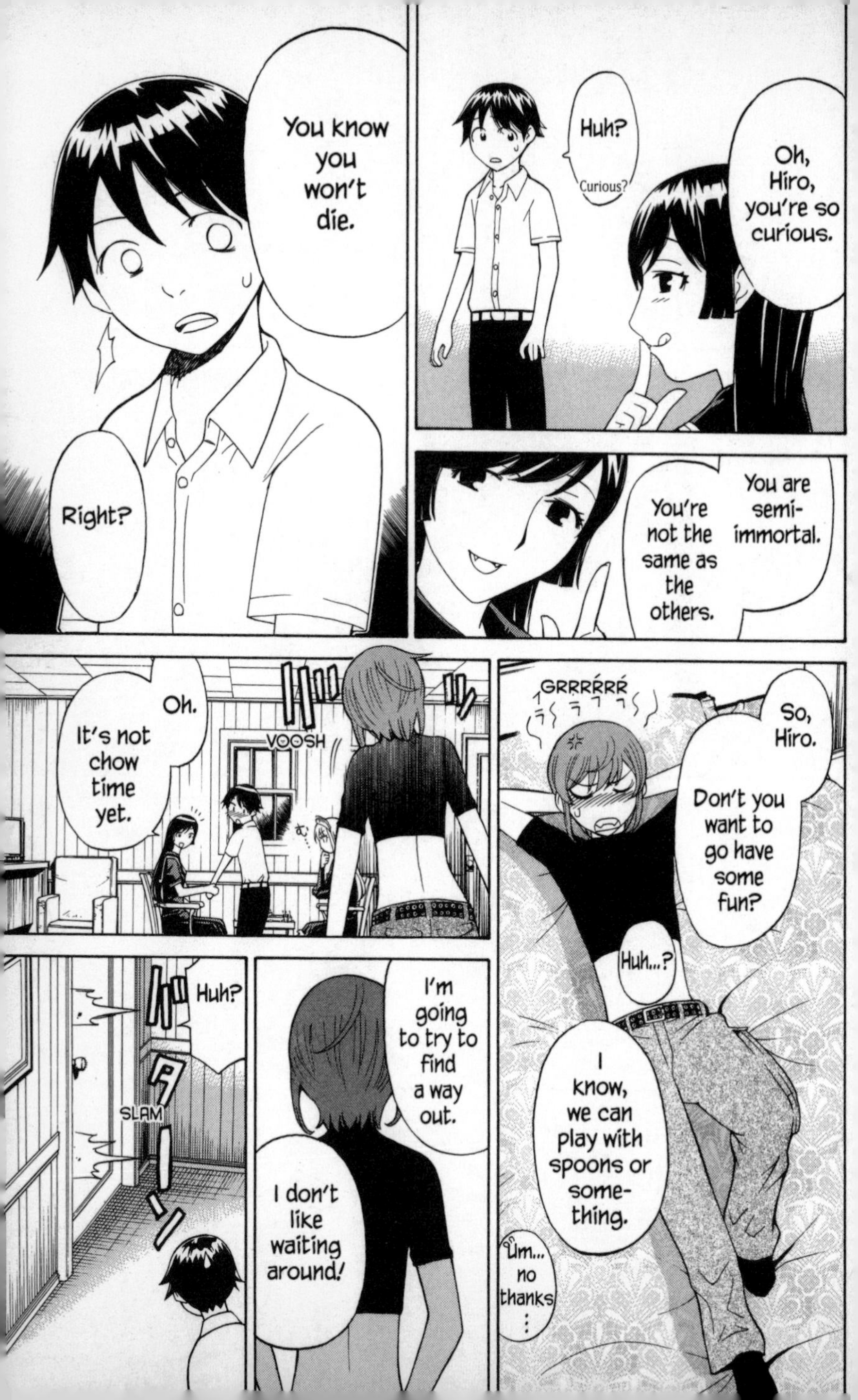

Oh, Hiro, you're so curious.
Huh?
Curious?
You are semi-immortal.
You're not the same as the others.
You know you won't die.
Right?
GRRRRR
So, Hiro.
Don't you want to go have some fun?
Huh...?
I know, we can play with spoons or something.
Um... no thanks...
Oh. It's not chow time yet.
VOOSH
I'm going to try to find a way out.
I don't like waiting around!
Huh?
SLAM

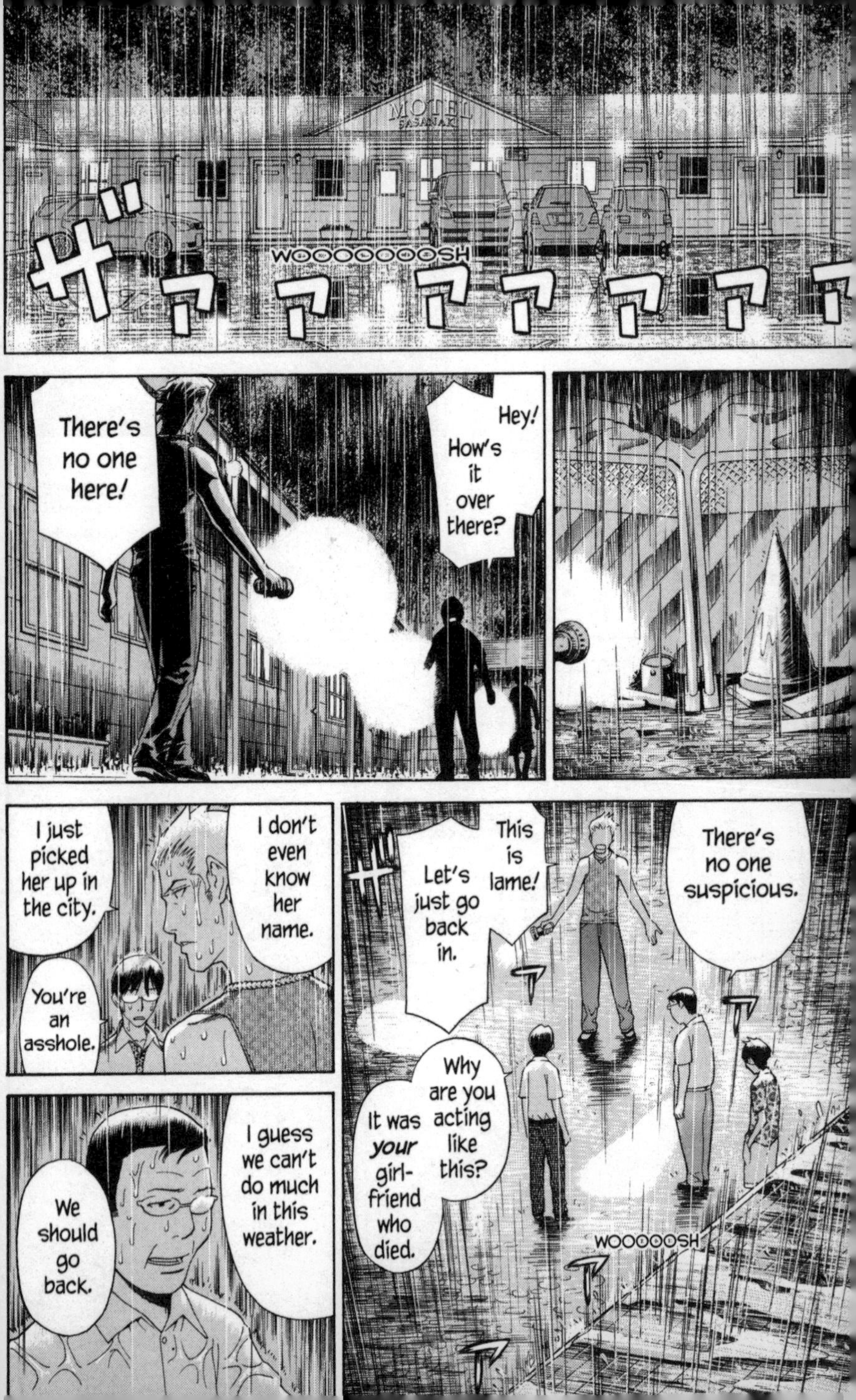
MOTEL
SASANAKI
WOOOOOOOOSH
ザァァァァァ
Hey! How's it over there?
There's no one here!
There's no one suspicious.
This is lame!
Let's just go back in.
Why are you acting like this?
It was *your* girlfriend who died.
WOOOOOSH
I don't even know her name.
I just picked her up in the city.
You're an asshole.
I guess we can't do much in this weather.
We should go back.

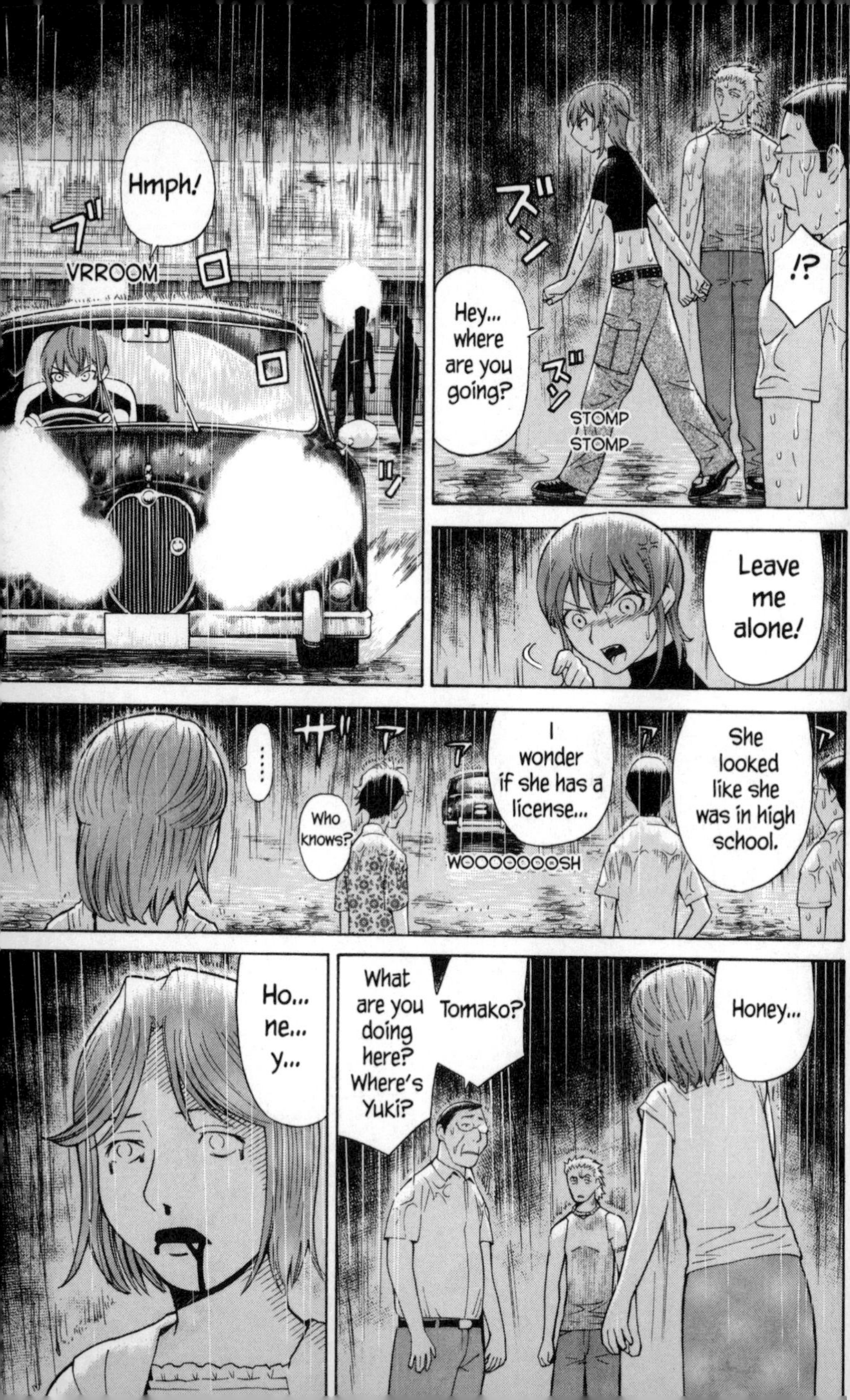

!?
Hey... where are you going?
STOMP STOMP
Leave me alone!
Hmph!
VRROOM
She looked like she was in high school.
I wonder if she has a license...
WOOOOOOOOSH
Who knows?
......
Honey...
Tomako?
What are you doing here? Where's Yuki?
Ho... ne... y...

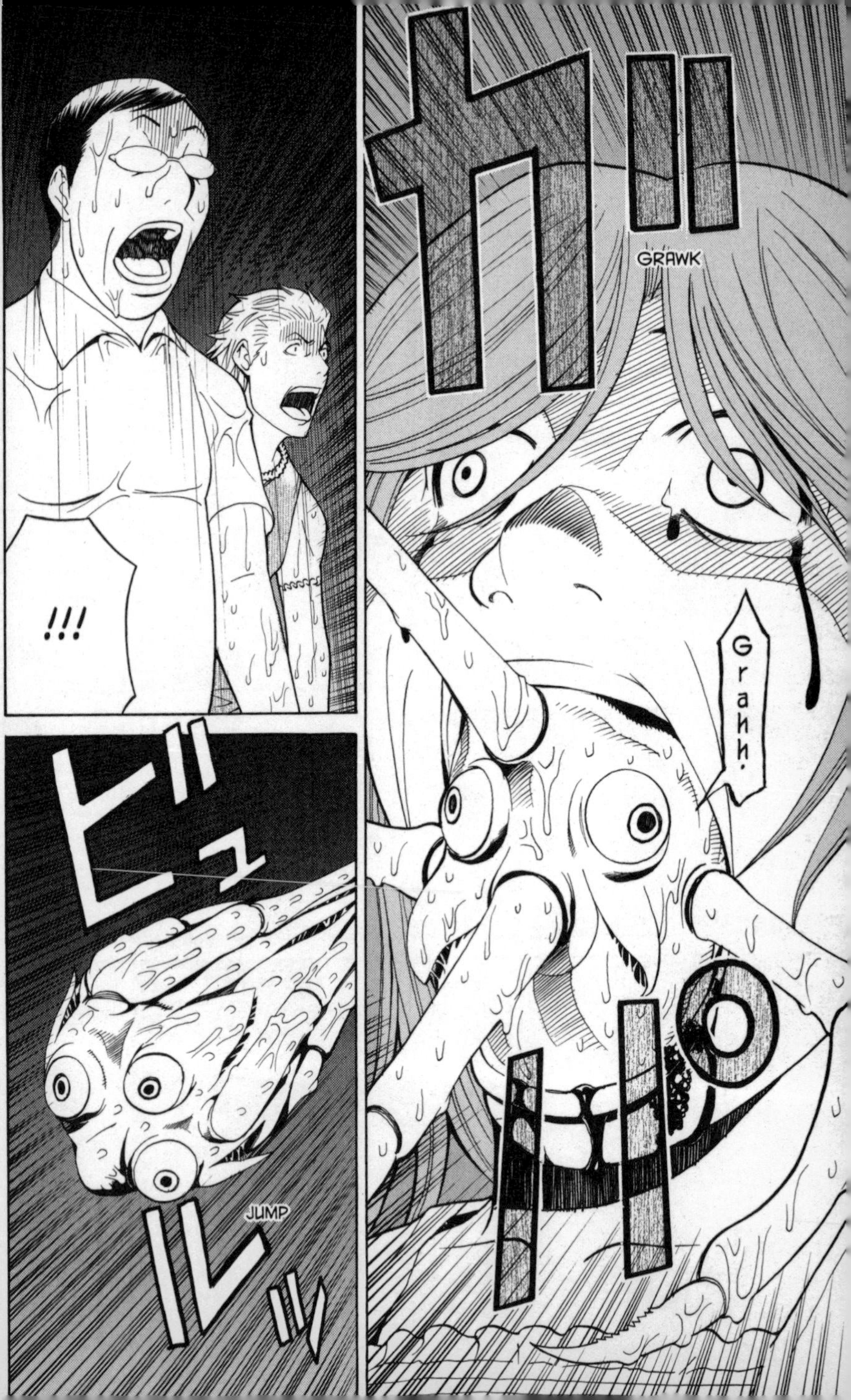
GRAWK
Granh.
!!!
JUMP

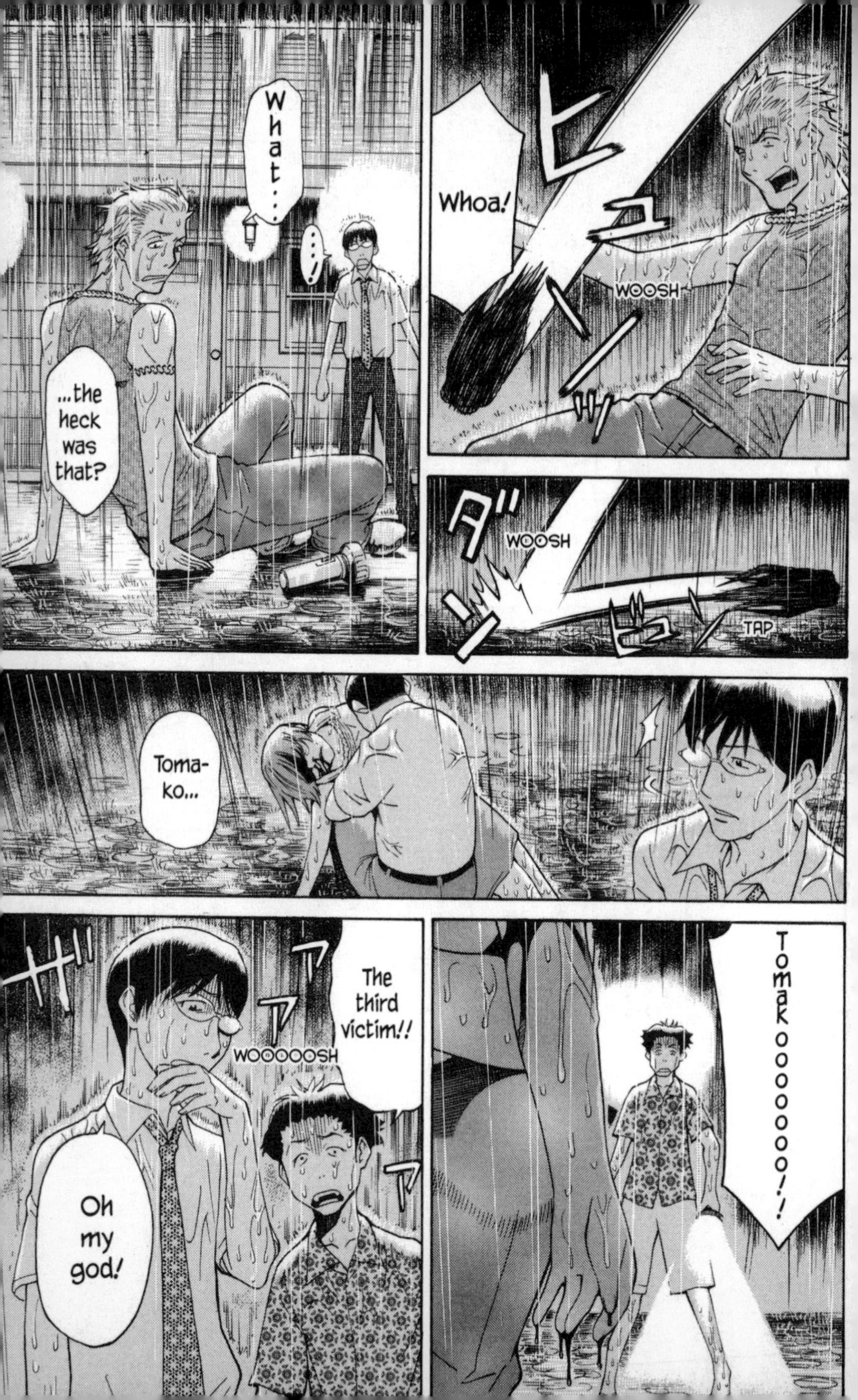

Whoa!
WOOSH
WOOSH
TAP
What...
...!
...the heck was that?
Tomako...
Tomakoooooooo!!
The third victim!!
WOOOOOSH
Oh my god!

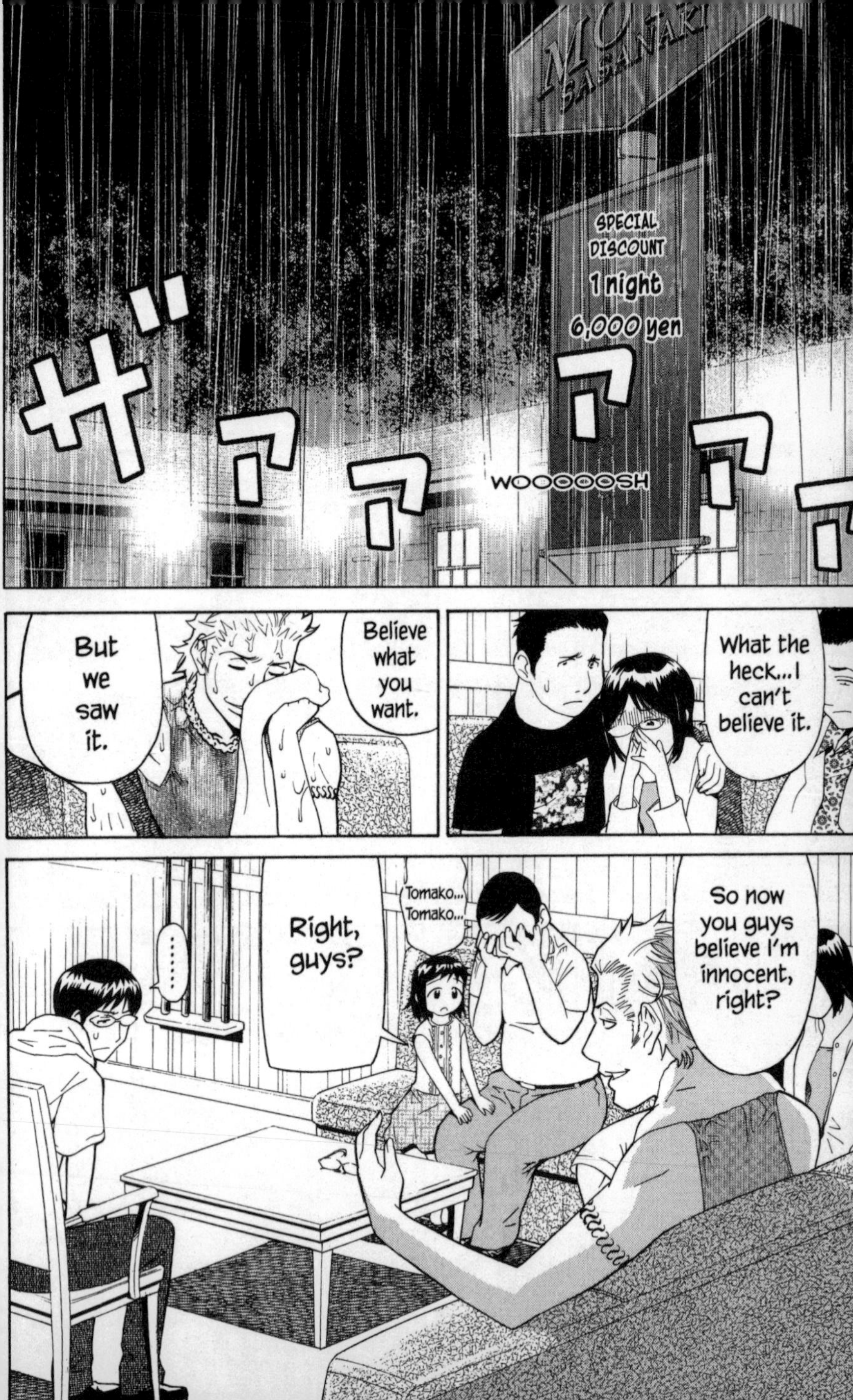
SPECIAL DISCOUNT
1 night
6,000 yen
ザァァァァ
WOOOOOOSH
What the heck...I can't believe it.
Believe what you want.
But we saw it.
So now you guys believe I'm innocent, right?
Tomako... Tomako...
Right, guys?
......

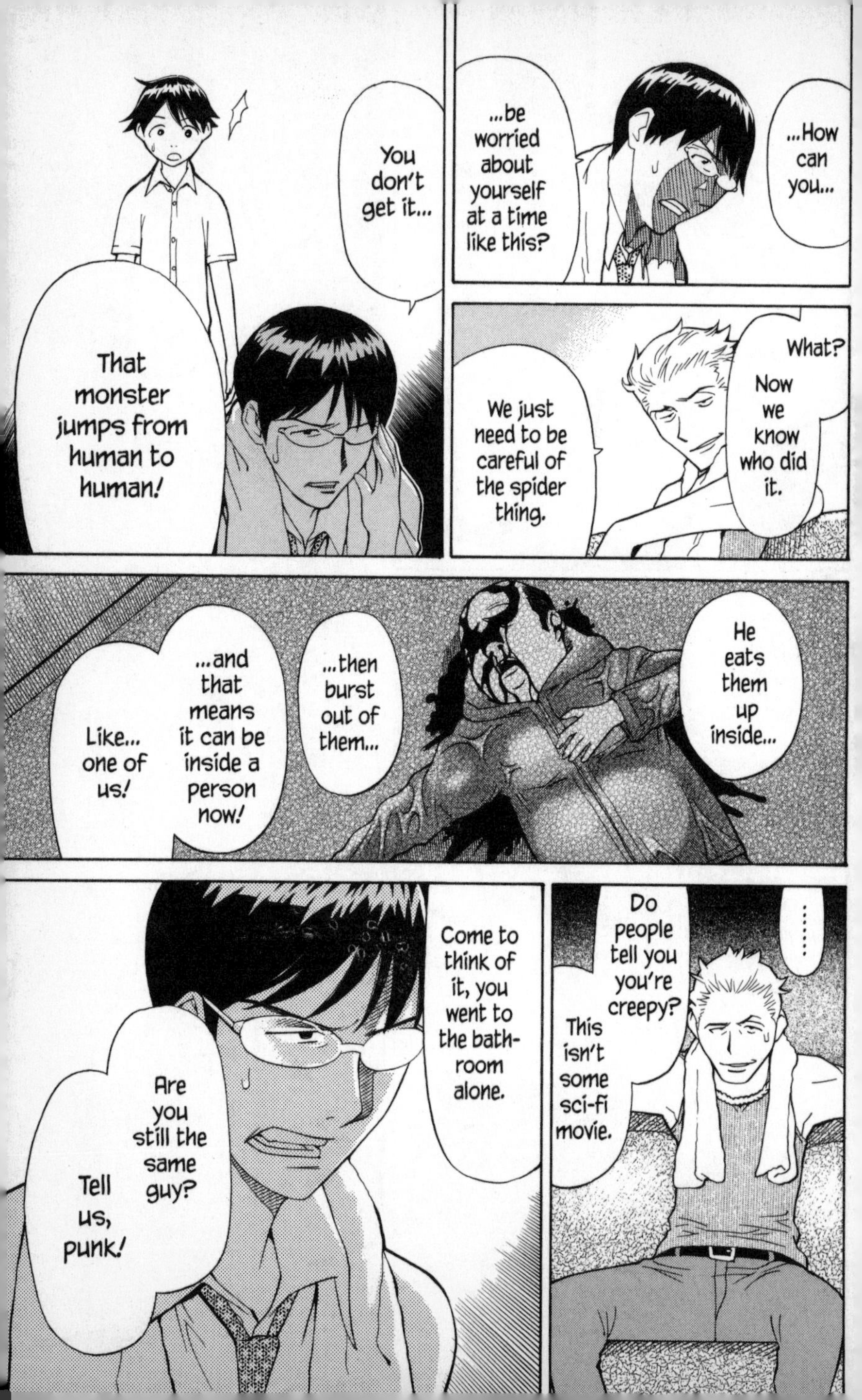
...How can you...
...be worried about yourself at a time like this?
What?
Now we know who did it.
We just need to be careful of the spider thing.
You don't get it...
That monster jumps from human to human!
He eats them up inside...
...then burst out of them...
...and that means it can be inside a person now!
Like... one of us!
......
Do people tell you you're creepy?
This isn't some sci-fi movie.
Come to think of it, you went to the bathroom alone.
Are you still the same guy?
Tell us, punk!

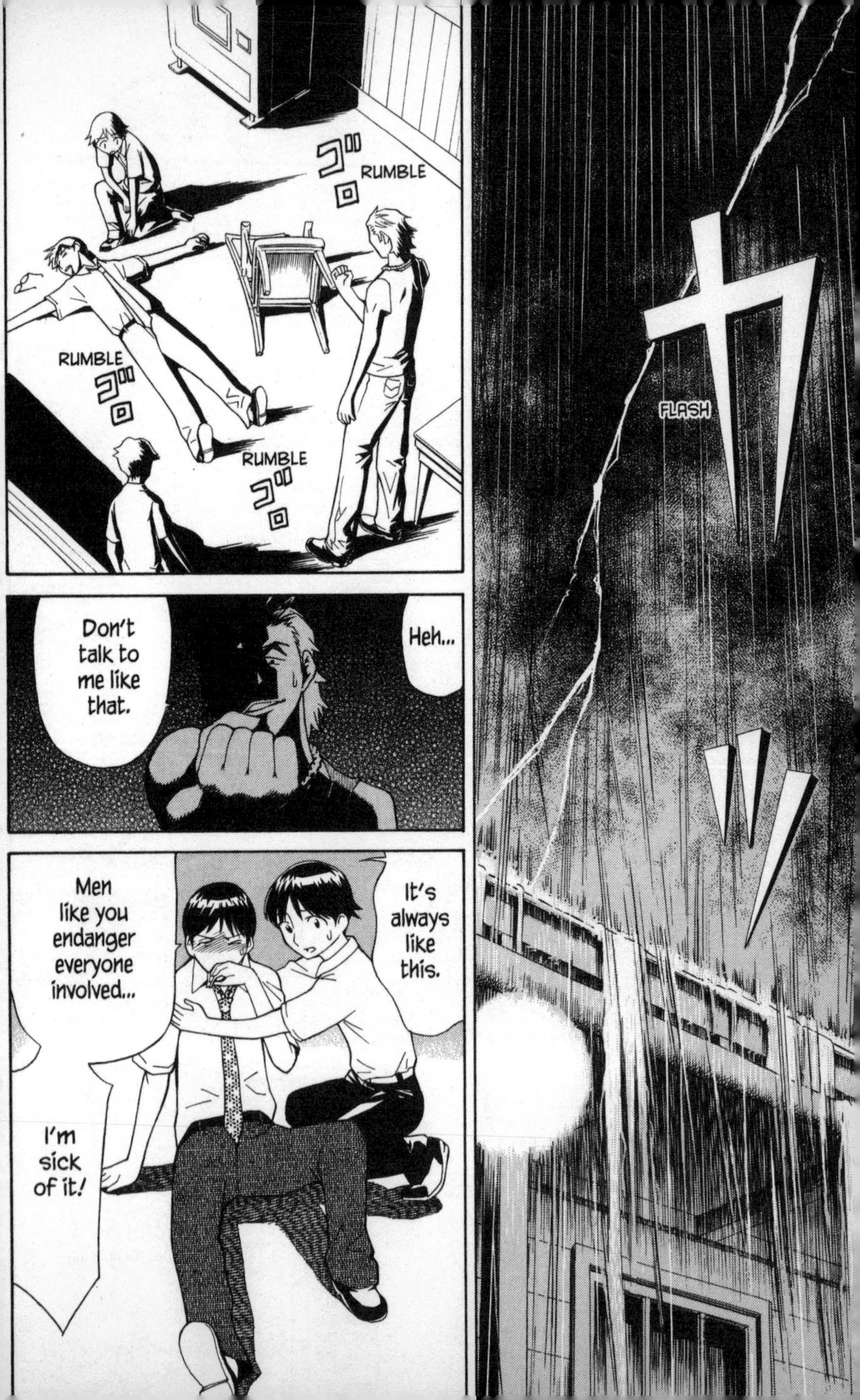
カッ
FLASH
ゴロ
RUMBLE
RUMBLE
ゴロ
RUMBLE
ゴロ
Heh...
Don't talk to me like that.
It's always like this.
Men like you endanger everyone involved...
I'm sick of it!

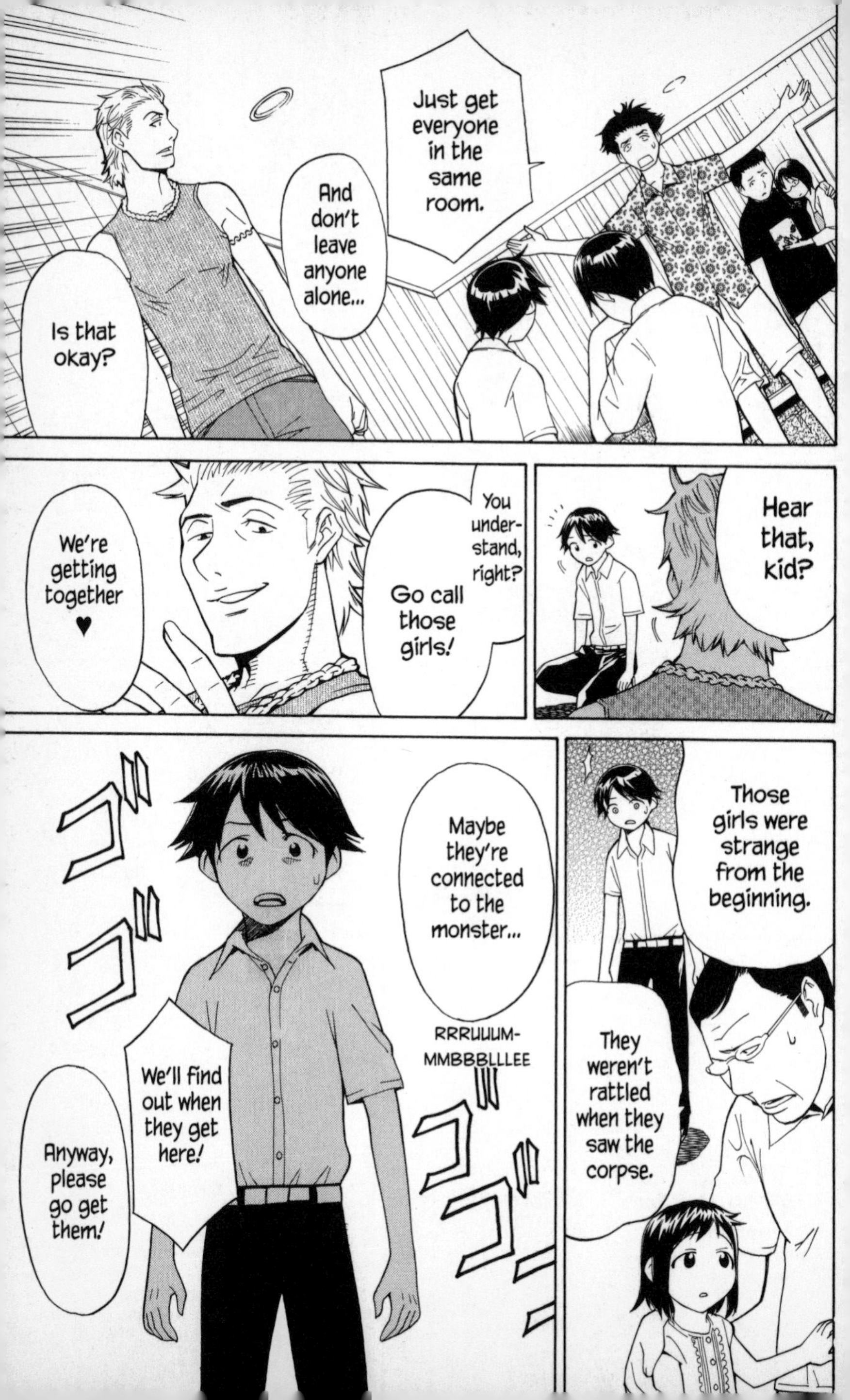
Just get everyone in the same room.
And don't leave anyone alone...
Is that okay?
Hear that, kid?
You under-stand, right?
Go call those girls!
We're getting together ♥
Those girls were strange from the beginning.
They weren't rattled when they saw the corpse.
Maybe they're connected to the monster...
RRRUUUM-MMBBBLLLEE
We'll find out when they get here!
Anyway, please go get them!

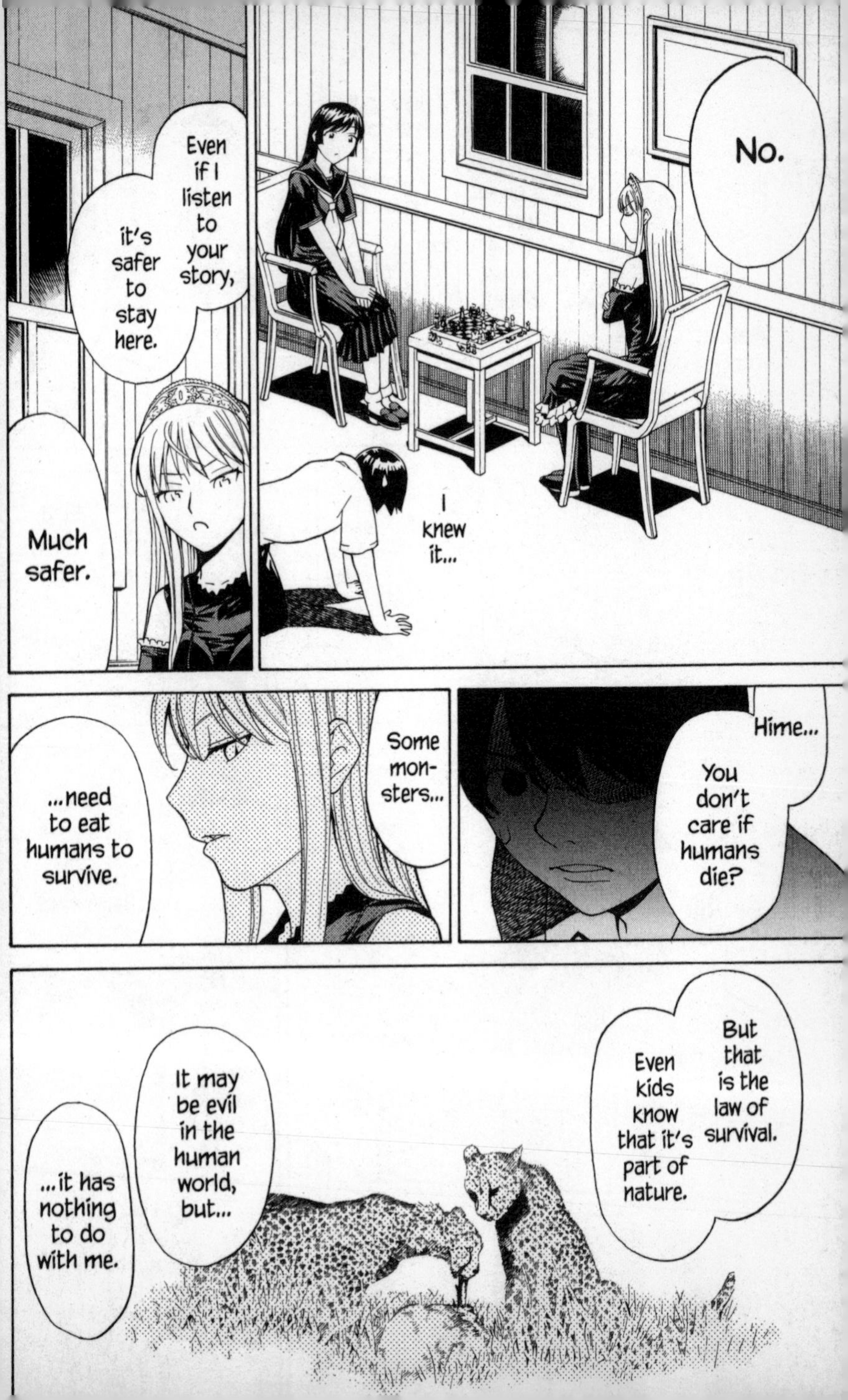
No.
I knew it...
Even if I listen to your story,
it's safer to stay here.
Much safer.
Hime...
You don't care if humans die?
Some monsters...
...need to eat humans to survive.
But that is the law of survival.
Even kids know that it's part of nature.
It may be evil in the human world, but...
...it has nothing to do with me.

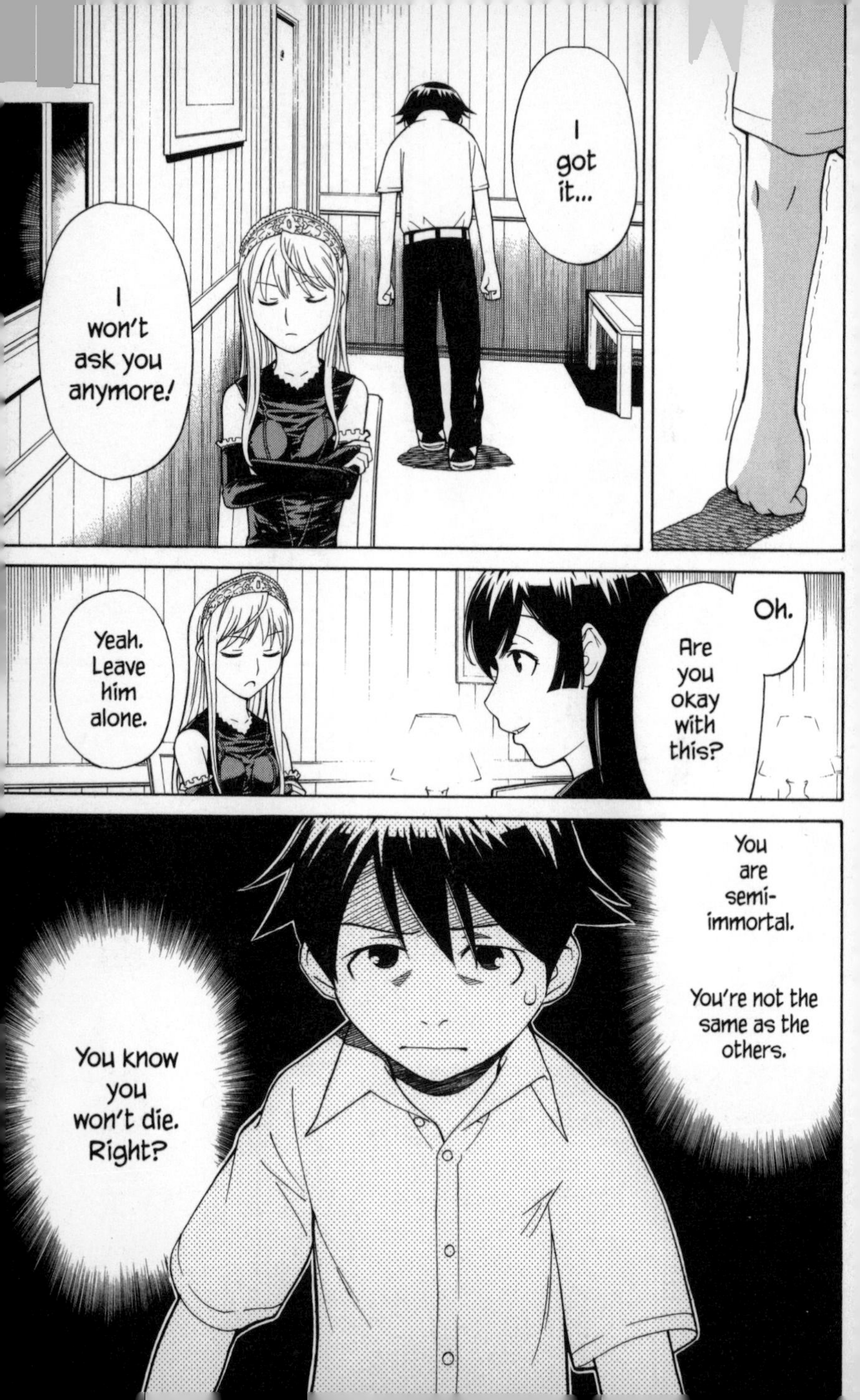
I got it...
I won't ask you anymore!
Oh. Are you okay with this?
Yeah. Leave him alone.
You are semi-immortal.
You're not the same as the others.
You know you won't die. Right?

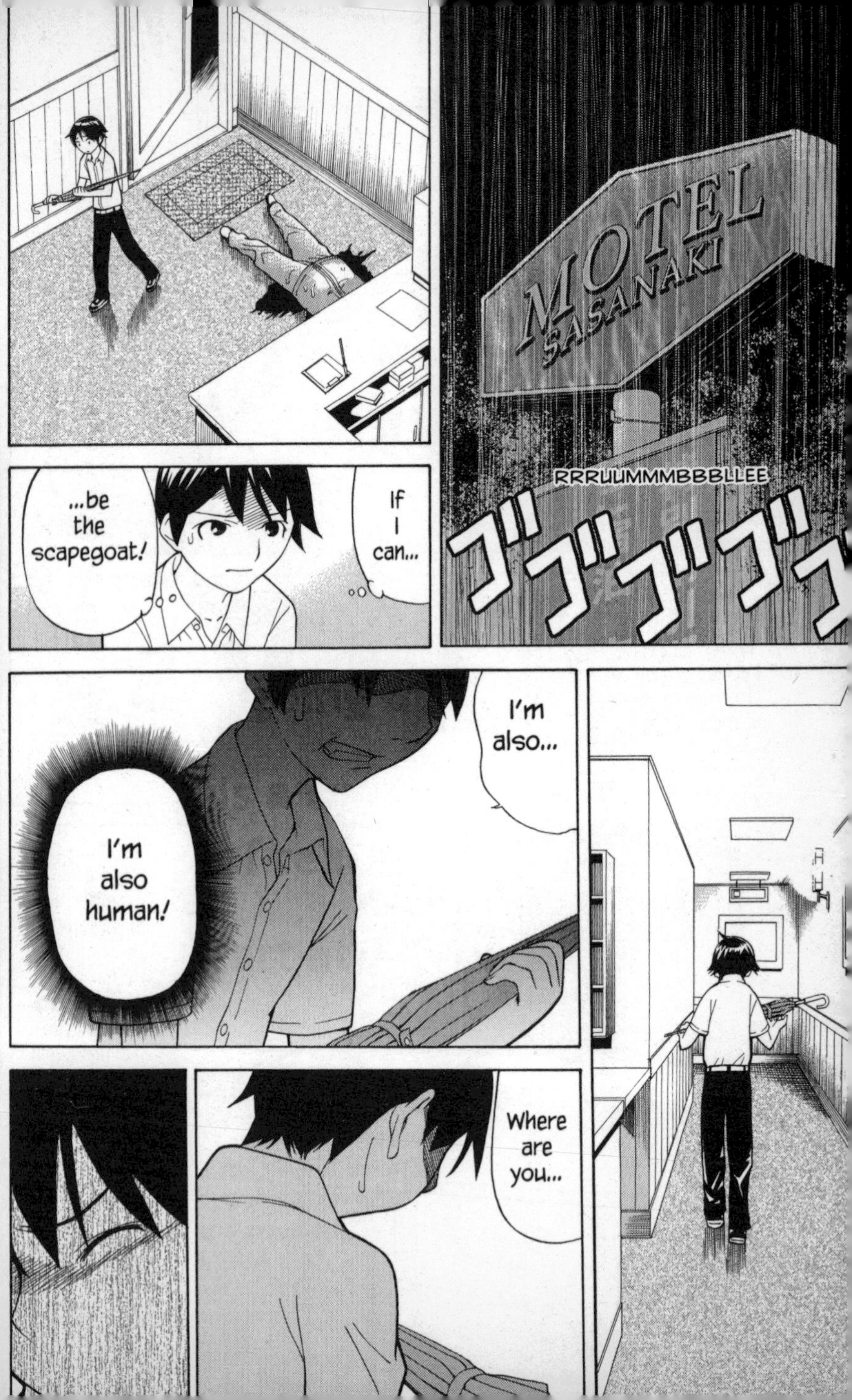
MOTEL
SASANAKI
RRRUUMMMBBBLLEE
ゴゴゴゴ
If I can...
...be the scapegoat!
I'm also...
I'm also human!
Where are you...

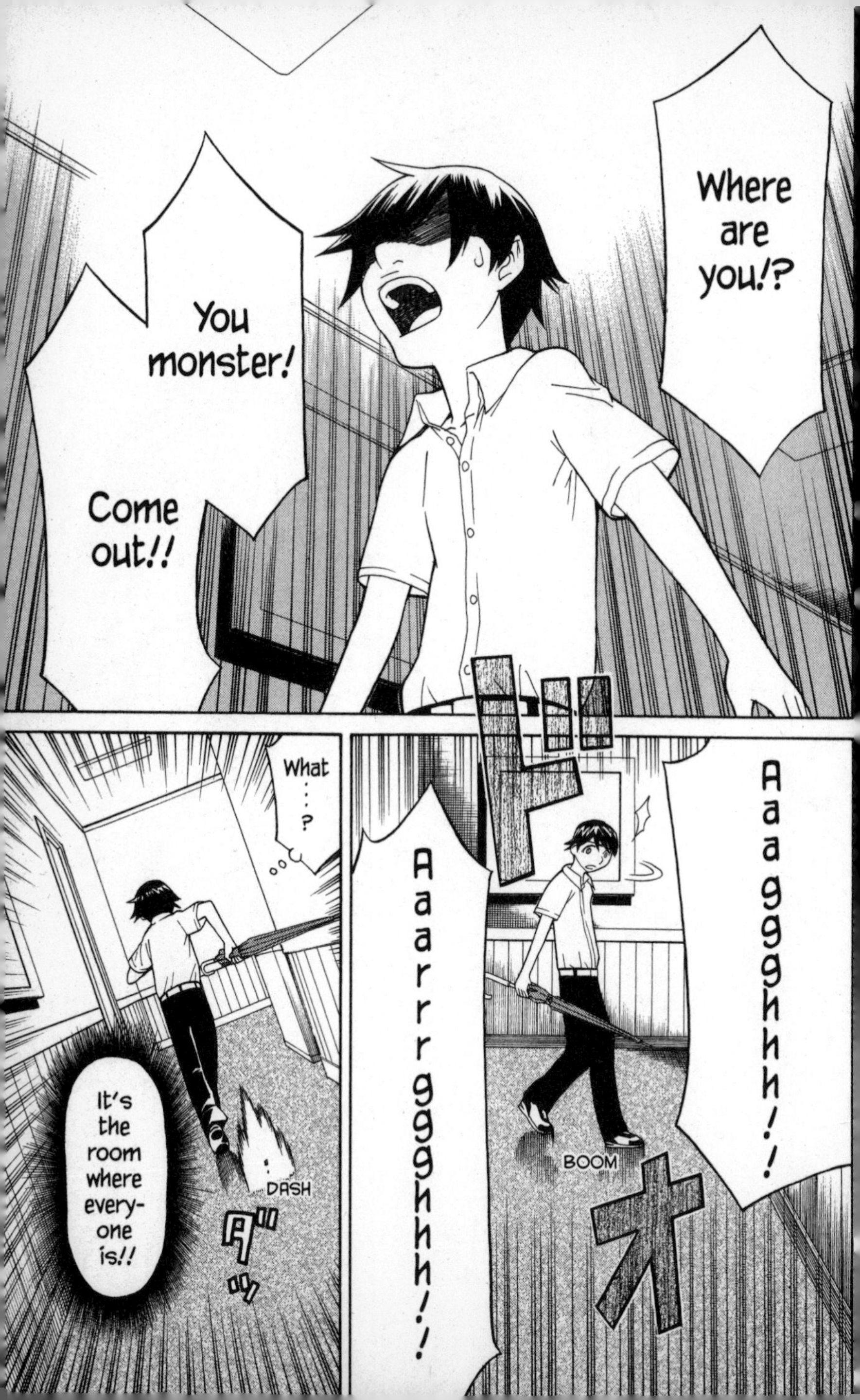
Where are you!?
You monster!
Come out!!
Aaaggghhh!!
Aaarrrggghhh!!
BOOM
What...?
It's the room where every-one is!!
DASH

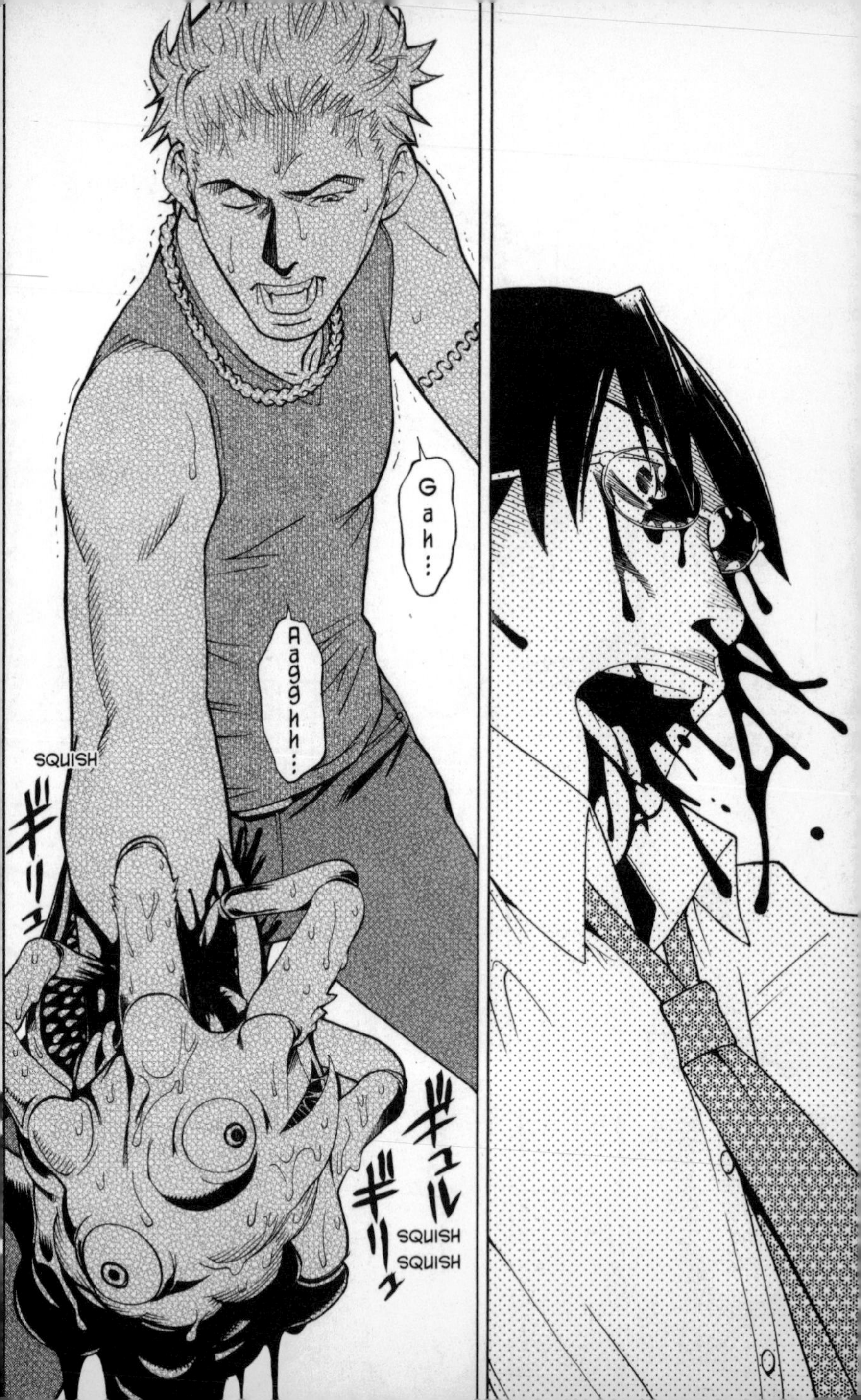
Gah...
Aagghh...
SQUISH
ギリュ
ギュル
ギリュ
SQUISH
SQUISH

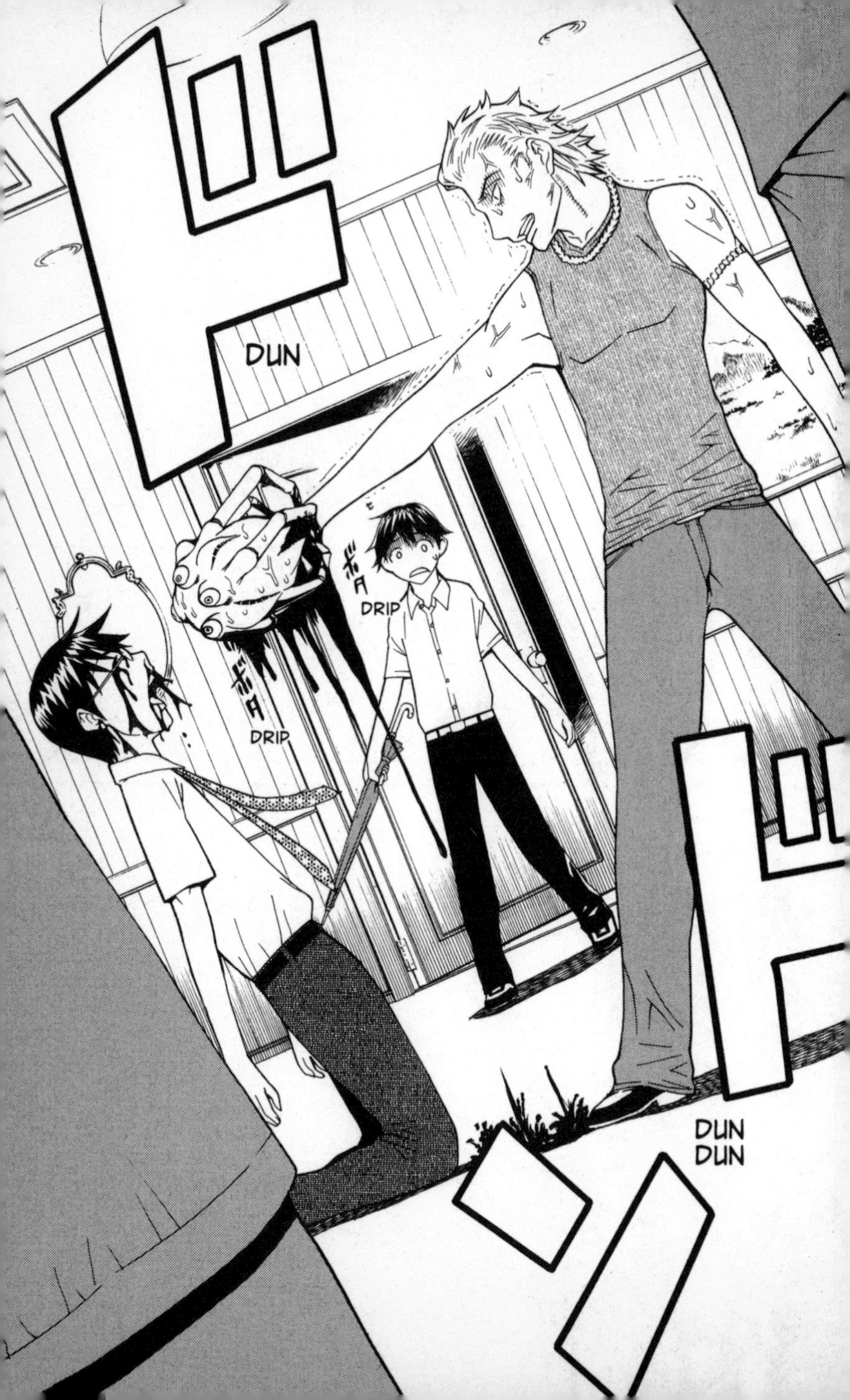
ド
DUN
ボタ
DRIP
ボタ
DRIP
ドド
ン
DUN
DUN

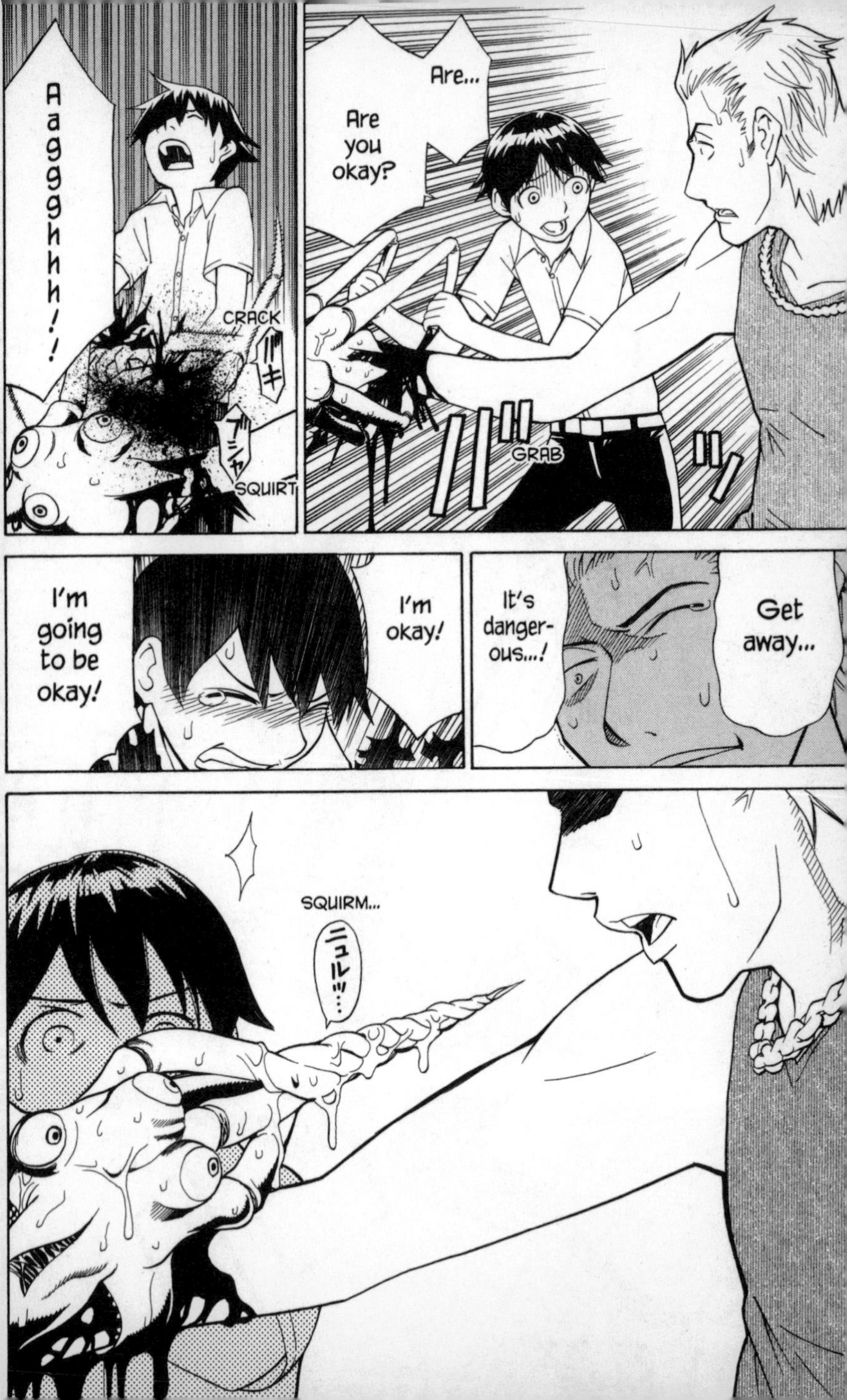
Are...
Are you okay?
GRAB
Aaggghhh!!
CRACK
バキ
ブシャ
SQUIRT
Get away...
It's danger-ous...!
I'm okay!
I'm going to be okay!
SQUIRM...
ニュルッ...

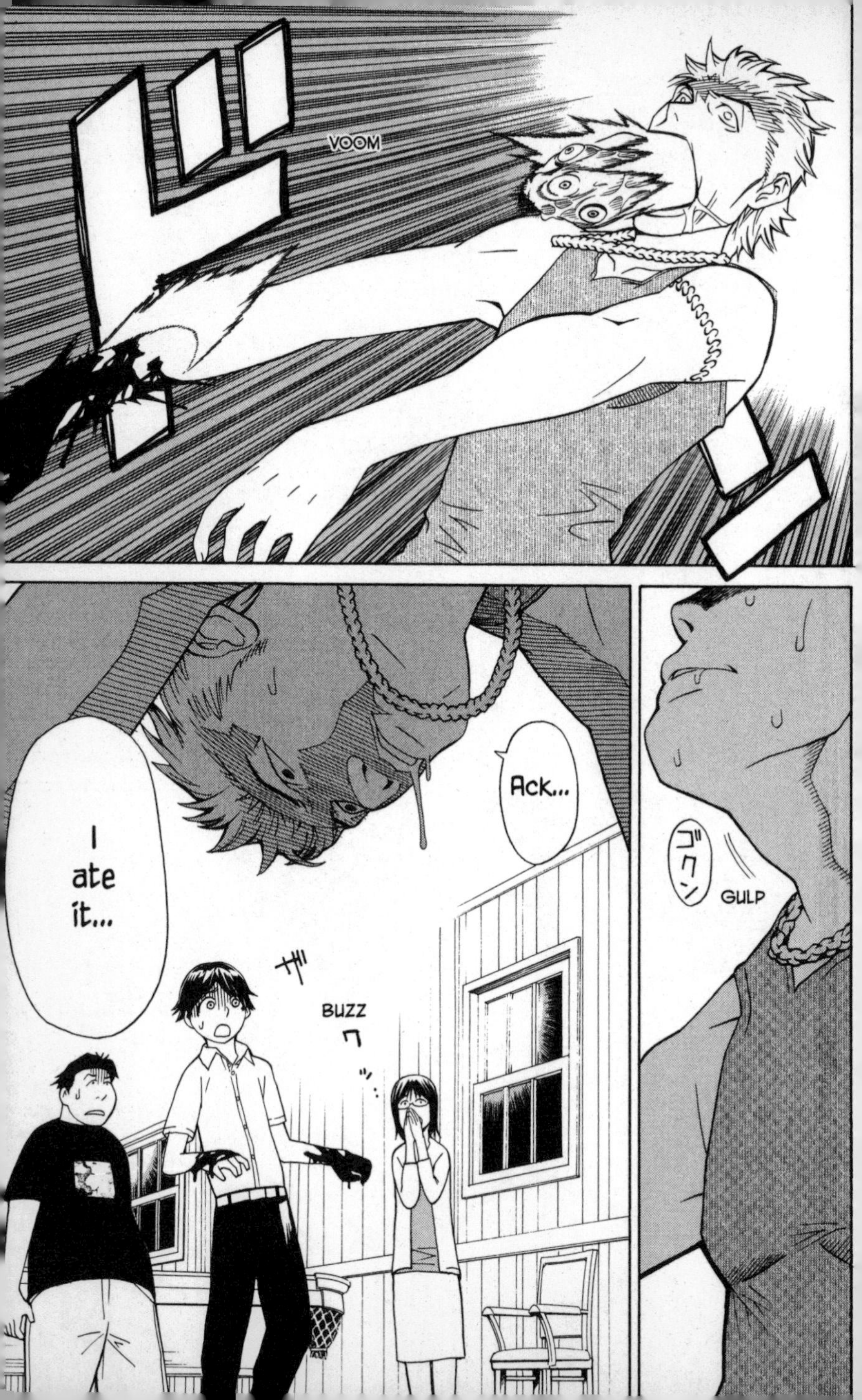

VOOM
ゴクン
GULP
Ack...
I ate it...
ザワッ..
BUZZ

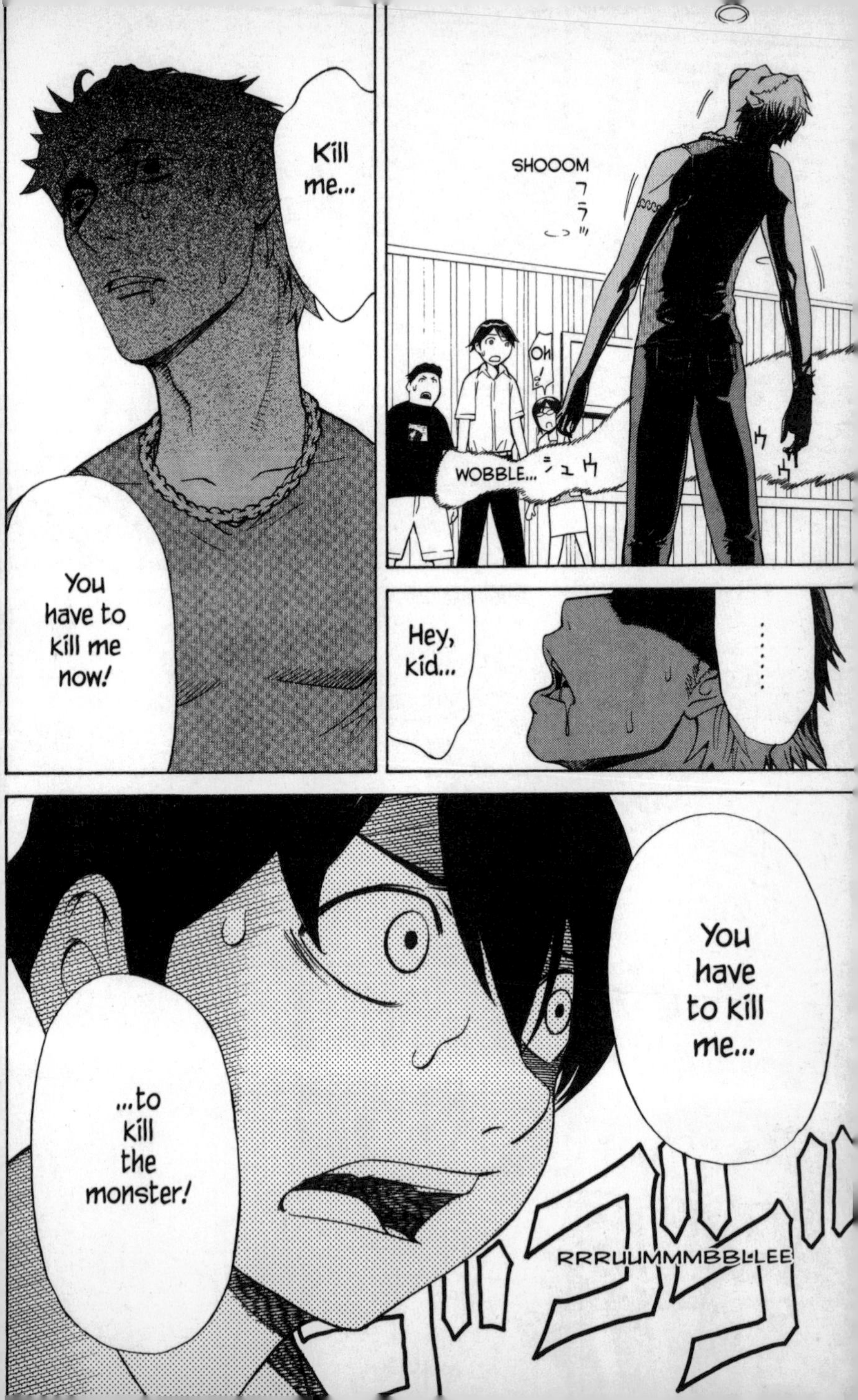
SHOOOM
フラッ
Oh!
WOBBLE...
シュウ
......
Hey, kid...
Kill me...
You have to kill me now!
You have to kill me...
...to kill the monster!
RRRUUMMMBBLLEE

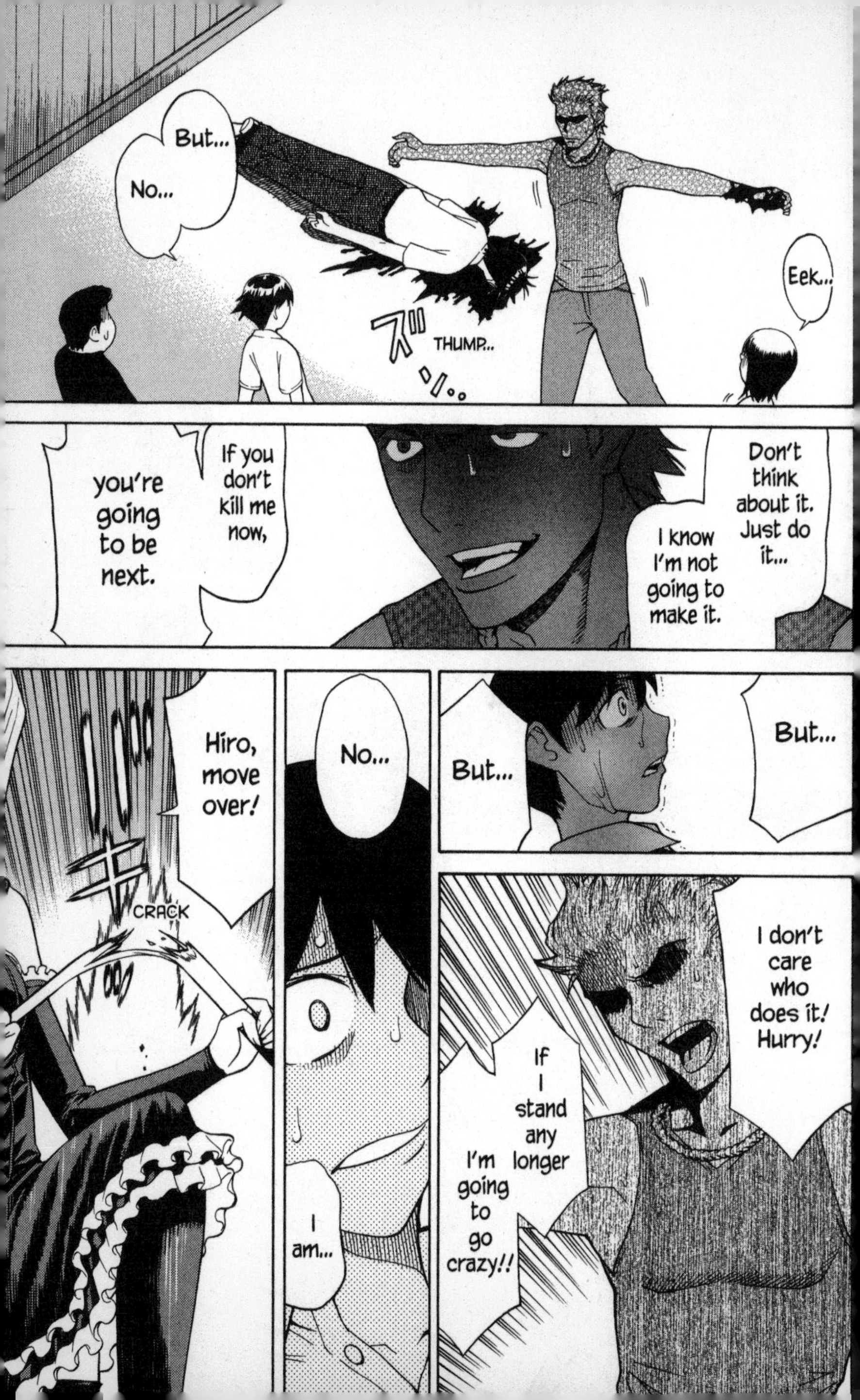
Eek...
THUMP...
But...
No...
Don't think about it. Just do it...
I know I'm not going to make it.
If you don't kill me now,
you're going to be next.
But...
But...
I don't care who does it! Hurry!
If I stand any longer I'm going to go crazy!!
No...
I am...
Hiro, move over!
CRACK

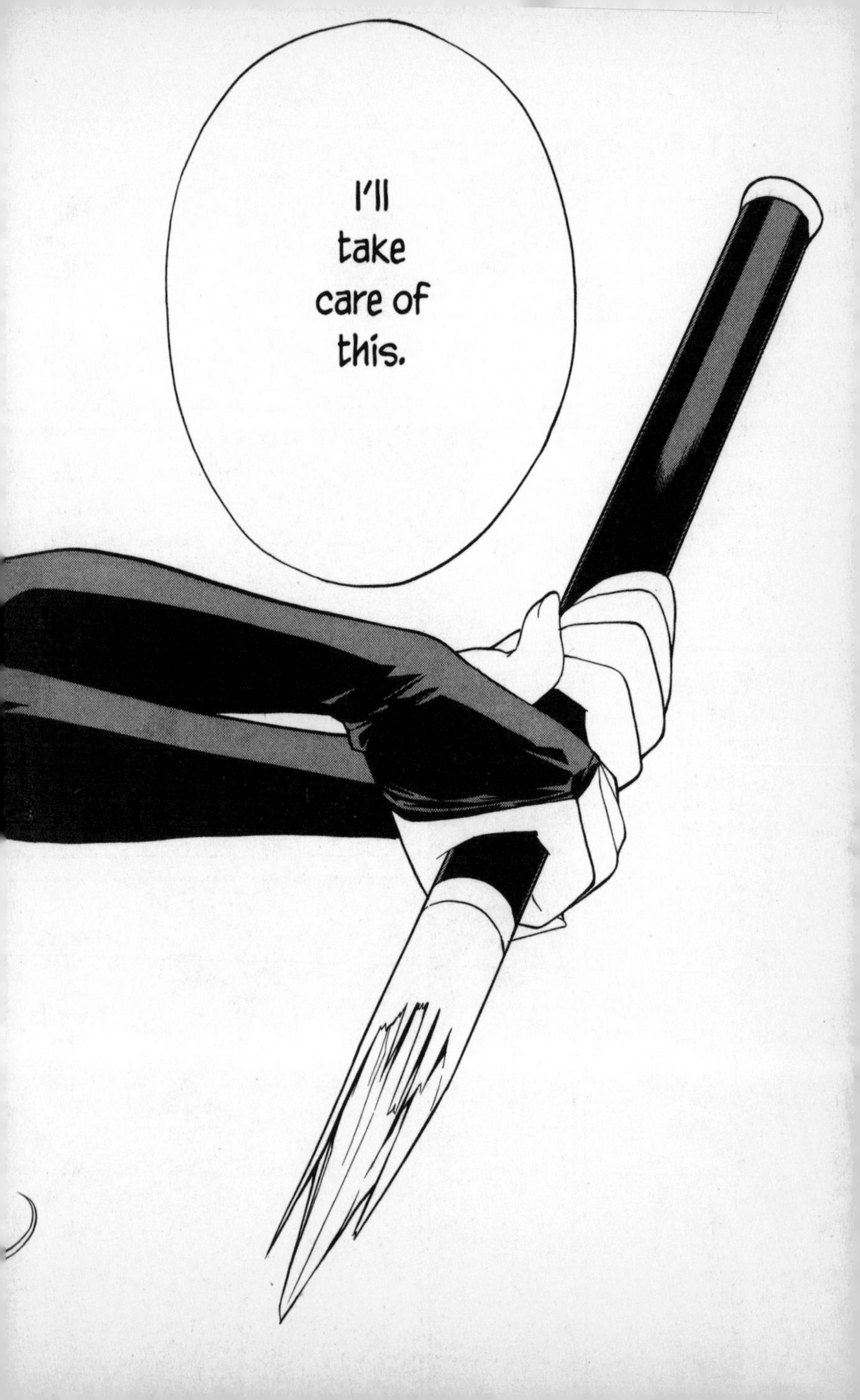
I'll take care of this.

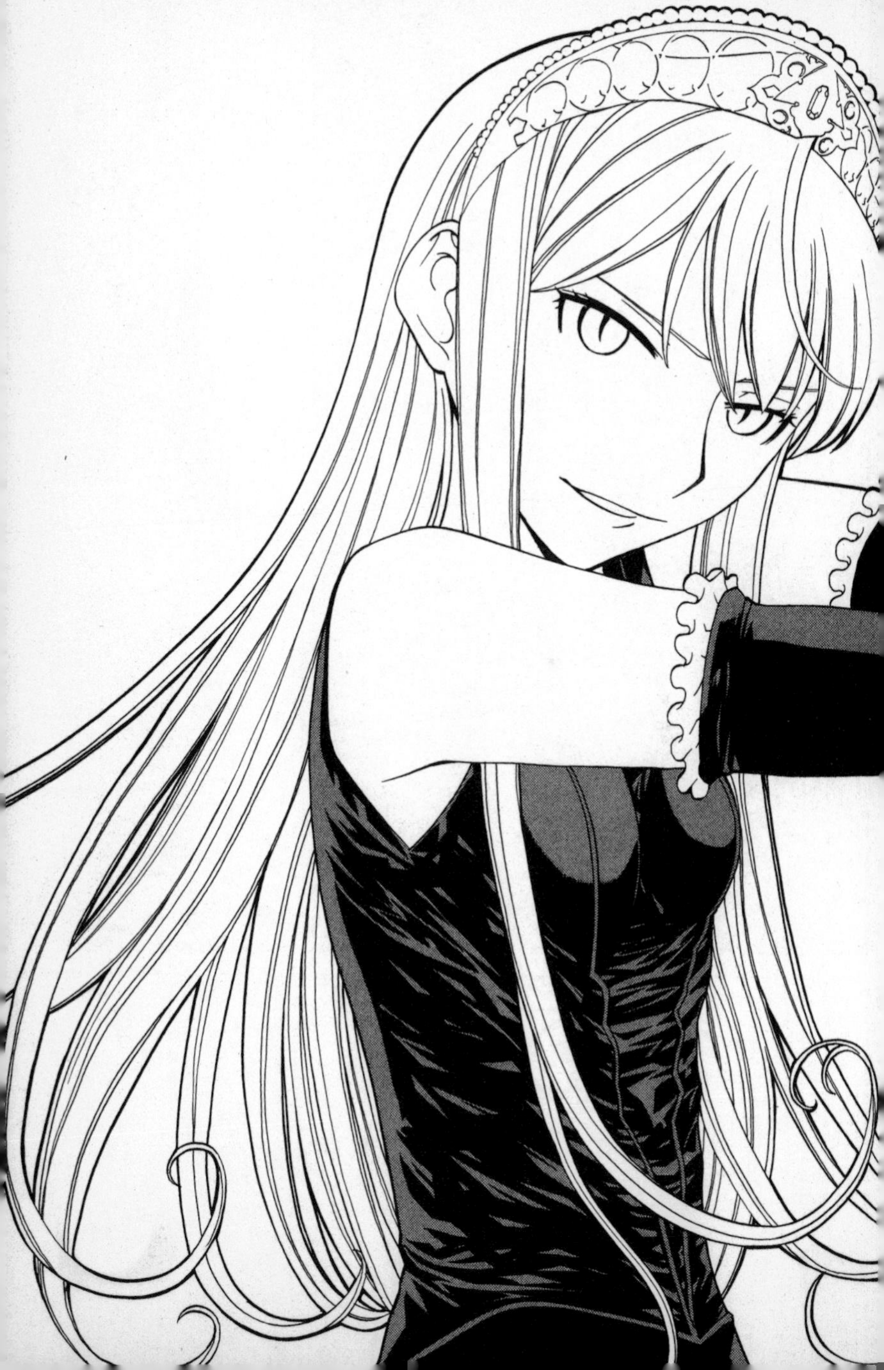

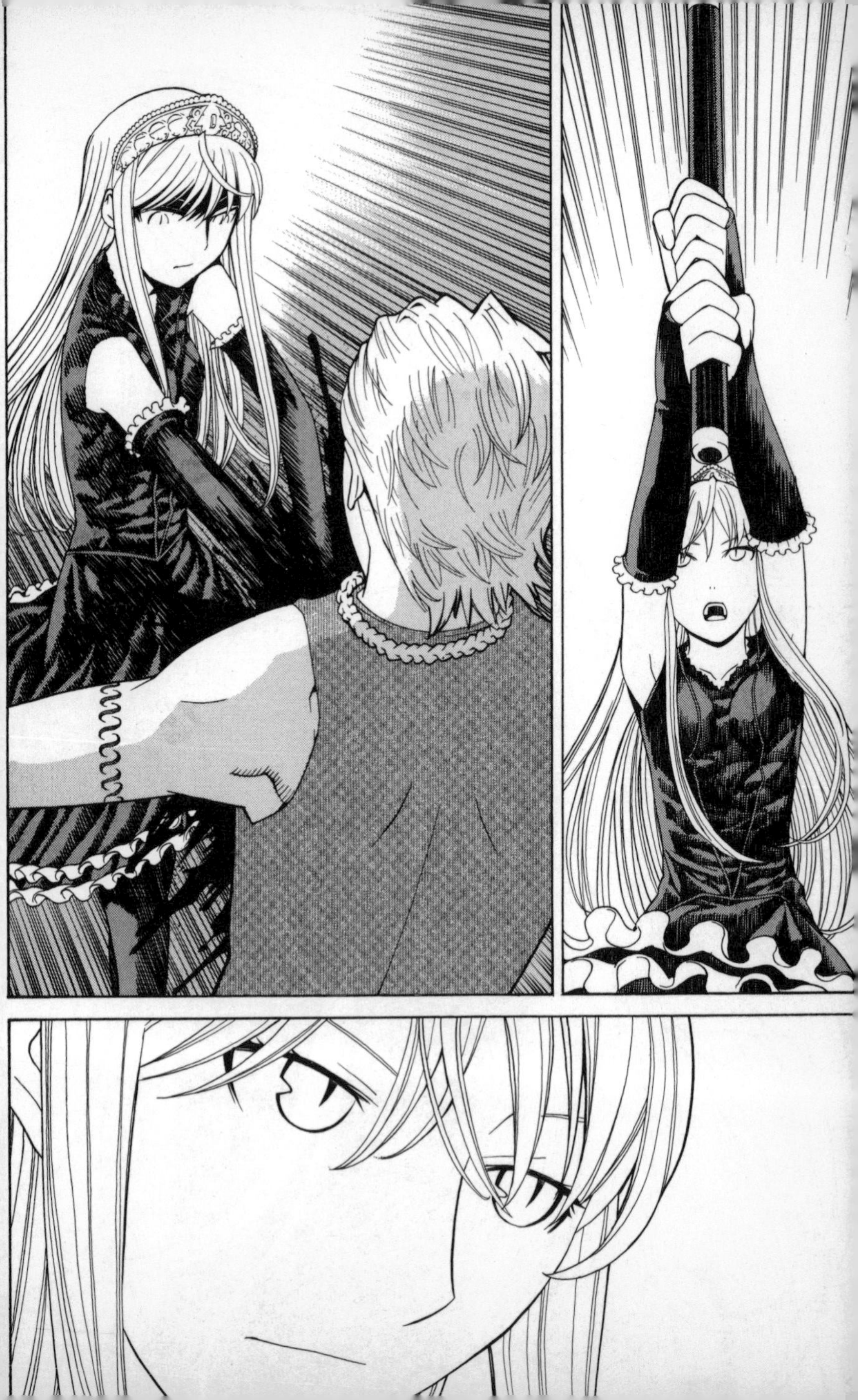

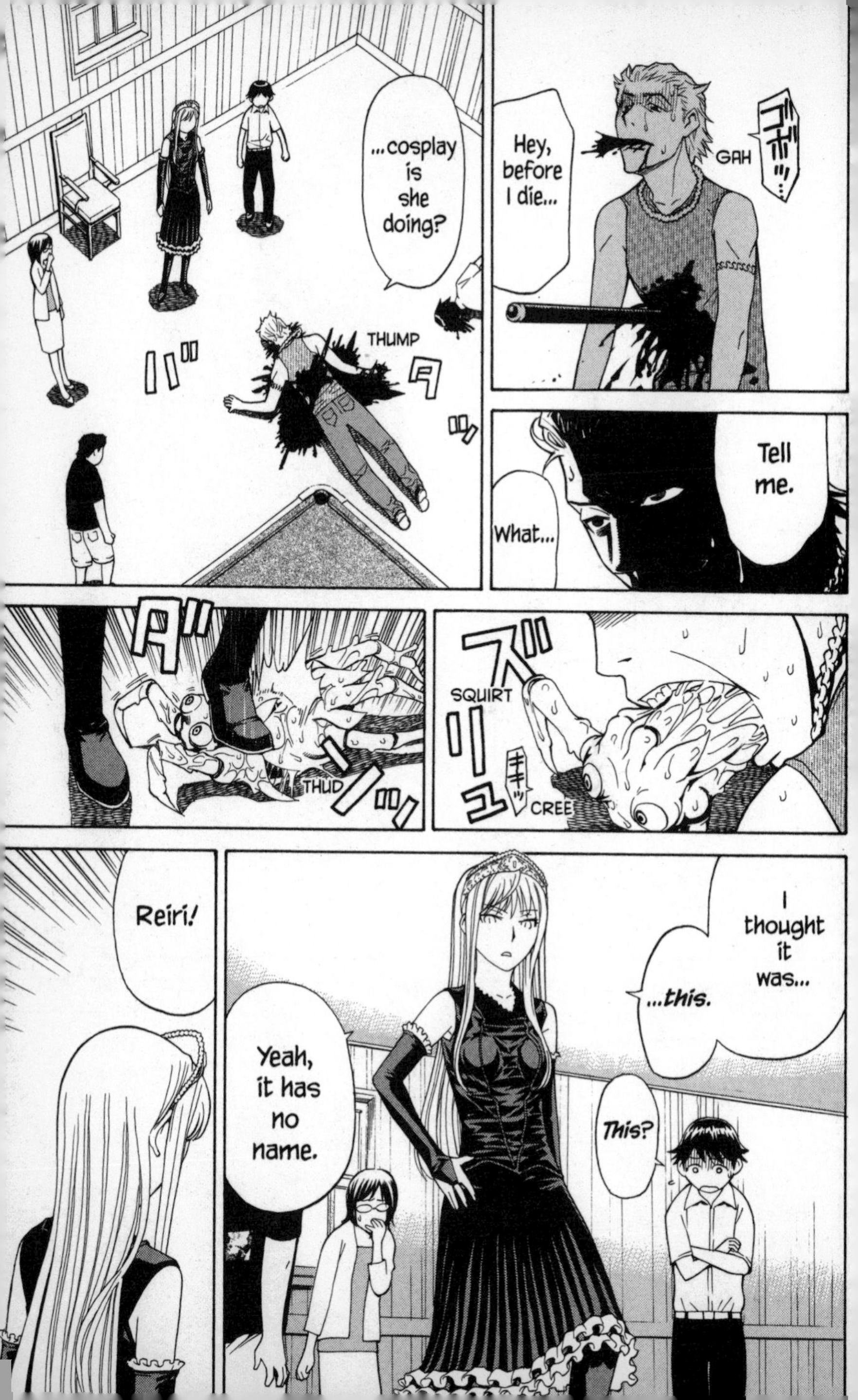
GAH
Hey, before I die...
Tell me.
What...
...cosplay is she doing?
THUMP
SQUIRT
CREE
THUD
I thought it was...
...this.
This?
Yeah, it has no name.
Reiri!

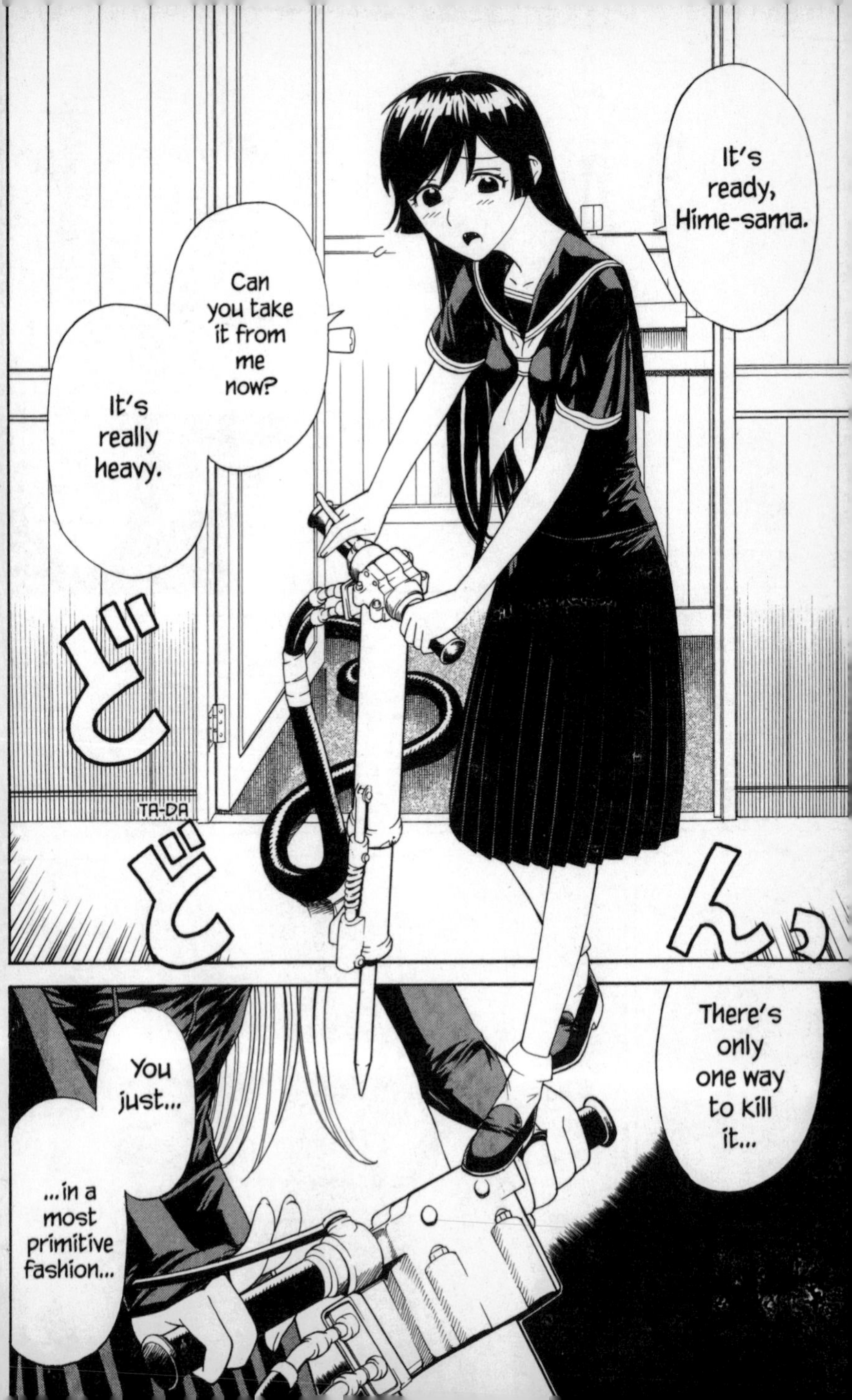
It's ready, Hime-sama.
Can you take it from me now?
It's really heavy.
どどんっ
TA-DA
There's only one way to kill it...
You just...
...in a most primitive fashion...

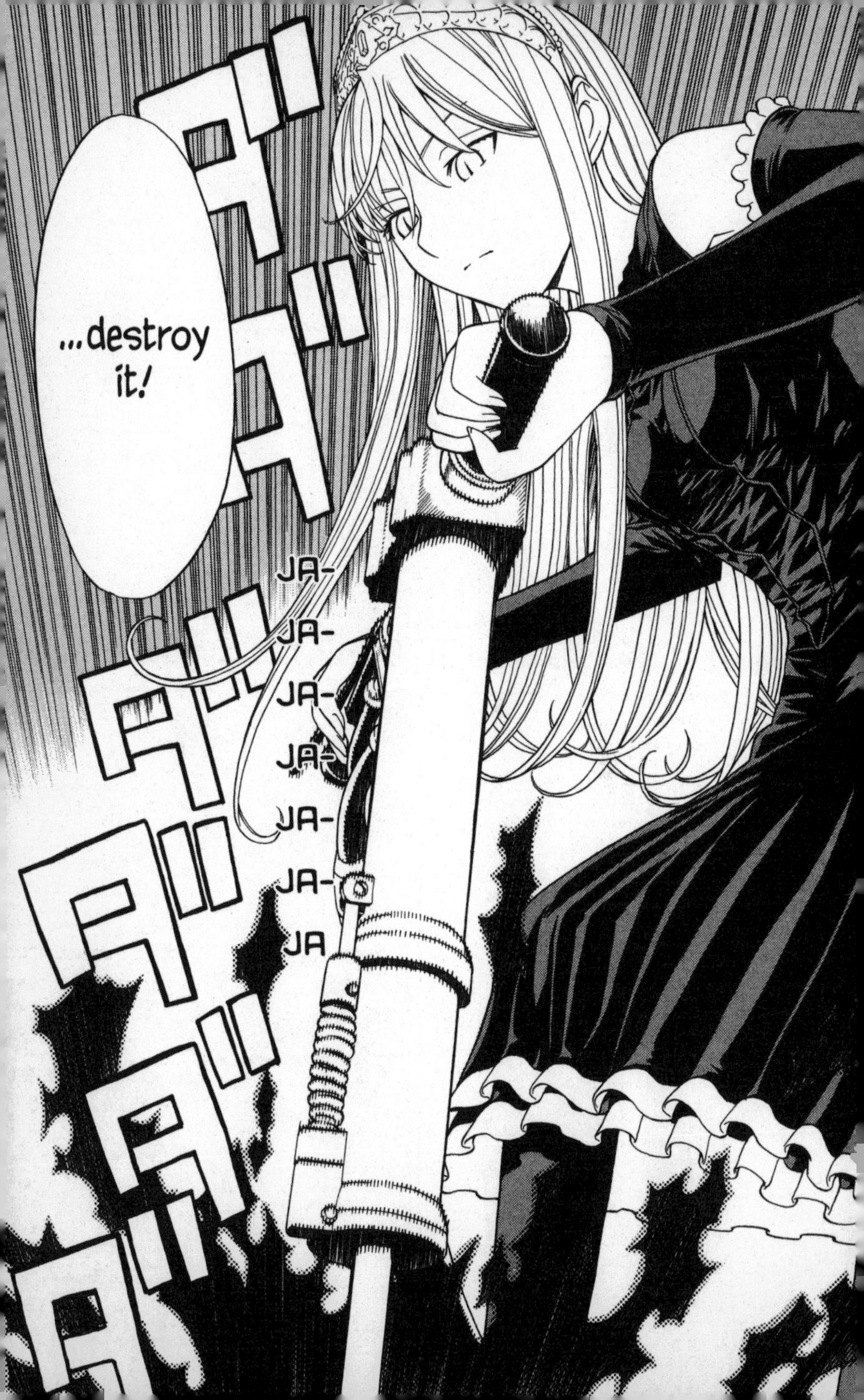
...destroy it!
JA-
JA-
JA-
JA-
JA-
JA-
JA

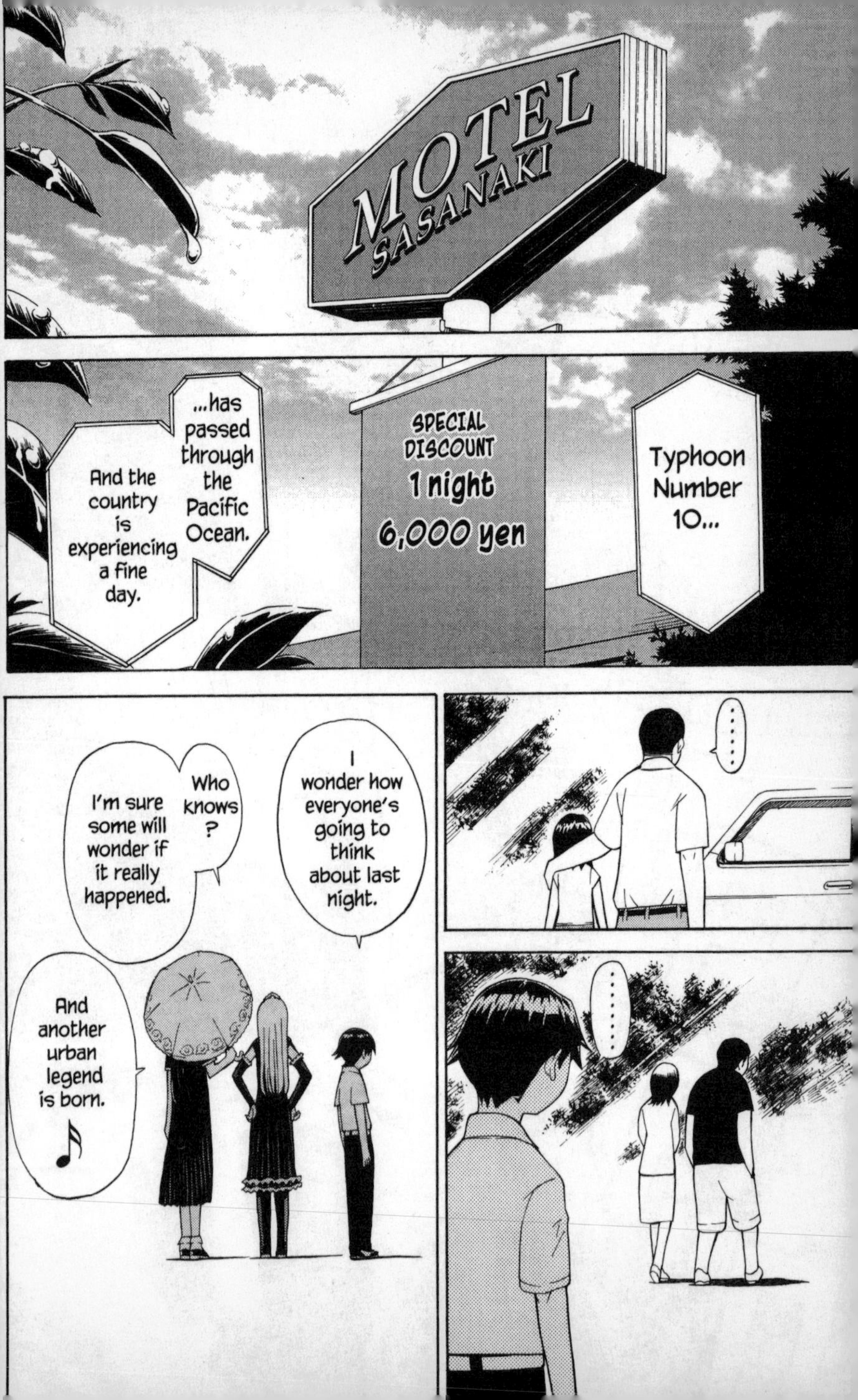
MOTEL
SASANAKI
Typhoon Number 10...
SPECIAL DISCOUNT 1 night 6,000 yen
...has passed through the Pacific Ocean.
And the country is experiencing a fine day.
......
......
I wonder how everyone's going to think about last night.
Who knows?
I'm sure some will wonder if it really happened.
And another urban legend is born. ♪

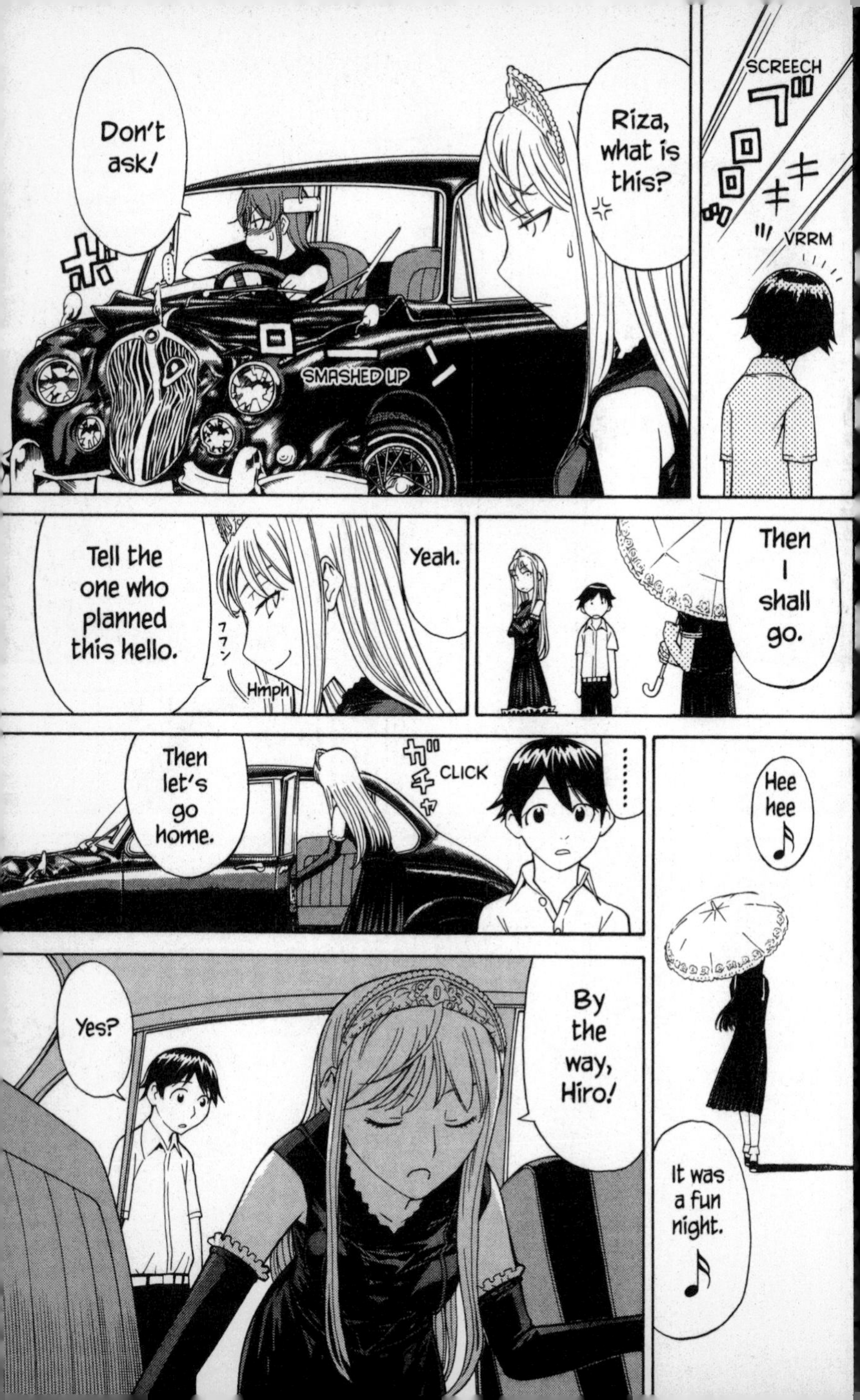
SCREECH
VRRM
Riza, what is this?
Don't ask!
SMASHED UP
Then I shall go.
Yeah.
Tell the one who planned this hello.
Hmph
Hee hee ♪
It was a fun night. ♪
......
CLICK
Then let's go home.
By the way, Hiro!
Yes?

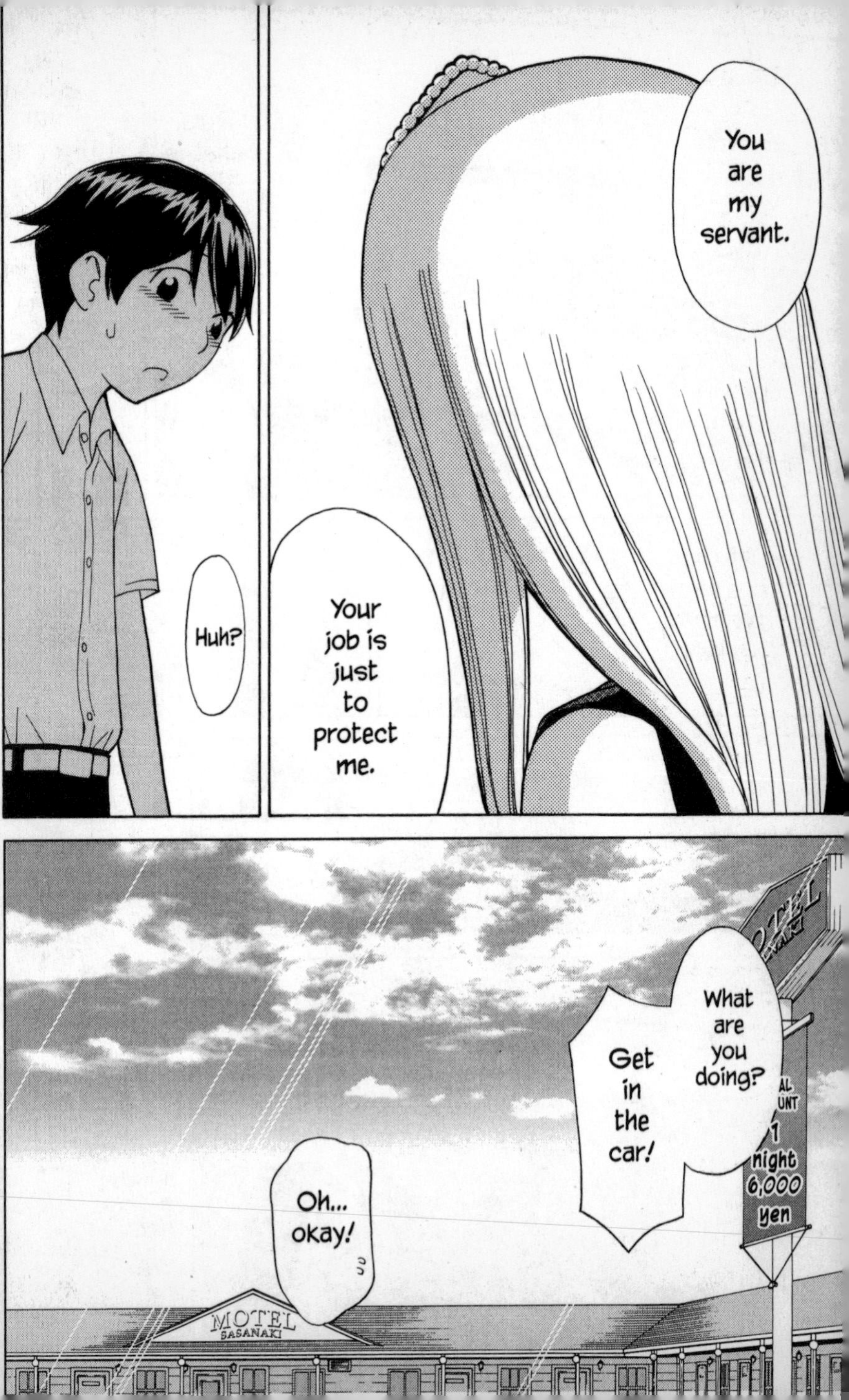
You are my servant.
Your job is just to protect me.
Huh?
What are you doing?
Get in the car!
1 night 6,000 yen
Oh... okay!
MOTEL SASANAKI

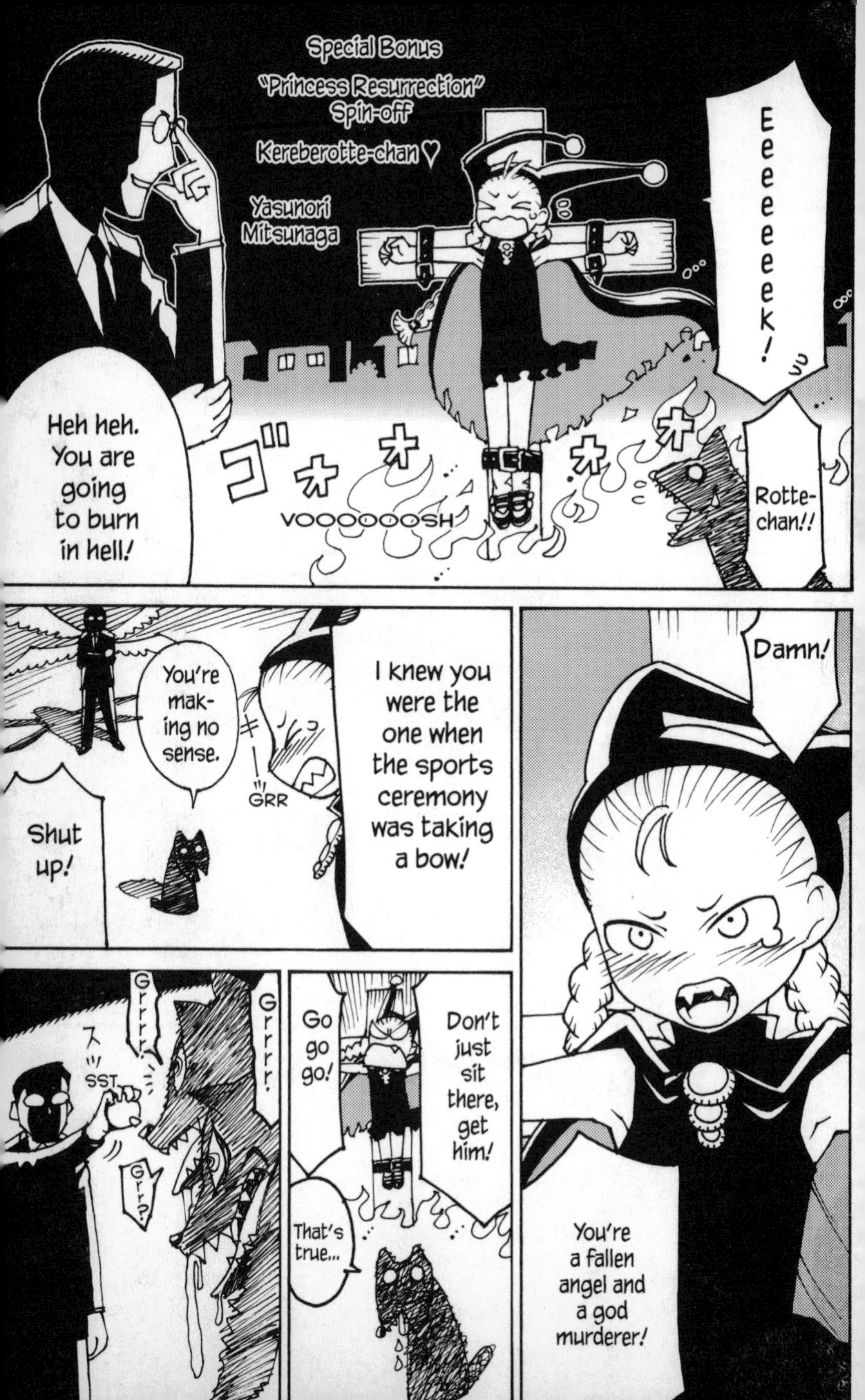
Special Bonus
"Princess Resurrection" Spin-off
Kereberotte-chan ♥
Yasunori Mitsunaga
Eeeeeeeek!
Rotte-chan!!
VOOOOOOOSH
Heh heh. You are going to burn in hell!
Damn!
You're a fallen angel and a god murderer!
I knew you were the one when the sports ceremony was taking a bow!
You're mak-ing no sense.
GRR
Shut up!
Don't just sit there, get him!
Go go go!
That's true...
Grrrr.
Grrrr.
SST
Grr?

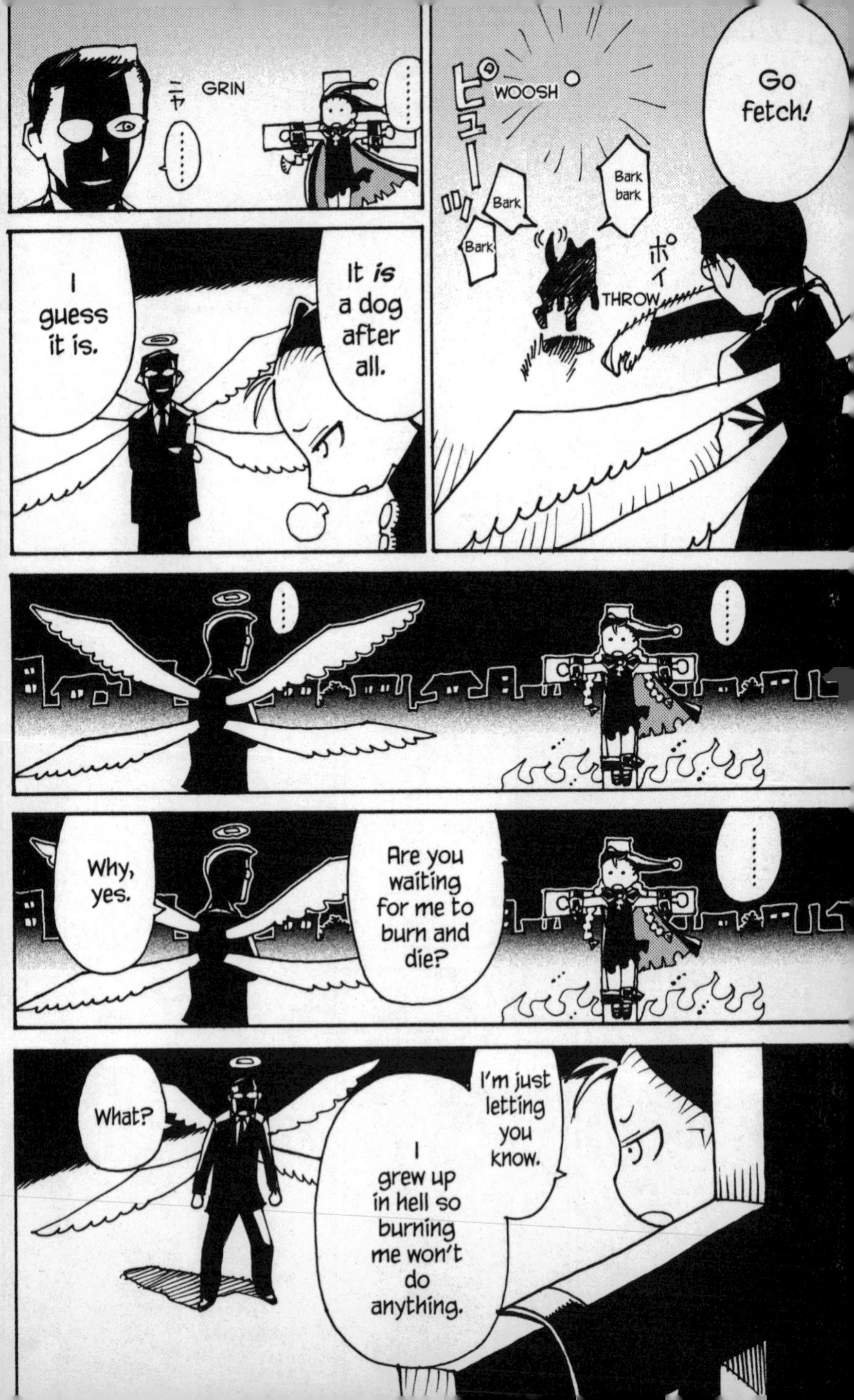
Go fetch!
Bark bark
ポイ THROW
ピュー WOOSH
Bark
Bark
......
ニヤ GRIN
......
It *is* a dog after all.
I guess it is.
......
......
Are you waiting for me to burn and die?
Why, yes.
I'm just letting you know.
I grew up in hell so burning me won't do anything.
What?

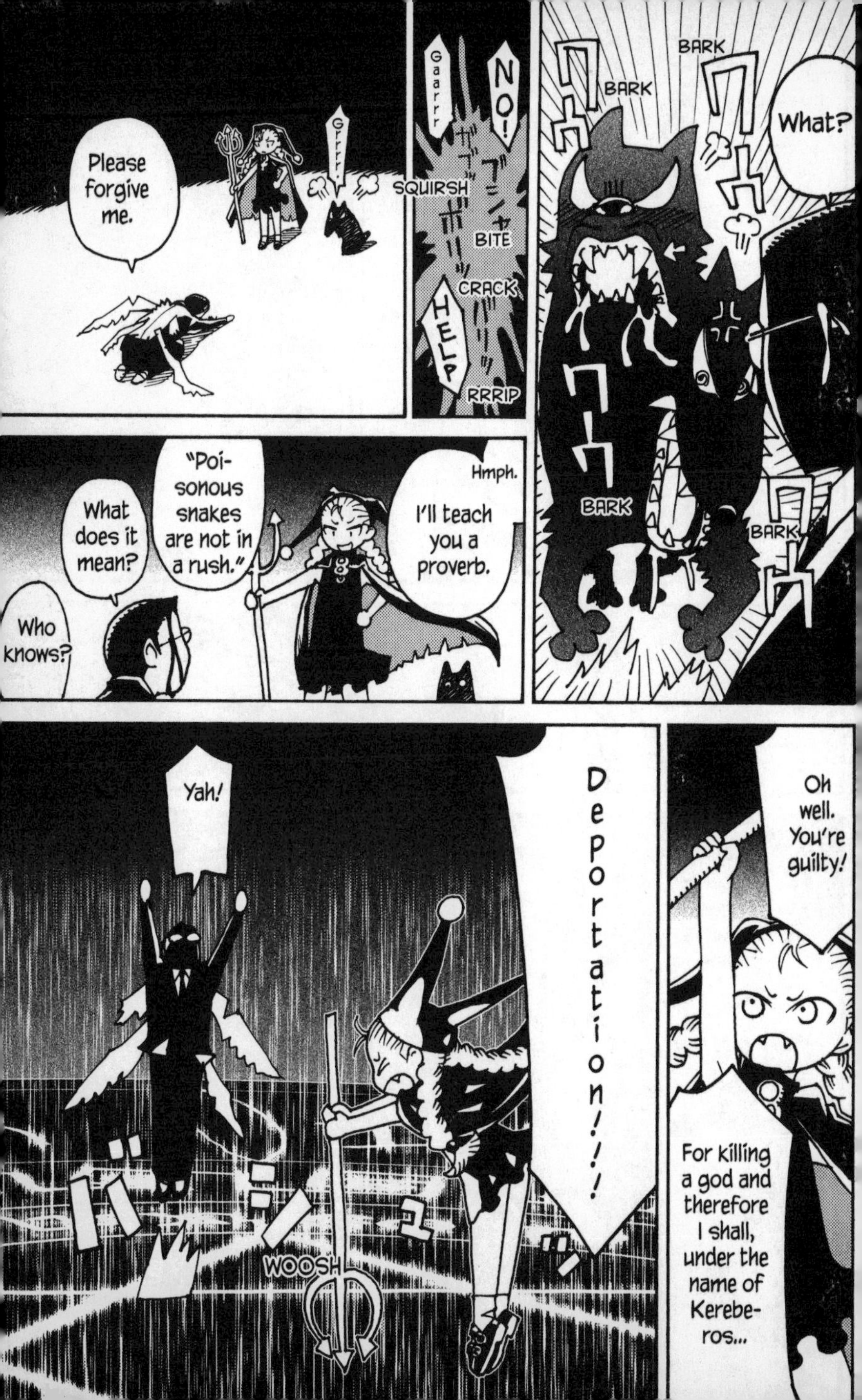

BARK
BARK
What?
BARK
BARK
NO!
Gaarrr
SQUIRSH
BITE
CRACK
HELP
RRRIP
Grrr
Please forgive me.
Hmph.
I'll teach you a proverb.
"Poisonous snakes are not in a rush."
What does it mean?
Who knows?
Oh well. You're guilty!
For killing a god and therefore I shall, under the name of Kereberos...
Deportation!!!
Yah!
WOOSH

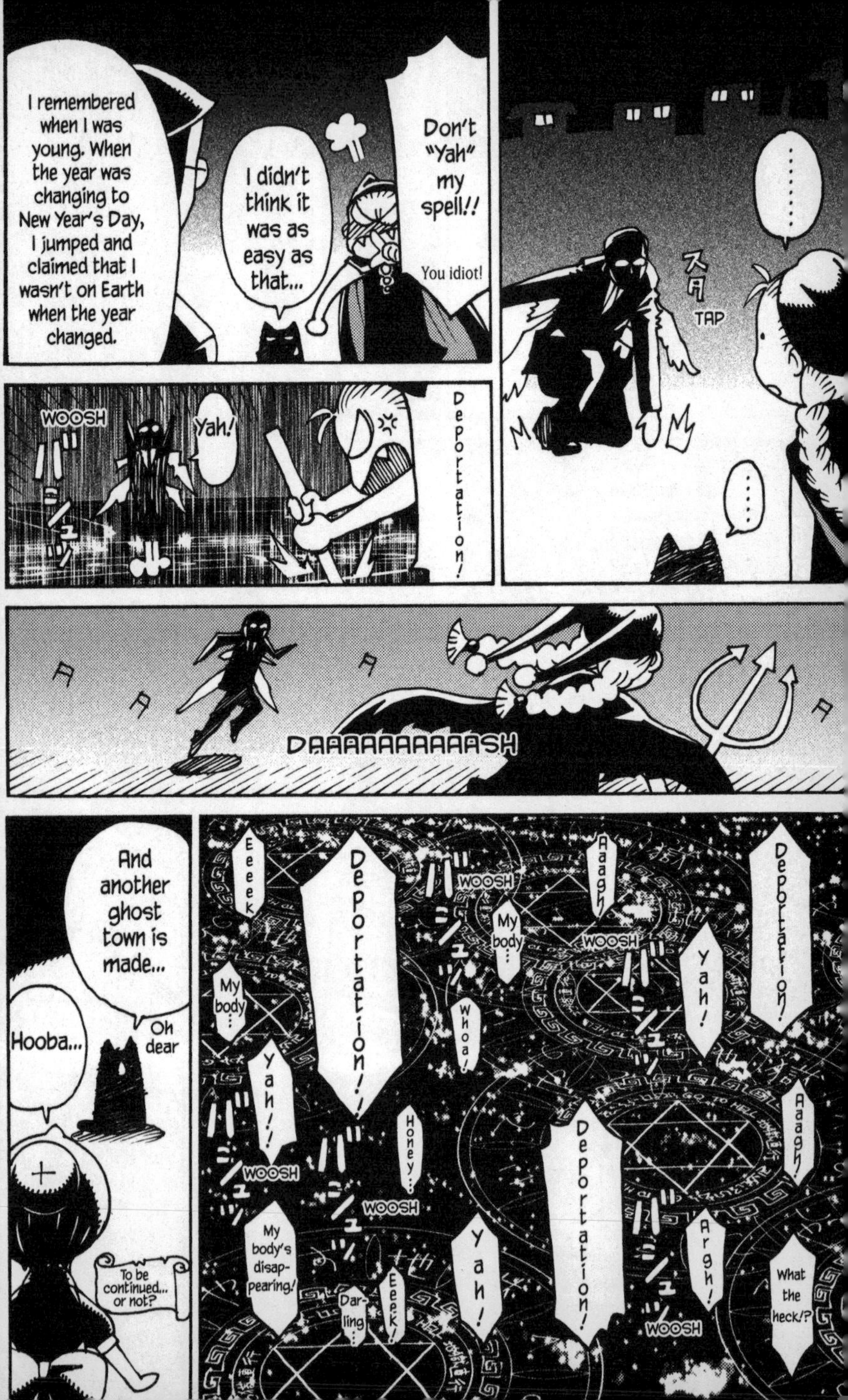
......
TAP
......
Don't "Yah" my spell!!
You idiot!
I didn't think it was as easy as that...
I remembered when I was young. When the year was changing to New Year's Day, I jumped and claimed that I wasn't on Earth when the year changed.
Deportation!
Yah!
WOOSH
DAAAAAAAAAASH
Deportation!
Aaagh
WOOSH
My body...
WOOSH
Yah!
Whoa!
Deportation!!
Eeeek
My body...
Yah!!
WOOSH
Honey...
WOOSH
Aaagh
Deportation!
Argh!
What the heck!?
WOOSH
Yah!
Eeek!
Darling...
My body's disappearing!
And another ghost town is made...
Oh dear
Hooba...
To be continued... or not?

Preview of the next volume!

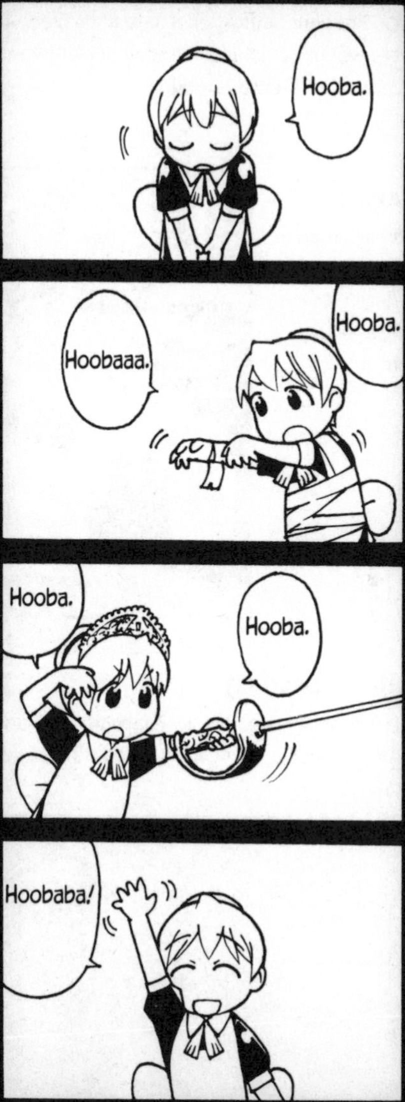
Hooba.
Hooba.
Hoobaaa.
Hooba.
Hooba.
Hoobaba!

Look forward to it!

Translation Notes

Japanese is a tricky language for most Westerners, and translation is often more an art than a science. For your edification and reading pleasure, here are notes on some of the places where we could have gone in a different direction, or where a Japanese cultural reference is used.

Onee-sama, page 3

Onee-sama is a term of respect meaning "older sister." However, it often has a negative implication, implying a "bratty girl," as it's used here.

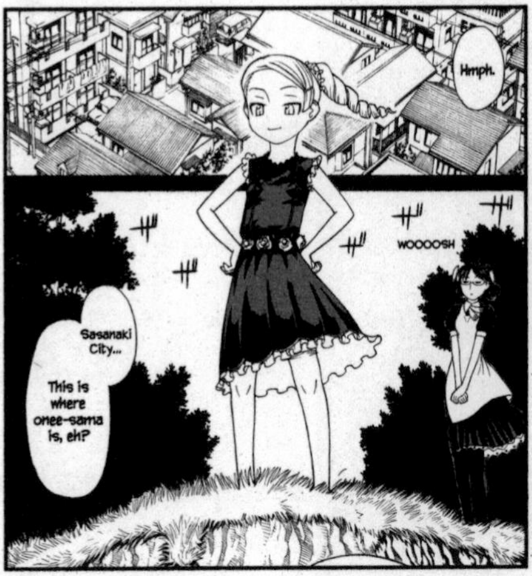
Hmph.
WOOOOSH
Sasanaki City...
This is where onee-sama is, eh?

"Monster's Ballad," page 123

"Monster's Ballad" is a popular song sung in elementary and junior high schools. A choral group known as Young 101 debuted with the song on a music show in 1972.

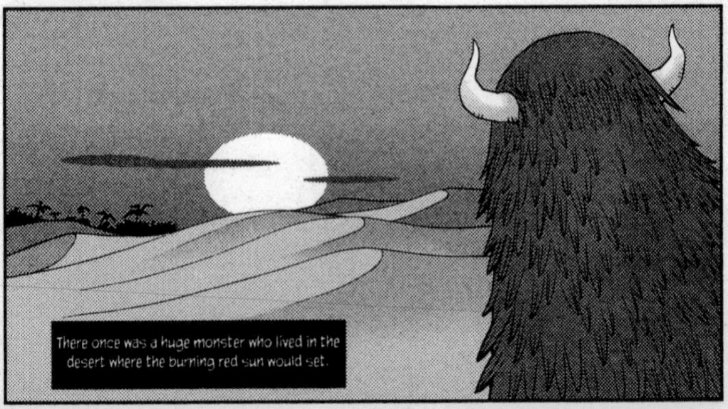
There once was a huge monster who lived in the desert where the burning red sun would set.

Cosplay, page 166

Cosplay is a term invented in Japan, joining the words "costume" and "play." It usually refers to a person who dresses up as a character from an anime or game.

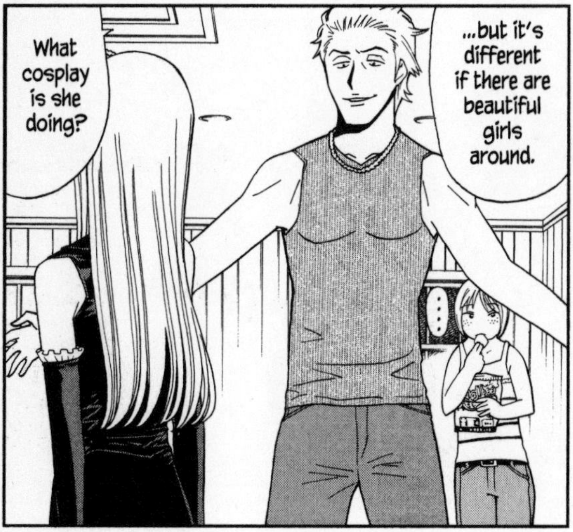
...but it's different if there are beautiful girls around.
What cosplay is she doing?

Preview of volume 3

We're pleased to present you with a preview of volume 3. Please check our website (www.delreymanga.com) to see when this volume will be available in English. For now you'll have to make do with the Japanese!

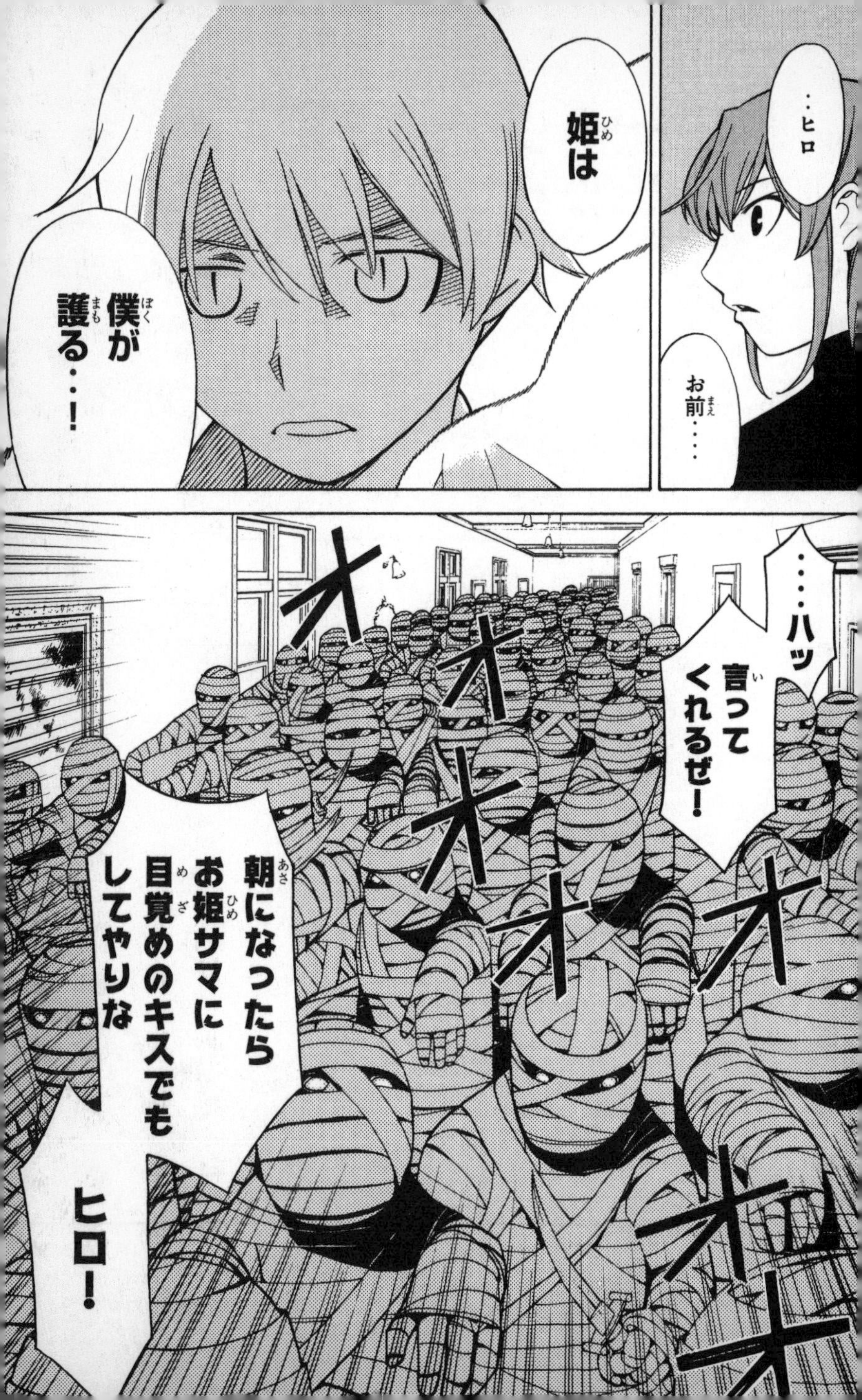
…ヒロ
お前….
姫は
僕が護る…!
……ハッ
言ってくれるぜ!
朝になったらお姫サマに目覚めのキスでもしてやりな
ヒロー!
オオオオオオオ

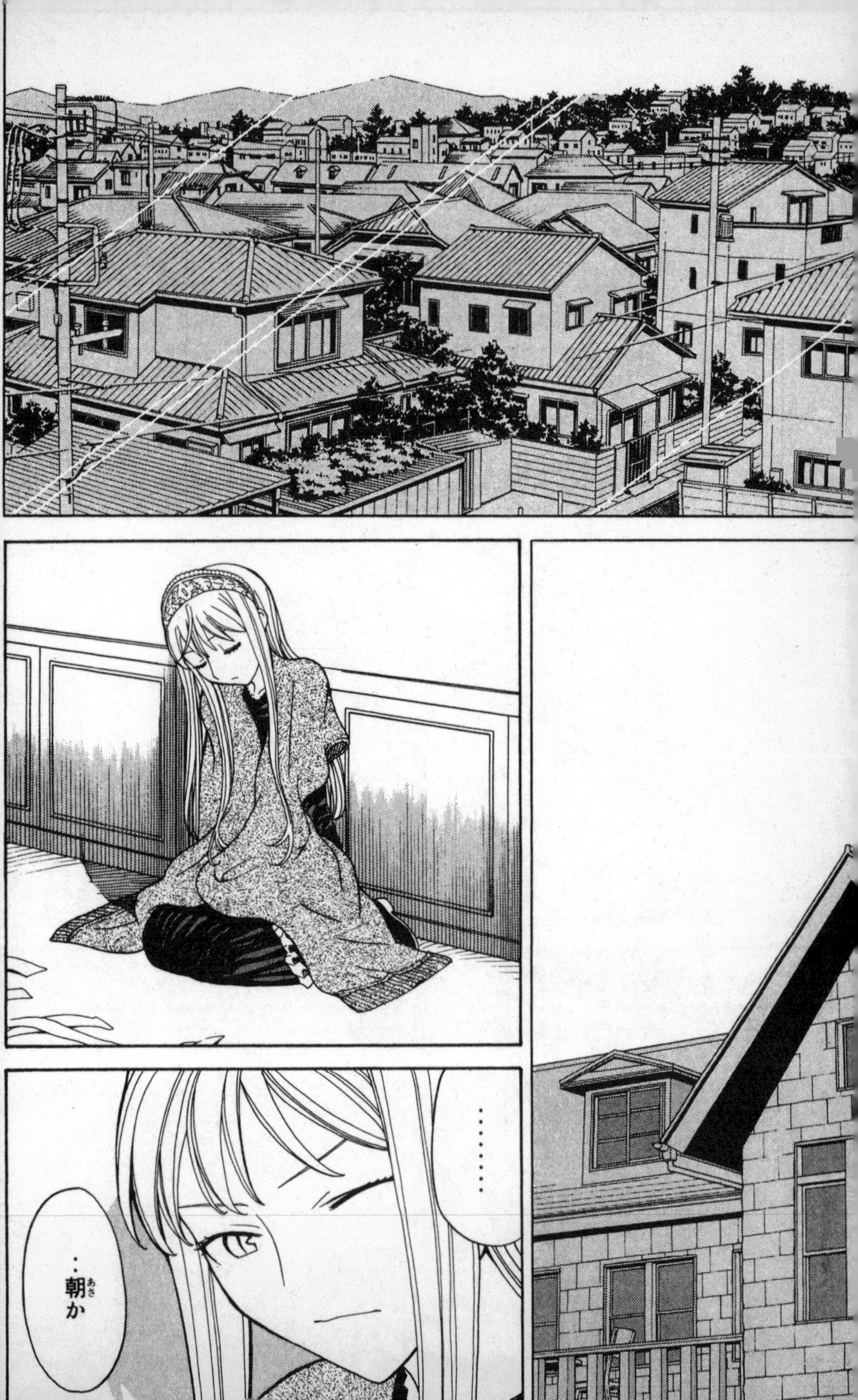
……
…朝か

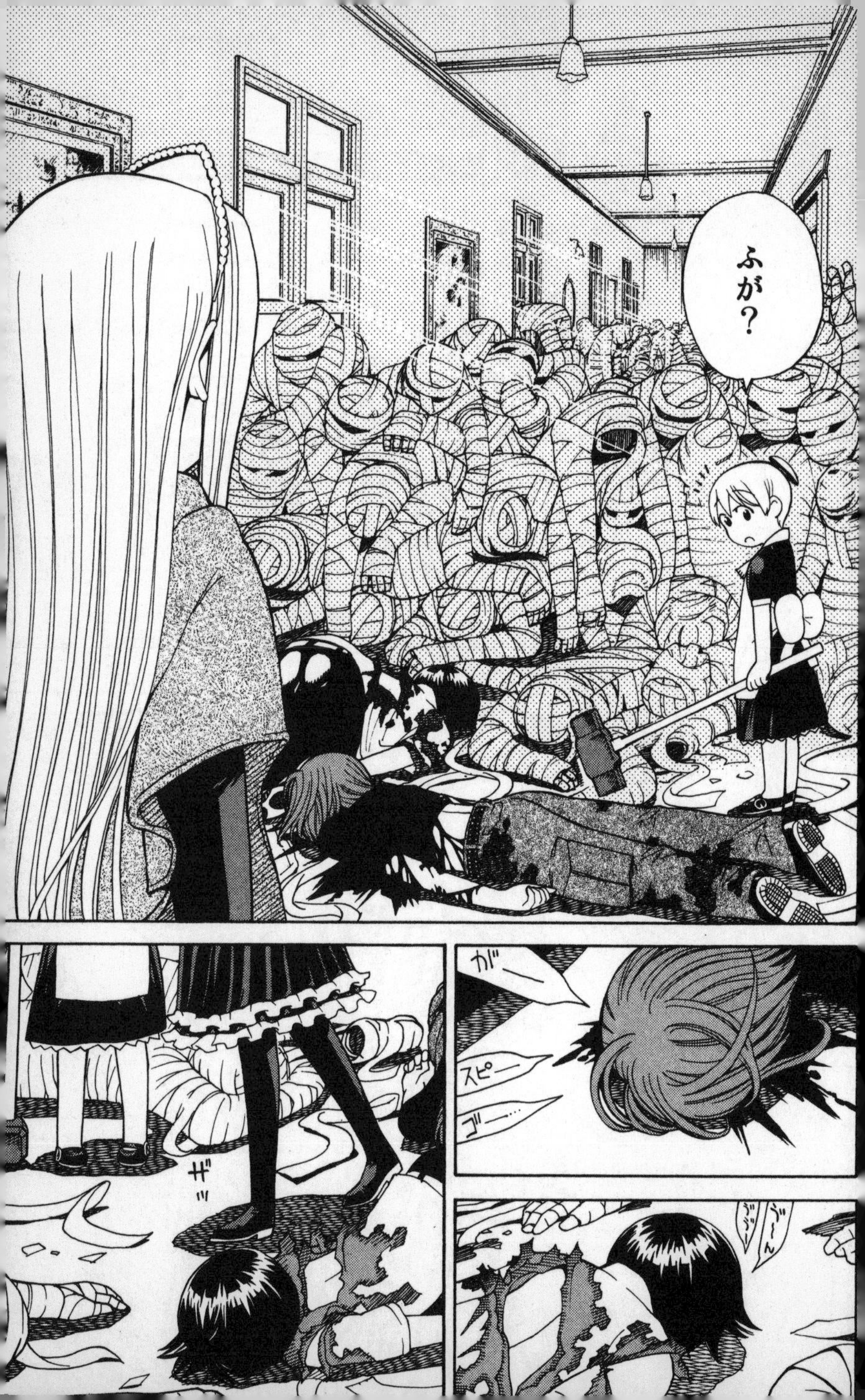
ふが？
ガー
スピー
ゴー…
う〜ん
うーう
ザッ

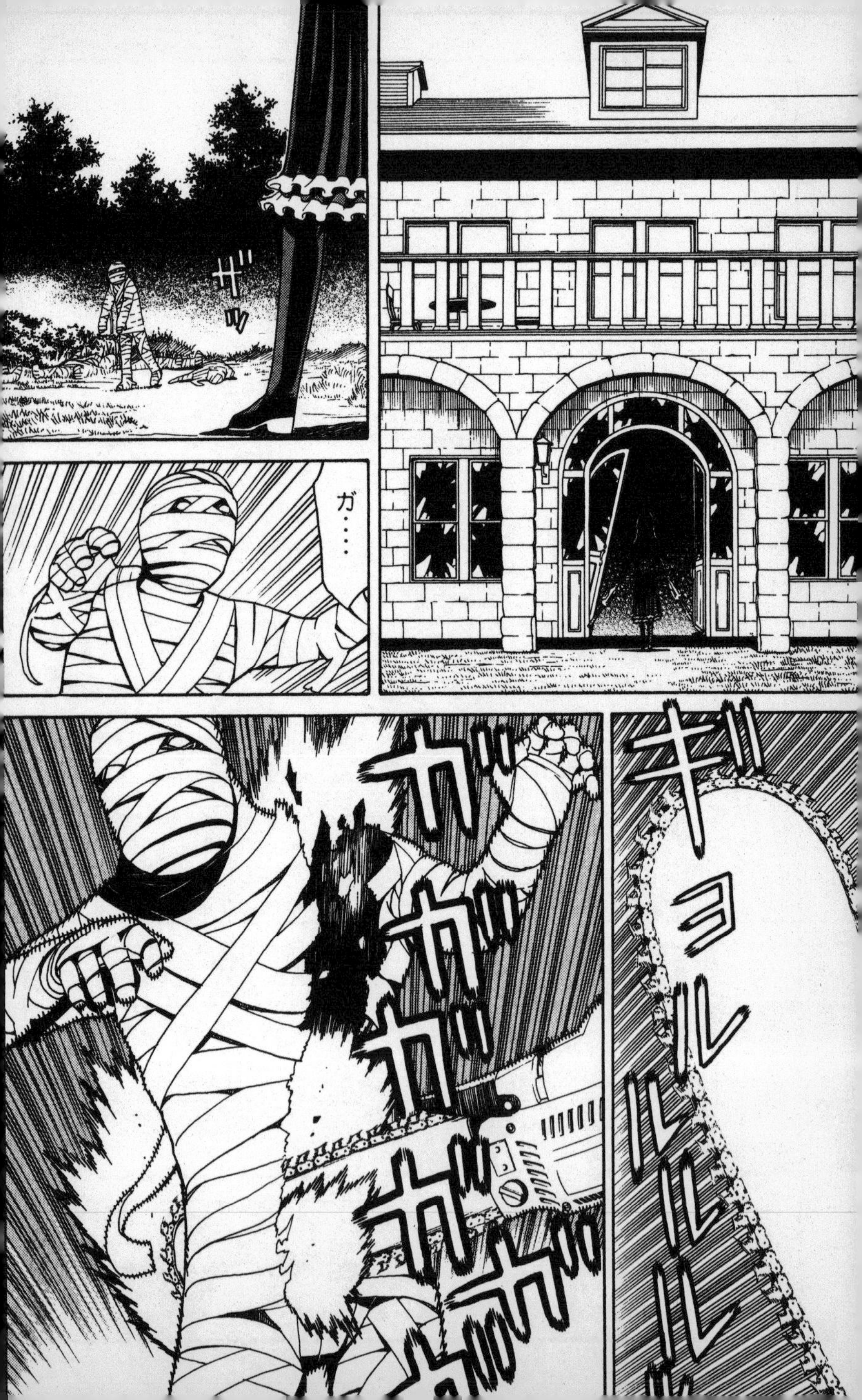
ザッ
ガ・・・・
ギョルルル
ガガガガガガガ

MANGA BY TORU ZEKU
ART BY YUNA TAKANAGI

DEFENDING THE NATURAL ORDER OF THE UNIVERSE!

The *shiki tsukai* are "Keepers of the Seasons"—magical warriors pledged to defend the planet's natural order against those who would threaten it.

When 14-year-old Akira Kizuki joins the *shiki tsukai,* he knows that it'll be a difficult life. But with his new friends and mentors, he's up to the challenge!

Special extras in each volume! Read them all!

VISIT WWW.DELREYMANGA.COM TO:
• Read sample pages
• View release date calendars for upcoming volumes
• Sign up for Del Rey's free manga e-newsletter
• Find out the latest about new Del Rey Manga series

RATING   T AGES 13+

The Otaku's Choice.™

Le Chevalier d'Eon

STORY BY TOU UBUKATA
MANGA BY KIRIKO YUMEJI

DARKNESS FALLS ON PARIS

A mysterious cult is sacrificing beautiful young women to a demonic force that threatens the entire country. Only one man can save Paris from chaos and terror, the king's top secret agent: The Chevalier d'Eon.

• Available on DVD from ADV Films.

Special extras in each volume! Read them all!

ALIVE

STORY BY TADASHI KAWASHIMA
ART BY TOKA ADACHI

SMART SCIENCE-FICTION SUSPENSE

Millions of people worldwide have taken their own lives, victims of a lethal alien pandemic visited upon the Earth.

But a group of Tokyo teens has somehow survived and now, facing a devastated world, must ask questions they never thought they'd have to ask:

Why did they abandon us?
Will we be next?
Why are we alive?

Special extras in each volume! Read them all!

TOMARE!

止まれ

[STOP!]

You're going the wrong way!

Manga is a completely different type of reading experience.

To start at the *beginning,* go to the end!

That's right! Authentic manga is read the traditional Japanese way—from right to left, exactly the *opposite* of how American books are read. It's easy to follow: Just go to the other end of the book, and read each page—and each panel—from right side to left side, starting at the top right. Now you're experiencing manga as it was meant to be!